FIAT
Owners
Workshop
Manual

J H Haynes
Member of the Guild of Motoring Writers

and Colin Barge

Models covered
All petrol-engine versions of the FIAT 131 Saloon and Estate
1297 cc, 1301 cc, 1367 cc, 1585 cc and 1995 cc; ohv, sohc and dohc

Does not cover diesel-engine models

ISBN 1 85010 165 5

Printed in England *(310-12L5)*

ABCDI

Haynes Publishing Group
Sparkford Nr Yeovil
Somerset BA22 7JJ England

Haynes Publications, Inc
861 Lawrence Drive
Newbury Park
California 91320 USA

British Library Cataloguing in Publication Data

Haynes, J. H.
Fiat 131 Mirafiori owners workshop manual
– (Owners Workshop Manual)
1 Fiat automobile
I. Title II. Barge, C.D. III. Series
629.28'722   TL215.F5
ISBN 1-85010-165-5

Acknowledgements

Thanks are due to FIAT UK Limited for the supply of technical information and certain illustrations, and to Crouch's Garage at Ilminster, Somerset, for their co-operation in supplying information. Thanks are also due to Castrol Limited who supplied lubrication data, and to the Champion Sparking Plug Company who supplied the illustrations showing the various spark plug conditions.

Lastly, a special thanks to all those people at Sparkford and Yeovil who helped in the production of this manual.

About this manual

Its aim

The aim of this manual is to help you get the best value from your car. It can do so in several ways. It can help you decide what work must be done (even should you choose to get it done by a garage), provide information on routine maintenance and servicing, and give a logical course of action and diagnosis when random faults occur. However, it is hoped that you will use the manual by tackling the work yourself. On simpler jobs it may even be quicker than booking the car into a garage and going there twice to leave and collect it. Perhaps most important, a lot of money can be saved by avoiding the costs the garage must charge to cover its labour and overheads.

The manual has drawings and descriptions to show the function of the various components so that their layout can be understood. Then the tasks are described and photographed in a step-by-step sequence so that even a novice can do the work.

Its arrangement

The manual is divided into thirteen Chapters, each covering a logical sub-division of the vehicle. The Chapters are each divided into Sections, numbered with single figures, eg 5; and the Sections into paragraphs (or sub-sections), with decimal numbers following on from the Section they are in, eg 5.1, 5.2, 5.3 etc.

It is freely illustrated, especially in those parts where there is a detailed sequence of operations to be carried out. There are two forms of illustration: figures and photographs. The figures are numbered in sequence with decimal numbers, according to their position in the Chapter – eg Fig. 6.4 is the fourth drawing/illustration in Chapter 6. Photographs carry the same number (either individually or in related groups) as the Section or sub-section to which they relate.

There is an alphabetical index at the back of the manual as well as a contents list at the front. Each Chapter is also preceded by its own individual contents list.

References to the 'left' or 'right' of the vehicle are in the sense of a person in the driver's seat facing forwards.

Unless otherwise stated, nuts and bolts are removed by turning anti-clockwise, and tightened by turning clockwise.

Vehicle manufacturers continually make changes to specifications and recommendations, and these when notified are incorporated into our manuals at the earliest opportunity.

Whilst every care is taken to ensure that the information in this manual is correct, no liability can be accepted by the authors or publishers for loss, damage or injury caused by any errors in, or omissions from, the information given.

Introduction to the Fiat 131

The FIAT 131 is available either as a two or four door saloon, or as a five door estate car. Furthermore the purchaser can choose between the basic and 'Special' versions of each model.

Externally the UK and USA models appear similar but the main difference lies in the engine compartment.

USA models are fitted with a double overhead camshaft (dohc) engine which is a development of the well proven FIAT 124 Sport engine.

UK models were originally available with the 1300 or 1600 overhead valve (ohv) engine which was developed from the popular FIAT 124 engine. Later 1300 and 1600 variants are fitted with a double overhead camshaft (dohc) engine. A two litre dohc engined model was also added to the range in 1978, known as the 'Sport'. The two litre engine is a direct descendant of the power unit of the FIAT 132.

When the FIAT 131 was introduced to the UK market in 1975, only a 4-speed manual gearbox was available. In 1976, however, a 5-speed gearbox became the standard fitting on 1600 models and later to all models in the range. The engine and gearbox are mounted in-line in the traditional manner, with a propeller shaft to take the drive to the rear axle.

This layout is extremely practical and, combined with its good handling characteristics, roomy interior and ample luggage capacity, makes the Mirafiori a vehicle well worth looking after.

Contents

Fiat 131 Mirafiori 1600 Special Estate

The FIAT 131 Mirafiori Special (UK 4 door model shown)

Use of English

As this book has been written in England, it uses the appropriate English component names, phrases, and spelling. Some of these differ from those used in America. Normally, these cause no difficulty, but to make sure, a glossary is printed below. In ordering spare parts remember the parts list may use some of these words:

English	American	English	American
Accelerator	Gas pedal	Leading shoe (of brake)	Primary shoe
Aerial	Antenna	Locks	Latches
Anti-roll bar	Stabiliser or sway bar	Methylated spirit	Denatured alcohol
Big-end bearing	Rod bearing	Motorway	Freeway, turnpike etc
Bonnet (engine cover)	Hood	Number plate	License plate
Boot (luggage compartment)	Trunk	Paraffin	Kerosene
Bulkhead	Firewall	Petrol	Gasoline (gas)
Bush	Bushing	Petrol tank	Gas tank
Cam follower or tappet	Valve lifter or tappet	'Pinking'	'Pinging'
Carburettor	Carburetor	Prise (force apart)	Pry
Catch	Latch	Propeller shaft	Driveshaft
Choke/venturi	Barrel	Quarterlight	Quarter window
Circlip	Snap-ring	Retread	Recap
Clearance	Lash	Reverse	Back-up
Crownwheel	Ring gear (of differential)	Rocker cover	Valve cover
Damper	Shock absorber, shock	Saloon	Sedan
Disc (brake)	Rotor/disk	Seized	Frozen
Distance piece	Spacer	Sidelight	Parking light
Drop arm	Pitman arm	Silencer	Muffler
Drop head coupe	Convertible	Sill panel (beneath doors)	Rocker panel
Dynamo	Generator (DC)	Small end, little end	Piston pin or wrist pin
Earth (electrical)	Ground	Spanner	Wrench
Engineer's blue	Prussian blue	Split cotter (for valve spring cap)	Lock (for valve spring retainer)
Estate car	Station wagon	Split pin	Cotter pin
Exhaust manifold	Header	Steering arm	Spindle arm
Fault finding/diagnosis	Troubleshooting	Sump	Oil pan
Float chamber	Float bowl	Swarf	Metal chips or debris
Free-play	Lash	Tab washer	Tang or lock
Freewheel	Coast	Tappet	Valve lifter
Gearbox	Transmission	Thrust bearing	Throw-out bearing
Gearchange	Shift	Top gear	High
Grub screw	Setscrew, Allen screw	Trackrod (of steering)	Tie-rod (or connecting rod)
Gudgeon pin	Piston pin or wrist pin	Trailing shoe (of brake)	Secondary shoe
Halfshaft	Axleshaft	Transmission	Whole drive line
Handbrake	Parking brake	Tyre	Tire
Hood	Soft top	Van	Panel wagon/van
Hot spot	Heat riser	Vice	Vise
Indicator	Turn signal	Wheel nut	Lug nut
Interior light	Dome lamp	Windscreen	Windshield
Layshaft (of gearbox)	Countershaft	Wing/mudguard	Fender

Buying spare parts and vehicle identification numbers

Buying spare parts

Spare parts can be obtained from many sources, for example: FIAT garages, other garages and accessory shops, and motor factors. Our advice regarding spare parts is as follows:

Officially appointed FIAT garages - This is the best source of parts which are peculiar to your car and otherwise not generally available (eg. complete cylinder heads, internal gearbox components, badges interior trim etc). It is also the only place you should buy your parts if your car is still under warranty; non-FIAT components may invalidate the warranty. To be sure of obtaining the correct parts it will always be necessary to give the partsman your car's engine number, chassis number and number for spares, and if possible take the old part along for positive identification. Remember that many parts are available on a factory exchange scheme - any parts returned should always be clean! It obviously make good sense to go to the specialists on your car for this type of part for they are the best equipped to supply you. They will also be able to provide their own Fiat service manual for your car should you require one.

Other garages and accessory shops - These are often very good places to buy material and components needed for the maintenance of your car (eg. oil filters, spark plugs, fan belts, oils and grease, touch-up paint, filler paste etc). They also sell general accessories, usually have convenient opening hours, charge lower prices and can often be found not far from home.

Motor factors - Good factors will stock all of the more important components which wear out relatively quickly (eg. clutch components, pistons, valves, exhaust systems, brake cylinders/pipes/hoses/seals/shoes and pads, etc). Motor factors will often provide new or reconditioned components on a part exchange basis - this can save a considerable amount of money.

Vehicle identification numbers

As already stated, when ordering new parts it is essential that the storeman has full information about your particular model of FIAT.

The bodyshell type and number is stamped on the right-hand side panel of the engine compartment.

The engine type and number is stamped on the cylinder block just above the oil filter extension housing.

Furthermore, a specification plate is fitted to the front right-hand side body panel and gives details of the following: Homologation reference number, version code, chassis type, number for spares, and paintwork colour code.

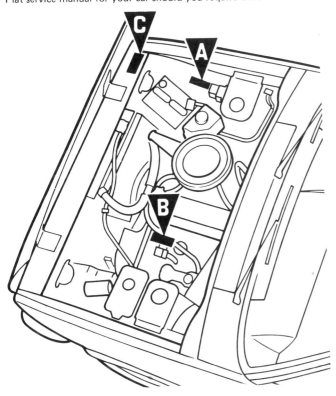

Location of vehicle identification plates

A: Body type and number stamped right-hand side panel of engine compartment

B: Engine type and number stamped on cylinder block above oil filter unit

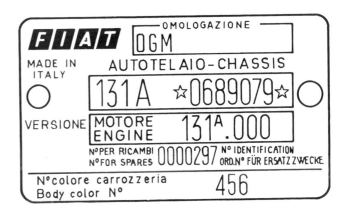

C: Specification plate (typical) fitted to front right-hand side body panel

Tools and working facilities

Introduction

A selection of good tools is a fundamental requirement for anyone contemplating the maintenance and repair of a motor vehicle. For the owner who does not possess any, their purchase will prove a considerable expense, offsetting some of the savings made by doing-it-yourself. However, provided that the tools purchased are of good quality, they will last for many years and prove an extremely worthwhile investment.

To help the average owner to decide which tools are needed to carry out the various tasks detailed in this manual, we have compiled three lists of tools under the following headings: *Maintenance and minor repair, Repair and overhaul,* and *Special*. The newcomer to practical mechanics should start off with the *Maintenance and minor repair* tool kit and confine himself to the simpler jobs around the vehicle. Then, as his confidence and experience grow, he can undertake more difficult tasks, buying extra tools as, and when, they are needed. In this way, a *Maintenance and minor repair* tool kit can be built-up into a *Repair and overhaul* tool kit over a considerable period of time without any major cash outlays. The experienced do-it-yourselfer will have a tool kit good enough for most repair and overhaul procedures and will add tools from the *Special* category when he feels the expense is justified by the amount of use these tools will be put to.

It is obviously not possible to cover the subject of tools fully here. For those who wish to learn more about tools and their use there is a book entitled *How to Choose and Use Car Tools* available from the publishers of this manual.

Maintenance and minor repair tool kit

The tools given in this list should be considered as a minimum requirement if routine maintenance, servicing and minor repair operations are to be undertaken. We recommend the purchase of combination spanners (ring one end, open-ended the other); although more expensive than open-ended ones, they do give the advantages of both types of spanner.

Combination spanners - 8, 9, 10, 11, 12, 13, 14, 15, 16 and 19 mm
Box spanners - 8, 12, 14, (long) and 21 mm
Adjustable spanner - 9 inch
Spark plug spanner (with rubber insert)
Spark plug gap adjustment tool
Set of feeler gauges
Plug/points file
Brake bleed nipple spanner
Screwdriver - 4 in long x ¼ in dia (flat blade)
Screwdriver - 4 in long x ¼ in dia (cross blade)
Combination pliers - 6 inch
Hacksaw, junior
Tyre pump
Tyre pressure gauge
Grease gun
Oil can
Fine emery cloth (1 sheet)
Wire brush (small)
Funnel (medium size)

Repair and overhaul tool kit

These tools are virtually essential for anyone undertaking any major repairs to a motor vehicle, and are additional to those given in the *Maintenance and minor repair* list. Included in this list is a comprehensive set of sockets. Although these are expensive they will be found invaluable as they are so versatile - particularly if various drives are included in the set. We recommend the ½ in square-drive type, as this can be used with most proprietary torque spanners. If you cannot afford a socket set, even bought piecemeal, then inexpensive tubular box wrenches are a useful alternative.

The tools in this list will occasionally need to be supplemented by tools from the *Special* list.

Sockets (or box spanners) to cover range in previous list, and ¾ in square drive 32 mm (1¼ in AF) and 44 mm
Reversible ratchet drive (for use with sockets)
Extension piece, 10 inch (for use with sockets)
Universal joint (for use with sockets)
Torque wrench (for use with sockets)
Mole wrench - 8 inch
Ball pein hammer
Soft-faced hammer, plastic or rubber
Screwdriver - 6 in long x 5/16 in dia (flat blade)
Screwdriver - 2 in long x 5/16 in square (flat blade)
Screwdriver - 1½ in long x ¼ in dia (cross blade)
Screwdriver - 3 in long x 1/8 in dia (electricians)
Pliers - electricians side cutters
Pliers - needle nosed
Pliers - circlip (internal and external)
Cold chisel - ½ inch
Scriber (this can be made by grinding the end of a broken hacksaw blade)
Scraper (this can be made by flattening and sharpening one end of a piece of copper pipe)
Centre punch
Pin punch
Hacksaw
Valve grinding tool
Steel rule/straight edge
Allen keys
Selection of files
Wire brush (large)
Axle-stands
Jack (strong scissor or hydraulic type)

Special tools

The tools in this list are those which are not used regularly, are expensive to buy, or which need to be used in accordance with their manufacturers' instructions. Unless relatively difficult mechanical jobs are undertaken frequently, it will not be economic to buy many of these tools. Where this is the case, you could consider clubbing together with friends (or a motorists' club) to make a joint purchase, or borrowing the tools against a deposit from a local garage or tool hire specialist.

The following list contains only those tools and instruments freely available to the public, and not those special tools produced by the vehicle manufacturer specifically for its dealer network. You will find occasional references to these manufacturers' special tools in the text of this manual. Generally, an alternative method of doing the job without the vehicle manufacturers' special tool is given. However, sometimes, there is no alternative to using them. Where this is the case and the relevant tool cannot be bought or borrowed you will have to entrust the work to a franchised garage.

Valve spring compressor (where applicable)
Piston ring compressor
Balljoint separator
Universal hub/bearing puller
Impact screwdriver
Micrometer and/or vernier gauge
Dial gauge
Stroboscopic timing light
Dwell angle meter/tachometer
Universal electrical multi-meter
Cylinder compression gauge
Lifting tackle
Trolley jack
Light with extension lead

Buying tools

For practically all tools, a tool dealer is the best source since he will have a very comprehensive range compared with the average garage or accessory shop. Having said that, accessory shops often offer excellent quality tools at discount prices, so it pays to shop around.

Remember, you don't have to buy the most expensive items on the shelf, but it is always advisable to steer clear of the very cheap tools. There are plenty of good tools around at reasonable prices, so ask the proprietor or manager of the shop for advice before making a purchase.

Care and maintenance of tools

Having purchased a reasonable tool kit, it is necessary to keep the tools in a clean serviceable condition. After use, always wipe off any dirt, grease and metal particles using a clean, dry cloth, before putting the tools away. Never leave them lying around after they have been used. A simple tool rack on the garage or workshop wall, for items such as screwdrivers and pliers is a good idea. Store all normal spanners and sockets in a metal box. Any measuring instruments, gauges, meters, etc, must be carefully stored where they cannot be damaged or become rusty.

Take a little care when tools are used. Hammer heads inevitably become marked and screwdrivers lose the keen edge on their blades from time to time. A little timely attention with emery cloth or a file will soon restore items like this to a good serviceable finish.

Working facilities

Not to be forgotten when discussing tools, is the workshop itself. If anything more than routine maintenance is to be carried out, some form of suitable working area becomes essential.

It is appreciated that many an owner mechanic is forced by circumstances to remove an engine or similar item, without the benefit of a garage or workshop. Having done this, any repairs should always be done under the cover of a roof.

Wherever possible, any dismantling should be done on a clean flat workbench or table at a suitable working height.

Any workbench needs a vice: one with a jaw opening of 4 in (100 mm) is suitable for most jobs. As mentioned previously, some clean dry storage space is also required for tools, as well as the lubricants, cleaning fluids, touch-up paints and so on which become necessary.

Another item which may be required, and which has a much more general usage, is an electric drill with a chuck capacity of at least 5/16 in (8 mm). This, together with a good range of twist drills, is virtually essential for fitting accessories such as wing mirrors and reversing lights.

Last, but not least, always keep a supply of old newspapers and clean, lint-free rags available, and try to keep any working area as clean as possible.

Spanner jaw gap comparison table

Jaw gap (in)	Spanner size
0.250	$\frac{1}{4}$ in AF
0.276	7 mm
0.313	$\frac{5}{16}$ in AF
0.315	8 mm
0.344	$\frac{11}{32}$ in AF; $\frac{1}{8}$ in Whitworth
0.354	9 mm
0.375	$\frac{3}{8}$ in AF
0.394	10 mm
0.433	11 mm
0.438	$\frac{7}{16}$ in AF
0.445	$\frac{3}{16}$ in Whitworth; $\frac{1}{4}$ in BSF
0.472	12 mm
0.500	$\frac{1}{2}$ in AF
0.512	13 mm
0.525	$\frac{1}{4}$ in Whitworth; $\frac{5}{16}$ in BSF
0.551	14 mm
0.563	$\frac{9}{16}$ in AF
0.591	15 mm
0.600	$\frac{5}{16}$ in Whitworth; $\frac{3}{8}$ in BSF
0.625	$\frac{5}{8}$ in AF
0.630	16 mm
0.669	17 mm
0.686	$\frac{11}{16}$ in AF
0.709	18 mm
0.710	$\frac{3}{8}$ in Whitworth; $\frac{7}{16}$ in BSF
0.748	19 mm
0.750	$\frac{3}{4}$ in AF
0.813	$\frac{13}{16}$ in AF
0.820	$\frac{7}{16}$ in Whitworth; $\frac{1}{2}$ in BSF
0.866	22 mm
0.875	$\frac{7}{8}$ in AF
0.920	$\frac{1}{2}$ in Whitworth; $\frac{9}{16}$ in BSF
0.938	$\frac{15}{16}$ in AF
0.945	24 mm
1.000	1 in AF
1.010	$\frac{9}{16}$ in Whitworth; $\frac{5}{8}$ in BSF
1.024	26 mm
1.063	$1\frac{1}{16}$ in AF; 27 mm
1.100	$\frac{5}{8}$ in Whitworth; $\frac{11}{16}$ in BSF
1.125	$1\frac{1}{8}$ in AF
1.181	30 mm
1.200	$\frac{11}{16}$ in Whitworth; $\frac{3}{4}$ in BSF
1.250	$1\frac{1}{4}$ in AF
1.260	32 mm
1.300	$\frac{3}{4}$ in Whitworth; $\frac{7}{8}$ in BSF
1.313	$1\frac{5}{16}$ in AF
1.390	$\frac{13}{16}$ in Whitworth; $\frac{15}{16}$ in BSF
1.417	36 mm
1.438	$1\frac{7}{16}$ in AF
1.480	$\frac{7}{8}$ in Whitworth; 1 in BSF
1.500	$1\frac{1}{2}$ in AF
1.575	40 mm; $\frac{15}{16}$ in Whitworth
1.614	41 mm
1.625	$1\frac{5}{8}$ in AF
1.670	1 in Whitworth; $1\frac{1}{8}$ in BSF
1.688	$1\frac{11}{16}$ in AF
1.811	46 mm
1.813	$1\frac{13}{16}$ in AF
1.860	$1\frac{1}{8}$ in Whitworth; $1\frac{1}{4}$ in BSF
1.875	$1\frac{7}{8}$ in AF
1.969	50 mm
2.000	2 in AF
2.050	$1\frac{1}{4}$ in Whitworth; $1\frac{3}{8}$ in BSF
2.165	55 mm
2.362	60 mm

Jacking and towing

Jacking

The jack supplied with the car tool kit should only be used for changing a roadwheel. Whenever repair or overhaul operations are being carried out, jack the car in the following positions and always supplement the jack with axle stands placed under the body side frame:

Raising front end: place the jack under the front crossmember.

Raising the rear end: place the jack under the tubular section of the axle casing as close to the trailing arm as possible.

Towing

Towing hooks are fitted to the front and rear of the car and any towing hooks or ropes should always be attached to these points only.

On cars fitted with automatic transmission the car may be towed with the gear selector in the N (neutral) position a distance of 30 miles at a speed not exceeding 30 mph (50 kph). If the car is to be towed over long distances or the transmission is faulty, the car must be towed with either the rear wheels suspended off the ground or with the propeller shaft removed.

Using the jack supplied with the car to raise the road wheel clear of the ground (the arrow indicates the jacking point location)

Raising the front of the car using a trolly jack placed under the front suspension crossmember. (The arrow shows the position of a 1¼ in (3 cm) wooden packing block)

Raising the rear of the car using a trolly jack placed under the differential casing

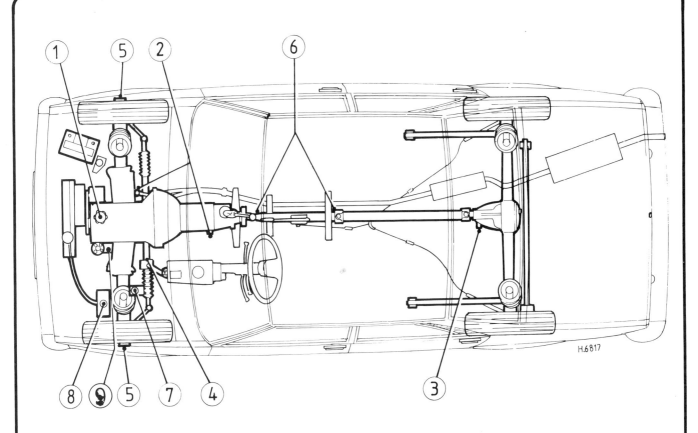

H.6817

Recommended lubricants and fluids

Recommended lubricants and fluids

Component or system	Lubricant type or specification
Engine (1)	Engine oil to API 'SE' SAE 15W/40
Manual transmission (2)	SAE 80W/90 not EP
Automatic transmission (2)	Dexron II transmission fluid
Rear axle, standard or limited slip differential (3)	SAE 80W/90 EP oil
Steering rack (4)	Lithium based grease
Wheel bearings (5)	Lithium based grease
Propeller shaft splines (6)	Lithium based grease N3
Brake fluid reservoir (7)	Hydraulic fluid to DOT 3
Cooling system (8)	Ethylene Glycol based
Power steering (9)	Dexron II transmission fluid

Note: *The above are general recommendations only. Lubrication requirements vary from territory to territory and depend on vehicle usage. If in doubt, consult the operator's handbook supplied with the vehicle, or your nearest dealer.*

Routine maintenance

For modifications, and information applicable to later models, see Supplement at end of manual

Maintenance is essential in the first instance to ensure safety and in the second instance, it is desirable to achieve the best possible value in terms of performance, economy and reliability. Due to technological developments over the years, the need for periodic lubrication - oiling, greasing etc, has been drastically reduced and in some cases totally eliminated. This unfortunately has led some owners to think that because no such action is required the items no longer exist or will last for ever. This is a serious delusion. It therefore follows that the cheapest and simplest element of maintenance is visual examination. A minor defect can be spotted and rectified before it can develop into a major fault and possible roadside breakdown.

In each of the maintenance instructions given below the figures in brackets refer to the Chapter/Section where further information on the particular service task can be found.

Weekly or before a long journey

Check engine oil level *(Chapter 1)*
Check operation of lights, direction indicators, horn, wipers and washers and rear window demister *(Chapter 10)*
Check engine coolant level *(Chapter 2)*
Check battery electrolyte level *(Chapter 10)*
Check washer reservoir fluid level(s)
Check tyre pressures and condition of tyres *(Chapter 11)*
Check brake fluid level in reservoir *(Chapter 9)*
Check automatic gearbox fluid level (where applicable) *(Chapter 6B)*
Check power steering fluid level (where applicable) *(Chapter 11)*

Every 6000 miles (10 000 km) or 6 months, whichever occurs first

Check brake and clutch pedals adjustment and front and rear brake linings for wear *(Chapters 9 and 5)*
Inspect seat belts for fraying, splits, oil contamination etc, and anchorage points for security *(Chapter 12)*
Drain the engine oil, renew the oil filter, and refill the engine with specified oil *(Chapter 1)*
Check oil level in gearbox and rear axle, topping up as necessary *(Chapters 6A and 8)*
Check spark plug gaps *(Chapter 4)*
Check contact breaker points (where applicable) *(Chapter 4)*
Check ignition timing *(Chapter 4)*
Check engine idling speed *(Chapter 3)*
Check power steering pump reservoir fluid level *(Chapter 13)*

Every 12 000 miles (20 000 km) or 12 months, whichever occurs first

Carry out those operations listed under the 6000 mile (10 000 km) service, in addition to the following:
Check operation of door locks, hinges, window winding mechanisms, bonnet and boot hinges, locks and catches. Lubricate and adjust as necessary

Check headlamp alignment *(Chapter 10)*
Check front wheel toe-in *(Chapter 11)*
Check all fuel and coolant hoses and pipes for leaks *(Chapters 2 and 3)*
Check condition of, and renew as necessary, exhaust system, brake hoses and steering linkage *(Chapters 3, 9 and 11)*
Check the oil levels in manual gearbox and rear axle *(Chapters 6 and 8)*
Lubricate propeller shaft sliding sleeve *(Chapter 7)*
Check and adjust handbrake lever *(Chapter 9)*
Check the condition of tyres, for uneven wear, tread depth, cuts, etc *(Chapter 11)*
Check front wheel bearings *(Chapter 11)*
Check brake calipers/cylinders for general condition and leaks *(Chapter 9)*
Check coolant level and strength of antifreeze mixture *(Chapter 2)*
Check for correct tension of alternator drive belt, and power steering and air conditioner belts, if fitted *(Chapter 10)*
Check condition of toothed timing belt — renew if necessary *(Chapter 1)*
Check valve clearances *(Chapter 1)*
Check cylinder compression *(Chapter 1)*
Renew the contact breaker points (where applicable) *(Chapter 4)*
Renew air filter element *(Chapter 3)*
Clean battery terminals and apply petroleum jelly *(Chapter 10)*
Check battery charge rate and efficiency *(Chapter 10)*
Check engine emission control system *(Chapter 3)*

Every 24 000 miles (40 000 km) or 24 months, whichever occurs first

Carry out those operations listed under the 12 000 mile (20 000 km) in addition to the following;

Renew the oil in the manual gearbox and rear axle *(Chapters 6A and 8)*
Renew the hydraulic fluid in the brake system *(Chapter 9)*
Renew the engine coolant fluid *(Chapter 2)*

Every 36 000 miles (58 000 km) or 36 months, whichever occurs first

Carry out those operations listed under the 12 000 mile (20 000 km) service in addition to the following:
Renew the automatic transmission fluid *(Chapter 6B)*
Renew the engine timing belt *(Chapter 1B)*
Renew air filter element (fuel injection system)

Every 48 000 miles (70 000 km) — carry out those operations listed under the 24 000 mile (40 000 km) service

Every 60 000 miles (96 000 km) — carry out those operations listed under the 12 000 mile (20 000 km) service

Oil level dipstick dohc engine

The cooling system expansion tank. (The arrow indicates the minimum level)

Location of the sump drain plug (B)

Removing the oil filter canister using a chain wrench

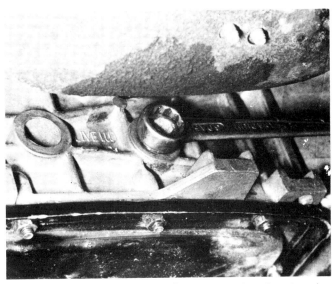

Undoing the gearbox filler/level plug (4-speed manual gearbox shown)

Remove plug 'A' to check/top-up gearbox oil level. Remove plug 'B' to drain gearbox oil (5-speed manual gearbox shown)

The rear axle filler/level and drain plug A: Filler/level plug B: Drain plug

Chapter 1 Part A: Overhead valve engine

For modifications, and information applicable to later models, see Supplement at end of manual

Contents

Specifications

General
Type ... ... Four cylinder, overhead valve, pushrod operated

Capacity
1300 (A.000) ... ... 1297 cc
1300 (A7.000) ... ... 1301 cc
1600 (A1.000) ... ... 1585 cc

Bore
1300 (A.000) ... ... 2.992 in (76 mm)
1300 (A7.000) ... ... 2.996 in (76.1 mm)
1600 (A1.000) ... ... 3.307 in (84 mm)

Stroke
1300 ... ... 2.81 in (71.5 mm)
1600 ... ... 2.81 in (71.5 mm)

Oil capacity, including filter ... ... 7 Imp pts (4 litres)

Firing order ... ... 1 - 3 - 4 - 2 (number 1 cylinder at front)

Compression ratio ... ... 9.2 : 1

Crankshaft and main bearings
Standard journal diameter ... ... 2.0860 - 2.0868 in (52.985 - 53.005 mm)
Maximum ovality (out of round) ... ... 0.0002 in (0.005 mm)
Crankshaft endfloat ... ... 0.0021 - 0.0120 in (0.055 - 0.305 mm)
Crankpin journal diameter (standard) ... ... 1.8986 - 1.8993 in (48.224 - 48.244 mm)
Maximum ovality (out of round) ... ... 0.0002 in (0.005 mm)

Main bearing thickness (standard)	0.0718 - 0.0721 in (1.825 - 1.831 mm)
Main bearing clearance	0.0020 - 0.0037 in (0.050 - 0.095 mm)

Camshaft

Cam lift

1300	0.389 in (9.90 mm)
1600	0.406 in (10.32 mm)

Journal diameter (standard size)

Front	1.8911 - 1.8927 in (48.033 - 48.058 mm)
Centre	1.7257 - 1.7266 in (43.833 - 43.858 mm)
Rear	1.4517 - 1.4527 in (36.875 - 36.900 mm)

Journal to bearing clearance

Front	0.0010 - 0.0028 in (0.026 - 0.071 mm)
Centre	0.0018 - 0.0036 in (0.046 - 0.091 mm)
Rear	0.0010 - 0.0028 in (0.026 - 0.071 mm)

Bearing inner diameter:

Front	1.8931 - 1.8939 in (48.084 - 48.104 mm)
Centre	1.7285 - 1.7292 in (43.904 - 43.924 mm)
Rear	1.4537 - 1.4545 in (36.926 - 36.946 mm)

Pistons

Piston diameter (measured at 52.4 mm from crown at right angles to gudgeon pin)

Piston diameter standard:	**1300***	**1600**
Grade A	2.9889 - 2.9892 in (75.92 - 75.93 mm)	3.3038 - 3.3042 in (83.92 - 83.93 mm)
Grade C	2.9896 - 2.9900 in (75.94 - 75.95 mm)	3.3046 - 3.3050 in (83.94 - 83.95 mm)
Grade E	2.9904 - 2.9908 in (75.96 - 75.97 mm)	3.3054 - 3.3058 in (83.96 - 83.97 mm)

***Note:** 1301 cc engines have a standard piston diameter of 2.996 in (76.10 mm)*

Oversize pistons available	0.0079 - 0.0157 - 0.0236 in (0.2, 0.4, 0.6 mm)
Piston ring groove width:	
Compression (TOP)	0.0604 - 0.0612 in (1.535 - 1.555 mm)
Oil control (CENTRE)	0.0798 - 0.0806 in (2.03 - 2.05 mm)
Oil scraper (BOTTOM)	0.1561 - 0.1569 in (3.967 - 3.987 mm)
Piston to bore clearance	0.0027 - 0.0035 in (0.070 - 0.090 mm)
Gudgeon pin boss offset	0.08 in (2.0 mm)
Gudgeon pin boss bore diameter	0.8660 - 0.8662 in (21.996 - 22.002 mm)

Piston rings

Ring thickness:

Top compression	0.0582 - 0.0587 in (1.478 - 1.490 mm)
Centre oil control	0.0778 - 0.0783 in (1.978 - 1.990 mm)
Bottom oil scraper	0.1544 - 0.1549 in (3.925 - 3.937 mm)

Clearance in groove:

Top compression	0.0018 - 0.0030 in (0.045 - 0.077 mm)
Centre oil control	0.0015 - 0.0028 in (0.040 - 0.072 mm)
Bottom oil scraper	0.0011 - 0.0024 in (0.030 - 0.062 mm)

Piston ring end gap in bore:	**1300**	**1600**
Top compression	0.0118 - 0.0196 in (0.30 - 0.50 mm)	0.0118 - 0.0177 in (0.30 - 0.45 mm)
Centre oil control	0.0118 - 0.0196 in (0.30 - 0.50 mm)	0.0118 - 0.0177 in (0.30 - 0.45 mm)
Bottom oil scraper	0.0078 - 0.0137 in (0.20 - 0.35 mm)	0.0098 - 0.0157 in (0.25 - 0.40 mm)

Piston gudgeon pins

Diameter (standard)	0.8658 - 0.8660 in (21.991 - 21.997 mm)
Oversize gudgeon pin	+ 0.0079 in (0.2 mm)
Pin to piston clearance	0.0007 - 0.0027 in (0.018 - 0.070 mm)
Pin to connecting rod clearance	0.0004 - 0.0006 in (0.010 - 0.016 mm)

Connecting rods

Small end bush inside diameter	0.8662 - 0.8665 in (22.004 - 22.010 mm)

Valves

Valve clearance (cold) inlet and exhaust	0.008 in (0.20 mm)

Valve head diameter:	**1300**	**1600**
Inlet	1.36 in (34.5 mm)	1.36 in (34.5 mm)
Exhaust	1.22 in (31.0 mm)	1.32 in (33.5 mm)

Valve stem diameter	0.314 - 0.315 in (7.974 - 7.992 mm)
Valve spring free length:	
Outer	1.97 in (50 mm)
Inner	1.54 in (39.2 mm)
Valve guide length:	
Exhaust	1.65 in (42.0 mm)

Inlet	1.79 in (45.5 mm)
Valve guide inner diameter	0.315 - 0.316 in (8.022 - 8.040 mm)
Valve stem/guide clearance	0.0012 - 0.0026 in (0.030 - 0.066 mm)
Valve guide interference fit	0.0025 - 0.0042 in (0.063 - 0.108 mm)
Valve guide outside diameter:	
Standard	0.5535 - 0.55425 in (14.06 - 14.078 mm)
Oversize	0.5606 - 0.5613 in (14.24 - 14.258 mm)
Valve seat angle	45° 30'
Valve seat width	0.078 in (2 mm)

Engine lubrication

Oil pump:	
Gears to housing clearance	0.0043 - 0.0070 in (0.110 - 0.180 mm)
Gear thickness (new)	1.1793 - 1.1806 in (29.956 - 29.989 mm)
Gear backlash between teeth	0.006 in (0.15 mm)
Gears to cover face clearance	0.0012 - 0.0045 in (0.031 - 0.116 mm)
Oil pressure relief valve spring:	
Free length	1.58 in (40.2 mm)
Minimum length and loading	0.83 at 11.06 lb (21 mm at 5 kg)
Oil pressure at 100°C (212°F)	49.78 - 71.12 psi (3.5 - 5 kg cm^2)

Torque wrench settings

	lbs f ft	kg f m
Cylinder head bolts	61.5	8.5
Connecting rod caps	36	5
Main bearing cap bolt (small)	58	8
Main bearing cap bolts (large)	83	11.5
Rocker shaft retainer nuts	28	4
Camshaft wheel bolt	87	12
Crankshaft wheel and pulley nut	144	20
Flywheel bolts	61.5	8.5
Manifold nuts	18	2.5
Front crossmember nut	25	3.5
Rear crossmember-to-body bolt	18	2.5
Rear crossmember-to-mounting nut	18	2.5
Rear mounting-to-gearbox nut	22	3

1 General description

The FIAT 131 is available with either a 1300 or 1600 ohv engine and only minor dimensional sizes distinguish them. The two engines are very similar to the engines fitted to the FIAT 124 and 124S.

The design of the engine is conventional. The crankshaft runs in five main bearings and the overhead inclined valves are operated by a belt driven camshaft, tappets, and pushrods through rockers pivoting on a shaft mounted on the aluminium cylinder head. The valve seats are cast iron inserts. The cylinder block is cast iron and the cylinders are bored directly into it.

Pistons are fitted with one compression and two oil control rings. The gudgeon pin is a push fit in the piston bosses and connecting rod small end bush. The gudgeon pin is retained in place by two circlips seated in grooves machined into the ends of the piston bosses.

The oil pump is of the gear type, drawing oil up from the engine sump. It is driven by a special drive sleeve in mesh with a skew gear on the camshaft. This sleeve has a splined internal bore and also drives the distributor.

The lubrication system is pressurised. The oil circulates under pressure from the gear type pump which drains oil from the sump and forces it through a full flow filter. The oil pressure is gauged after it has passed through the filter. From the filter it flows to a longitudinal galley cast in the crankcase and five branches from the galley run direct to the main crankshaft bearings. Oilways in the crankshaft allow oil to pass to the connecting rod big end bearings. From the main bearings oil also passes from further oilways to the camshaft bearings.

From the centre camshaft bearing oil passes through another oil-way vertically through the cylinder head into the hollow rocker shaft. This acts as a gallery and feeds oil out to lubricate the rocker arms.

Oil pressure is lost at this point, and the oil drains back down from the head through the pushrod apertures to the sump. It lubricates the tappets and cams on the way. Maintenance of the oil pressure is dependent on the tolerances of the bearings and journals, the viscosity of the oil and the efficiency of the pump. A relief valve in the pump prevents excessive pressure from cold oil damaging the filter and a relief valve in the filter permits oil to continue circulating if the filter gets blocked.

The engine is supported, together with the transmission unit, at three places, one on each side of the engine between the crankcase and the chassis rails and underneath the gearbox by a crossmember bolted to the underframe.

2 Major operations possible with the engine installed

The following work may be carried out with the engine in place:

a) *Removal and refitting of the cylinder head assembly.*
b) *Removal and refitting of the clutch assembly.*
c) *Removal and refitting of the engine front mountings.*

The following work can be carried out with the engine in place but is inadvisable unless there are very special reasons:

a) *Removal and refitting of the sump (the engine must be raised first).*
b) *Removal and refitting of the big end bearings (after sump removal).*
c) *Removal and refitting of pistons and connecting rods (after removing cylinder head and sump).*
d) *Removal and refitting of the timing belt and timing wheels (after removal of the radiator).*
e) *Removal and refitting of the oil pump (after removal of the sump).*

3 Major operations for which the engine must be removed

1 Removal and refitting of the crankshaft and main bearings.
2 Removal and refitting of the flywheel.
3 Removal and refitting of the rear crankshaft oil seal.

4 Methods of engine removal

1 The engine, complete with gearbox, can be lifted as a unit from the

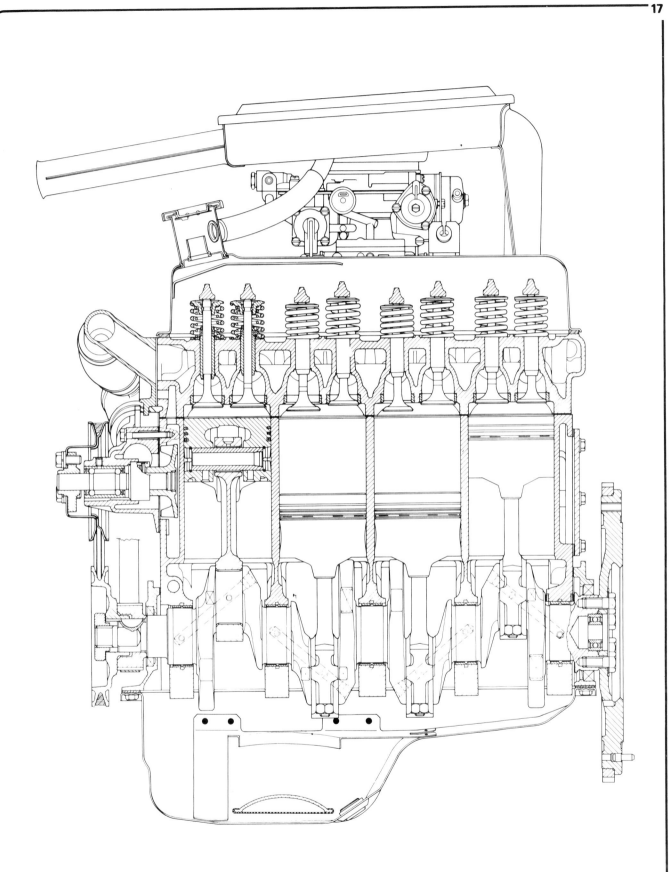

Fig. 1.1. A longitudinal section through the 1600 (type A1.000) engine

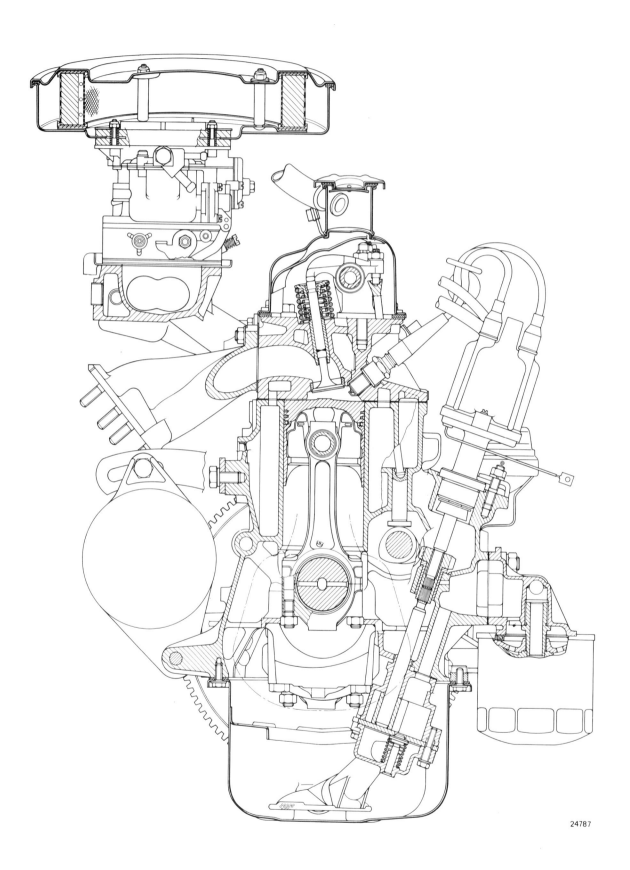

24787

Fig. 1.2. A sectioned end view of the 1300 (type A000) engine

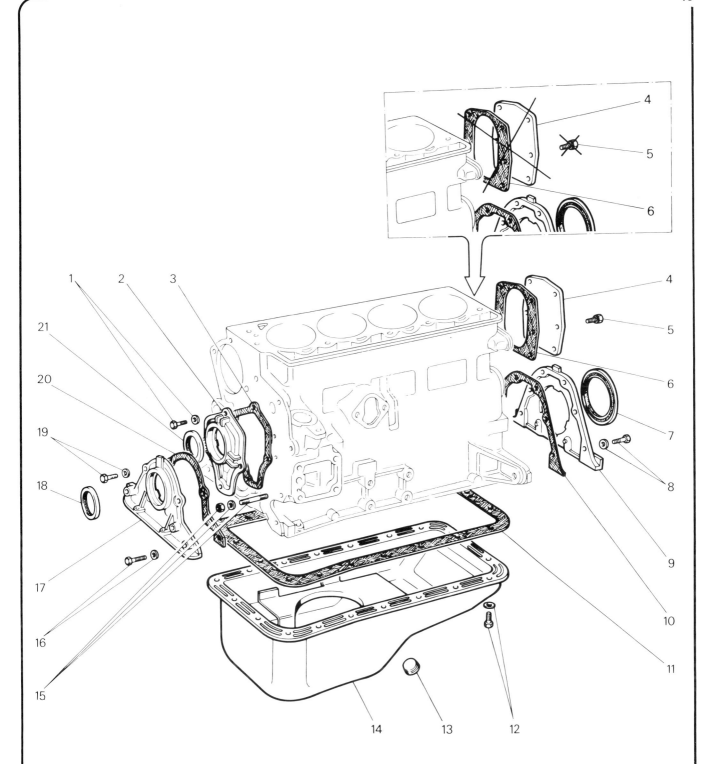

Fig. 1.3 Engine cylinder block covers and sump

1 Bolt and washer
2 Camshaft cover
3 Camshaft cover gasket
4 Water gallery blanking plate
5 Bolt
6 Blanking plate gasket
7 Crankshaft rear cover oil seal

8 Bolt and washer
9 Crankshaft rear cover
10 Crankshaft rear cover gasket
11 Sump gasket
12 Bolt and washer
13 Sump drain plug
14 Sump

15 Stud, washer, and nut
16 Bolt and washer
17 Crankshaft front cover
18 Crankshaft front cover oil seal
19 Bolt and washer
20 Crankshaft front cover gasket
21 Camshaft cover oil seal

NOTE: 4, 5 and 6 are only fitted to block type A1.000 (1600 engine)

engine compartment. Alternatively, the engine and gearbox can be split at the front of the bellhousing, the gearbox supported and left in position, and the engine removed. Whether or not components such as the carburettor, manifolds, generator and starter are removed first depends to some extent on what work is to be done.

5 Engine removal - with gearbox

The do-it-yourself owner should be able to remove the engine fairly easily in about 3½ hours. It is essential to have a good hoist, and two strong axle stands if a pit is not available. Engine removal will be made much easier if you have someone to help you. Before beginning work, it is worthwhile to get all the accumulated dirt and grease cleaned off the engine unit at a service station which is equipped with steam or high pressure air and water cleaning equipment. It helps to make the job quicker, easier and of course, much cleaner. Decide whether you are going to jack up the car and support it on axle stands or raise the front on wheel ramps. If the latter, run the car up now (and chock the rear wheels) whilst you still have the engine power available. Remember that with the front wheels supported on ramps the working height and engine lifting height is going to be increased.

1   Open the bonnet and prop it up to expose the engine and ancillary components. Disconnect the battery leads and lift the battery out of the car. This prevents accidental short circuits while working on the engine.
2   Mark the location of the hinges with a soft leaded pencil, to make refitting easier. Undo the nuts and bolts from the hinges and lift the bonnet off. Place it somewhere safe where it will not be damaged.
3   Drain the cooling system as described in Chapter 2.
4   Remove the sump drain plug and drain the oil out of the engine into a container (an old one gallon oil can with the side cut out will do).
5   Disconnect the HT and LT leads from the coil to the distributor.
6   Disconnect the leads from the alternator, starter motor, low oil

pressure indicator and water temperature sender units.
7   Disconnect the accelerator and choke cables at the carburettor.
8   Disconnect the fuel pipe line to the pump inlet side.
9   Disconnect the exhaust pipe by removing the four nuts at the manifold flange joint.
10 Disconnect the water hoses to the radiator and remove the radiator as described in Chapter 2.
11 Remove the air cleaner assembly.
12 Disconnect the servo vacuum hose at the inlet manifold.
13 Remove the engine to chassis earth strap.
14 Disconnect the heater hoses from the engine.
15 From inside the car remove the gearlever assembly as described in Chapter 6.
16 From under the car disconnect the forward end of the propeller shaft from the gearbox as described in Chapter 7.
17 Remove the wires from the reverse lamp switch.
18 If the car is fitted with an automatic transmission refer to Chapter 6, Part B for information of the parts to be disconnected.
19 Release the speedometer cable from the gearbox.
20 Disconnect the clutch cable from the clutch release lever and draw the cable out through the bellhousing.
21 Undo the exhaust pipe support clip from the rear of the transmission.
22 Support the gearbox with a jack and remove the supporting cross-member from beneath it.
23 Now sling the engine to whatever lifting device you are using and support the weight. Undo the engine mounting nuts, the upper one on the right and the lower one on the left (photo). This will allow the studs to disengage easily from the body mountings. It is important to sling the engine fairly well forward so that when lifted the whole unit will tilt at an acute angle for lifting out. At the same time there should be no possibility of the unit slipping out of the sling. Make sure that there is sufficient headroom to lift the unit out.
24 Lift steadily and carefully, watching that the lifting slings do not

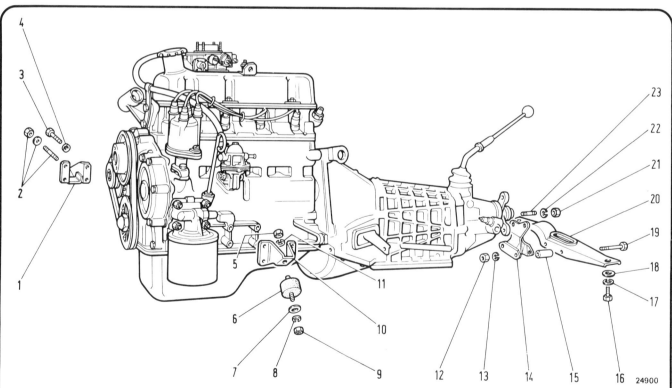

Fig. 1.4. An exploded view of the engine and gearbox mounting attachments (Sec. 4)

1	Right-hand bracket	7	Plain washer	13	Spring washer	19	Bolt
2	Stud, washer and nut	8	Spring washer	14	Gearbox rear mounting	20	Crossmember
3	Bolt	9	Nut	15	Spacer	21	Nut
4	Washer	10	Left-hand bracket	16	Bolt	22	Spring washer
5	Nut	11	Spring washer	17	Spring washer	23	Stud
6	Front engine mounting flange	12	Nut	18	Washer		

strain against ancillaries on the engine which could be damaged.

6 Engine removal - without gearbox

1   Begin by following the instructions in Section 5, paragraph 1 to 14 inclusive.
2   Disconnect also the starter motor cables and remove the bolts holding the starter motor to the transmission unit. Lift the starter motor out.
3   Remove the bolts retaining the flywheel lower cover plate to the front of the transmission case.
4   Support the front of the gearbox on a jack and remove the four bolts holding it to the engine block assembly.
5   Sling the engine with the lifting tackle in such a way that it will not tilt and then take the weight. Undo the engine mounting stud nuts as described in paragraph 23 of the previous Section.
6   Pull the engine forward, supported by the sling, until it disengages from the gearbox input shaft and then lift it up clear and out. If some difficulty is experienced in drawing the engine forward do not impose any lifting or lowering strains which could damage the gearbox input shaft.
7   Where the vehicle is fitted with an automatic transmission (1600 models only) refer to Chapter 6, Part B for details of disconnecting the engine from the transmission.

7 Engine dismantling - general

1   Owners who dismantle a lot of engines will probably have a stand on which to mount them, but most will make do with a work bench. This should be large enough on which to spread the inevitable bits and pieces and tools, and strong enough to support the engine weight. If the floor is the only possible place, try and ensure that the engine rests on a hardwood platform, or similar, rather than concrete (or beaten earth!!).
2   Spend some time on cleaning the unit. If you have been wise this will have been done before the engine was removed, at a service bay. Good solvents, such as 'Gunk', will help to 'float' off caked dirt/grease under a water jet. Once the exterior is clean, dismantling may begin. As parts are removed clean them in petrol or paraffin (do not immerse parts with oilways in paraffin. Paraffin, which could possibly remain in oilways, would dilute the oil for initial lubrication after reassembly).
3   Where components are fitted with seals and gaskets it is always best to fit new ones - but do not throw the old ones away until you have the new ones to hand. A pattern is then available if they have to be specially made. Hang them on a convenient hook.
4   In general it is best to work from the top of the engine downwards. In any case support the engine firmly so that it does not topple over when you are undoing stubborn nuts and bolts.

5   Always place nuts and bolts back together on their components or place of attachment if possible - it saves so much confusion later. Otherwise put them in small, separate pots or jars so that their groups are easily identified.

8 Engine dismantling - ancillary components

1   If you are obtaining a reconditioned engine all ancillaries must come off first - just as they will if you are doing a thorough engine inspection/overhaul yourself. These are:
   Alternator (Chapter 10)
   Distributor (Chapter 4)
   Oil filter (this Section)
   Carburettor (Chapter 3)
   Inlet manifold (this Section)
   Exhaust manifold (this Section)
   Water pump (Chapter 2)
   Fuel pump (Chapter 3)
   Engine mounting brackets (this Section)
2   If you are obtaining what is termed a 'short engine' (or 'half-engine') comprising cylinder block, crankshaft, pistons, and connecting rods, all assembled, then the cylinder head, flywheel, sump and oil pump will need to be removed from the worn engine.
3   Remove all the ancillaries according to the removal instructions described in the various Chapters and Sections as indicated in paragraph 1.
4   To remove the oil filter cartridge simply unscrew it. If it is tight put a piece of chain around it and a screwdriver locked in the links to act as a lever.
5   The inlet and exhaust manifolds can be taken off after removing the carburettor and the seven securing nuts and washers.
6   The oil filter extension housing can be removed by removing the two nuts and bolts securing it to the cylinder face (photo).
7   The engine mounting brackets are bolted to the crankcase. They can be removed without taking the engine from the car if the engine is supported and raised a little.

9 Valve rocker shaft assembly - removal

1   Undo the valve rocker cover retaining nuts and take the cover off.
2   The rocker shaft assembly is held in place by four nuts.
3   Slacken the nuts evenly and remove them.
4   Now lift the rocker shaft assembly off the mounting studs.

10 Cylinder head - removal

Assuming that the engine has not been taken out of the car proceed

5.23 Undo the front engine mounting nuts

8.6 The oil filter extension housing

as follows:
1 Disconnect both battery leads.
2 Drain the cooling system as detailed in Chapter 2.
3 Remove the hoses from the water pump.
4 Remove the carburettor air cleaner unit.
5 Remove the valve rocker gear as detailed in Section 9 of this Chapter.
6 Disconnect the HT leads from the spark plugs.
7 Disconnect the carburettor connections (accelerator, choke and fuel lines).
8 Disconnect the lead to the water temperature sender unit.
9 Remove the carburettor (not essential but merely to prevent damage).
10 Lift out the pushrods.
11 Slacken off the head retaining bolts evenly in the reverse order to the tightening sequence shown on Fig. 1.13. Remove the cylinder head bolts.
12 Now lift off the head. If it is stuck, it is possible (with the engine in the car) to re-connect the battery and turn the engine over so that the cylinder compression will break the seal. Do not try to force anything between the head and block or damage will result. Hit the side of the head with a soft faced mallet if necessary.

11 Valves - removal

1 Remove the cylinder head as described in the previous Section.
2 The valves are located by a collar on compressed springs which grip two collets (or a split collar) into a groove in the stem of the valve. The springs must be compressed with a special G clamp in order to release the collets and the valve. Place the specifically shaped end of the clamp over the spring collar with the end of the screw squarely on the face of the valve. Screw up the clamp to compress the springs and expose the collets on the valve stem. Sometimes the collar sticks and the clamp screw cannot be turned. In such instances, with the clamp pressure still on, give the head of the clamp (over the springs) a tap with a hammer, at the same time gripping the clamp frame firmly to prevent it slipping off the valve.

Take off the two collets, release the clamp, and the collar and springs can be lifted off. The valve can then be pushed out through its guide and removed. If the end of the valve sticks at the guide when removing it, it is due to burring. Carefully grind off the corner of the stem to permit it to pass through the guide. If you force it through it will score the guide. Make sure that each valve is kept in such a way that position is known for refitting. Unless new valves are to be fitted each valve **must** go back where it came from. The springs, collars and collets should also be kept with their respective valves. A piece of card with eight holes punched in it is a good way to keep the valves in order.

12 Valve guides - inspection and renewal

If the valves are very slack in the guides and the slackness cannot be attributed to wear of the valve stems then new guides will have to be fitted along with new valve guide oil seals.

Removal of the guide necessitates the use of a special stepped drift to drive the guide out of the cylinder head casting. As the guide is an interference fit in the head it will be necessary to heat the head casting to approximately 100°C during the removal and refitting of the guide. Finally, after the new guides have been fitted, new valve guide seals will need to be installed using two further special tools.

It is therefore advisable to entrust the removal and fitting of new valve guides to your nearest FIAT dealer as they will have available the special tools mentioned. Attempts to do this operation by makeshift means may cause costly damage to the cylinder head.

13 Sump - removal

1 The engine should be out of the car in order to remove the sump. Otherwise disconnect the front engine mountings and jack the engine up until sufficient clearance is available to remove it once the securing screws are taken out.
2 With the engine out, it is better to wait until the cylinder head is removed. Then invert the engine and undo the set screws holding the

sump to the crankcase and lift it off. If the cylinder head is not being removed (for example, if the oil pump only is being removed) the engine should be placed on its side.

14 Crankshaft pulley, timing cover, gearwheels and timing belt - removal

The timing gear is accessible with the engine in the car but the strip down procedure is performed more easily with the engine removed.
1 Unlock the tab washer and undo the large nut which holds the fan belt driving pulley to the crankshaft. It will be necessary to prevent the crankshaft from turning by locking the flywheel with a bar in the starter ring teeth against one of the dowel pegs in the end of the crankcase.
2 Another method is to block one of the crankshaft journals with a piece of wood against the side of the crankcase. To remove the bolt, when the engine is still fitted in the car, put the car in gear to prevent the crankshaft from turning.
3 The pulley should pull off easily. If not, lever it off with two screwdrivers at 180° to each other. Take care not to damage either the pulley wheel or timing case cover which is made of light alloy.
4 Remove the bolts holding the timing case cover in place and take it off.
5 Slide the toothed rubber timing belt off the pulleys.
6 Now remove the camshaft gearwheel retaining bolt. FIAT recommend that tool A.60457 must be used to lock the camshaft while slackening or tightening the camshaft gearwheel retaining bolt.
7 An alternative method of slackening the camshaft retainer bolt is to use a ring spanner and a soft mallet. Ensure that the ring spanner is a good fit on the bolt. Now deliver a sharp blow on the end of the ring spanner with the mallet, turning the bolt in an anticlockwise direction to slacken it.
8 The two pulley gearwheels can now be carefully levered off. However, if they are very tight a puller may be necessary to draw them off.

15 Pistons, connecting rods and big-end bearings - removal

1 As it is necessary to remove the cylinder head and the sump from the engine in order to remove the pistons and connecting rods, the

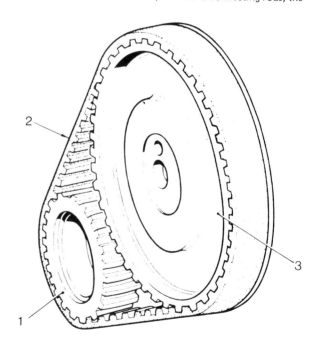

Fig. 1.5. The timing wheels and timing belt (Sec. 14)

1 Crankshaft timing wheel   3 Camshaft timing wheel
2 Timing belt

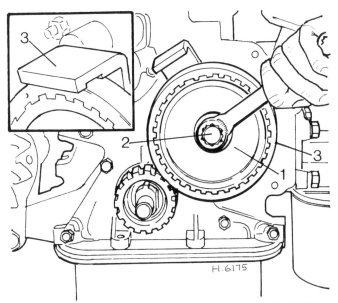

Fig. 1.6. Slackening the camshaft wheel retaining bolt using FIAT Tool A60457 to lock the timing wheel

1 *Camshaft timing wheel*
2 *Camshaft timing wheel retaining bolt*
3 *FIAT Tool A60457*

removal of the engine is the logical thing to do first. With the engine on the bench and the cylinder head and sump removed, stand the block inverted (with crankshaft uppermost).

2 Each connecting rod and its bearing cap is matched, and held by two high tensile steel bolts. Before anything else, mark each connecting rod and cap with its cylinder number and relationship - preferably with the appropriate number of dabs of paint. Using punch or file marks may be satisfactory, but it has been known for tools to slip - or the marks even to cause metal fatigue in the connecting rod. Once marked, undo the bearing cap bolts using a good quality socket spanner. Lift off each bearing cap and put it in a safe place. Carefully turn the engine on its side. Each piston can now be pushed out from the block by its connecting rod. Clean a small area on the front of each piston crown and place an indicative dab of paint. Do not use a punch, or file marks, on the pistons under any circumstances. The shell bearings in the connecting rods and caps can be removed simply by pressing the edge of the end opposite the notch in the shell and they will slide round ready to be lifted out.

16 Pistons - removal from connecting rods

The pistons are joined to the connecting rods by gudgeon pins which in turn are retained by circlips in each end of the piston bosses.
1 To remove the circlips turn them to the cut out position and remove them using circlip pliers.
2 The gudgeon pin can now be pushed out through the piston and the connecting rod released. To facilitate easy removal of the gudgeon pins, should they be tight in the piston bosses, immerse the pistons in hot water to expand them sufficiently, allowing the gudgeon pin to slide out easily.

17 Piston rings - removal

1 With the piston assemblies removed, the piston rings may be removed by opening each of them in turn, just enough to enable them to ride over the lands of the piston body.
2 In order to prevent the lower rings dropping into an empty groove higher up the piston as they are removed, it is helpful to use two or three narrow strips of tin or old feeler blades inserted behind the ring at equidistant points and then to employ a twisting motion to slide the ring from the piston.
3 Note from where each ring has been removed if they are to be used again.

Fig. 1.7. The piston and connecting rod assembly

1	Gudgeon pin	6	Piston
2	Circlip	7	Connecting rod
3	Oil scraper ring	8	Connecting rod cap
4	Oil control ring	9	Big-end bearing shell
5	Compression ring		

18 Flywheel - removal

1 The flywheel can be removed with the engine in the car but it is not recommended, and the following procedure prevails when the engine has been lifted out:
2 Remove the clutch assembly (Chapter 5).
3 Lock the crankshaft in position with a piece of wood and undo the six bolts in the centre of the flywheel.
4 Using a soft headed mallet, tap the periphery of the flywheel progressively all round, drawing it off the crankshaft boss. Do not allow it to assume a skew angle as the fit on the flange has very close tolerances to maintain proper balance and concentricity with the crankshaft. Make sure it is well supported so that it does not drop.

19 Oil pump - removal

1 Remove the engine from the car (preferably - although one may detach the sump with the engine in place if the engine is disconnected from the front mountings and jacked up).
2 Remove the sump.
3 Undo the bolts securing the pump and suction pipe unit to the crankcase and withdraw the pump.

20 Camshaft - removal

1 Remove the engine from the car.
2 Remove the valve gear and pushrods, sump, fan belt pulley, timing case cover, pulley gearwheels and timing belt, oil pump, distributor and driving gear.
3 Remove the fuel pump.
4 If the cylinder head has been removed stand the engine inverted, if not, lie it on its right-hand side and rotate the crankshaft several times to push the tappets (cam followers) out of the way.
5 Remove the four bolts retaining the camshaft endplate and seal.
6 Remove the camshaft endplate and carefully draw the camshaft out. Care must be taken when drawing the cam lobes past the tappets to prevent damage to either the cam lobes or the tappets. This will be easy if the engine is completely inverted. If, however, it is lying on its side with the tappets in such a position that they could fall out under their own weight, more care is necessary. When withdrawing the shaft care must be taken not to damage the camshaft bearings with the edges of the cam lobes.

21 Tappets - removal

1   The tappets can only be removed from their bores in the crankcase after the camshaft has been removed. Section 20 of this Chapter details the camshaft removal operation.
2   Once the camshaft has been removed the tappets can be lifted away from their housings. Note that the shape of the tappet dictates it can only be fitted or removed from the bottom of the crankcase bore.

22 Crankshaft and main bearings - removal

1   With the engine removed from the car, remove the sump, oil pump, timing belt and timing gearwheels, and flywheel.
2   Now remove the crankshaft front and rear cover plates which both incorporate oil seals.
3   Remove the connecting rod bearing caps. This will already have been done if the pistons have been removed.
4   Remove the two cap bolts from each of the main bearing caps.
5   Lift the caps off and carefully note their positions, marking them with paint spots if necessary.
6   Grip the crankshaft at each end and lift it out. Remove the shell bearings from the crankcase bearing caps and also the semi-circular crankshaft thrust washers.

23 Crankshaft - examination and renovation

1   Examine all the crankpins and main bearing journals for signs of scoring or scratches. If all surfaces are undamaged, check that all the bearing journals are round. This can be done with a micrometer or caliper gauge, taking readings across the diameter at six or seven points for each journal. If you do not own, or know how to use a micrometer, take the crankshaft to your local engineering works and ask them to 'mike it up' for you.
2   If the crankshaft is ridged or scored, it must be reground. If the ovality exceeds 0.002 in (0.05 mm) on measurement, but there are no signs of scoring or scratching on the surfaces, regrinding may be necessary. It would be advisable to ask the advice of the engineering works to whom you would entrust the work of regrinding in such instances.
3   Check also that the oilway plugs are secure (photo).

24 Big-end (connecting rod) bearings and main bearings - examination and renovation

1   Big-end bearing failure is normally indicated by a pronounced knocking from the crankcase and a slight drop in oil pressure. Main bearing failure is normally accompanied by vibration, which can be quite severe at high engine speeds, and a more significant drop in oil pressure. Oil pressure drop can only be verified, of course, if a gauge is fitted.
2   The shell bearing surfaces should be matt grey in colour with no sign of pitting or scoring (photo).
3   New shell bearings are supplied in a series of thicknesses dependent on the degree of regrinding that the crankshaft requires, which is done in multiples of 0.01 in (0.25 mm). So, depending on how much it is necessary to grind off, bearing shells are supplied 0.01 in (0.25 mm) undersize and so on. The engineering works regrinding the crankshaft will normally supply the correct shells with the reground crankshaft.
4   If an engine is removed for overhaul, it is worthwhile renewing big-end bearings and main bearings as a matter of course. This will add many thousands of miles to the life of the engine before regrinding of the crankshaft becomes necessary. Make sure that the new bearing shells are of the standard dimension if the crankshaft has not been reground.

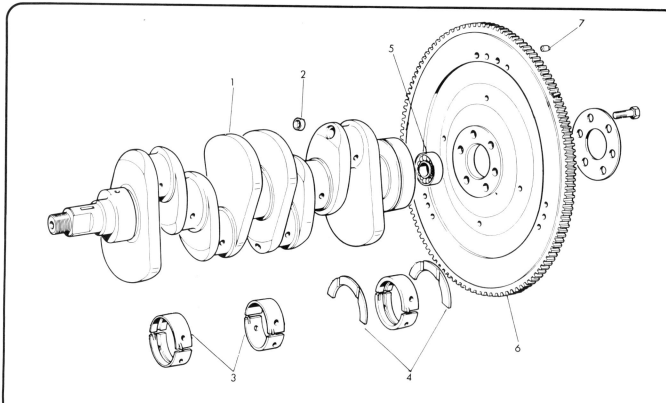

Fig. 1.8. Crankshaft components (Sec. 22)

1 Crankshaft	4 Crankshaft thrust washers	6 Flywheel
2 Oilway blanking plug	5 Spigot bearing	7 Clutch plate locating dowel
3 Main bearing shells		

23.3 The pointer marks the crankshaft oil way plug

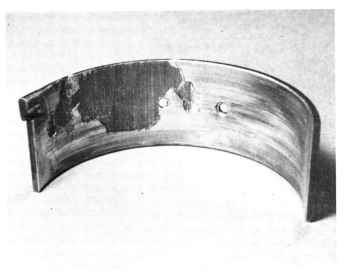

24.2 A badly worn big-end shell bearing

25 Cylinder bores - examination and renovation

1   The cylinder bores must be examined for taper, ovality, scoring and scratches. Start by carefully examining the top of the cylinder bores. If they are at all worn a very slight ridge will be found on the thrust side. This marks the top of the piston travel. The owner will have a good indication of the bore wear prior to dismantling the engine, or removing the cylinder head. Excessive oil consumption accompanied by blue smoke from the exhaust is a sure sign of worn cylinder bores and piston rings.
2   Measure the bore diameter just under the ridge with a micrometer and compare it with the diameter at the bottom of the bore, which is not subject to wear. If the difference between the two measurements is more than 0.006 in (0.15 mm) then it will be necessary to fit special piston rings or to have the cylinders rebored and oversize pistons and rings fitted. If no micrometer is available, remove the rings from a piston and place the piston in each bore in turn about three quarters of an inch below the top of the bore. If a 0.010 in (0.25 mm) feeler gauge can be slid between the piston and the cylinder wall on the thrust side of the bore then remedial action must be taken. Oversize pistons are available in the following sizes:

+ 0.0079 in (0.2 mm)
+ 0.0157 in (0.4 mm)
+ 0.0236 in (0.6 mm)

3   These are accurately machined to just below these measurements so as to provide correct running clearances in bores machined out to the exact oversize dimensions.
4   If the bores are slightly worn but not so badly worn as to justify reboring them, special oil control rings can be fitted to the existing pistons which will restore compression and stop the engine burning oil. Several different types are available and the manufacturer's instructions concerning their fitting must be followed closely.

26 Pistons and rings - examination and renovation

1   Examine the pistons (with the rings removed as described in Section 17) for signs of damage on the crown and around the top edge. If any of the piston rings have broken, there could be quite noticeable damage to the grooves, in which case the piston must be renewed. Deep scores in the piston walls also call for renewal. If the cylinders are being rebored, new oversize pistons and rings will be needed anyway. If the cylinders do not need reboring and the pistons are in good condition, only the rings need to be checked.
    Pistons should be measured across the diameter at right angles to the gudgeon pin 2 in (52 mm) down from the piston crown.

2   To check the existing rings, place them in the cylinder bore and press each one down in turn to the bottom of the bore. In this case a distance of 2½ in (65 mm) from the top of the cylinder will be satisfactory. Use an inverted piston to press them down square. With a feeler gauge, measure the gap for each ring which should be as given in the Specifications at the beginning of this Chapter. If the gap is too large, the rings will need renewal.
3   New pistons are not usually fitted in an un-rebored block. If they are the precautions for fitting new rings should be considered as indicated in the following paragraphs.
4   When new rings are fitted in untouched bores the top ring normally has a cutaway step to prevent the top ring fouling any ridge which there may be in the bore. If the top ring does not have such a feature then the ridge should be scraped or ground away. If this is not done the ring will break when it hits the ridge.
5   New rings should be placed in the bores as described in paragraph 2, and the gap checked. Any gaps which are too small should be increased by filing one end of the ring with a fine file. Be careful not to break the ring as they are brittle (and expensive). On no account make the gap less than specification. If the gap should close when under normal operating temperatures, the ring will break.
6   The groove clearance of new rings in old pistons should be within the specified tolerances. If it is not enough, the rings could stick in the piston grooves causing loss of compression.

27 Camshaft, camshaft bearing and tappets - examination and renovation

1   With the camshaft removed, examine the bearings for signs of obvious wear and pitting. If there are signs, then the three bearings will need renewal. This is not a common requirement, and to have to do so is indicative of severe engine neglect at some time. As special removal and refitting tools are necessary to do this work properly it is recommended that the work be given to a specialist machine shop or a FIAT dealer. Check that the bearings are located properly so that the oilways from the bearing housings are not obstructed.
2   The camshaft itself should show no marks on either the bearing journals or the cams. If it does, it should be renewed. Check that the overall height of each cam from base to peak is within the specifications. If not the camshaft should be renewed.
3   Examine the skew gear for signs of wear or damage. If the gear is badly worn then it will mean renewing the camshaft.
4   Carefully examine the tappets for wear on the face that bears on the camshaft. In addition check that there are no apparent cracks or chips and test the fit of the tappet in the cylinder tappet bores.
5   Note that whenever a **new** camshaft is fitted the old tappets should be discarded and a **new** set of tappets fitted. This is very important as old tappets will very quickly destroy a new camshaft by wearing off the case hardening.

28 Timing gearwheels and timing belt - examination and renovation

1   There are two types of camshaft timing wheel fitted to these
engines. On some engines the timing wheel is manufactured from
cast iron, while on others it is made from a plastic material. Check both
the camshaft and crankshaft gearwheels for damage and the timing
belt for stretching, cracks and wear. As there is no timing belt adjuster
or tensioner fitted to these engines it is imperative that the timing belt
is in first class condition.
2   If during carrying out these checks any component is found faulty
then it should be renewed.

29 Valve rocker shaft assembly and pushrods - examination and renovation

1   Thoroughly clean the rocker shaft assembly before dismantling it.
2   Remove the snap-ring from the end of the shaft and remove the
rocker posts, rocker arms and springs.
3   Check the rocker shaft for wear and straightness, The straightness
of the shaft can be checked by rolling it on a piece of glass. If the
shaft is out of true it should be renewed. The surface of the shaft
should be free from any wear ridges caused by the rocker arms. If any
wear is present, renew the shaft.
4   Check the rocker arms for wear of the rocker bushes, for wear at
the rocker arm face which bears on the valve stem, and for wear of the
ball ended adjusting screws. Wear in the rocker arm bush can be
checked by gripping the rocker arm tip and holding the rocker arm in
place on the shaft, noting if there is any lateral rocker arm movement.
If movement is present, and the arm is very loose on the shaft, a new
bush or rocker arm must be fitted.
5   Check the tip of the rocker arm where it bears on the valve head
for cracking or serious wear of the case hardening. If none is present
the rocker arm is still serviceable. Check the ball end of the rocker arm

adjusting screw for wear or damage.
6   Check the pushrods for straightness by rolling them along a flat
surface and renew any that are bent.

30 Connecting rods - examination and renovation

1   Examine the small end bushes for wear and fit. If any of the bushes
require renewal then the defective connecting rods should be taken to
the nearest FIAT dealer. They will have the necessary tools and equipment to remove the worn bushes and fit and ream the new ones to
size.
2   If it is suspected that a connecting rod is bent or twisted, the
suspected rod should be taken to the nearest FIAT dealer for an
alignment test on a special jig.

31 Flywheel starter ring gear - examination and renovation

1   If the teeth on the flywheel ring gear are badly worn, or if some are
missing, then it will be necessary to fit a new ring gear. The ring gear is
supplied as an individual spare and is a shrink fit on the flywheel.
2   To remove the ring gear use a sharp cold chisel and a heavy hammer.
The greatest care should be taken to prevent damaging the flywheel
during this process. It is sometimes advantageous to drill a ¼ in (6
mm) hole at the intersection point of two teeth, and to strike this
point with the cold chisel.
3   To fit a new ring gear, heat it gently and evenly to a temperature of
170° to 175°C (338° - 347°F) in an oil bath or oven; do not exceed
this temperature as the case hardening will be weakened.
4   With the ring at this temperature, fit it to the flywheel with the
front teeth facing the flywheel register. The ring should be tapped
gently down onto its register and left to cool naturally, when the
shrinkage of the metal on cooling will ensure that it is a permanent and
secure fit.

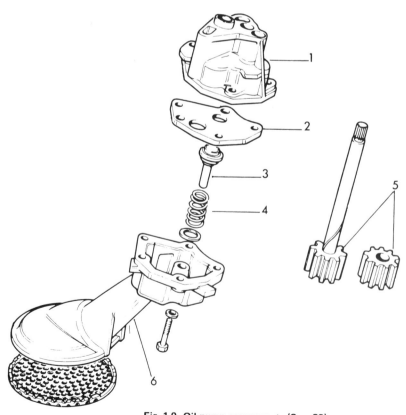

Fig. 1.9. Oil pump components (Sec. 32)

1 Pump housing	3 By-pass relief valve
2 Pump gear cover plate	4 Valve spring

5 Pump gears	
6 Suction horn and strainer	

32 Oil pump - dismantling, examination and renovation

1 With the oil pump removed from the engine, undo and remove the three bolts and spring washers securing the suction horn to the pump housing.
2 Thoroughly clean all the component parts in petrol and then check the gear endfloat and tooth clearances in the following manner.
3 With the two gears in position in the pump, place the straight edge of a steel rule across the joint face of the housing and measure the gap between the bottom of the straight edge and the top of the gears with a feeler gauge. The clearance should not exceed 0.0045 in (0.116 mm).
4 Check the backlash between the two gears and this should not exceed 0.006 in (0.15 mm).
5 Fit a new oil pump if the clearances are incorrect.

33 Decarbonisation

1 Modern engines, together with modern fuels and lubricants, have virtually nullified the need for the engine to have a 'de-coke' which was common enough only a few years ago. Carbon deposits are formed mostly on the modern engine only when it has to do a great deal of slow speed, stop/start running, for example in busy traffic conditions. If carbon deposit symptoms are apparent, such as pinking or pre-ignition and running on after the engine has been switched off, then a good high speed run on a motorway or straight stretch of road is usually sufficient to clear these deposits out. It is beneficial to any motor car to give it a good high speed run from time to time.
2 There will always be some carbon deposits, of course, so if the occasion demands the removal of the cylinder head, for some reason or another, it is a good idea to remove the carbon deposits when the opportunity presents itself. Carbon deposits in the combustion chambers of the cylinder head can be dealt with as described under the Section heading 'Cylinder head - inspection and renovation'. The other carbon deposits which have to be dealt with are those on the crowns of the pistons. This work can easily be carried out with the engine in the car, but great care must be taken to ensure that no particles of dislodged carbon fall either into the cylinder bores and down past the piston rings or into the water jacket orifices in the cylinder block.
3 Bring the first piston to the top of its stroke and then, using a sheet of strong paper and some self adhesive tape, mask off the other three cylinders and surrounding block to prevent any particles falling into the open orifices in the block. To prevent small particles of dislodged carbon from finding their way down the side of the piston which is actually being decarbonised, press grease into the gap between the piston and the cylinder wall. Carbon deposits should then be scraped away carefully with a flat blade from the top of the crown of the piston and the surrounding top edge of the cylinder. Great care must be taken to ensure that the scraper does not gouge away into the soft aluminium surface of the piston crown.
4 A wire brush, either operated by hand or a power drill should not be used if decarbonising is being done with the engine still in the car. It is virtually impossible to prevent carbon particles being distributed over a large area and the time saved by this method is very little.
5 In addition to the removal of carbon deposits on the pistons, it is a good time also to make sure that traces of gasket or any sealing compound are removed from the mating face of the cylinder block top face.
6 After each piston has been attended to, clean out the grease and carbon particles from the gap where it has been pressed in. As the engine is revolved to bring the next piston to the top of its stroke for attention, check the bore of the cylinder which has just been decarbonised and make sure that no traces of carbon or grease are adhering to the inside of the bore.

34 Valves, valve seats and valve springs - examination and renovation

1 Examine the heads of the valves for pitting and burning, especially the heads of the exhaust valves. The valve seatings should be examined at the same time. If any pitting on the valve and seat is very slight, the marks can be removed by grinding the seats and valves together with coarse, and then fine, valve grinding paste.
2 Where bad pitting has occurred to the valve seats it will be

34.3 Grinding an exhaust valve into its seat

necessary to recut them and fit new valves. This latter job should be entrusted to the local FIAT agency or engineering shop. In practice it is very seldom that the seats are so badly worn. Normally, it is the valve that is too badly worn to be refitted, and the owner can easily purchase a new set of valves and match them to the seats by valve grinding.
3 Valve grinding is carried out as follows: Smear a trace of coarse carborundum paste on the seat face and apply a suction grinder tool to the valve head. With a semi-rotary motion, grind the valve head to its seat (photo), lifting the valve occasionally to redistribute the grinding paste. When a full matt even surface finish is produced on both the valve seat and the valve, then wipe off the paste and repeat the process with fine carborundum paste, lifting and turning the valve to redistribute the paste as before. A light spring placed under the valve head will greatly ease this operation. When a smooth unbroken ring of light grey matt finish is produced, on both valve and valve seat faces, the grinding operation is complete. It is important though that the seat widths of the grinding do not exceed specification. If they do the valve will need renewal and the seat recutting by a specialist.
4 Scrape away all carbon from the valve head and the valve stem. Carefully clean away every trace of grinding compound, taking great care to leave none in the ports or in the valve guides. The simplest way is to flush with paraffin and then hose out with water.
5 Check that all valve springs are intact. If any one is broken, all should be renewed. Check that the free height of the springs is within specifications. If some springs are not within specifications, renew them all. Springs suffer from fatigue and it is a good idea to renew them even if they look all right.

35 Cylinder head - examination

1 With the valves removed and all carbon deposits cleaned away, the valve seats must be examined for signs of cracking or pitting. Mild pitting can be cured by grinding in the valves with carborundum paste, but any hair line cracks or severe ridging and pitting mean that at least the seats will need recutting or renewing. This is a specialist task. Cracks visible anywhere else in the head, mean that it must be scrapped.
2 The head must be perfectly flat where it joins the cylinder block. Use a metal straight edge at various positions along and across the head to see if it is warped in any way. The least one can expect from a warped head is persistent blowing of gaskets and loss of coolant.
3 Check the valve guides (Section 12).
4 See that all water passages are clear and scrape away any visible hard deposits. Note that a chemical de-scaler might be worth using after the engine is reassembled.
5 Make sure also that the other mating flange surfaces (for manifolds etc) are clean, flat and unpitted.

36 Engine reassembly - general

1   To ensure maximum life with minimum trouble from a rebuilt engine, not only must everything be correctly assembled, but everything must be spotlessly clean, all the oilways must be clear, locking washers and spring washers must always be fitted where indicated and all bearing and other working surfaces must be thoroughly lubricated during assembly.
2   Before assembly begins renew any bolts or studs, the threads of which are in any way damaged, and whenever possible use new spring washers.
3   Apart from your normal tools, a supply of clean rag, an oil can filled with engine oil (an empty plastic detergent bottle thoroughly cleaned and washed out, will do), a new supply of assorted spring washers, a set of new gaskets, and a torque spanner, should be collected together.

37 Crankshaft - refitting

1   Ensure that the cylinder block is thoroughly clean and all the oil-ways are clear. If possible blow the drillings out with compressed air.
2   Clean the crankshaft in the same manner and then inject engine oil into the crankshaft oilways.
3   Fit the upper halves of the five main bearing shells into the cylinder block housings so that the notches on the bearing shells fit into the cut-outs provided. Note that the centre bearing shell has no oil groove in it. When fitting new shell bearings soak them in paraffin and wipe them dry before fitting to remove any surface preservative. When in position lubricate them with clean engine oil (photos).
4   The crankshaft endfloat thrust washers are semi-circular and fit each side of the cylinder block No. 5 (rear) bearing housing. The thrust washer grooves should face outwards. Hold the washers in place with a dab of grease (photos).
5   Lower the crankshaft into position taking care not to dislodge the thrust washers.
6   Clean the main bearing caps and fit the shell bearings remembering that the plain bearing goes in the centre. Refit the caps having first lubricated the journals. The caps are identified by markings and the paint spots put on earlier. No. 1 cap (front), however, is not marked (except by the paint spot). Nos. 2 - 5 are centre punched 1 - 4 (photos).
7   Refit the main bearing cap bolts and do them up finger tight.
8   Test the crankshaft for freedom of rotation. Should it be very stiff to turn, or possess high spots, a most careful inspection must be made, preferably by a skilled mechanic with a micrometer to trace the cause of the trouble. It is very seldom that any trouble of this nature will be experienced when fitting the crankshaft.
9   Continue to tighten the main bearing bolts down evenly making frequent checks to see if the crankshaft is still free to rotate.
10 Tighten the main bearing bolts to the torque wrench setting shown in the Specifications at the beginning of this Chapter. Note that one of the bolts retaining the No. 1 bearing cap is smaller and has a different torque setting than the other bolts (photo).
11 If during the tightening sequence the crankshaft binds and will not rotate stop tightening the bolts and investigate the cause.
12 Finally, test the crankshaft endfloat which should be within the limits as detailed in the Specifications. If the endfloat exceeds these limits then oversize thrust washers will need to be fitted.

38 Pistons and connecting rods - reassembly

1   If the original pistons are being used, they must be matched with the same connecting rod and gudgeon pin from which it was removed. If new pistons are being installed it does not matter to which connecting rod they are fitted.
2   It is important that the piston and connecting rod are assembled in the correct way to ensure that the offset of the piston is on the thrust side of the cylinder. The offset side of the piston is on the same side as the oil jet hole which is bored into the shoulder of the connecting rod. Therefore, the connecting rod reference numbers will face away from the camshaft.
3   Now lubricate the gudgeon pin and small end bush and place the piston on top of the connecting rod. Align the piston bosses with the small end and slide the gudgeon pin through. If necessary, heat the pistons in hot water first. Now ensure that the piston is fitted the

correct way round as described in paragraph 2.
4   FIAT recommend that tool A.60303 be used to refit the gudgeon pin circlips. However, the circlips can be fitted using a pair of circlip pliers and a small screwdriver.
5   With the circlips now in place ensure that the ends of the circlip are not in line with the special slots machined into the piston bosses which enable the circlip to be easily removed.

39 Piston rings - refitting

1   Ensure that the piston and piston rings have been inspected and renewed in accordance with the procedure described in Section 26 of this Chapter.
2   Check that the ring grooves are completely clean.
3   Fit the rings over the top of the piston, starting with the bottom oil control ring.
4   The ring may be spread with the fingers sufficiently to go around the piston, but it could be difficult getting the bottom past the other two grooves. It is well worth spending a little time cutting a strip of thin tin plate from any handy can, say 1 in (25 mm) wide and slightly shorter in length than the piston circumference. Place the ring around this and then slide the strip with the ring on it over the piston, until the ring can be conveniently slipped off into its groove.
5   Repeat this operation in the same manner with the other two rings, making sure that they are fitted the right way up.
6   The words 'TOP' or 'BOTTOM' may be marked on the rings and indicate which way up the ring fits in its groove in the piston, ie. the side marked 'TOP' should face the top of the piston, and does not mean that the ring concerned should necessarily go into the top piston groove.

40 Pistons - refitting in cylinder bores

1   The pistons, complete with connecting rods and new shell bearings can be fitted to the cylinder bores in the following manner.
2   With a piece of lint free rag wipe the cylinder bores clean. If new rings have been fitted, any surface oil 'glaze' on the bore walls should be removed by rubbing with a very fine abrasive. This can be a very fine grade of emery cloth, or a fine cutting paste used for rubbing down paintwork. This operation will enable the new piston rings to speedily bed into the cylinders properly. Make sure that all traces of abrasive are confined to the cylinder bores and are completely removed when the pistons are refitted to the cylinder.
3   Now generously lubricate the pistons, rings and cylinder bores with clean engine oil.
4   The pistons, complete with connecting rods, are fitted to the bores from above. First fit the bearing shell into the connecting rod engaging the notch in the cut-out and ensure that the oil holes are aligned (photo).
5   To fit the piston into the bore it is necessary to compress the piston rings using a piston ring clamp (Fig. 1.10). Alternatively, if a piston ring clamp is not available, then a piece of thin tin wide enough to cover the rings adequately and long enough to wrap around the piston with a substantial overlap used in conjunction with a large Jubilee clip is sufficient.
6   As each piston is inserted into its bore, ensure that it is the correct piston/connecting rod assembly for that particular bore. The oil drilling in the connecting rod shoulder, faces the thrust side (left) of the cylinder. The matching numbers of the connecting rod and cap face the other side of the cylinder (Fig. 1.11).
7   Compress the rings and gently tap the piston crown with a hammer handle, continue to drive the piston down until the complete piston is in the bore. Take care during this operation to ensure that the piston ring gaps have been spaced at 90° to each other before they are compressed with the tool.
8   If new pistons and rings are being fitted to the rebored block, the clearances are very small and care has to be taken to make sure that no part of a piston ring catches the edge of the bore before being pressed down. They are very brittle and easily broken. For this reason it is acceptable practice to chamfer the lip of the cylinder very slightly to provide a better ease of entry for the rings into the cylinder. The chamfer should be at an angle of 45° and should not be cut back too much.

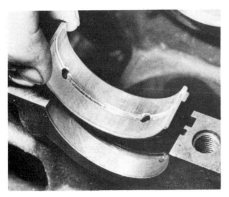

37.3A Fitting a main bearing shell into the crankcase

37.3B The centre main bearing shell has no oil groove

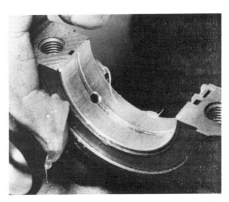

37.4A Applying grease to hold the crankshaft thrust washer in place

37.4B Fitting one of the crankshaft thrust washers at the side of No. 5 main bearing

37.6A Main bearing caps show identifying marks

37.6B Fitting a main bearing cap

37.10 Tightening a main bearing cap bolt

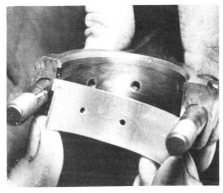

40.4 Fitting a big-end bearing shell into a connecting rod

41 Connecting rods to crankshaft - reassembly

1   If the original big-end bearing shells are nearly new and are being reused, then ensure that they are refitted in their correct locations on the respective connecting rods.

2   Generously lubricate the crankshaft journal with clean engine oil, and turn the crankshaft so that the journal is in the most advantageous position for the connecting rod to be drawn onto it.

3   Wipe the connecting rod bearing cap and back of the bearing shell clean, and fit the bearing shell in position ensuring that the locating tongue at the back of the bearing engages with the locating groove in the connecting rod cap.

4   Make sure the correct cap is fitted to its respective rod by checking the matching numbers (photo).

5   Lubricate the bearing shell and offer up the connecting rod cap to the connecting rod (photo).

6   Fit the connecting rod nuts and tighten the nuts evenly to the torque wrench setting specified at the beginning of this Chapter.

7   After tightening each cap nut, rotate the crankshaft to ensure that the bearings are not binding.

8   Oil the cylinder bores liberally for initial lubrication purposes.

9   Repeat the above operation for the other three connecting rod assemblies and then ensure that the engine rotates smoothly by hand.

42 Crankshaft front and rear cover plates and oil seals - refitting

1   When overhauling the engine it is always advisable to renew the oil seals. The crankshaft has a front and rear oil seal fitted into a housing bolted to each cylinder block end.

2   The two seals are pressed into their respective housings and rest against centralising lugs at the rear.

3   With the housings removed from the cylinder block drive the seals out from their housings.

4   Correct fitting of the new oil seals is essential. The seals are marked with an arrow to denote the direction of rotation of the crankshaft.

Fig. 1.10. Replacing the piston using a piston ring compressor (Sec 40)

1   Piston   *2   Piston ring compressor tool*

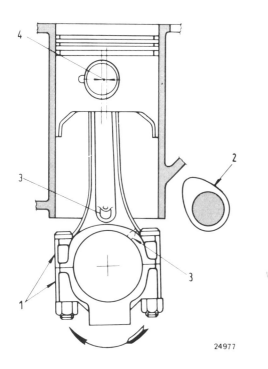

Fig. 1.11. Installation of piston - connecting rod assembly (Sec. 40)

1   Location of connecting rod matching number with cylinder
2   Camshaft
3   Lubrication hole
4   Gudgeon pin boss offset (2 mm)

The seals should be fitted so that the arrow is visible from the outside of the seal and should be checked for correct crankshaft rotation in relation to the arrow (photo).

5   When refitting the housing always use new paper gaskets taking care that the retaining bolts are tightened evenly (photo).

Note: It is also recommended that the crankshaft surface on which the lip of the seal will run is lubricated with engine oil prior to fitting the housings.

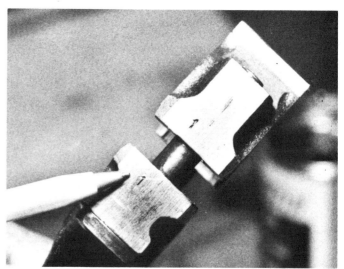

41.4 Each connecting rod and cap has corresponding marks

41.5 Fitting a big-end bearing cap with a new bearing shell onto the connecting rod

43 Tappets/camshaft - refitting

1   If you are fitting a new camshaft it is recommended that new tappets are fitted with it.
2   Invert the engine or tip it on its side and refit the tappets after lubricating them with clean engine oil.
3   Wipe the camshaft bearing journals clean and lubricate them generously.
4   Insert the camshaft into the cylinder block, taking care not to damage the camshaft bearings with the cam lobes (photo).
5   Fit a new oil seal into the camshaft cover housing having removed all traces of old gasket from the face of the cylinder block and the cover housing.
6   Prior to fitting the housing cover it is recommended that the camshaft surface on which the lip of the oil seal runs is lubricated with engine oil.
7   Refit the camshaft cover housing using a new paper gasket and tighten the housing bolts to the recommended torque wrench setting (photo).

44 Timing wheels and timing belt - refitting

1   This Section describes the refitting procedure as part of the general

41.6 Tightening the big-end bearing cap nuts

42.4 The seal in the rear cover plate has an arrow (indicated) in the direction of shaft rotation

42.5 Fitting the front crankshaft cover plate and seal using a new gasket

43.4 Replacing the camshaft into the cylinder block

43.7 Refitting the camshaft cover housing using a new seal and gasket

overhaul of the engine, and assumes that the engine is removed from the car.

2   Refit both the crankshaft and camshaft gearwheels. The crankshaft gearwheel is located on a Woodruff key while the camshaft gearwheel has a small hole drilled near its centre which locates with a dowel peg on the camshaft. Ensure that the gearwheels are fitted the correct way round with the timing marks facing outwards.

3   FIAT recommend that too A.60457 be used to prevent rotation of the camshaft when tightening the camshaft gearwheel retaining bolt. If this tool is not available and some other means is employed to lock the camshaft take care not to damage the camshaft gearwheel as in some applications it is made of plastic.

4   With the gearwheels now in position rotate the crankshaft until No. 1 and 4 pistons are at the top of the bore and the timing mark on the crankshaft gearwheel is in line with the timing mark cast into the crankshaft front cover housing.

5   Now rotate the camshaft gearwheel until the timing mark on its periphery is aligned with the other timing mark cast into the crankshaft front cover housing.

6   Now slide the rubber timing belt evenly over both the gearwheels taking care that all of the reference marks remain aligned.

7   Now refit the timing case cover and finally refit the fan belt drive pulley and locknut and tab washer.

8   Prevent the crankshaft from rotating and tighten the fan belt drive pulley securing nut to the recommended torque wrench setting. Now knock back the tab washer to lock the nut in place.

45 Oil pump - refitting

1   Before refitting the oil pump it is as well to check first that the bushing for the drive gear inside the cylinder block is in good condition (photo).

2   This can be done by refitting the pump/distributor drive gear, using a suitable guide rod, and verifying that there is no excessive play. It may be necessary to rotate the camshaft to locate the drive gear with the gear on the camshaft (photo).

3   Before fitting the oil pump it is sound practice to prime the pump

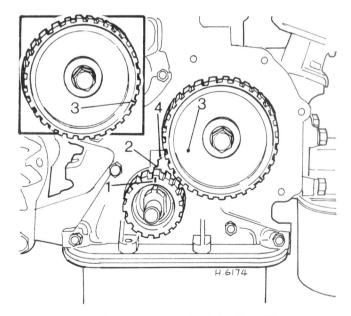

H.6174

Fig. 1.12. Setting the valve timing (Sec. 44)

1   Notched reference mark on crankshaft timing wheel
2   Notched reference mark on crankshaft front cover plate
3   Reference mark on cast iron camshaft timing wheel
3   (Inset diagram) Reference mark on plastic (alternative type) Camshaft timing wheel
4   Notched reference mark on crankshaft front cover plate

45.1 View of the oil pump/distributor drive gear bush in the cylinder block, looking down through the distributor mounting hole

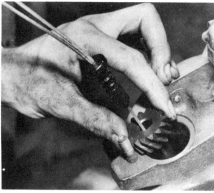
45.2 Refitting the oil pump/distributor drive gear into its bushing using a guide rod - in this case the engine oil dipstick

45.4A Replacing the oil pump ...

45.4B ... not forgetting to fit a new gasket

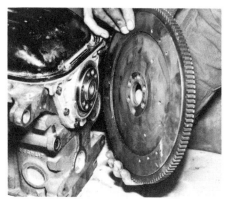
46.2 Fitting the flywheel to the crankshaft

47.2 Fit the sump onto the new gasket

48.3 Replacing the steel disc before the valve springs

48.5A Replacing the inner and outer valve springs

48.5B Putting the upper spring seat in position

48.5C Compressing the valve springs with the clamp screw on the valve head

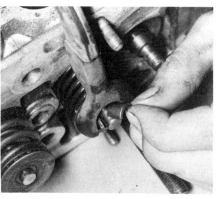
48.6 With the springs clamped the split collets are replaced

48.7 Release the compressor and see that the collets remain in position

with engine oil. Find a clean container large enough in which to immerse the suction horn of the oil pump. Partially fill the container with clean engine oil and immerse the suction horn in the oil. Now rotate the pump drive spindle so that the oil is drawn through the pump. It is then primed.

4   Place the mounting bolts through the oil pump, and offer the pump up to the cylinder block, remembering to fit a new gasket between the mating faces (photos).

5   Tighten the mounting bolts evenly to the specified torque wrench setting.

46 Flywheel and clutch assembly - refitting

1   The flywheel has a special dimple mark near the edge on the clutch side. This should be at 12 o'clock with Nos. 1 and 4 pistons at TDC (Top Dead Centre).

2   Carefully place the flywheel in position on the end of the crankshaft. Now refit the special washer and six securing bolts. Tighten the bolts evenly to the recommended torque wrench setting (photo).

3   Refit the clutch assembly as detailed in Chapter 5.

47 Sump - refitting

1   Ensure that the two mating faces are absolutely clean.

2   Place the new gasket in position without using any gasket cement to hold it. Place the sump in position (photo).

3   Refit the securing screws and special washers. The washers should have their convex/serrated sides towards the bolt heads.

4   Tighten the screws evenly and not too tightly.

48 Valves and valve springs - refitting to cylinder head

1   Gather together all the new or reground valves and ensure that where the original valves are being reused, they will be returned to their original positions.

2   Ensure that all the valves and springs are clean and free from carbon deposits and that the ports and valve guides in the cylinder head have no carbon dust or valve grinding paste left in them.

3   Fit the steel discs which form the lower seating surface of the springs against the cylinder head (photo).

4   Place the valve in the guide, having smeared the stem with molybdenum grease or oil first.

5   Fit the inner and outer valve springs and retainer collar and compress the springs with a valve spring compressor until the grooved part of the valve stem is clear of the retainer (photos).

6   Fit the two split collets, tapered lip inwards so that they engage in the valve stem recess snugly. Use a dab of grease to hold them in place if necessary (photo).

7   Slowly release the compressor and see that the split collets remain in position. Tap the valve stem with a mallet after assembly just to ensure that the collets are correctly seated (photo).

8   Repeat the above operations until all the valves have been assembled in the cylinder head.

49 Oil filter and adaptor housing - refitting

1   Ensure that both faces are clean and free from the remains of the old gasket.

2   Fit a new gasket and mount the unit on the studs screwed into the block. The filter cartridge mounting face should be facing the bottom of the engine (engine inverted in photo).

3   Before fitting the new oil filter canister wet its sealing ring with engine oil.

4   Screw the filter up until it just contacts the sealing ring then tighten it a further ¾ of a turn.

50 Cylinder head - refitting

1   With the valves and springs refitted, examine the head to make sure that the mating face is perfectly clean and smooth and that no traces

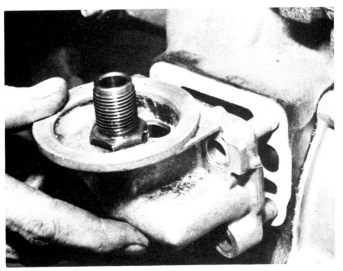

49.2 Refit the oil filter adaptor housing

50.4 Installing the cylinder head on top of the new head gasket

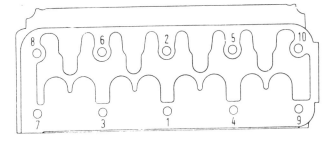

Fig. 1.13. Cylinder head bolt tightening sequence

of gasket or other compounds are left on it. Any scores, grooves or burrs should be carefully cleaned up with a fine file.

2   Examine the face of the cylinder block in the same manner as the head.

3   Most head gaskets indicate which side is the top, so check that the gasket is being fitted the correct way up.

4   Place the gasket in position and carefully lower the cylinder head onto it (photo). Refit the cylinder head bolts.

5   Evenly tighten down the bolts, using a torque wrench, in the progressive order as indicated in Fig. 1.13. The tightening sequence

should continue at ¼ - ½ a turn of the bolts until the recommended torque wrench setting is reached. The object of this procedure is to keep the tightening stresses even over the whole head, so that it settles level and undistorted.

51 Valve rocker shaft assembly and pushrods - refitting

1   Refit the eight pushrods through the head so that the lower ball ends fit into the tappet recesses (photo).
2   Place the rocker assembly over the head and line up the four mounting pedestals with the four studs and lower it. It will not go all the way down as some valves will have to be opened under pressure from the rocker arms when tightening the pedestal nuts (photo).
3   Engage the ends of the pushrods into the rocker arms and then tighten down the four securing nuts and washers a little at a time so that the whole assembly goes down evenly. It is a good idea to slacken off the valve clearance adjuster locknuts at this stage and back off the screws.
4   Tighten the nuts holding the rocker shaft assembly in position evenly, until the recommended torque wrench setting is reached (photo).
5   Adjust the valve clearances as described in Section 52 of this Chapter.

6   Finally refit the rocker cover using a new gasket and taking care not to overtighten the securing nuts.

52 Valve clearance - adjustment

1   Clearances should be set as soon as the rocker shaft is reassembled to the head. After the engine has been refitted and run for a while they should be checked again.
2   The recommended valve clearance, with the engine cold, for both inlet and exhaust valves is 0.008 in (0.20 mm).
3   There are different ways of ensuring the valves are in the correct position for clearance checking. One method is to turn the engine until No. 1 cylinder is at TDC on the exhaust/inlet stroke. This can be ascertained by checking to see that the exhaust valve is almost fully closed and the inlet valve is just beginning to open, the valves are then said to be 'on the rock.' When No. 1 cylinder is in this position both valves for No. 4 cylinder are ready to be checked and adjusted if necessary. This arrangement is reciprocal for Nos. 1 and 4 cylinders and Nos. 2 and 3 cylinders in the same way. Alternatively some may find it easier to follow the table below which gives an individual checking order which involves the minimum turning of the engine crankshaft. No. 1 valve is the first valve of the engine on No. 1 cylinder.

51.1 Putting back the pushrods through the cylinder head

51.2 Refitting the rocker shaft assembly on the cylinder head

51.4 Tightening the rocker shaft assembly securing nuts

52.5 Checking and adjusting the valve clearances

Valve fully open	Valve clearance to check
No. 8	No. 1 (exhaust)
No. 6	No. 3 (inlet)
No. 4	No. 5(exhaust)
No. 7	No. 2 (inlet)
No. 1	No. 8 (exhaust)
No. 3	No. 6 (inlet)
No. 5	No. 4 (exhaust)
No. 2	No. 7 (inlet)

4   To adjust the clearance undo the locknut with a ring spanner just enough to enable the screw to be turned using a small spanner.
5   Place the 0.008 in (0.20 mm) feeler blade between the rocker arm and the valve stem and turn the adjusting screw until the feeler blade can just be moved with slight drag. Hold the screw and tighten the locknut with the feeler blade still in position. Check the clearance again to ensure the screw did not move, when the locknut was tightened. (photo).

53 Inlet and exhaust manifolds - refitting

1   Ensure that the mating faces are clean.
2   Position the gasket over the studs and slide the manifolds onto the studs.
3   Refit the retaining nuts and washers and tighten the nuts to the recommended torque wrench setting.

54 Engine reassembly - fitting ancillaries

The ancillaries which were removed at the first stage of dismantling may now be refitted before the engine is put back in the vehicle. One possible exception is the carburettor which is somewhat vulnerable and relatively fragile. Details of removal and refitting of these items are dealt with in the appropriate Chapters as mentioned in Section 8 of this Chapter. It is much easier to refit the alternator and fan belt at this stage and similarly to set the static ignition timing which is necessary when refitting the distributor.

55 Engine - refitting and initial starting after overhaul or major repair

1   Whether or not the engine has been removed together with the gearbox it is easier to refit them as individual units.

2   Place a sling around the engine so that it stays horizontal when lifted and lower it carefully into the engine compartment.
3   It is important when connecting the engine to the gearbox that no strain is imposed on the gearbox primary shaft when it is being engaged in the clutch assembly (For automatic transmission refer to Part B of Chapter 6 for details).
4   It may be necessary to turn the engine a little to engage the primary shaft in the clutch assembly but if the clutch assembly has been aligned correctly (see Chapter 5) there should be little difficulty.
5   Refit the bellhousing to gearbox bolts and refit and tighten the engine mountings.
6   Now refit all the ancillaries, wiring connections, controls and hoses etc.
7   Before attempting to start the engine ensure that the battery is fully charged, and that all coolants, lubricants and fuel are replenished.
8   If the fuel system has been dismantled it will require several revolutions of the engine on the starter motor to pump the petrol up to the carburettor. The easiest way is to remove the plugs and spin over the engine. This will also ensure that oil will be pumped around the system before the initial start.
9   As soon as the engine fires allow it to run at a fast tickover only, and bring it up to the normal operating temperature.
10 As the engine warms up there will be odd smells and some smoke from parts getting hot and burning off oil deposits. The signs to look for are leaks of water or oil which will be obvious if serious. Check also the exhaust pipe and manifold connections, as they do not always 'find' their exact gas tight position until the warmth and vibration from the engine have acted upon them, and it is almost certain that they will need further tightening. This should be done, of course, with the engine stopped.
11 When the normal running temperature has been reached, adjust the engine idling speed as described in Chapter 3.
12 Stop the engine and wait a few minutes to see if any lubricant or coolant is dripping out when the engine is stationary.
13 Road test the car to check that the timing is correct and that the engine is giving the necessary smoothness and power. **Do not race the engine** - if new bearings and/or pistons have been fitted it should be treated as a new engine and run in at a reduced speed for the first 500 miles (850 Km).

56 Fault diagnosis - engine

Refer to Section 113 at the end of the second part of this Chapter.

Chapter 1 Part B:Twin overhead camshaft engine

For modifications, and information applicable to later models, see Supplement at end of manual

Contents

Specifications

General

Type	Four cylinder, double overhead camshaft
Identification: *	
1975 and 1976 models	132 A1.040.5
1977 and 1978 models	132 A1.040.6
Capacity	1756 cc (107.13 cu in)
Bore (standard)	3.31 in (84 mm)
Stroke	3.12 in (79.2 mm)
Firing order	1 - 3 - 4 - 2
Compression ratio	8 : 1
Horsepower rating (SAE) net:	
Catalytic converter models	83
Non-catalytic converter models	86

*Note: *Models fitted with catalytic converters have second digital group 031 in place of 040*

Crankshaft and main bearings

Main journal diameter (standard)	2.0860 - 2.0868 in (52.985 - 53.005 mm)
Crank pin journal diameters (standard)	1.9993 - 2.0001 in (50.782 - 50.802 mm)
Maximum ovality (out of round)	0.0002 in (0.005 mm)
Main bearing shell thickness (standard)	0.0718 - 0.0721 in (1.825 - 1.831 mm)
Main bearing to journal clearance	0.0020 - 0.0037 in (0.050 - 0.095 mm)
Crankshaft regrind diameters	−0.010, −0.020, −0.030, −0.040 in (−0.0254, −0.508, −0.762, −1.016 mm)
Crankshaft endfloat	0.0021 - 0.012 in (0.055 - 0.305 mm)

Camshaft

Cam lift:	
Inlet	0.3824 in (9.714 mm)
Exhaust	0.3824 in (9.714 mm)

Journal diameter (standard):	
Front	1.1788 - 1.1795 in (29.944 - 29.960 mm)
Centre	1.8013 - 1.8020 in (45.755 - 45.771 mm)
Rear	1.8171 - 1.8178 in (46.155 - 46.171 mm)
Journal to bearing clearance:	
Front	0.0019 - 0.0035 in (0.049 - 0.090 mm)
Centre	0.0011 - 0.0027 in (0.029 - 0.070 mm)
Rear	0.0011 - 0.0027 in (0.029 - 0.070 mm)
Bearing inner diameter:	
Front	1.1814 - 1.1824 in (30.009 - 30.034 mm)
Centre	1.8031 - 1.8042 in (45.800 - 45.825 mm)
Rear	1.8189 - 1.8198 in (46.200 - 46.225 mm)
Tappet shim thicknesses available	0.1299 to 0.1850 in (3.30 to 4.70 mm) in 0.10 mm increments

Pistons

Piston diameter (measured at 1.18 in (30 mm) from crown at right angles to gudgeon pin)

Piston diameter (standard):	
Grade A	3.3051 - 3.3055 in (83.950 - 83.960 mm)
Grade C	3.3059 - 3.3063 in (83.970 - 83.980 mm)
Grade E	3.3066 - 3.3070 in (83.990 - 84.000 mm)
Oversize pistons available	0.0079, 0.0157, 0.0236 in (0.2, 0.4, 0.6 mm)
Piston ring groove width:	
Compression (top)	0.0604 - 0.0612 in (1.535 - 1.555 mm)
Oil control (centre)	0.0798 - 0.0806 in (2.030 - 2.050 mm)
Oil scraper (bottom)	0.1561 - 0.1569 in (3.967 - 3.987 mm)
Piston to bore clearance	0.0016 - 0.0024 in (0.040 - 0.060 mm)
Gudgeon pin boss inner diameter	0.8660 - 0.8662 in (21.996 - 22.002 mm)

Piston rings

Ring thickness:	
Top (compression)	0.0582 - 0.0587 in (1.478 - 1.490 mm)
Centre (oil control)	0.0779 - 0.0787 in (1.980 - 2.000 mm)
Bottom (oil scraper)	0.1544 - 0.1549 in (3.925 - 3.937 mm)
Clearance in groove:	
Top (compression)	0.0018 - 0.0030 in (0.045 - 0.077 mm)
Centre (oil control)	0.0011 - 0.0027 in (0.030 - 0.070 mm)
Bottom (oil scraper)	0.0011 - 0.0024 in (0.030 - 0.060 mm)
Piston ring end gap in bore:	
Top (compression)	0.0118 - 0.0177 in (0.30 - 0.45 mm)
Centre (oil control)	0.0118 - 0.0177 in (0.30 - 0.45 mm)
Bottom (oil scraper)	0.0098 - 0.0157 in (0.25 - 0.40 mm)

Piston gudgeon pins

Diameter	0.8658 - 0.8660 in (21.991 - 21.997 mm)
Oversize pin	+ 0.0079 in (+ 0.2 mm)
Pin to piston clearance	0.0001 - 0.0003 in (0.002 - 0.008 mm)
Pin to connecting rod clearance	0.0004 - 0.0006 in (0.010 - 0.016 mm)

Connecting rods

Small end bush inside diameter:	
Class 1	0.8662 - 0.8665 in (22.004 - 22.010 mm)
Class 2	0.8664 in (22.006 mm)

Valves

Valve clearances set cold	
Inlet valve	0.018 in (0.45 mm)
Exhaust valve	0.023 in (0.60 mm)
Valve head diameter:	
Exhaust	1.42 in (36 mm)
Inlet	1.67 in (42.4 mm)
Valve face angle	45° 30' ± 5'
Valve seat angle	45° ± 5'
Valve stem diameter	0.3139 - 0.3146 in (7.974 - 7.992 mm)
Valve guide inner diameter	0.3158 - 0.3165 in (8.022 - 8.040 mm)
Valve stem/guide clearance	0.0012 - 0.0026 in (0.030 - 0.066 mm)
Valve guide interference fit in cylinder head	0.0008 - 0.0026 in (0.021 - 0.066 mm)
Valve guide OD (standard)	0.5905 - 0.5912 in (14.998 - 15.016 mm)
Valve guide OD (oversize)	+ 0.0079 in (+0.2 mm)
Valve seat width in head	0.079 in (2 mm)
Valve spring free length:	
Outer	2.122 in (53.9 mm)
Inner	1.646 in (41.8 mm)

Auxiliary driveshaft

Bush inside diameter:
Front ...   .   1.8930 - 1.8938 in (48.08 - 48.10 mm)
Rear   ...   .   1.5354 - 1.5362 in (39.00 - 39.02 mm)
Shaft journal diameters:
Front ...   .   1.8903 - 1.8913 in (48.013 - 48.038 mm)
Rear   ...   .   1.5326 - 1.5336 in (38.929 - 38.954 mm)

Engine lubrication

Oil pump type   ...   .   High capacity gear type
Gears to housing clearance ...   .   0.0043 - 0.0070 in (0.110 - 0.180 mm)
Gear thickness (new)   ...   .   1.1793 - 1.1806 in (29.956 - 29.989 mm)
Gear backlash between teeth   ...   .   0.006 in (0.15 mm)
Gears to cover face clearance   ...   .   0.0012 - 0.0045 in (0.031 - 0.116 mm)
Oil pressure relief valve spring:
Free length   ...   .   1.58 in (40.2 mm)
Minimum length and loading   ...   .   0.8 in (21 mm) at 11 lb (5 kg)
Oil pressure at 100°C (212°F)   ...   .   49 - 71 psi (3.5 - 5 kg/cm^2)
Oil filter type   ...   .   Full flow, renewable cartridge
Oil capacity   ...   .   8.4 US pints, 4 litres, 7 Imp pints (approx)

Torque wrench settings*

	lb f ft	kg f m
Cylinder head bolts	54 (61)	7.5 (8.5)
Manifold stud nuts	18	2.5
Camshaft housing nuts	14.5	2
Camshaft timing wheel bolts	87	12
Idler/tensioner wheel retaining nut	32.5	4.5
Crankshaft timing/pulley wheel nut	87	12
Auxiliary shaft wheel	87	12
Connecting rod cap nuts	47 (37)	6.5 (5.2)
Main bearing cap bolt (small)	58	8
Main bearing cap bolts (large)	83	11.5
Flywheel to crankshaft bolts	62 (105)	8.5 (14.5)
Sparking plug	29	4

*Figures in brackets are applicable torque wrench settings for 1978 vehicles onwards.

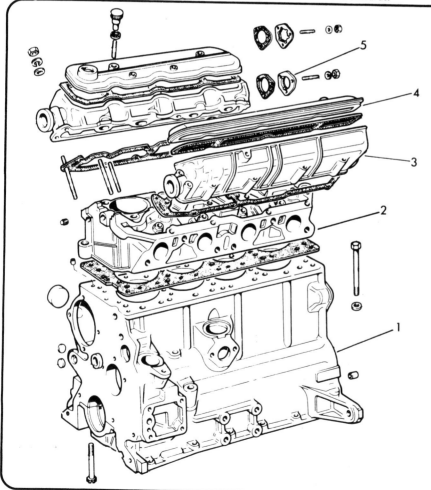

Fig. 1.14. Main static components of engine

1   Crankcase/cylinder
2   Cylinder head
3   Camshaft housing
4   Camshaft housing cover
5   Camshaft locating plate

57 General description

The FIAT 131 models available in the USA are all fitted with a 1756 cc (107.13 cu in) twin overhead camshaft engine.

The carburation consists of a single progressive twin-choke down-draught Weber carburettor. The inlet manifold feeds four inlet ports in the cylinder head and it has fittings to provide for the vacuum operated servo assisted brakes. The inlet ports lead to valves angled at 45° and a hemispherical combustion chamber in the cylinder head. The exhaust valves lead to four exhaust ports in a cast iron exhaust manifold. The two rows of valves are operated by separate camshafts situated on the cylinder head and the camshafts are driven by a toothed belt running on a pulley mounted at the front end of the crankshaft. Belt tension is maintained by an idler wheel. The same toothed belt drives the auxiliary shaft mounted on the right-hand

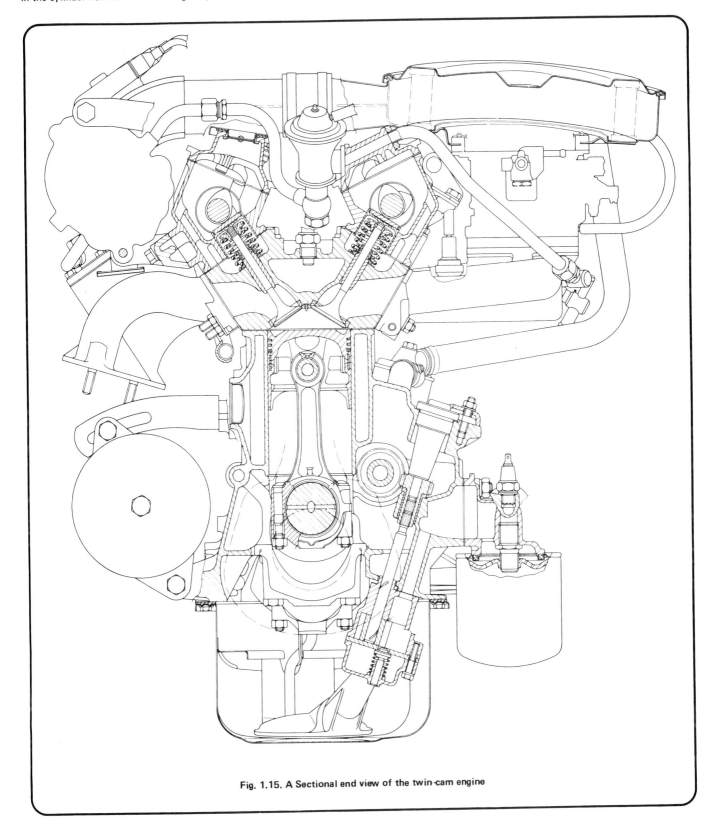

Fig. 1.15. A Sectional end view of the twin-cam engine

side of the cylinder block. This shaft drives the oil pump through a skew type drive gear. The distributor is mounted to the exhaust camshaft housing and driven through a gear machined on the camshaft.

The statically and dynamically balanced steel crankshaft rotates in five renewable main bearings which are individually fed with oil at pressure from the oil pump. Drillings in the crankshaft take oil from the main journals to the crankpin/big-end bearings. Drillings in the cylinder block transport oil from the crankshaft main bearings to the camshaft bearings.

The auxiliary driveshaft bearings are also lubricated with oil direct from the pump. The oil pressure relief valve is situated within the oil pump.

Various electrical transducers are used to monitor the water temperature and oil pressure.

All models are fitted with emission control equipment as standard and cars destined for California have in addition a catalytic converter incorporated in the exhaust system. The emission control system falls into three main categories: the (CEC) Crankcase Emission Control, the (EEC) Exhaust Emission Control and the (FEEC) Fuel Evaporative Emission Control.

Starting the engine is accomplished by a pre-engaged type of starter motor. It is situated low on the right-hand side of the engine and the pinion meshes with a ring gear shrunk onto the steel flywheel attached to the rear end of the crankshaft.

Power is taken from the engine flywheel and transmitted through a conventional clutch on manual transmission models or through a torque converter on automatic transmission models.

58 Major operations - engine in place

The following major operations can be carried out on the engine with it in place in the car:
1　Removal and refitting of the cylinder head assembly.
2　Removal and refitting of the sump.
3　Removal and refitting of the timing belt.
4　Removal and refitting of the big-end bearing shells.
5　Removal and refitting of the camshafts.
6　Removal and refitting of the water pump.
7　Removal and refitting of the oil pump.
8　Removal and refitting of the pistons and con-rods.

59 Major operations - engine removed

The following operations can only be carried out with the engine out of the car and on a bench:
1　Removal and refitting of the main bearings.
2　Removal and refitting of the crankshaft.
3　Removal and refitting of the auxiliary driveshaft.
4　Removal and refitting of the flywheel.

60 Methods of engine removal

1　The engine can be removed either attached to the gearbox or disconnected from it. Both methods are described but the photo sequence shows removal with gearbox attached because it was considered the easiest method to employ.
2　It is essential that adequate clearance under the car is provided. If a pit is used for the removal operation then there will be sufficient clearance under the car. Where a pit is not available raise the front and rear of the car and support the car on axle stands.
3　In addition a strong hoist will be required to lift the engine and gearbox out. Remember that the engine and gearbox have a combined weight of over 200 lbs.
The engine/gearbox removal sequence described is intended for cars fitted with a manual gearbox. If the vehicle, however, is fitted with an automatic transmission, refer to the second part of Chapter 6 which contains details of the removal sequence for the automatic transmission.
4　Certain models may have air conditioning equipment fitted and it will be necessary to take the car to a specialist to have the refrigerant charge removed from the system before removing the engine. After refitting the engine the car will need to be returned to the air conditioning specialist to recharge the system.

Do not attempt to discharge the system yourself. It requires specialist equipment.

61 Engine removal - with gearbox

1　Position the car and raise it to provide adequate clearance underneath. Remember to support the vehicle with wooden packing blocks or axle stands. Never rely on a hydraulic jack alone to support the vehicle especially when you will be working underneath it.
2　Open the bonnet and prop it up.
3　Disconnect the battery leads and remove the battery.
4　With a soft-leaded pencil mark the position of the hinges to the bonnet and with the help of an assistant to hold the bonnet, undo the nuts and bolts from the bonnet hinges and lift the bonnet off.
5　Drain the cooling system as detailed in Chapter 2.
6　Remove the engine sump plug and drain the oil into a suitable container. Remove the oil filter.
7　Disconnect the HT and LT leads from the ignition coil to the distributor.
8　Disconnect the leads from the alternator, starter motor and low oil pressure indicator switch. Before removing any wires note their colours and positions. If you are at all doubtful tie a small label to each wire stating on the label the component and position from which it was removed.
9　Remove the air cleaner assembly.
10　Unbolt the carburettor from the manifold and place it to one side complete with its attached pipes and linkage (photo). Make a careful note of the exact location points of each hose.
11　Now disconnect the wires from the thermo valve and switch screwed into the bottom of the inlet manifold (photo).
12　Disconnect the wires from the thermostatic switch fitted into the bottom of the radiator.
13　Remove the radiator complete with electric cooling fan as detailed in Chapter 2 (photo).
14　On cars fitted with air conditioning equipment disconnect the two hoses which run across the top of the radiator. Read paragraph 4 of Section 60 first. Plug the ends of the pipes and their unions to prevent the ingress of dirt and moisture. Undo and remove the nuts and bolts retaining the air conditioning compressor. Remove the two pulley belts and lift the compressor free.
15　Now disconnect the exhaust manifold clamp (photo).
16　Remove the nuts from the front engine mounting rubbers and disconnect the engine earth strap (photo).
17　Disconnect the heater hoses from the engine. Refer to Chapter 2 and detach and remove the radiator.
18　From within the car remove the gear lever assembly as described in Chapter 6.
19　Now disconnect the forward end of the propeller shaft and rubber coupling from the gearbox spider (photo).
20　Disconnect the various wires from the gearbox sender switches.
21　Disconnect the clutch cable from the clutch release lever and draw the cable out through the bellhousing.
22　Undo the exhaust pipe support clip from the rear of the gearbox casing.
23　Support the gearbox with a jack and remove the gearbox supporting crossmember.
24　From within the engine compartment disconnect the speedometer drive cable from its connection at the odometer switch (cars fitted with a catalytic converter only) (photo).
25　Cars not fitted with catalytic converters must have the speedometer cable disconnected at the gearbox end (photo).
26　Attach the sling around the engine and support the weight. To ease the removal operation it will be beneficial to completely remove one of the front engine mounting rubbers.
27　Before lifting the engine and gearbox further ensure that there are no wires, hoses or brackets still attached which would prevent the engine from being lifted. Also check that you have allowed enough ground clearance under the car as the engine/gearbox unit will need to be tipped at an acute angle to remove it (photo). Remove the support jack from under the gearbox.
28　Lift steadily, carefully watching that the lifting slings do not strain against ancillaries on the engine which could be damaged.
29　Now rest the engine and gearbox on a strong bench ready for dismantling (photo).

61.10 The carburettor and its associate pipe connections

61.11 The thermo valve and thermo switch fitted to the underside of the inlet manifold

61.13 Lift the radiator clear

61.15 The exhaust manifold clamp viewed from below

61.16 The engine to chassis earthing strap

61.19 Disconnecting the forward end of the propeller shaft and rubber coupling from the gearbox spider

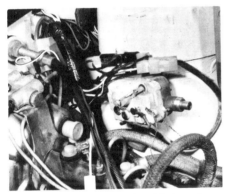

61.24 Disconnect the speedo cable from the odometer switch box (cars fitted with catalytic converter)

61.25 Disconnect the speedo cable from the rear gearbox housing (cars not fitted with a catalytic converter)

61.27 Lifting the engine out. Note the acute angle which it must be tipped to clear

62 Engine removal - without gearbox

1   Begin by following the instructions in Part A, Section 5 from paragraphs 1 - 17 inclusive.
2   Remove the bolts holding the starter motor to the transmission bellhousing and lift the starter motor out.
3   Remove the bolts retaining the flywheel lower cover plate to the front of the gearbox case.
4   Support the front of the gearbox with a jack and remove the four bolts holding it to the engine block assembly. If the car is fitted with automatic transmission then refer to Chapter 6, Part B for details of disconnecting the transmission from the engine.
5   Place a sling around the engine in such a way that it will not tilt and then take the weight. Undo the front engine mounting nuts and remove one of the engine mounting rubbers.
6   Pull the engine forward, supported by the sling, until it fully disengages from the gearbox primary input shaft and then lift it up

and clear. If some difficulty is experienced in drawing the engine forward do not impose any lifting or lowering strains which could cause damage to the gearbox primary shaft.

63 Engine dismantling - general

1   Refer to the procedure given in Part A, Section 7 of this Chapter for details of preparing the engine ready for dismantling.

64 Engine dismantling - ancillary components

1   Details of the components to be removed are given in Part A, Section 8 of this Chapter. However, ignore the fuel pump as the twin-cam engine has an electric fuel pump fitted at the rear of the car.
2   In addition to the ancillaries quoted all components relating to the emission control equipment will have to be removed. Details of these components are covered in Chapter 3.

61.29 The engine gearbox resting on a strong bench ready for dismantling

64.4 The oil/vapour separator unit

64.6 The arrow indicates the dipstick tube sleeve nut

65.4 The alloy water pipe elbow fitted to the front of the cylinder head

65.7 The idler wheel tensioner assembly. The arrows indicate the bolt and nut which have to be loosened when releasing the belt tension

3   The timing belt and its associate gear wheels will have to be removed. The removal sequence is given in Part B, Section 65 of this Chapter.
4   Now remove the oil/vapour separator from the cylinder block below the inlet manifold. The separator is retained by a single bolt through its centre and rubber elbow hoses at its side (photo).
5   The tensioner idler wheel and spring can be removed by undoing the nut and bolt securing it to the block face.
6   Remove the engine oil level dipstick and its tube. The dipstick tube is located by a bracket at the top and by a sleeve nut screwed into the cylinder block at its base (photo).

65 Timing belt - removal, refitting and adjustment

The timing belt will need to be renewed at 3 yearly or 37,000 mile intervals at the most and will therefore be one of the more frequent major tasks undertaken. FIAT state that timing belts cannot be reused and if at any time the tension on the belt is relieved it must be renewed.
1   Begin by draining the cooling system and remove the radiator as described in Chapter 2.
2   Remove the spark plugs and set the engine at TDC with No. 4 cylinder on the compression stroke. A check will show that the timing marks on the camshaft gearwheels are aligned with the cast marks on the support behind the gearwheels.
3   Slacken the alternator mountings to loosen and remove the alternator/water pump drivebelt, referring to Chapter 2, Section 5 if necessary. At this stage undo the nut that retains the crankshaft pulley and remove the pulley.
4   On cars fitted with air conditioning equipment, slacken the compressor retaining bolts and remove the drivebelts.
5   Now disconnect one end of the hose between the thermostat and water pump. Also remove the two bolts securing the water pipe elbow to the front of the cylinder head (photo). The union elbow can now be removed complete with attached hoses and thermostat.
6   Remove the timing belt cover. It is retained by three bolts and a nut.
7   With the cover now removed proceed to slacken the air pump mounting bolts and remove the air pump drivebelt.

8   Loosen the nut at the centre of the tensioner idler wheel and the bolt attached to the tensioner spring (photo).
9   Lever the idler wheel to the left and tighten the nut to hold the idler wheel in place (Fig. 1.19).
10 Remove the belt and check that the timing marks are still in line. The hole drilled into the auxiliary shaft wheel is approximately lined up with the bolt for the tensioner spring.
11 Loosely install the timing belt cover and check that the mark on the crankshaft pulley is in line with the TDC mark on the cover.
12 Remove the cover and fit the new timing belt. Ensure that the slack in the belt is between the exhaust camshaft gear wheel and the idler wheel tensioner.
13 Loosen the nut on the tensioner to take out the slack in the belt.
14 Rotate the crankshaft through two complete turns bringing the timing marks back in line.
15 Tighten the nut on the idler wheel and the bolt on the tensioner spring.
16 Finally check that the timing marks on the camshaft gearwheels, auxiliary shaft pulley, and crankshaft pulley are still properly aligned.
17 Reassembly is now the reversal of the dismantling procedure. Readjust the fanbelt and air conditioning compressor drivebelt (where applicable) on refitting. Check coolant system for leaks, on completion.

66 Cylinder head removal - engine in car

1   Drain the cooling system and remove the radiator as described in Chapter 2 having first disconnected the battery negative (earth) lead.
2   Slacken the alternator and remove the drivebelt. If the car is fitted with air conditioning equipment the compressor drivebelts should be removed before removing the alternator drivebelt.
3   Now remove the timing belt cover as detailed in Section 65, followed by the removal of the timing belt.
4   Remove all HT leads to the spark plugs and identify them as necessary. Remove the electrical connections to the various sender units fitted into the cylinder head.
5   Remove the air cleaner assembly and the accelerator rod linkage.
6   It is advisable to remove the carburettor from the manifold and

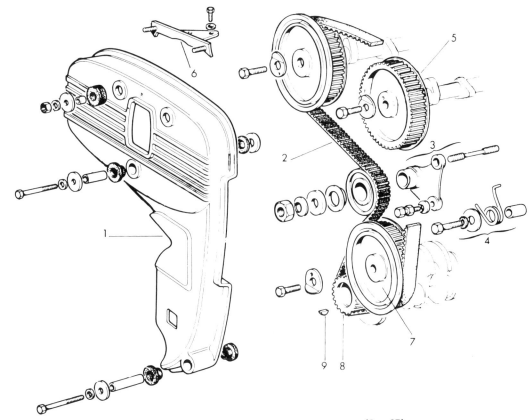

Fig. 1.16. Timing belt components (Sec 65)

1   Timing belt cover
2   Timing belt
3   Idler wheel bearing bracket

4   Idler wheel spring tensioner assembly
5   Camshaft timing wheel
6   Timing cover support bracket

7   Auxiliary shaft wheel
8   Crankshaft timing wheel
9   Woodruff locating key

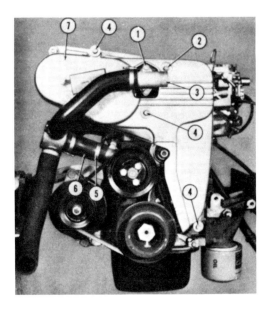

Fig. 1.17. Timing belt cover location and surrounding components
(Sec 65)

1   Bolts retaining the alloy water elbow to the cylinder head
2   Cover retaining nut
3   Alloy water elbow fitting
4   Cover retaining bolts
5   Hose clip
6   Hose water pump to thermostat

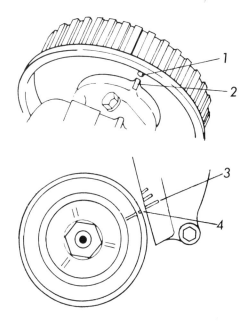

Fig. 1.18. Timing the camshafts (Sec. 65)

1   Reference mark on the rear of the timing wheel
2   Reference mark on camshaft housing
3   TDC reference mark on timing cover casing
4   Reference timing mark on crankshaft front pulley

Fig. 1.19. The timing belt and associated pulley wheels (Sec 65)

1   Inlet camshaft timing wheel
2   Timing belt
3   Idler/tensioner pulley wheel
4   Tensioner bracket
5   Tensioner locking bolt
6   Auxiliary shaft wheel
7   Crankshaft pulley wheel
8   Idler/tensioner pulley wheel locking nut
9   Exhaust camshaft timing wheel

66.11 Removing the camshaft cover plates

place it to one side complete with its attached pipes. However, make
a careful note of the location of each of the pipes.
7   Disconnect the exhaust manifold clamp allowing the exhaust
pipe to fall free from the manifold.
8   Remove the vacuum servo hose from the inlet manifold connection.
9   Disconnect the metal pipe, flexible hose and bracket from the
EGR valve assembly.
10   Ancillaries such as the distributor, air pump, exhaust and inlet
manifolds can be removed before removing the head.
11   Remove the pipes, unions and brackets attached to the cam housing
cover plates (photo).
12   Now remove the ten bolts and washers holding the cylinder head
in position. Slacken the bolts off evenly and in the reverse order to
that used for tightening the head down.
13   Before removing the cylinder head ensure that all attaching
brackets, pipes and electrical wires are removed.
14   Finally lift the cylinder head assembly off. If the head appears to
be stuck to the cylinder block, under no circumstances attempt to
free it by levering it off with a screwdriver or chisel. Tap the head
firmly with a plastic or wooden headed hammer.
15   The mild shocks should break the bond between the cylinder head,
gasket and cylinder block, allowing the cylinder head to be lifted clear.
16   Under no circumstances attempt to free the cylinder head by turning the engine over with the starter motor. As the timing belt has been
removed, damage to the valves that are open could result from the
pistons as the engine is revolved.

67 Cylinder head removal - engine out of car

Follow the instructions given in Section 66 and, depending on
extent of engine dismantling during removal, ignore the items which
do not apply.

68 Cylinder head - dismantling

1   The cylinder head assembly is made of aluminium alloy and comprises three sub assemblies: the head and the two overhead camshaft
assemblies.
The head comprises the combustion chambers, inlet and exhaust
ports and the valve assemblies. The two camshaft assemblies comprise
the camshafts, camshaft housings, tappets and housing covers.
2   Once the cylinder head has been removed from the engine, place it
on a clean bench and commence removal of the inlet and exhaust
manifolds, unless they have already been removed.
3   The inlet manifold is retained by four bolts and two nuts and the
exhaust manifold is retained by four nuts.
4   Once the manifolds have been removed, the camshaft housing
covers are next removed with the aid of a large Allen key.
5   Now remove the two bolts that retain the water extension elbow
to the front of the cylinder head.
6   The camshaft housings are each located on the cylinder head by
ten studs and retained by nuts. The tappet barrels should remain in
the bores when the camshaft housings are removed.

69 Valve - removal

Valve removal on the twin-cam engine is identical to the valve
removal sequence detailed in Part A, Section 11 of this Chapter.

70 Valve guide - inspection and renewal

Refer to Part A, Section 12 of this Chapter for details of valve
guide inspection and renewal.

71 Camshafts, camshaft gear wheels and tappets - removal

1   Since the camshafts are withdrawn from the rear end of the housings,
it will be necessary to remove the camshaft gearwheel at the forward
end first. FIAT recommend that tool A60446 be used to lock the camshaft gearwheel when removing the lock bolt. An alternative method is
given in the following text.

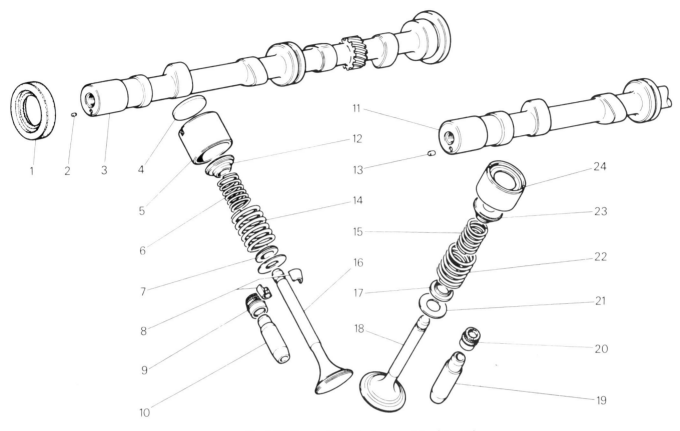

Fig. 1 20. Camshafts and valve assemblies (Sec 71)

1	Camshaft oil seal	7	Valve spring cup
2	Dowel peg	8	Cotters
3	Exhaust camshaft	9	Oil seal
4	Tappet shim	10	Valve guide
5	Tappet barrel	11	Inlet camshaft
6	Inner valve spring	12	Retainer collar

13	Dowel peg	19	Valve guide
14	Outer valve spring	20	Oil seal
15	Inner valve spring	21	Washer
16	Exhaust valve	22	Outer valve spring
17	Valve spring cup	23	Retainer collar
18	Inlet valve	24	Tappet barrel

2   The gearwheels are locked to their respective camshafts by a single bolt. Grasp the gearwheel gently in a soft jawed vice and undo the bolt.

3   Remove the bolt and washer which keeps the wheel/shaft alignment dowel peg in place. Ease the wheel off the shaft and take care not to lose the alignment dowel.

4   Next, at the rear of the housing, the camshaft retaining plate is held on by three nuts. Once removed the camshaft can be carefully withdrawn from the rear of the housing.

5   Be careful not to damage the camshaft bearing bores in the housing when removing the shaft. The housing is of aluminium alloy whereas the shaft is steel.

6   The tappets can be pushed out of their bores and as with the valves it is wise to store the tappets and shims so that they may be refitted into their original locations.

72 Sump - removal

1   Refer to Section 13 in Part A of this Chapter for details of removing the sump.

2   After removing the sump, assuming that the engine is being dismantled, remove the two bolts and washers retaining the oil tube. Now draw the tube out.

73 Oil pump - removal

Refer to Part A, Section 19 of this Chapter for details of oil pump removal.

74 Auxiliary shaft - removal

1   Remove the engine from the car (Sections 60 and 61).

2   Remove the timing belt (Section 64).

3   Remove the sump (Section 72).

4   Remove the oil pump (Section 73).

5   Remove the auxiliary shaft gearwheel. The gearwheel can be prevented from rotating by wrapping the old timing belt around it while the securing bolt is undone (Fig. 1.21).

6   Now remove the gearwheel taking care not to lose the locating dowel which should still be in place on the end of the auxiliary shaft.

7   Undo the four bolts securing the auxiliary shaft cover housing and remove it.

8   Now remove the clamp plate and remove the blanking cap followed by the oil pump gear. To facilitate easy removal of the gear rotate the auxiliary shaft and draw the gear out through the casing using a pair of long nosed pliers.

9   Now undo the two bolts holding the auxiliary shaft retainer plate in position.

10 With the 'U' shaped retainer plate now removed, the auxiliary shaft can be withdrawn from the cylinder block. Take great care when drawing the shaft out to prevent damage to the auxiliary shaft bearings fitted into the cylinder block.

75 Pistons, connecting rods and big-end bearings - removal

Refer to Part A, Section 15 of this Chapter for details of the removal sequence.

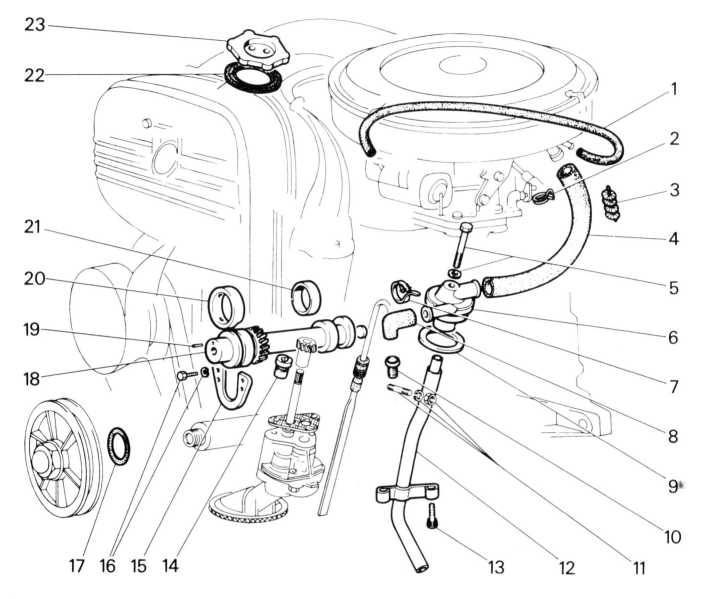

Fig. 1.21. The auxiliary shaft, oil pump and oil vapour separator assemblies (Sec 74)

1	Blow-by gas and oil vapour hose	9	Gasket	16	Bolt and spring washer
2	Hose clip	10	Cylinder block connection pipe	17	Washer
3	Flame trap	11	Stud, spring washer and nut	18	Auxiliary shaft
4	Breather pipe	12	Breather tube	19	Dowel peg
5	Retainer bolt and washer	13	Bolt	20	Front bush
6	Oil vapour separator body	14	Drive gear bush	21	Rear bush
7	Hose clip	15	Retainer plate	22	Seal
8	Elbow hose			23	Oil filler cap

76 Piston - removal from connecting rod

Refer to Part A, Section 16 of this Chapter for details of the removal operation.

77 Piston rings - removal

Refer to Part A, Section 17 of this Chapter for details of piston ring removal.

78 Flywheel - removal

Refer to Part A, Section 18 of this Chapter for details of the flywheel removal operation.

79 Crankshaft and main bearings - removal

Refer to Part A, Section 22 of this Chapter for details.

80 Crankshaft - examination and renovation

Refer to Part A, Section 23 of this Chapter for details, but note that the crankshaft journals of the 2.0 litre model and certain high performance ohc engine variants are given a tuff-triding treatment when new to improve the wear characteristics. When it is necessary to regrind these crankshafts, FIAT recommend that this treatment be repeated on the undersize journals. Your FIAT dealer will be able to advise you on this.

81 Big-end (connecting rod) bearings and main bearings - examination and renovation

Refer to Part A, Section 24 of this Chapter for details.

82 Cylinder bores - examination and renovation

Refer to Part A, Section 25 of this Chapter for details.

83 Pistons and rings - examination and renovation

Refer to Part A, Section 26 of this Chapter for details.

84 Camshaft and camshaft bearing - examination and renovation

1 Carefully examine the camshaft bearings for wear. If the bearings are obviously worn or pitted or the metal underlay is just showing through, then they must be renewed. This is an operation for your local FIAT agent or automobile engineering works, as it demands the use of specialised equipment. The bearings are removed using a special drift after which the new bearings are pressed in, care being taken that the oil holes in the bearings line up with those in the block. With another special tool the bearings are then reamed in position.
2 The camshaft itself should show no signs of wear, but, if very slight scoring marks on the cams are noticed, the score marks can be removed by very gentle rubbing down with a very fine emery cloth or an oil stone. The greatest care should be taken to keep the cam profiles smooth.

85 Timing wheels and belt - examination

1 The belt has a rubber surface and is reinforced for strength, and as a consequence it is most unlikely that the wheels will need anything more than a clean in an oil/grease solvent and wiping dry.
2 The idler wheel which maintains the tension in the timing belt runs on a prepacked ball bearing race. Whenever the timing belt is being changed or attended to, it is advisable to check for excessive play of the wheel and bearing. The wheel bearing assembly should be renewed if discernable play is felt.
3 The belt however, does not wear but fatigues, and because failure of this belt would be catastrophic for the engine, it must be renewed at regular intervals even though on the surface it might appear serviceable.
4 The timing belt must be renewed at intervals **NOT** exceeding 37,000 miles - FIAT justifiably recommend that it should be renewed every 25,000 miles.
5 It is important to remember that when handling a new belt - when fitting - to avoid bending it to a sharp angle or the fibres which reinforce the belt will be seriously weakened.

86 Tappets - examination and renovation

Examine the bearing surface of the tappets which lie on the camshaft. Any indentation in this surface or any cracks indicate serious wear, and the tappets should be renewed. Thoroughly clean them out removing all traces of sludge. It is most unlikely that the sides of the tappets will be worn, but, if they are a very loose fit in their bores and can be readily rocked, they should be discarded and new tappets fitted. It is very unusual to find worn tappets and any wear present is likely to occur only at very high mileages.

87 Connecting rods - examination and renovation

Refer to Part A, Section 30 of this Chapter for details.

88 Flywheel starter ring gear - examination and renovation

Refer to Part A, Section 31 of this Chapter for details.

89 Oil pump - dismantling, examination and renovation

Refer to Part A, Section 32 of this Chapter for details.

90 Decarbonisation

Refer to Part A, Section 33 of this Chapter for details.

91 Valves, valve seats and valve springs - examination and renovation

Refer to Part A, Section 34 of this Chapter for details.

92 Cylinder head - examination

Refer to Part A, Section 35 of this Chapter for details.

93 Engine reassembly - general

Refer to Part A, Section 36 of this Chapter for details.

94 Crankshaft - refitting

Refer to Part A, Section 37 of this Chapter for details.

95 Pistons and connecting rods - reassembly

Refer to Part A, Section 38 of this Chapter for details.

96 Piston rings - refitting

Refer to Part A, Section 39 of this Chapter for details.

97 Piston - refitting to cylinder

Refer to Part A, Section 40 of this Chapter for details.

98 Connecting rod to crankshaft - reassembly

Refer to Part A, Section 41 of this Chapter for details.

99 Crankshaft front and rear plates and oil seals - refitting

1 Refer to Part A, Section 42 of this Chapter for fitting instructions of the cover plates and oil seals.
2 With the covers now in position, refit the crankshaft gearwheel followed by the crankshaft pulley fitted with a new rubber 'O' ring.
3 Tighten the crankshaft pulley retaining nut to the recommended torque wrench setting.

100   Auxiliary shaft - refitting

1   Lubricate the auxiliary shaft cylinder block bushes and refit the auxiliary shaft.
2   Refit the 'U' shaped retainer plate securing it with two bolts and washers.
3   Fit a new oil seal to the auxiliary shaft cover plate and refit the cover plate along with a new gasket ensuring that the mating faces are clean.
4   Refit the auxiliary shaft gearwheel ensuring that the dowel peg locates with the hole drilled into the gearwheel. Refit the securing bolt and washer and tighten the bolt to the recommended torque wrench setting. The gearwheel can be prevented from rotating while the bolt is tightened by holding the gearwheel with the old timing belt.

101   Oil pump - refitting

1   Refer to Part A, Section 45 of this Chapter for details. Note that the twin cam engine has the auxiliary shaft fitted where the ohv engine has its camshaft fitted and that the drivegear on the auxiliary shaft only drives the oil pump. Remember that the distributor of the twin cam engine is driven from the exhaust camshaft in the head.
2   After installing the oil pump, remember to refit the distributor blanking piece and clamp to the hole in the cylinder block (photo).

102   Sump - refitting

Before refitting the sump as detailed in Part A, Section 47 of this Chapter ensure that the oil tube, and front and rear crankshaft cover plates are in position.

103   Flywheel and clutch assembly - refitting

1   Refer to Part A, Section 46 of this Chapter for details of the flywheel refitting procedure.
2   Refer to Chapter 5 for details of refitting the clutch assembly.

104   Water pump and oil vapour separator - refitting

1   Refer to Chapter 2 for details of refitting the water pump.
2   Now fit the rubber elbow hose and breather pipe to the separator and clean the mating faces of the housing and cylinder block.
3   Fit a new gasket to the separator and position the assembled separator onto the cylinder block.
4   Now refit the single bolt retaining the separator to the cylinder block.
5   Finally tighten the elbow hose and breather pipe clips (photo).

105   Valves and valve springs - reassembly to cylinder head

Refer to Part A, Section 48 of this Chapter for details.

106   Camshafts, tappets and camshaft gearwheel - refitting

1   Wipe the camshaft bearing journals and cam lobes and liberally lubricate with engine oil.
2   Wipe the inside bearing bores of each camshaft housing and lubricate with engine oil.
3   Carefully insert the camshafts into the housings so that the surfaces of the bearings in the housing are not scratched by the cam lobes as they pass through.
4   Fit the camshaft endplate and tighten the three securing bolts to the torque specified.
5   Refit the respective camshaft gearwheel onto the shaft projecting through the front of the housing. The wheel is located by a dowel pin and secured by a single bolt. A tag washer is fitted beneath the bolt and this serves not only to lock the bolt when it is tightened later, but also to retain the dowel pin in its bore.
6   Generously lubricate the tappets internally and externally and insert them into the bores from which they were removed.

107   Cylinder head - reassembly

The cylinder head assembly comprises:

1   *Basic head casting with valves and springs fitted.*
2   *The two camshaft assemblies.*
3   *The camshaft housing covers.*
4   *Water outlet elbow.*
5   *Spark plugs.*
6   *Water temperature sender unit.*
7   *Exhaust manifold.*
8   *Inlet manifold, carburettor and various sender switches fitted into the inlet manifold.*

Before commencing reassembly, ensure that the correct gaskets have been obtained. Compare their shape with the old gaskets and joint faces to which they are to be fitted. When purchasing new gaskets always quote the engine type and serial number.
1   Clean the mating faces of the cylinder head and camshaft housing.
2   Place the camshaft assembly onto the head, over the studs which locate it in the correct position having first fitted a new gasket.
3   Now fit the spring washers and nuts, progressively tightening them to the specified torque wrench setting (photo).
4   Do not fit the camshaft housing covers until the tappet/cam clearance has been adjusted, see Section 108.
5   The water elbow and cylinder head joint faces should be cleaned and the elbow refitted along with a new gasket.
6   Secure the elbow with nuts and spring washers and tighten to the specified torque wrench setting.
7   The spark plugs should be screwed into the cylinder head next and tightened to the recommended torque wrench setting.

101.2 Refitting the distributor dummy piece and clamp

104.5 Tighten the hose clip joining the oil separator elbow hose to the crankcase

107.3 Tightening the camshaft housing nuts

8 The water temperature sender unit can also be refitted at this stage.
9 The exhaust manifold can now be refitted using a new gasket and check that both mating faces are clean and free from the remains of the old gasket. The exhaust gasket should be fitted dry without any jointing compound and the nuts tightened to the recommended torque wrench setting.
10 The inlet manifold may or may not be fitted with the carburettor assembly, but in any event use new gaskets and ensure that the mating faces are free from fragments of the old gasket. Air leaks in the inlet manifold could present running problems and at its worst a seized engine! Again tighten the securing nuts to the recommended torque wrench setting.

108 Tappet/camshaft clearance setting - engine in or out of car

1 Remove the camshaft housing covers.
2 Rotate the camshaft (by rotating the crankshaft - if this task is performed with the engine in the car) until the cam which moves the tappet to be checked is perpendicular to the tappet face and the valve is closed.
3 Measure the existing tappet clearance and record the measurement so that the required thickness of the tappet shim can be calculated.
4 If the gap is not between 0.017 - 0.019 in (0.43 - 0.48 mm) inlet valve and 0.019 - 0.021 in (0.48 - 0.53 mm) exhaust valve when the engine is cold proceed as follows.
5 Rotate the camshaft until the valve is fully open then insert FIAT tool A60422 or alternatively a bent screwdriver to hold the tappet barrel down (photo).
6 Rotate the camshaft again so that the tappet shim may be extracted from the top of the tappet with a thin small screwdriver inserted into two grooves in the side of the tappet barrel.
7 Measure the thickness of the tappet cam plate with a micrometer. Add or subtract as appropriate the difference between the measured gap (paragraph 3) and the desired gap (paragraph 4) from the thickness of the tappet shim to obtain the thickness which is required to produce the desired clearance.
8 The specification section lists the range of thicknesses of tappet shims available from FIAT dealers. There are 15 different thicknesses and the thickness is marked on one face of the shim. This face must be on the tappet barrel side when fitted, and it is well to check that the plate is the thickness marked.
9 Insert the new tappet shim into the recess in the top of the tappet barrel. Turn the camshaft again so that the spacing tool or bent screwdriver (paragraph 5) can be extracted. Turn the camshaft again to the position indicated in paragraph 2 and check that the desired tappet/cam clearance has been achieved.
10 Repeat this procedure for the remaining seven valve tappets.
11 Finally refit the camshaft housing covers.

108.5 Using a bent screwdriver to hold the tappet down

109 Cylinder head - refitting to cylinder block

1 It is essential to position the camshafts in the cylinder head and the crankshaft in the engine block in their correct relative positions before the head is lowered onto the engine. Once the head has been fitted it is equally important that the camshafts are not turned until they have been coupled by the timing belt to the crankshaft. There will be a severe, possibly damaging, mechanical collision of valves and pistons if these precautions are not taken.
2 Turn the camshafts until the marks on their rear faces line up with the datum marks cast onto the cam housings. The cylinder head is now in the correct condition for refitting to the engine.
3 Turn the crankshaft until No 1 and 4 pistons are at top dead centre. The engine is now in the correct condition to accept the cylinder head.
4 Place a new cylinder head gasket on the engine block, having smeared it with a little grease first. The gasket is marked as to which way up it should be.
5 Lower the head carefully onto the engine. Take care not to knock the open valves against the engine block face, they may bend.
6 A couple of dummy studs screwed into the cylinder block will aid the task of lowering the cylinder head safely onto the block.
7 With the cylinder head in position, the retaining bolts can be inserted and tightened in a progressive manner, using a torque wrench and in the sequence shown in Fig. 1.22. The torque wrench setting is given in the Specifications at the start of Chapter 1, Part B.
8 The timing belt and tensioner should now be refitted as described in Section 110.

110 Timing belt, and tensioner reassembly

1 Having checked the condition of the tensioner idler wheel bearing and overhauled the tensioner as necessary refit it loosely to the block face.
2 Now fit the new rubber timing belt as described in Section 65.

111 Final assembly

1 Refit the water pump pulley.
2 Refit the air pump and drivebelt.
3 Refit the alternator and fan belt.
4 Refit the air conditioning compressor and belts where applicable.
5 Refit the oil filter adapter housing along with a new oil filter canister. Finally, refit any other ancillary which may be fitted more easily with the engine removed. It is recommended that the carburettor is fitted after the engine has been fitted in the car to prevent damage.

112 Engine - refitting and initial starting after overhaul or major repair

Refer to Part A, Section 55 of this Chapter for details.

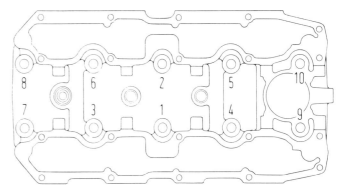

Fig. 1.22. Cylinder head retaining bolts tightening sequence (Sec. 109)

113   Fault diagnosis - engine

Symptom	Reason/s
Engine will not turn over when starter switch is operated	Flat battery. Bad battery connections. Starter motor jammed. Bad connections at solenoid. Defective solenoid. Starter motor defective.
Engine turns over normally but fails to start	No spark at plugs. No fuel reaching engine. Too much fuel reaching the engine (flooding).
Engine starts but runs unevenly and misfires	Ignition and/or fuel system faults. Incorrect valve clearances. Valves burnt out. Worn out piston rings.
Lack of power	Ignition and/or fuel system faults. Incorrect valve clearances. Valves burnt out. Worn out piston rings.
Excessive oil consumption	Oil leaks from crankshaft oil seals, auxiliary/camshaft oil seals, valve cover gaskets, sump, oil filter, oil drain plug. Worn piston rings or cylinder bores resulting in oil being burnt by engine. Worn valve guides and/or defective valve stem seals.
Excessive mechanical noise from engine	Wrong valve clearances. Worn rocker arm levers (OHV engine) Worn crankshaft bearings. Worn cylinders/piston (piston slap).

Chapter 2 Cooling system

For modifications, and information applicable to later models, see Supplement at end of manual

Contents

Specifications

Type of system	Pressurized spill return with belt driven centrifugal water pump
Cooling fan type	
1300 Basic model	Directly coupled to water pump, belt driven
Other models	Electric motor driven, coupled to a thermostatic switch
Thermostatic switch	
Cut in temperature	Approx. 90^{0} - 94^{0}C (194^{0} - 201^{0}F)
Cut out temperature	Approx. 85^{0} - 89^{0}C (185^{0} - 192^{0}F)
Thermostat	
Nominal opening temperature	Approx. 81^{0} - 85^{0}C (178^{0} - 185^{0}F)
Temperature when fully open	Approx. 92^{0}C (199^{0}F)
Valve stroke at 92^{0}C	Approx. 0.29 in (7.5 mm)
Cooling system capacity	Approx. 1.6 Imp. gals (7.5 litres), (16 US pts)
Antifreeze type	Ethylene glycol with inhibitors for mixed metal engines
Radiator cap relief pressure	11 lbf in (0.8 kgf cm)

1 General description

The engine cooling water, termed 'coolant', is circulated by a belt driven water pump, and the coolant is pressurised. Pressurising the system is necessary to prevent premature boiling of the coolant and to allow the engine to operate at its most efficient running temperature.

The overflow pipe from the radiator is connected to the expansion tank which makes the task of topping up the system virtually unnecessary. The coolant expands when hot, and instead of it being forced down the overflow pipe and lost, it flows into the expansion tank. As the engine cools the coolant contracts and, because of the pressure differential, is drawn back into the top tank of the radiator.

The cooling system comprises radiator, water pump, thermostat, interconnecting hoses and the waterways in the cylinder head and block assemblies.

A cooling fan is fitted to provide additional cooling by drawing the ambient air through the radiator core. All models utilize an electrically driven cooling fan, except the basic 1300 model. The electric fan circuit comprises a relay and a temperature sensing sender switch fitted into the lower part of the radiator. The 1300 basic model, however, has fan blades bolted directly to the water pump drive pulley.

2 Cooling system - draining and refilling

With the car on level ground, drain the system as follows:

1 If the engine is cold, remove both the radiator cap and the expansion chamber filler cap by turning them anticlockwise. If the engine is hot, turn the expansion tank filler cap slightly, to relieve pressure in the system, but use a rag over the cap for protection against any escaping steam. If the engine is very hot, the sudden release of the cap (causing a drop in pressure) can result in the coolant boiling. After relieving the system pressure, remove the radiator cap and the expansion chamber filler cap.

2 If antifreeze is used in the cooling system, and has been in use for less than two years, drain the coolant into a suitably sized receptacle. This is done by simply undoing the radiator drain tap (photo).

3 There is an additional drain tap located under the exhaust manifold on the engine. Open this tap also and drain the engine block (photo).

4 When refilling the system use clean water (mixed with antifreeze when appropriate as detailed in Section 6) and fill the system slowly to minimize the possibility of air locks. Fill the radiator right up to the top and refit the cap. Then fill the expansion tank about 3 in (75 mm) above the minimum mark (photo).

3 Cooling system - flushing

1 With the passing of time, the cooling system will gradually lose its efficiency as the radiator becomes choked with rust, scale deposits from the coolant and other sediment. To clear the system out, initially drain the system as described previously, then allow water from a hose to run through the top hose connection and out of the bottom hose connection for several minutes. Close the cylinder block drain tap while this is being done.

2 Refit the hoses and top up the system with fresh 'soft' water, (use rainwater if possible) and a proprietary flushing compound, following the manufacturer's instructions carefully. (Refer to Section 4).

3 If the cooling system is very dirty, reverse flush it, by forcing water

52

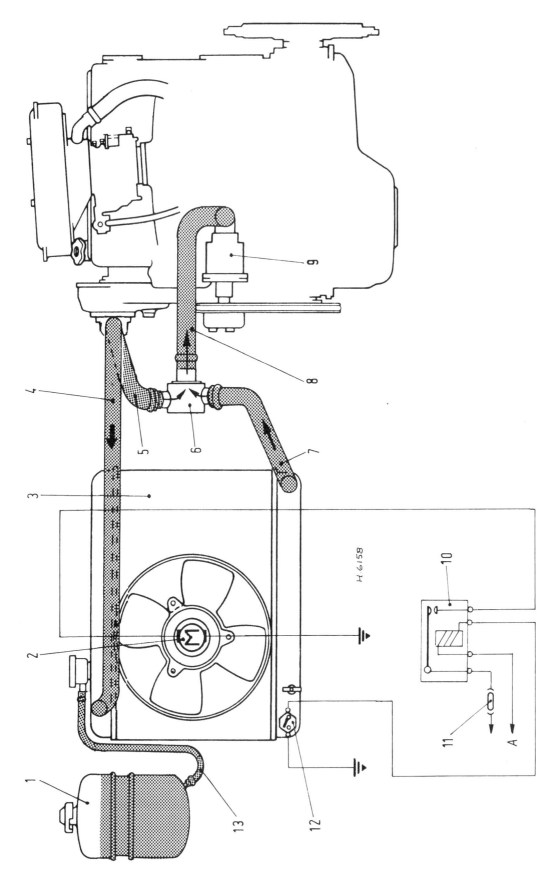

Fig. 2.1. The water flow path and the electric cooling fan circuit

1 Expansion tank
2 Cooling fan motor
3 Radiator
4 Top hose

5 Hose cylinder head outlet to thermostat
6 Thermostat
7 Lower hose

8 Hose thermostat to water pump
9 Water pump
10 Electric fan motor relay

11 Fuse
12 Thermostatic control switch
13 Tube radiator to expansion tank

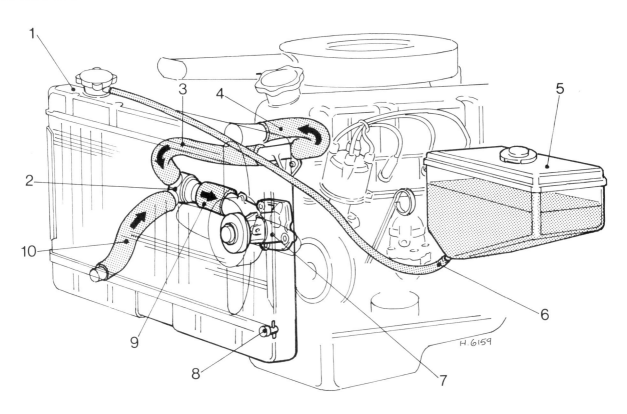

Fig. 2.2. The cooling system layout 1300 basic model

1 Radiator	4 Top hose	6 Tube radiator to expansion bottle
2 Thermostat	5 Expansion tank	7 Water pump
3 Hose water outlet to thermostat		

8 Radiator drain tap	
9 Hose thermostat to water pump	
10 Bottom hose	

2.2 Location of the radiator drain tap

2.3 Location of cylinder block drain tap

2.4 Fill the expansion tank about 3 inches (75 mm) above the minimum level

from a hose up through the bottom hose connection for about five to ten minutes, then complete the operation as described in paragraph 2, of this Section.

4   Refill the system as described in Section 2 of this Chapter.

4   Antifreeze solution

1   Where temperature is likely to drop below freezing point, the cooling system must be adequately protected. Even if you keep the engine warm at night it is possible for water to freeze in the radiator with the engine running in very cold conditions, particularly if the engine cooling is being adequately dealt with by the heater. The thermostat stays closed and the radiator water does not circulate.

2   It is best to drain the coolant completely and flush out the system first. Then treat the system with a proprietary flushing compound as described in Section 3.

3   Most proprietary antifreeze solutions marketed are suitable for aluminium engines but make sure. The amount required in solution varies little between makes and is always marked on the container. As a guide the following table gives the quantities needed for various protection levels based on the cooling capacity of 7.5 litres/13.19 Imp. pts/15.8 US pts.

%	Quantity	Complete Protection
25	1.9 lts/3.2 Imp. pts	-11^oC
35	2.6 lts/4.5 Imp. pts	-19^oC
45	3.4 lts/5.8 Imp. pts	-29^oC

4   Mix the antifreeze with half the total coolant capacity and pour it

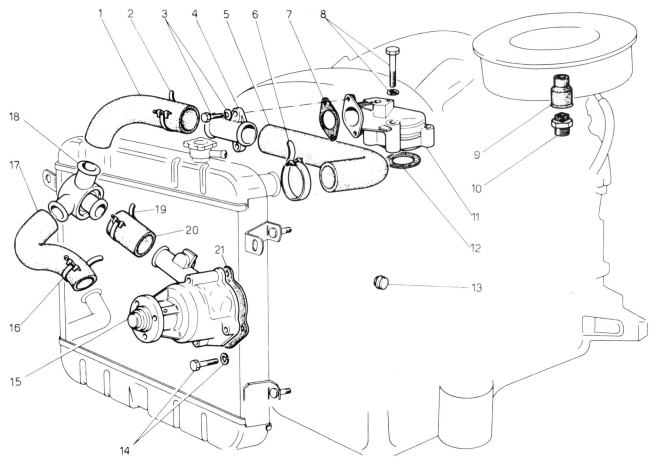

Fig. 2.3. Typical layout of the connecting hoses and associate parts

1	Hose cylinder head outlet to thermostat	8	Bolt and spring washer	15	Water pump
2	Hose clip	9	Cover	16	Hose clip
3	Bolt and spring washer	10	Sender unit	17	Lower hose
4	Union	11	Outlet elbow	18	Thermostat unit
5	Top hose	12	Gasket	19	Hose clip
6	Hose clip	13	Blanking plug	20	Hose thermostat to water pump
7	Gasket	14	Bolt and washer	21	Water pump gasket

in. Top up with clean water and run the engine up to normal working temperature with the heater control lever in the 'on' position.

---

5   Fan belt - removal, refitting and adjustment

If the fan belt is over stretched or worn it should be renewed. The most usual reason for renewal is that the belt has broken. It is therefore recommended that a spare belt is always carried in the car. Refitting is a reversal of the removal sequence, but if refitting due to breakage follow the procedure given below.

1   Loosen the alternator pivot and slotted link bolts and move the alternator towards the engine. (On cars fitted with air conditioning equipment it will be necessary to remove the air conditioning compressor drive belt when attempting to remove or refit the engine fan belt).

2   Carefully fit the belt over the crankshaft, water pump and alternator pulleys.

3   Adjust the belt until there is 0.5 in (13 mm) of lateral movement at the midpoint position between the alternator pulley and the water pump pulley (photo).

4   Retighten the pivot and link bolts (on air conditioned cars now refit and adjust the compressor drive belt).

5   **Note:** After fitting a new fan belt it will require adjustment after 250 miles (400 km).

5.3 Typical front view of the fan belt and alternator slotted adjuster bracket

6 Radiator - removal and refitting

1 Drain the system as described in Section 2.
2 Slacken the clip securing the expansion tank hose to the radiator. Carefully ease the hose from the union pipe on the radiator.
3 Slacken the top and bottom hose clips and ease the hoses off from their radiator connections.
4 On cars fitted with an electric cooling fan remove the wires from the thermostatic switch fitted into the bottom of the radiator.
5 On air conditioned cars unclip the compressor pipes running along the top of the radiator.
6 Remove the two nuts and washers retaining the radiator and lift it out carefully from its lower mounting cushion (photos).

7 Refitting is the reverse of the dismantling procedure.
8 Refill the system as described in Section 2 of this Chapter.

7 Electric cooling fan and motor - removal and refitting

1 Drain the system as detailed in Section 2.
2 Remove the radiator as detailed in Section 6.
3 The motor and fan are mounted on a frame on the rear face of the radiator.
4 The fan motor support frame is detached from the radiator after undoing the three nuts and bolts securing it to the radiator. The fan motor is removed from the frame, after unscrewing the three nuts which locate the motor (photo).

6.6A Lift the radiator clear

6.6B The radiator bottom cushion mounting

7.4 The electric cooling fan and its mounting frame

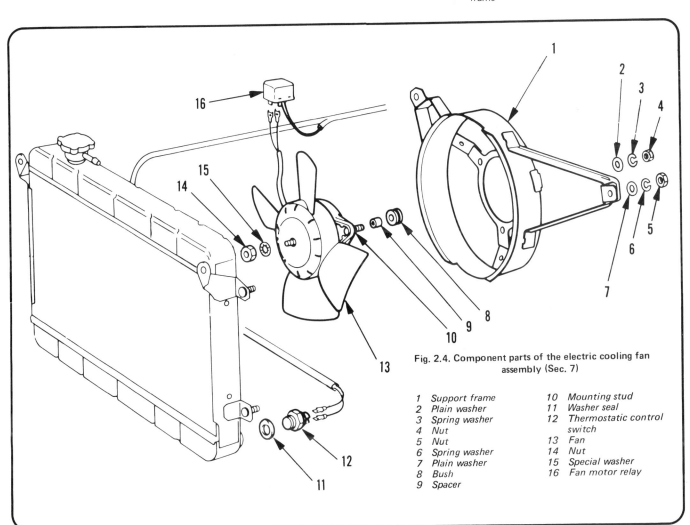

Fig. 2.4. Component parts of the electric cooling fan assembly (Sec. 7)

1 Support frame
2 Plain washer
3 Spring washer
4 Nut
5 Nut
6 Spring washer
7 Plain washer
8 Bush
9 Spacer
10 Mounting stud
11 Washer seal
12 Thermostatic control switch
13 Fan
14 Nut
15 Special washer
16 Fan motor relay

5   Refitting the motor assembly follows the reversal of the dismantling procedure.

6   The motor, if suspected of being faulty, can be tested in situ by removing the wires from the thermostatic radiator switch and, using jump leads, supplying the fan motor with a direct feed from the battery.

8   Thermostat - removal, testing and refitting

1   To remove the thermostat drain the cooling system as described in Section 2 of this Chapter.

2   Slacken the three hose clips connecting the lower radiator hose, the cylinder head by-pass hose and the thermostat to water pump hose.

3   Carefully pull the hoses off from the thermostat assembly and remove it (photo).

4   Test the thermostat for correct functioning by suspending it together with a thermometer on a string in a container of cold water. Heat the water and note the temperature at which the thermostat begins to open. The opening temperature should be between 81° and 85°C and the thermostat valve should be fully open at 92°C. The valve stroke at 92°C will be approximately 0.29 in (7.5 mm) if the valve has fully opened.

5   Discard the thermostat if it opens too early, or does not close when the water cools down. If the thermostat is stuck open when cold it will be apparent when it is first exposed.

9   Water pump - removal, overhaul and refitting

1   If the water pump starts to leak, shows excessive movement of the spindle, or is noisy during operation, the pump may be dismantled and overhauled. Make sure before you begin that the suspected faulty parts are readily available as spares. Generally it is now the policy for garages not to hold pump parts in stock, but to supply the whole pump unit ready to refit on the engine.

2   For safety reasons disconnect the battery negative earth lead.

3   Drain the cooling system as detailed in Section 2.

4   Remove the radiator as detailed in Section 6.

5   Remove the fan belt as detailed in Section 5.

6   On 1300 basic models the cooling fan blades are bolted directly to the water pump pulley. Remove the three locating bolts and release the blades and pulley.

7   On other models the bolts only retain the water pump pulley.

8   Slacken the hose clip and pull the large hose off the water pump.

9   Now remove the two bolts holding the heater pipe to the pump body.

10 Remove the four pump retaining bolts and lift the pump away from the engine.

11 Assuming you have obtained the necessary parts and have access to

FIAT tool A40026 or a conventional puller, the pump can be dismantled.

12 Holding the pump body lightly in a vice and using either FIAT tool A40026 or a conventional puller, withdraw the pump impeller from the shaft.

13 The set screw which locates the bearing in the pump body is now removed, to allow the shaft, together with the pulley hub and bearings, to be gently driven out.

14 The water seal may be tapped out of the pump body using an ordinary drift.

15 Using the puller again, the pulley hub may be removed from the shaft if necessary.

16 Clean all the components and inspect them for wear or damage. Renew parts as necessary.

17 To assemble the pump, carefully insert the water seal into the pump body. Do not use excessive force, and be careful not to damage the carbon seal block and face. The seal block is very fragile and if scratched or damaged will allow water to escape past the mating face of the pump impeller into the bearing assembly in the pump.

18 Refit the pulley hub onto the pump shaft which is complete with the bearing assembly; the shaft is now ready to be inserted into the pump body. When offering up the shaft assembly to the body ensure that the hole in the bearing outer race is aligned to accept the set screw which locates the shaft assembly in position in the pump. Carefully drive the assembly into the pump and screw in the set screw.

8.3 Remove the lower hose from the thermostat unit

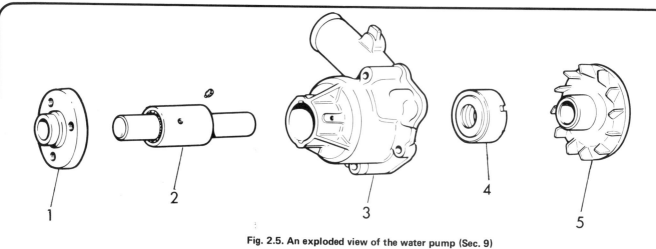

Fig. 2.5. An exploded view of the water pump (Sec. 9)

1   Pump drive fitting, the hub of the pulley
2   Pump shaft and bearing assembly
3   Pump housing
4   Pump seal
5   Centrifugal Impeller

19 Finally press the impeller onto the shaft until the free clearance between the impeller vanes and the pump body is 0.040 in (1 mm).
20 The body is now ready for refitting. When refitting the pump use a new gasket and ensure that the mating faces between the pump body and cylinder block are clean.
21 Refitting is the reversal of the dismantling procedure.

10 Fault diagnosis - cooling system

Symptom	Reason/s
Overheating	Low coolant level.
	Slack fan belt.
	Thermostat not operating.
	Defective water pump.
	Cylinder head gasket blowing.
	Radiator core clogged with flies or dirt.
	Radiator blocked internally.
	Electric cooling fan inoperative.
	Kinked or partially collapsed hose.
	Binding brakes.
	Bottom hose or tank frozen.
Engine running too cool	Defective thermostat.
	Electric cooling fan does not cut out.
	Faulty water temperature gauge.
Loss of coolant	Leaking radiator or hoses.
	Defective radiator or cylinder block drain taps.
	Cylinder head gasket leaking.
	Water pump or gasket leaking.
	Cylinder block core plug leaking.

Chapter 3 Carburation;
fuel, exhaust and emission control systems

For modifications, and information applicable to later models, see Supplement at end of manual

Specifications

Fuel pump
Type ... ...   Mechanical diaphragm type or electrical type depending on model

Fuel tank
Capacity
    UK models ... ...   11 Imp. gal (50 litres)
    USA models ... ...   12.2 US gal.

Fuel filters
dohc engine ... ...   Line filter with disposable element and wire mesh filter at carburettor fuel inlet

ohv engines ... ...   Gauze filter in fuel pump and wire mesh filter at carburettor fuel inlet

Air cleaner ... ...   Renewable paper element

Carburettor specifications (USA models)

Type ... ...   Weber 32ADFA 1/100, 3/100, 4/100, 6/100, 11/100, 3/101, 4/101, 6/101, 13/102, 14/101, 16/102

	Primary	Secondary
Bore	1.260 in (32 mm)	1.260 in (32 mm)
Venturi	0.787 in (23 mm)	0.905 in (25 mm)
Main jet	0.041 in (1.25 mm)	0.051 in (1.40 mm)
Emulsion tube type	F74	F74
Accelerator pump delivery	0.41 to 0.68 cu in (6.75 to 11.25 cm^3) per 10 pumps of accelerator pedal	
Needle valve seat	0.069 in (1.75 mm)	
Choke calibration	77°F (25°C)	
Float level: distance between float and cover lid with gasket held in vertical position	0.2165 to 0.2953 in (5.5 to 7.5 mm)	

Carburettor specifications (UK models)

All measurements given in millimetres

Type ... ...   **Weber 32 ADF 3/200 or Weber 32 ADF 3/100***

	Primary	Secondary
Choke tube diameter	32	32
Venturi diameter	23	23
Auxiliary venturi diameter	4.5	4.5
Main jet size	120	125
Air correction jet size	165	160
Emulsion tube size	F73	F73
Idling speed jet size	0.5	0.5
Idling speed air bleed size	160	0.7
Accelerator pump jet size	0.5	—
Power fuel jet diameter	—	1.00
Power mixture outlet diameter	—	2.50
Needle valve seat size	1.75	
Float level**	6.00	

*Air conditioned models
**Measured from float to cover gasket in vertical position

Type

	Solex C32 TEIE/42	
	Primary	Secondary
Choke tube diameter	32	32
Venturi diameter	23	23
Auxiliary venturi diameter	3.4	3.4
Main jet size	127.5	135
Air correction jet size	155	155
Emulsion tube size	N64	N64
Idling speed jet size	0.45	0.45
Idling speed air bleed size	110	0.70
Accelerator pump jet size	0.55	—
Power fuel jet diameter	—	0.80
Power mixture outlet diameter	—	2.00
Anti-syphon bleed size	140	—
Needle valve seat size	160	—
Float level	6.5 to 7.5*	
Accelerator pump output (10 strokes)	8 to 10 cc	

*Using gauge A.95148

Idling speed and CO values (USA models)

	Manual	Automatic
Normal idling speed rpm		
Standard exhaust	800 - 900	700 - 750
Catalytic converter	800 - 850	700 - 750
CO reading		
Standard exhaust	0.5 + 0.2%	0.7 + 0.2%
Catalytic converter	3 + 0.5%	3 + 0.5%
Fast idling speed rpm		
Manual	1600 + 50	
Automatic	1300 + 50	

Idling speed and CO values (UK models)

Weber carburettor

	Manual	Automatic
Normal idling speed rpm	800 + 50	800 + 50
Fast idle (air conditioned cars only)	1600 + 50	1300 + 50
CO value	2 - 2.5%	

Solex carburettor

	Manual	
Normal idling speed	850	
CO value	2 - 2.5%	

1 General description

The system is conventional and consists of a fuel tank mounted at the rear. The fuel pump fitted to USA models is electrical and mounted at the rear of the car close to the fuel tank. UK models are fitted with a mechanical lift pump bolted to the engine crankcase and operated by an eccentric on the engine camshaft.

A Solex or Weber dual-choke, down draught carburettor is fitted to the alloy inlet manifold. Several model types of carburettor are used and each type is suited to an individual application.

All USA import models have full emission control systems fitted, while those destined for California have in addition a catalytic converter. The function of each system is described later in the Chapter.

2 Air filter - removal, servicing and refitting

1 To change the paper air filter element and clean the interior of the housing it is only necessary to remove the three nuts and cover plate (photo). The old element can be taken out and the interior wiped out (photo). Element renewal is normally required after 6,000 miles, but in dusty or industrially polluted conditions it will be necessary more often. It is important not to run with a choked filter or without one at all. Either of these conditions will upset the mixture balance of the carburettor.

2 The lower half of the filter case is secured to the carburettor by four nuts. Remove the nuts and lift off the filter housing stiffening plate.

3 Now remove the two nuts retaining the air cleaner pipe to the camshaft housing.

4 Lift the air cleaner body and remove the two pipes joining it at the base (photo).

5 Refitting the assembly is the reverse of the dismantling procedure.

Fig. 3.1. Removing the air cleaner (typical) (Sec. 2)

1 Cover	4 Nuts retaining air cleaner pipe
2 Cover nuts	5 Air pipe
3 Air cleaner	

3 Carburettor - description and general principles

All the carburettors fitted to the FIAT 131 range are of the 'fixed choke' design and are manufactured by Weber or Solex. The term 'fixed choke' relates to the throat (venturi) into which the main petrol

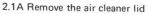

2.1A Remove the air cleaner lid

2.1B Remove the filter element

2.4 Lift air cleaner unit clear of carburettor and disengage hoses

jet sprays the fuel, and because on these carburettors this venturi is a fixed size, several other jets are incorporated in the carburettor to enrich the fuel/air mixture passing into the engine as and when necessary. All fuel jets take the form of inserts screwed into the carburettor body.

The carburettors function is as follows: Petrol is pumped into the float chamber and is regulated by the needle valve actuated by the float. As air is sucked into the engine a slight vacuum - proportional to air flow - is created in the venturi of the carburettor; this vacuum draws a corresponding amount of fuel from the float chamber through the main jet screwed into the bottom of the float chamber. The fuel is then drawn through the emulsion tube where it mixes with the small amount of air coming from the air correction jet. The fuel air emulsion passes on through the spray tube and into the main air stream in the venturi of the carburettor.

The flow of air through the carburettor is controlled by the butterfly valves operated by the accelerator linkage and cable. A feature of this type of carburettor is that the accelerator linkage does not open the butterfly valves in the two throats simultaneously. The principle employed here is that only one barrel is used when the air/petrol requirements are low and the second barrel is opened only when extra power is required.

The engines power and economy is dependent upon, and is in proportion to, the amount of air and fuel drawn into the engine. On the fixed choke carburettor the proportions of fuel and air are controlled by the sizes of the main jets, carburettor throat 'venturi', and the other minor enrichment jets. All these sizes are fixed and decided by the engine designers. The only adjustment or trim to the fuel/air mixture available is provided by the accelelerator's butterfly valve stop and the 'idling mixture control screw'. Section 5 describes the procedure for carburettor adjustments.

As mentioned earlier, fixed jet carburettors require additional jets to enrich the air/fuel mixture when necessary, such as for accelera-tion. An accelerator pump device is fitted to the carburettor and operated by levers connected to the accelerator linkage. The pump supplies fuel under pressure to a fuel spray nozzle projecting into the venturi throat.

In addition to the jets already mentioned there is the idling jet. The flow of fuel through this jet is adjustable. When the engine is idling and the accelerator butterfly valve is almost closed, the slight vacuum in the inlet manifold sucks air and fuel via the pilot jet through the idling jet orifice. The three minor jets therefore provide the mixture enrichment necessary when accelerating, maintaining high speed and engine idling.

Arrangements for cold starting consist of a choke flap above the main jet and venturi. To start the engine when cold, appreciably more fuel is required to overcome the losses due to condensation of the fuel vapour in the inlet manifold ducts. By closing the choke valve an increased vacuum is created in the carburettor barrel and this causes a greater amount of fuel to be drawn out of the main jet system. The choke flap is closed through a system of links and levers operated by a bi-metallic coiled spring. Joined to the compartment in which the bi-metallic spring is housed is a reservoir of engine coolant with inlet and outlet connections. When the engine and coolant are cold the bi-metallic spring will coil itself up due to contraction, and will, through the interconnecting linkage, close the choke flap. As the engine warms up the temperature of the coolant flowing through the system

rises and causes the bi-metallic spring to expand and thus unwind itself. This progressive expansion and unwinding of the spring will eventually fully open the choke flap rendering it ineffective as the engine reaches a pre-determined temperature.

Cars fitted with air conditioning equipment and emission control equipment will have a fast idling device fitted.

This device consists of a diaphragm unit attached to the throttle linkage. One side of the diaphragm is connected by a pipe to the inlet manifold. When the throttle is closed such as when idling or cruising down hill in gear the depression in the inlet manifold draws the diaphragm control unit upwards, thus compressing the return spring and partially opens the primary throttle flap valve. The fast idling speed is adjustable by turning the slotted screw attached to the diaphragm control rod.

In addition to the above unit, vehicles fitted with emission control equipment will have an electro magnetic fuel shut-off valve fitted. Unfortunately the engine has a tendency to run-on after the ignition is switched off. The valve is screwed into the fuel gallery in the carburettor main body. The valve consists of two parts, the solenoid in the cylindrical casing operated by switching on and off the ignition and the needle valve which is moved under the influence of the solenoid. When the ignition is switched off the solenoid is de-magnetised and the needle valve under the influence of a control spring moves forward and shuts off the fuel supply to the idling jet.

The valve also shuts off the fuel supply to prevent the catalytic converter from overheating when the throttle is closed during deceleration from above 2650 $\pm$ 50 rpm. The tachymetric switch which is located under the right-hand side of the dashpanel senses the engine speed from the ignition coil and the vacuum depression in the inlet manifold. During the deceleration period the electro magnetic fuel shut off device is de-energised and as already mentioned the return spring forces the needle valve into the idling jet and shuts off the fuel supply.

4 Carburettor - removal and refitting

1 Both the Weber and Solex carburettor may be removed easily, with the engine in the car, for inspection and cleaning. Under certain circumstances it may be wise to remove the carburettor from the inlet manifold before removing the engine.

2 The removal procedure described in this Section is primarily for cars fitted with emission control equipment. As all the cars in the FIAT 131 range are fitted with carburettors of a similar design these instructions can be adopted. Note that some carburettors will not have the same fittings or pipe connections. It is advisable before disconnecting any of the pipe connections to take note of their locations to avoid incorrect refitting at a later time. A small label attached to the pipe with a written description is ideal.

3 Remove the air cleaner assembly as described in Section 2 (photo).

4 Now disconnect the two electric feed wires to the carburettor (emission control type only).

5 Disconnect the fuel inlet and return pipes (photo).

6 Disconnect the vapour hose situated to the side of the inlet and return fuel pipes (emission control type only).

7 Now disconnect the fast idle vacuum hose pipe (where applicable). (photo).

4.3 The air cleaner assembly removed

4.5 Disconnect the fuel inlet and return pipe connections (arrowed)

4.7 Disconnecting the fast idle control vacuum hose (where applicable)

4.8 Disconnecting the automatic choke water hoses

4.13 The apparently complicated maze of pipes attached to the carburettor of a dohc engine which has emission control systems fitted

Remember to always fit a new gasket between the carburettor and inlet manifold. Take care when tightening the four retaining nuts. They should be tightened evenly to prevent any possible distortion of the carburettor base flange occurring.
13 On emission control models ensure that the various pipes and hoses have been reconnected to their original positions (photo).
14 If the carburettor has been dismantled it will need adjusting as described in Section 5.

5 Carburettor - setting and adjustment

Note: On models imported to the USA it must be appreciated that any adjustments to the fuel (and emission control) systems may infringe federal or local laws, and should only be carried out when absolutely necessary. In all cases, adjustments should be checked by a suitably equipped FIAT agent or carburation specialist at the first possible opportunity.

Idling speed and mixture adjustments using a CO meter
1 Run the engine until the normal operating temperature is reached. On cars fitted with a catalytic converter disconnect the air hose from the valve on the air manifold.
2 Ensure that all the remaining carburettor and emission control pipes are satisfactorily connected.
3 On cars with automatic transmission, apply the handbrake, and place the gear selector lever in 'Drive'. Using a tachometer check that the idling speed is as stated in the Specifications. Cars fitted with manual transmission should be in Neutral when checking the normal idling speed.
4 Adjust the idling screw until the engine idling speed is set at the recommended setting specification.
5 Now connect the CO meter to the vehicle exhaust and adjust the idle mixture screw to obtain the lowest CO output, which should be within the limits recommended in the Specifications Section.
6 After setting the CO output it will be necessary to repeat the idling speed adjustment operation.

Fig. 3.2. Removing the Weber carburettor (typical for emission control types) (Sec. 4)

1 Carburettor
2 Water hoses
3 Throttle linkage connection
4 Wire
5 Vacuum hose to activated carbon trap
6 EGR vacuum hose
7 Nut
8 Wires to fuel shut-off solenoid
9 Fuel inlet pipe
10 Fuel return pipe
11 Vacuum hose for fast idle
12 Vapour vent hose

8 Disconnect the two water hoses connected to the automatic choke (photo).
9 Disconnect the accelerator rod from the throttle linkage.
10 Finally undo the four nuts retaining the carburettor to the inlet manifold.
11 Now lift the carburettor upwards off the mounting studs.
12 Refitting the carburettor is the reverse of the removal procedure.

7   Finally, reconnect the air hose, where applicable, to the valve on the air manifold.

Idling speed and mixture adjustments without a CO meter
8   Follow the instructions detailed in paragraphs 1 - 4 of this Section.
9   With the engine still running rotate the carburettor idle mixture

screw clockwise until the engine almost stops due to the mixture being too weak. Now back the adjusting screw off, counting the number of turns, until the engine almost stalls due to a mixture strength which is too rich. The theoretical correct mixture strength is midway between these two limits.
10 With the mixture screw now adjusted to this mid-point position it may be necessary to readjust the idling speed screw once more.

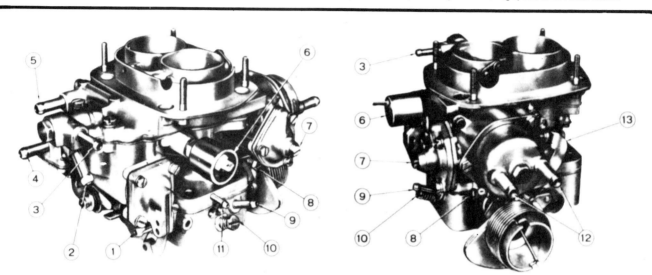

Fig. 3.3. The Weber carburettor showing typical pipe connections and adjusting screws (Sec. 5)

1 Blow-by vapour connection	7 Diaphragm unit for partially	10 Idling mixture screw
2 Fuel inlet pipe	opening of the choke valve	11 EGR pipe connection
3 Fuel return pipe	8 Basic idling speed adjusting screw	12 Water connections to automatic
4 Fast vacuum connection	9 Connection for hose from activated	choke mechanism
5 Float chamber vent pipe	carbon trap	13 Choke fast idle adjusting screw
6 Fuel shut-off device		

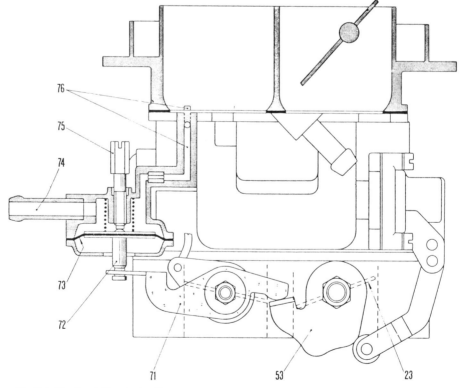

Fig. 3.4. The fast idling device (fitted to emission control and air conditioned cars only) (Sec. 5)

23 Primary throttle valve	72 Tie rod	74 Connection for vacuum feed pipe
53 Fast idle cam lever	73 Diaphragm controlling opening at	from inlet manifold
71 Actuating lever for opening	primary throttle	75 Fast idle adjusting screw
primary throttle flap valve during fast idling		76 Air passage

Fast idle adjustment

11 Place the transmission in Neutral.

12 Press and hold the emission control button (where applicable) (photo).

13 Increase the engine speed to approximately 2,000 rpm and allow it to return to the idling position.

14 Adjust the fast idle adjustment screw until the engine speed is within the limits specified for the fast idling speed.

---

6 Carburettor - dismantling, inspection and reassembly

1 The dismantling procedure described in this Section is primarily for the Weber carburettor (Fig. 3.6). As the Solex carburettor is very similar in both appearance and function the following instructions can be applied to this make also (Fig. 3.5). Where possible any differences between the two makes are mentioned in the text. Note that some components mentioned are applicable only to vehicles fitted with emission control equipment.

2 Do not dismantle the carburettor unless systematic diagnosis indicates that there is a fault with it. The internal mechanism is delicate and finely balanced and unnecessary tampering with it will probably do more harm than good.

3 If the automatic choke mechanism is suspected of being faulty then it is advisable to entrust the rectification of the fault to your nearest FIAT dealer who will have the necessary calibrated service tools to correctly set up the unit. It is for this reason that the dismantling and adjustment of the automatic choke device is not detailed in this manual.

4 Although certain parts may be removed with the carburettor still attached to the engine, it is considered safer to remove it as a complete unit and work with it on a clean bench.

5 Removal of the carburettor is described in Section 4.

6 The top or lid of the carburettor is retained by four slotted screws. These screws are made of a comparatively soft metal and will damage very easily unless the correct size of screwdriver is used to remove them.

7 Undo the four screws and lift the lid carefully off. Note that the automatic choke, choke flap, float and check valve are all connected to the lid.

8 The float is retained to the lid by a pivot pin which is easily removed.

9 With the float removed check that it is not punctured by either shaking it and listening for the sound of fuel splashing around inside, or by immersing in clean warm water and watching for air bubbles escaping from it.

10 The check valve is screwed into the carburettor lid and is easily removed using a suitable sized socket or box spanner. Note that a sealing washer is sandwiched between the check valve and carburettor lid.

11 A fuel filter is fitted into the carburettor lid and can be removed after undoing the blanking plug.

12 Before removing the choke valve flap from the choke spindle check the free play between the spindle and the carburettor lid. If there is no excessive play between the two parts then it will not be necessary to remove them from the lid. The flap valve is retained to the slotted spindle by two small screws. Remove the screws and draw the flap valve out. The spindle can now be removed.

13 It is not advisable to tamper with the automatic choke unit unless, as already mentioned, access is available to the special calibrating service tools.

14 Further dismantling of the carburettor main body can take place after the gasket has been removed. Most of the jets have screwdriver slots cut into their heads and are easily removed. Note carefully from which positions the jets are removed.

15 The accelerator pump diaphragm housing is retained to the carburettor main body by four screws. Remove the screws and lift the housing and spring from the main body.

16 Cars fitted with either emission control or air conditioning equipment will have a fast idle diaphragm unit. Disconnect the link clip from the base of the fast idle unit and remove the screws retaining it to the main carburettor body. Lift the unit away.

17 Before removing the throttle spindles check for any excessive wear between the spindles and the carburettor body. Excessive wear at these points will cause erratic running and a weak mixture. Excessive wear at these points is also a fair indication of the overall general condition of the carburettor. This check can be made without dis-

5.12 The emission control button used when adjusting the fast idle speed

mantling the carburettor or removing it from the engine.

18 If the throttle spindles are to be removed, it will be necessary to remove the throttle linkage, spacers, springs and throttle flap valves.

19 On Solex carburettors the main carburettor body is detachable from the base unit and the primary and secondary venturi are removable after having removed the accelerator pump injector and the auxiliary venturi. The auxiliary venturi are retained in position by locking screws projecting through the main carburettor body.

20 Thoroughly clean all the components with petrol and dry them with compressed air.

21 Inspect the diaphragms for splits or perforations and renew any suspect parts.

22 Check the jets for blockage or damage. If the jets are blocked they should be cleared using compressed air and not by a piece of wire. If the compressed air fails to clear the blockage then a new jet should be obtained.

23 It is impossible to be absolutely certain that the various drillings or passageways in the main carburettor body are free from obstructions. It is advisable to blow through them with compressed air in the direction of flow to dislodge any particles.

24 Examine the carburettor body for cracks or damage, bearing in mind that if the wear on the throttle spindle bosses is excessive then a new unit must be obtained.

25 Reassembling the carburettor is the reverse of the dismantling procedure. Remember to fit new gaskets and do not use any form of jointing compound on them.

26 Before reassembling the carburettor lid check the condition of the check valve and seat. If in doubt about its condition renew it.

27 Now refit the float and its pivot pin.

28 Before refitting the carburettor lid it will be necessary to check the float height, measured between the lid and the base of the float. When checking the float height of the Weber carburettor it is necessary to hold the lid vertically, with the float facing downwards. Now using a ¼ in (6 mm) twist drill as a gauge rod, lay it across the carburettor lid directly under the float. The float should just clear the drill shank (Fig. 3.7). Note that the lid gasket should be in place when carrying out this check. Adjustment of the float height is carried out by carefully bending the float arm. The float height of the Solex C32 TEIE/42 carburettor is checked and if necessary adjusted in a similar fashion, using special gauge number A95148 or a 6.5 to 7.5 mm twist drill shank.

The Solex C32 TEIE/1 and TEIE/2 types must be checked/set at a clearance of 0.354 to 0.394 in (9 to 10 mm); the shank of an equivalent twist drill will again suffice as a gauge.

29 Refit the carburettor to the manifold as described in Section 4 and adjust it as described in Section 5.

---

7 Mechanical fuel pump - removal, overhaul and refitting

1 Mechanical fuel pumps are fitted to all FIAT 131 models which

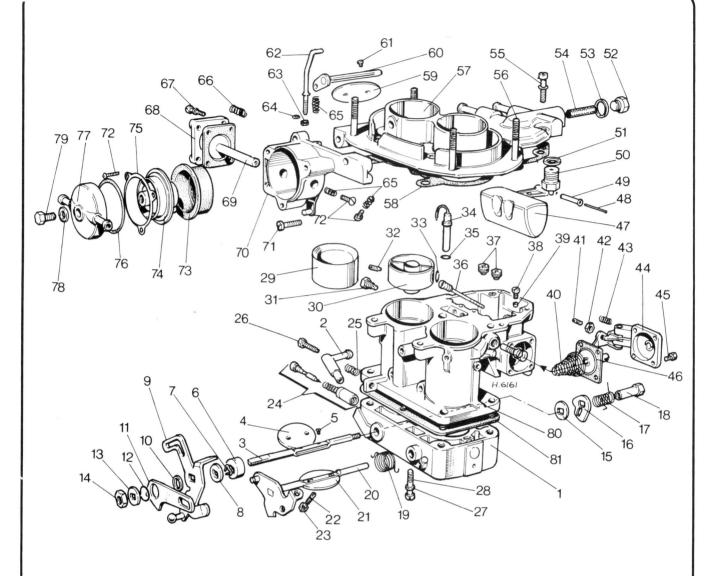

Fig. 3.5. An exploded view of the Solex twin-Choke carburettor (Sec. 6)

1	Carburettor base unit	28	Retaining screw	55	Screw
2	Elbow union	29	Choke tube (venturi)	56	Stud
3	Secondary throttle spindle	30	Auxiliary choke tube	57	Lid
4	Throttle flap valve	31	Pilot jet	58	Gasket
5	Screw	32	Lock screw	59	Choke flap valve
6	Spacer	33	Washer	60	Choke spindle
7	Rubber ring	34	Pump jet tube	61	Screw
8	Spacer	35	Seating washer	62	Link rod
9	Lever	36	Emulsion tube and air correction jet	63	Nut
10	Spacer	37	Main jets	64	Washer
11	Lever	38	Pump back bleed	65	Spring
12	Spacer	39	Ball	66	Spring
13	Washer	40	Pump spring	67	Screw
14	Nut	41	Adjusting screw	68	Diaphragm cover plate
15	Spacer	42	Locknut	69	Automatic choke diaphragm unit
16	Plate	43	Spring	70	Automatic choke body
17	Spring	44	Pump cover	71	Screw
18	Sleeve nut	45	Screw	72	Screw
19	Spring	46	Accelerator pump diaphragm	73	Cover
20	Primary throttle spindle	47	Float	74	Thermostatic control spring unit
21	Throttle flap valve	48	Float spindle	75	Lockplate ring
22	Adjusting screw	49	Bush	76	Gasket
23	Locknut	50	Check valve	77	Automatic choke housing
24	Idling mixture adjuster screw assembly	51	Seating washer	78	Sealing washers
25	Spring	52	Plug	79	Bolt
26	Idling speed adjustment screw	53	Sealing washer	80	Carburettor body
27	Spring washer	54	Filter	81	Gasket

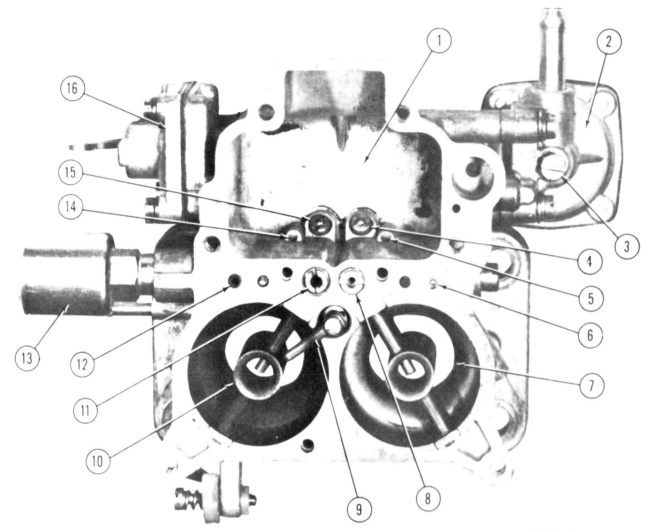

Fig. 3.6. The Weber twin-choke carburettor with the lid and gasket removed (typical) (Sec. 6)

1 Float chamber
2 Fast idling diaphragm unit
3 Fast idling adjustment screw
4 Main jet secondary choke
5 High speed gas inlet
6 High speed air passage

7 Secondary auxiliary venturi
8 Air correction jet secondary choke
9 Accelerator pump nozzle
10 Primary choke auxiliary venturi
11 Air correction jet primary choke

12 High speed air passage
13 Fuel shut-off solenoid
14 High speed gas inlet
15 Main jet primary choke
16 Accelerator pump housing

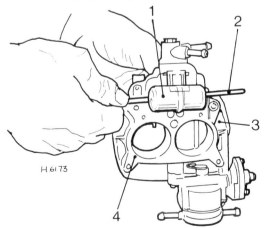

Fig. 3.7. Checking the float height of the
Weber varburettor using a gauge rod of
6 mm dia (¼ in approx) (Sec. 6)

1 Float
2 6 mm dia gauge
   rod
3 Lid
4 Lid gasket

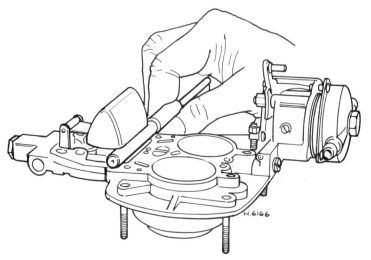

Fig. 3.8. Checking the float height of the
Solex carburettor using tool 6990117 (Sec. 6)

The carburettor cover must be in a horizontal position

utilise either the 1300 or 1600 ohv engine. The pump is bolted to the cylinder block and operated by a rocker arm which rides on an eccentric formed on the camshaft.

2   The fuel pump will need to be removed in order to overhaul, but the filter can be cleaned with the pump in situ. Disconnect the fuel inlet and outlet pipes from the pump (photo).

3   Undo the two nuts, holding the pump flange to the cylinder block, and take the pump off. Keep the spacer and gaskets together and do not discard them. If necessary blank off the fuel line from the tank to prevent loss of fuel.

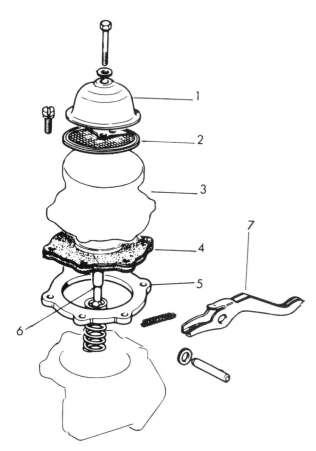

Fig. 3.9. The component parts of the mechanical fuel pump (Sec. 7)

1   Cover
2   Filter screen
3   Pump body incorporating one-way valves
4   Pump diaghragm
5   Gasket
6   Diaphragm actuating rod
7   Pump lever and pivot

4   Before dismantling the pump, clean the exterior thoroughly and mark the edges of the two halves of the body.

5   Undo the cover retaining bolt and lift the cover off. The gasket and gauze filter may now be removed.

6   Remove the eight screws and washers holding the two halves of the pump together and the top half may be lifted off.

7   The diaphragm and pushrod should be removed next but you will have to remove the pump lever and its spindle to release it. This is done by releasing one of the spindle circlips. This can prove to be very awkward but with patience and a strong blunt penknife blade, the circlip can be levered off. Push the spindle through and pull out the lever. Retrieve the lever spring. Lift out the diaphragm and its rod carefully. This spindle is usually known as the rocker arm pivot pin.

8   If there are any signs of wear in the rocker arm pivot, rocker arm and link bushes then they should be renewed.

9   The valve assemblies should only be removed from the upper body if renewal is necessary. They are staked into the body and usually destroyed when levered out.

10 Examine the diaphragm for signs of cracking or perforation and renew if necessary.

11 Overhaul kits are available for all pumps and are supplied complete with a new diaphragm, valves and sealing rings.

12 When fitting new valve assemblies to the body, first place the sealing washers in position and then fit the valves, making sure that they are the correct way up according to inlet and outlet. The valves will have to be restacked at six (different) places around the edge so that they are firmly held in their locations. If this is not done correctly and leakage occurs between the valve assembly and the sealing ring the pump will not operate efficiently.

13 To refit the diaphragm and lever arm, place the diaphragm spring in the body of the pump. Then the diaphragm and its rod. Press the diaphragm spring down and fit the spring, push in the lever (the right way up) and connect over the top of the machined stop on the rod. Push in the rocker arm pivot pin and push through the lever. Refit the circlip on the pivot pin using a new circlip.

14 Fit the upper half of the pump body and line up the mating marks. In order to assemble the two halves and the diaphragm correctly, push the rocker arm upwards so that the diaphragm is drawn level. Then place the eight screws in position lightly. It is best if the base of the pump is held lightly in a vice whilst the rocker arm is pushed right up to bring the diaphragm to the bottom of its stroke. A short piece of tube over the rocker arm will provide easy leverage. In this position the eight screws should be tightened evenly and alternatively.

15 Fit a new filter bowl gasket carefully in the groove of the upper body, making sure that it does not twist or buckle in the process. Refit the cover and retaining bolt.

16 When the pump is reassembled the suction and delivery pressure can be felt at the inlet and outlet ports when the rocker arm is operated. Be careful not to block the inlet port completely when testing the suction. If the rocker arm is operated strongly and the inlet side is blocked the diaphragm could be damaged.

17 Refitting is the reversal of the removal procedure. Make sure that the total thickness of gaskets and spacer is the same as originally fitted (photos).

18 Refit the fuel pipes and start the engine and check that the fuel line connections are not leaking.

7.2 Mechanical fuel pump with outlet pipe disconnected

7.17A Fuel pump showing outer gasket and spacer block being assembled

7.17B Fitting the fuel pump with the new gaskets fitted on either side of the spacer block

8 Electric fuel pump - removal and refitting

1 FIAT 131 models having the twin overhead camshaft engine are fitted with an electric fuel pump mounted at the rear of the car, close to the fuel tank (photo).
2 To remove the pump first disconnect the two hose clips and pull the pipes off.
3 Now disconnect the electric feed cable.
4 Undo the two nuts which hold the pump body to the insulators and lift the earth wire off the mounting stud.
5 The pump can now be removed.
6 Refitting the pump is the reversal of the removal sequence. Remember that after refitting and the engine has been started, to check that there are no leaks from the pipe connections.

9 Fuel filter and element - removal and refitting

1 Two types of fuel filter are fitted to cars having an electric fuel pump. In one type the renewable element is fitted inside a glass bowl, whereas the other type has a renewable canister filter screwed onto a cover housing similar in design to the oil filter (photo).
2 Removing the canister is straightforward. Unscrew the old unit and discard and screw on the new unit.
3 Renewing the element on the other type of filter is also relatively simple and is achieved by holding the glass bowl with one hand and releasing the handle at the base of the unit with the other.
4 Lift off the bowl and element. Clean the bowl and renew the element.
5 Refitting the bowl and filter is the reverse of the dismantling

Fig. 3.10. The electric fuel pump mounting and pipes (Sec. 8)

1 Support bracket
2 Wiring connector block
3 Fuel hose
4 Fuel pump
5 Mounting nut
6 Insulator block

Fig. 3.11. Fuel filter with disposable element (Sec. 8)

1 Retaining nuts
2 Support bracket
3 Fuel inlet pipe from fuel pump
4 Element inside of glass bowl
5 Handle and clamp assembly
6 Fuel outlet pipe to carburettor

8.1 The electric fuel lift pump located at the rear of the car

9.1 The line fuel filter with canister type disposable filter

procedure.

6   It is important with both types of filter to run the engine after refitting the units to check for any fuel leakage.

7   Removal of the filter head is carried out after having disconnected the fuel pipes. Remove the two retaining nuts and washers and lift the unit clear.

8   Refitting is a reverse of the removal procedure.

10 Fuel tank - removal and refitting

The removal sequences described are for cars fitted with fuel evaporative emission control systems, however, these instructions can be applied to cars not having these systems.

Saloon car

1   Drain the fuel tank after having first disconnected the battery earth lead.

2   Remove the rear seat cushion.

3   Remove the rear seat backrest and top shelf.

4   Disconnect the overfill hose and two fuel hoses from the sender unit.

5   Disconnect the two wires from the sender unit.

6   Disconnect the two vapour hoses from the tank.

7   From the outside of the car, remove the filler cap.

8   Now remove the two screws holding the plastic cap on the filler neck.

9   Pull the filler neck out of the tank.

10 From inside the car remove the nut and washer from the stud which retains the fuel tank strap to the top shelf.

11 From inside the boot lift the tank out.

12 Refitting the tank is the reverse of the removal procedure. Before refitting the seats and top shelf start the engine and check for any fuel leakage.

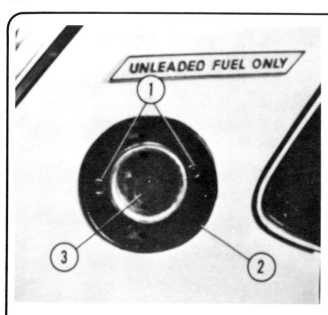

Fig. 3.12. The fuel tank filler neck and retaining ring (USA model shown) (Sec. 10)

1   Retaining screws   3   Filler neck
2   Plastic retainer ring

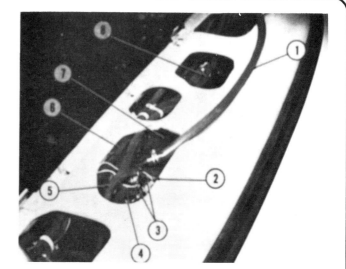

Fig. 3.13. The fuel and vapour hose connections to the saloon car (USA model shown) (Sec. 10)

1   Overfill hose   5   Fuel hose
2   Sender unit   6   Vapour hose
3   Wiring connections   7   Fuel tank
4   Fuel hose   8   Vapour hose

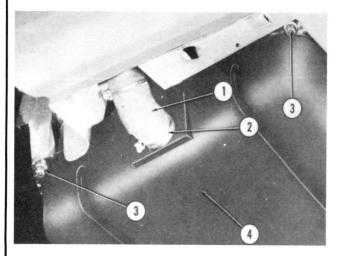

Fig. 3.14. The fuel tank mounting of the estate car as viewed from below (USA model shown) (Sec. 10)

1   Filler tube   3   Retaining nuts
2   Hose clip   4   Fuel tank

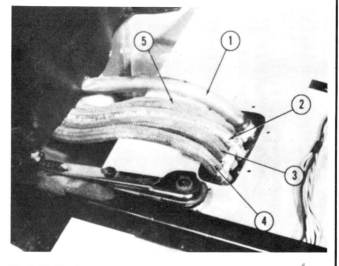

Fig. 3.15. The fuel and vapour hose connections of the estate car (USA model shown) (Sec. 10)

1   Overfill hose   4   Vapour hose
2   Vapour hose   5   Vapour hose separator to
3   Vapour hose   3-way valve

Estate car

13 Drain the fuel tank after having first disconnected the battery earth lead.

14 Lift up the rear floor deck.

15 Now disconnect the overfill hose and the three other fuel pipes noting the location of each pipe.

16 From underneath the car, which should be raised and supported, remove the cover plate screwed to the bodyshell.

17 With the pipe cover plate removed, slacken off the hose clips and release the hose from the tank.

18 Support the tank and remove the four nuts and washers holding the fuel tank to the body.

19 Carefully lower the tank and disconnect the two fuel hoses and wires from the sender unit.

20 The tank is now free from its mountings and connections and can be removed.

21 Refitting the tank is the reverse of the dismantling procedure. Before screwing the cover plate back up to the body shell recouple the various hoses and refill the fuel tank. Now start the engine and check the pipe connections for any signs of leakage.

---

11 Fuel tank sender unit - removal and refitting

Saloon car

1 Remove rear seat cushion and backrest.

2 Remove the top shelf.

3 Disconnect the fuel hoses and wiring connections.

4 Undo the six nuts retaining the sender unit to the fuel tank and lift the sender unit out complete with gasket.

5 When refitting the sender unit ensure that the tubes are pointing towards the left side of the car and that the hose connections and earth wire are secured correctly. The grey/red wire should be connected to the terminal marked 'W' and the orange/yellow wire is connected to the terminal marked 'T' on the sender unit.

Estate car

6 Remove the fuel tank as described in Section 10.

7 Now undo the six nuts securing the sender unit to the tank.

8 Lift out the sender unit and remove the gasket.

9 When fitting the sender unit ensure that the tubes fitted to the sender unit are pointing towards the left side of the car.

10 Refitting the tank is the reverse of the dismantling procedure.

---

12 Inlet manifold - removal and refitting

1300 and 1600 models

The inlet and exhaust manifolds fitted to the ohv engine are retained to the cylinder head by nuts and large washers.

1 Remove the air cleaner assembly as described in Section 2.

2 Remove the carburettor as described in Section 4.

3 Disconnect the water hoses and servo vacuum hose from the manifold.

4 Undo the manifold retaining nuts and remove together with the large washers and lift the inlet manifold carefully away from the cylinder head studs.

5 In some cases it will be found easier to remove the exhaust manifold together with the inlet manifold. Remember, however, to fit a new gasket when refitting the manifolds.

1800 models

6 The inlet manifold fitted to the dohc engine is fitted to the left-hand side of the cylinder head and retained by nuts and washers.

7 Remove the air cleaner assembly as detailed in Section 2.

8 Remove the carburettor as detailed in Section 4.

9 Disconnect the two vacuum pipes from the top of the manifold just behind the carburettor mounting (photo).

10 Disconnect the feed wires to the two switches screwed into the bottom of the inlet manifold.

11 Disconnect the EGR pipe and any remaining vacuum hoses joined to the manifold.

12 Undo the four bolts and two nuts retaining the inlet manifold to the cylinder head and remove the manifold.

13 When refitting the manifold always use a new gasket and ensure the mating faces are clean. Furthermore, do not use any jointing compound on the gasket and tighten the nuts and bolts evenly to prevent any distortion occurring.

14 Refit the carburettor and its associate pipes and connections as detailed in Section 4.

15 Refit the air cleaner as detailed in Section 2.

---

13 Exhaust manifold - removal and refitting

1300 and 1600 models

1 Disconnect the battery earth lead, then raise the left-hand side of the car for access to the front exhaust pipe/manifold flange nuts.

2 Remove the four flange securing nuts.

3 Lower the car to the ground.

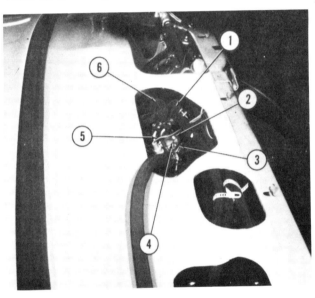

Fig. 3.16. Removing the sender unit of saloon car (USA model shown) (Sec. 11)

1 Fuel hose	4 Sender unit
2 Nuts securing sender unit to tank	5 Wiring connections
3 Earth wire	6 Fuel hose

12.9 Disconnect the two vacuum hoses from the inlet manifold

4 Now remove the nuts retaining the manifold to the cylinder head. Note that the large plain washers under the nuts also retain the inlet manifold.

5 With the nuts removed lift the manifold off the mounting studs and up through the engine compartment. Note that a gasket is fitted between the exhaust pipe and manifold.

6 In some instances it may be beneficial to remove the inlet manifold and exhaust manifold as one unit. In this case the various hoses, air filter and petrol pipes will have to be disconnected from the carburettor.

7 Refitting is the reverse of the dismantling procedure.

1800 model

8 The 1800 twin cam engine utilises a conventional two-part clamp to retain the front exhaust pipe to the manifold flange (photo).

9 Disconnect the manifold flange clamp.

10 Now disconnect the EGR pipe union bolt and union from the top of the exhaust manifold (photo).

11 Finally remove the nuts which secure the manifold to the cylinder head and lift the manifold from the engine compartment.

12 Refitting the manifold is the reverse of the removal procedure.

14 Exhaust system and catalytic converter

1 The exhaust systems fitted to the FIAT 131 models are conventional in their layout except for Californian import models which will have a catalytic converter incorporated in the system.

2 The system is clamped together in sections and incorporates two silencer boxes.

3 Use only the original type exhaust clamps and proprietary made parts of the system. When part of the exhaust system needs renewal it often follows that the rest of the system is as bad and it is recommended that the whole system be renewed.

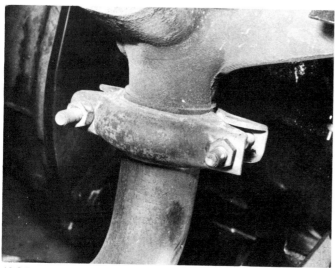

13.8 The exhaust manifold clamp fitted to the dohc engine

13.10 The exhaust manifold of the dohc engine with the exhaust flange clamp and pipe removed

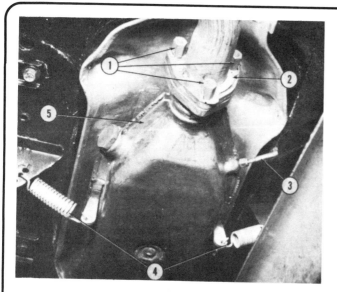

Fig. 3.17. The catalytic converter (Californian models only) (Sec. 14)

1 Flange nuts
2 Locking plate
3 Thermocouple cable
4 Springs
5 Catalytic converter

Fig. 3.18. The odometer switch (Californian models with catalytic converter only) (Sec. 14)

1 Locating screw
2 Odometer switch
3 Speedometer cable from transmission
4 Wiring harness
5 Lock wire
6 Cap covering reset screw
7 Fuse holder
8 Speedometer cable to speedometer head

4   It is most important when fitting exhaust systems that the twists and contours are correctly positioned and that each connecting joint overlaps the correct distance. Any stresses or strains imparted in order to force the system to fit the hanger rubbers will result in early fractures or failures.

5   When fitting a new part or a complete system it is well worth removing the whole system from the car and cleaning up all the joints so that they will fit together easily. The time spent struggling with obstinate joints whilst lying flat on your back under the car is less and the likelihood of distorting or even breaking a section is greatly reduced. Do not waste time trying to undo rusted clamps and bolts. Cut them off. New ones will be required anyway if they are bad.

6   The catalytic converter fitted to Californian models is joined into the exhaust system by a flange coupling.

7   Due to the high temperature at which the converter operates it is essential to allow the converter to cool down before attempting to touch it.

8   The catalytic converter will require renewal at 25,000 mile intervals. Indication of this mileage is given by a warning light on the dashpanel marked 'Catalyst' which only lights up when the contacts in the odometer switch close, causing a fuse to blow. Two cam drums driven by the speedometer cable turn gradually and at 25,000 mile intervals close the contacts in the odometer switch as already mentioned.

9   To remove the catalytic converter first ensure that it has cooled down.

10 Now disconnect the thermocouple cable.

11 Bend back the locking washer at the flange couplings and remove the three flange nuts from either end of the converter.

12 Disconnect the two support springs and lift the converter away from the pipes.

13 Refitting the converter is the reverse of the removal operation.

14 If the converter is being renewed then it will be necessary to reset the odometer switch as follows:

15 Remove the lockwire and unscrew the cap.

16 Now either turn the switch to 50 or if the switch is already on 50, turn it back to 25.

17 Renew the fuse.

15 Emission control systems - general description

1   The emission control systems enable cars, manufactured for the North American market, to conform with all Federal Regulations governing the emission of hydrocarbons, carbon monoxide, nitric oxide and fuel vapours from the crankcase, exhaust and fuel systems.

2   With the exception of the catalytic converter and its associate parts, the items described are fitted to all models.

Crankcase breather system

3   Crankcase breathing and removal of 'blow-by' vapours is achieved by making use of the inherent partial vacuum in the carburettor. In

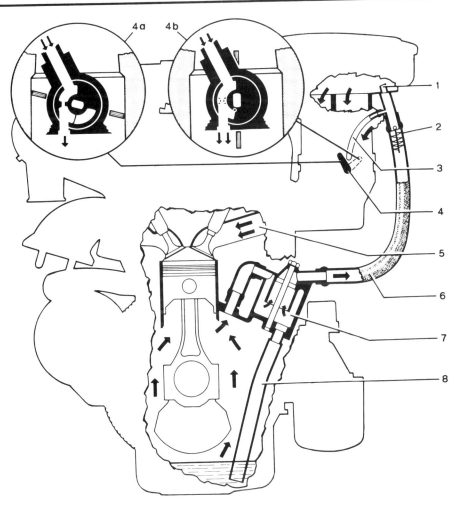

Fig. 3.19. Crankcase emission control system (fitted to all FIAT 131 models) (Sec. 15)

1 Emission feed to air cleaner	4a Control valve - engine idling	6 Oil separator to air cleaner line
2 Flame trap	4b Control valve - engine speed above idling	7 Liquid/vapour separator
3 Air cleaner to control valve line	5 Inlet manifold	8 Oil drain pipe back to sump

this way, emissions are burnt in the combustion process. An oil/vapour separator unit is fitted into the crankcase and a connecting pipe joins the separator to the air filter and carburettor (photo). A control valve fitted to the carburettor diverts some of the vapours directly into the carburettor at wide throttle openings. A flame trap is fitted into the pipe line joining the carburettor to the separator.

Air injection and EGR system
4 This system is used to reduce the emissions of hydrocarbons, nitric oxide and carbon monoxide in the exhaust gases, and comprises an air pump, diverter valve, check valve and air manifold.
5 A rotary vane type pump is belt driven from the engine and delivers air to each of the four exhaust ports (photo).
6 The diverter/relief valve ejects air from the pump to the atmosphere during deceleration, being controlled in this operation by inlet

manifold vacuum. Excessive pressure is discharged to atmosphere by operation of the relief valve (photo).
7 The check valve is a diaphragm - spring operated non-return valve. Its purpose is to protect the pump from exhaust gas pressures both under normal operation and in the event of a drivebelt failure.
8 The air manifold is used to direct the air into the engine exhaust ports.

Evaporative control system
9 This system prevents the release of fuel vapours from the fuel tank and carburettor into the atmosphere. The fuel tank and carburettor are vented through an activated carbon trap which absorbs the vapours which are drawn back into the intake manifold and burnt in the combustion process. The system comprises the following units:

15.3 The oil/vapour separator unit (shown fitted to the dohc engine)

15.5 The air pump (arrowed) fitted to the exhaust camshaft housing of the American market engine

15.6 The diverter/relief valve (A) and the electric valve control unit (B)

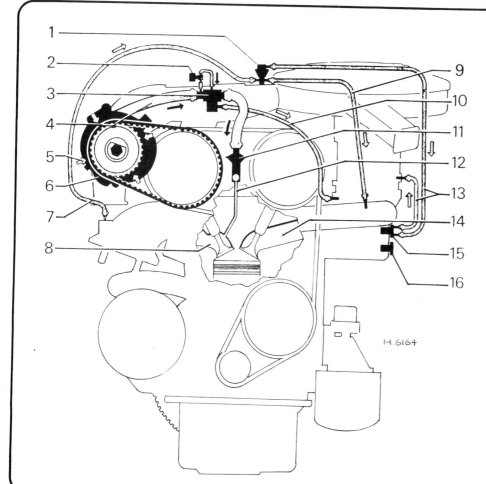

Fig. 3.20. Air injection and EGR system

1 Exhaust gas recirculation (EGR) control valve
2 Electro valve for diverter valve
3 Diverter valve
4 Air hose connecting air pump to diverter valve
5 Air intake
6 Air pump manifold
7 Exhaust gas tapping line
8 Exhaust port in cylinder head leading to exhaust manifold
9 Line to inlet manifold for exhaust gas recirculation
10 Vacuum line tapping in inlet manifold for diverter valve
11 Non-return valve
12 Air injector
13 Vacuum tapping line, in carburettor, for EGR valve
14 Inlet manifold
15 EGR control valve thermovalve
16 Electrovalve

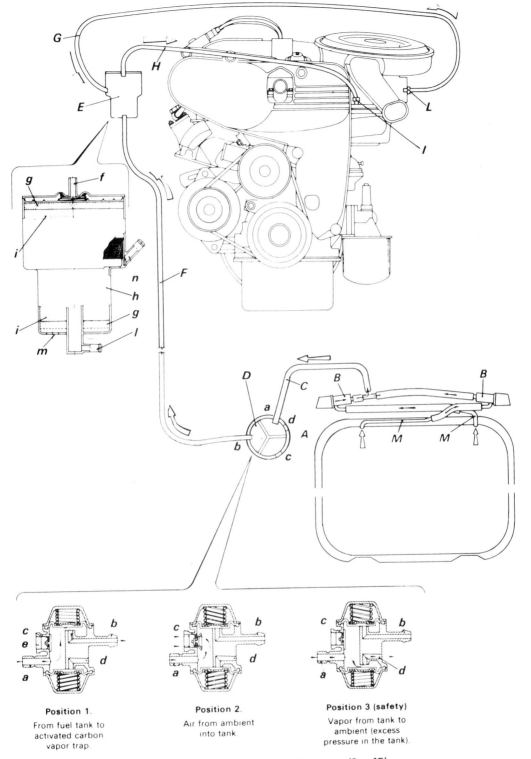

Position 1.

From fuel tank to
activated carbon
vapor trap.

Position 2.

Air from ambient
into tank.

Position 3 (safety)

Vapor from tank to
ambient (excess
pressure in the tank).

Fig. 3.21. Fuel vapour recirculation system (Sec. 15)

A Fuel tank
B Liquid/vapour separator
C Line from separator to 3-way valve
D 3-way control valve
E Activated carbon trap
F Line from 3-way valve to carbon trap
G Vent line from carburettor float chamber
H Line from carbon trap to carburettor below level of throttle
I Connection point on carburettor
L Connection point at carburettor float chamber vent
M Lines between tank and separator

a From fuel tank
b To activated carbon trap
c Fuel tank air inlet
d Safety outlet
e Air filter
f To carburettor below throttle level
g Synthetic filter
h Activated carbon trap
l Activated carbon
l Fuel vapour inlet from fuel tank
m Hot air purge inlet
n Inlet for fuel vapours from carburettor

a) Sealed fuel tank filler cap.
b) Limited filling tank.
c) Tank outlet vapour/liquid separator unit.
d) Carburettor vent pipe line.
e) Activated carbon trap (photo).
f) Three-way control valve.

10 The activated carbon trap is simply a canister filled with carbon and positioned in the engine compartment. There are three pipe connections, one from the fuel tank vent system, one from the inlet manifold, and the last one from the air filter. The fuel vapours 'soak' into the carbon, which is purged off the vapour when the engine is running. The vacuum in the inlet manifold draws warm air from the air filter unit through the carbon taking the vapour into the engine through the inlet manifold pipe. Between the petrol tank and the carbon canister there is a three-way valve. The valve allows air into the vent system to compensate for consumption of fuel. The valve also allows vapours to pass along the vent line to the carbon canister and engine. The third mode of operation of the valve is to allow vapour to vent directly to atmosphere in the event of a blockage in the vent pipe to the canister.

Exhaust gas recirculation (EGR) system
11 To minimise nitric oxide exhaust emissions, the peak combustion temperatures are lowered by recirculating a metered quantity of exhaust gas through the inlet manifold.
12 A control signal is taken from the throttle edge tapping of the carburettor. At idle or full load no recirculation is provided, but under part load conditions a controlled amount of recirculation is provided according to the vacuum signal profile of the metering valve. The EGR valve is mounted to the inlet camshaft cover (photo).
13 An EGR thermovalve control unit is mounted to the inlet manifold and cuts the vacuum signal when the choke is in operation.

Throttle positioner system ('fast idling system')
14 The object of this system is to maintain a flow of air through the carburettor which will allow the carburettor to meter the fuel efficiently and not give a slightly rich mixture as normally occurs in engine over-run and slow idling conditions.
15 The system comprises a throttle positioner diaphragm unit, an electro valve and electro valve actuating switches. There are in all four switches operating the electro valve;
   Switch A - fitted to the clutch pedal.
   Switch B - screwed into the gearbox casing operated when 3rd and 4th gears are selected.
   Switch C - screwed into the gearbox casing and operated through the gearshift (contacts open with transmission in neutral).
   Switch D - a push button manual control switch fitted to the brake cylinder reservoir mounting plate. This switch is used when the fast idling speed needs adjustment and actuates the electro valve directly.

Catalytic converter
16 To further reduce the emission of carbon monoxide and hydro carbons, a catalytic converter is fitted in the exhaust system of certain models. The catalytic converter consists of a steel outer shell inside which is housed pellets coated with an oxidation type catalyst. The catalyst is protected from overheating by a fuel shut off device when the throttle is either closed or the engine speed is higher than 2650 ± 50 rpm. This is achieved by means of a tachymetric switch linked to the ignition coil. The tachymetric speed switch, when activated, will complete an electric circuit and thus energise the fuel cut off solenoid valve. A thermocouple fitted to the catalytic converter is activated, when the unit reaches about 1800°F (982°C), and sends current to a warning light marked 'Slow Down' on the dashboard causing the light to flash. As the unit gets hotter so the frequency of the warning light increases.
17 The following precautions should be taken with cars fitted with a catalytic converter:

a) Avoid heavy impacts to the casing which can cause damage to the internal ceramic material.
b) Never use anything but unleaded fuel, or the emission control system efficiency will be seriously impaired.
c) The catalytic converter becomes extremely hot during operation of the car. Avoid contacting combustible materials such as long grass when parking, and allow the converter to cool before touching it during any repair or maintenance operations.

18 If misfiring of the engine occurs, the cause must be traced and rectified immediately to prevent damage to the catalytic converter.

16 Emission control systems - repair and maintenance operations

Oil/vapour separator unit - removal, cleaning and refitting
1   The removal and refitting of this unit is detailed in Chapter 1, part B, Section 64.
2   After removing the unit and cleaning it inspect the joining hoses for damage and remember to clean the flame trap fitted into the hose joining the separator to the air filter.

Activated carbon trap - removal and refitting
3   Disconnect the three pipes noting their exact positions.
4   Undo and remove the two mounting bolts and lift the unit free.
5   Refitting the unit is the reverse of the removal operation.

Air pump - removal and refitting
6   Remove the timing belt cover.
7   Disconnect the hose from the rear of the air pump (photo).
8   Remove the air pump drivebelt.

15.9e The activated carbon trap mounted to the bodyshell

15.12 The EGR exhaust gas recirculation valve

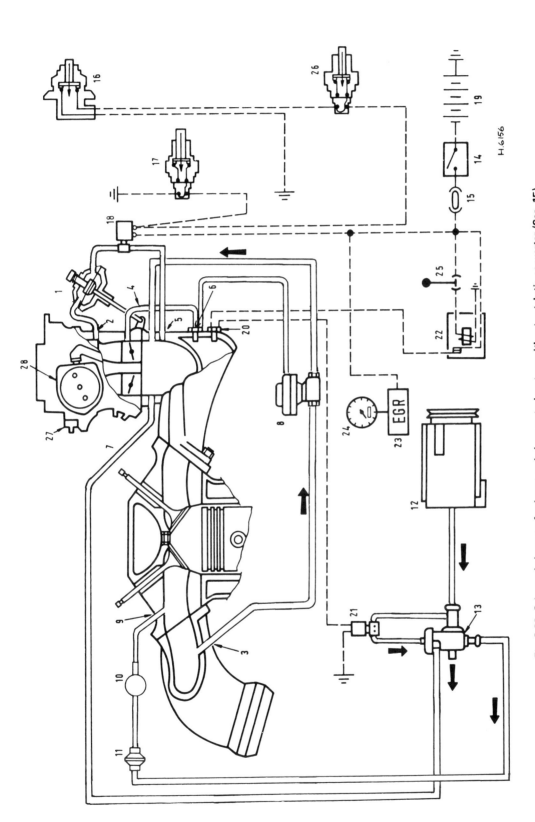

H.6156

Fig. 3.22. Schematic layout of exhaust emission control system without catalytic converter (Sec. 15)

1 Fast idle control unit
2 Carburettor tapping line above
   throttle level
3 Exhaust gas recirculation intake
4 EGR valve control vacuum inlet
5 Fast idle control vacuum inlet
6 EGR valve thermovalve control
7 Diverter valve control vacuum inlet

8 EGR valve
9 Air injector
10 Air injection manifold
11 Check valve
12 Air pump
13 Diverter valve
14 Switch
15 Fuse

16 Switch closed by engaging transmission
   3rd and 4th gear
17 Fast idle control switch
18 Electrovalve
19 Battery
20 Thermoswitch
21 Electrovalve
22 Relay switch contacts

23 EGR maintenance warning device
24 Odometer
25 Gear lever switch operated when
   transmission is in neutral
26 Switch closed when clutch is engaged
27 Fuel shut-off solenoid
28 Automatic choke

76

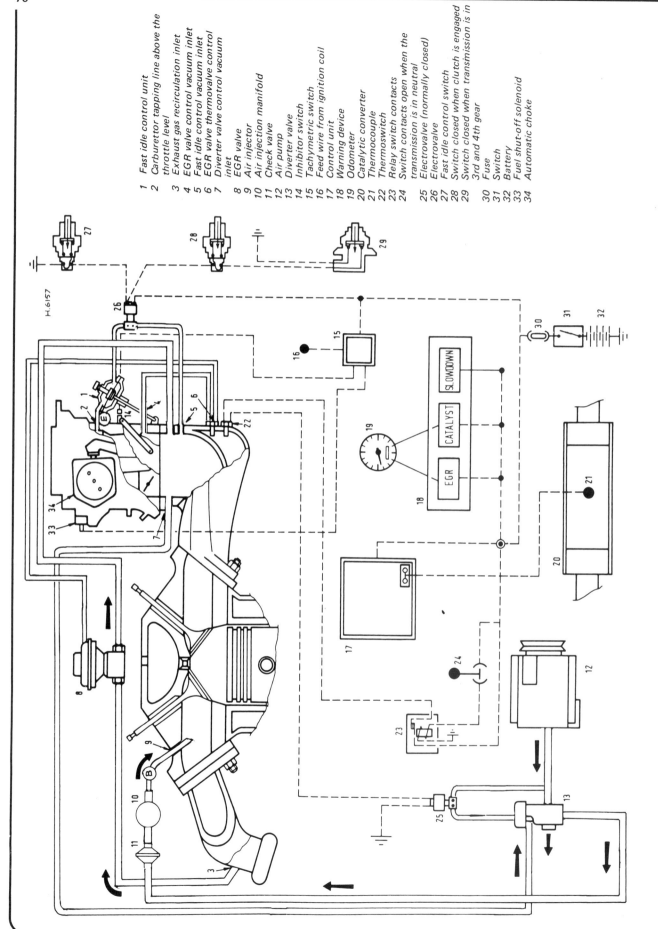

1 Fast idle control unit
2 Carburettor tapping line above the throttle level
3 Exhaust gas recirculation inlet
4 EGR valve control vacuum inlet
5 Fast idle control vacuum inlet
6 EGR valve thermovalve control vacuum inlet
7 Diverter valve control vacuum inlet
8 EGR valve
9 Air injector
10 Air injection manifold
11 Check valve
12 Air pump
13 Diverter valve
14 Inhibitor switch
15 Tachymetric switch
16 Feed wire from ignition coil
17 Control unit
18 Warning device
19 Odometer
20 Catalytic converter
21 Thermocouple
22 Thermoswitch
23 Relay switch contacts
24 Switch contacts open when the transmission is in neutral
25 Electrovalve (normally closed)
26 Electrovalve
27 Fast idle control switch
28 Switch closed when clutch is engaged
29 Switch closed when transmission is in 3rd and 4th gear
30 Fuse
31 Switch
32 Battery
33 Fuel shut-off solenoid
34 Automatic choke

Fig. 3.23. Schematic layout of exhaust emission control system with catalytic converter (Sec. 15)

16.7 The air pump mounted to the exhaust camshaft housing. Note the outlet pipe

Fig. 3.24. The air injection manifold assembly (Sec. 16)

1 Check valve   4 Bolt
2 Tubes   5 Bracket
3 Air manifold

16.21 The check valve (arrowed) screwed into the air manifold

9 Undo the nut holding the pump to the upper support bracket.
10 Undo the nut and bolt and remove the shield holding the pump to the cylinder head.
11 Lift the pump away.
12 It will be noted that the air pump drivebelt is not adjustable so if it is worn or stretched it must be replaced by a new belt.
13 Refitting the air pump is straightforward and follows the reverse

of the removal sequence. Remember to fit the shield to the rear of the mounting lug.

Air distribution manifold - removal and refitting
14 Remove the air filter assembly as described in Section 2.
15 Disconnect the hose to the check valve.
16 Undo the nut and bolt securing the air manifold to the support bracket fitted to the cam housing cover.
17 Using either a specially cranked spanner or FIAT tool A50146, undo the four manifold union nuts.
18 The manifold, complete with check valve can now be removed.
19 If necessary, hold the manifold in a vice, and unscrew the check valve.
20 Refitting is the reverse of the removal procedure.

Check valve - removal, testing and refitting
21 Disconnect the air hose at the check valve (photo).
22 Using an open ended spanner, unscrew the check valve but take care not to put undue strain on the manifold.
23 If necessary the valve can be checked by blowing air (by mouth only) through the valve. Air should pass through from the hose connection end but not from the manifold end. Renew the valve if defective.
24 Refitting is the reverse of the removal procedure.

Diverter and relief valve - removal and refitting
25 The diverter valve and its activating electro valve are mounted to a bracket attached to the right-hand upper strut mounting.

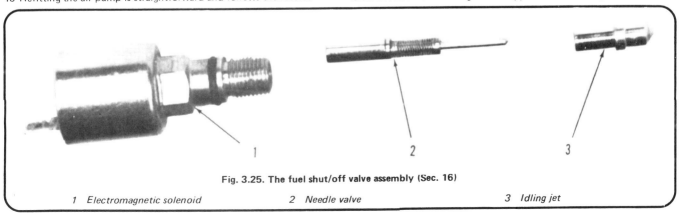

Fig. 3.25. The fuel shut/off valve assembly (Sec. 16)

1 Electromagnetic solenoid   2 Needle valve   3 Idling jet

26 Release the hose connections and remove the two nuts and bolts retaining it to the bracket.
27 The diverter valve electro-valve is retained to the bracket by two bolts and is removed once the two electrical connections and hoses have been released.
28 Refitting is a reverse of the removal procedure.

Exhaust gas recirculation (EGR) valve - removal and refitting
29 Loosen the clip and remove the hose from the EGR valve.
30 Undo the metal pipe union to the EGR valve.
31 Remove the nut, bolt and washer holding the EGR valve pipe bracket to the exhaust camshaft housing.
32 Remove the two bolts and spring washers retaining the EGR valve

to the camshaft cover.
33 Remove the EGR valve and gasket.
34 Refitting is the reverse of the removal operation.

Electro-magnetic fuel shut off valve
35 The valve is removed from the carburettor.
36 To test the valve operation remove the valve and reconnect the electric cable.
37 Now earth the body of the valve and switch the ignition on and off. The needle valve should move back and forward if the unit is functioning correctly.
38 If the unit does not function check that power is flowing through the supply cable and if it is the solenoid must be renewed.

17 Fault diagnosis - fuel system

Unsatisfactory engine performance and excessive fuel consumption are not necessarily the fault of the fuel system or carburettor. In fact they more commonly occur as a result of ignition faults. Before acting on the fuel system it is necessary to check the ignition system first. Even though a fault may lie in the fuel system it will be difficult to trace unless the ignition is correct.
The table below therefore, assumes that the ignition is in order.

Symptom	Reason/s
Smell of petrol when engine is stopped	Leaking fuel lines or unions. Leaking fuel tank.
Smell of petrol when engine is idling	Leaking fuel lines between carburettor and fuel pump. Overflow of fuel from float chamber due to wrong level setting. Ineffective needle valve or punctured float.
Difficult starting, uneven running, lack of power, cutting out	Incorrectly adjusted carburettor. Float chamber fuel level too low or needle valve sticking. Fuel pump not delivering sufficient fuel. Intake manifold gaskets leaking or manifold fractured.

18 Fault diagnosis - emission control systems

Symptom	Reason/s
Low CO content of exhaust gases (weak or lean mixture)	Fuel level incorrect in carburettor. Incorrectly adjusted carburettor.
High CO content of exhaust gases (rich mixture)	Incorrectly adjusted carburettor. Choke control mechanism sticking. Activated carbon trap blocked. Fuel level incorrect in carburettor. Air injection system fault.
Noisy air injection pump	Belt worn and stretched. Relief valve faulty. Diverter faulty. Check valve faulty.

Chapter 4 Ignition system

For modifications, and information applicable to later models, see Supplement at end of manual

Contents

Specifications

Spark plugs

1800	AC Delco 41-2XLS, Marelli CW78LP, Champion N7Y
1300 and 1600 ohv	Marelli CW7LP, Bosch W175T30, Champion N9Y, Fiat 1 L4J
Electrode gap	0.024 - 0.027 in (0.6 - 0.7 mm)

Coil type and application

1800	Marelli BES200A or Martinetti G37 SU
1300 and 1600 ohv	Marelli BE200A or Martinetti G52S

Primary winding resistance at 20°C

Marelli BES200A	2.59 - 2.81 ohms
Martinetti G37SU	2.60 - 2.95 ohms
Marelli BE200A	3.1 - 3.4 ohms
Martinetti G52S	3.0 - 3.3 ohms

Secondary winding resistance at 20°C

Marelli BES200A	6,750 - 8,250 ohms
Martinetti G37SU	7,000 - 8,500 ohms
Marelli BE 200A	5,670 - 6,930 ohms
Martinetti G52S	6,500 - 8,000 ohms

Distributor

1800	Marelli S144 CAY
1300 and 1600 ohv	Marelli S147A, 408RI or 408PI
	Ducellier HUS08R or HUS08P

Contact breaker points gap

1800	Starting contacts 0.012 - 0.019 in (0.31 - 0.49 mm)
	Normal contacts 0.014 - 0.017 in (0.37 - 0.43 mm)
1300 and 1600 ohv	0.014 - 0.017 in (0.37 - 0.43 mm)

Static advance

All UK models	$10°$
1756 cc engine (USA)	$0°$

Automatic advance

All ohv engines	$20° \pm 2°$
1800 engine (USA)	$36° \pm 1° \ 30'$

Dwell angle

I models (except electronic ignition versions)	$55° \pm 3°$

Firing order

All models	1—3—4—2 (No 1 cyl at front)

Torque wrench setting

	lb f ft	kg f m
Spark plugs	28	3.9

1 General description

The 1300 and 1600 ohv engines are fitted with a conventional distributor whereas the 1800 dohc engine is fitted with a distributor which has two sets of contact breaker points. One set is used for starting and the other set for normal running. The dual points provide both a retarded and advanced timing point.

Under normal running conditions both types of ignition system function in the same manner.

In order that the ignition system can operate correctly, the spark which ignites the air-fuel charge in the combustion chamber must be delivered at precisely the correct time. The correct time is that which will allow for the charge to burn sufficiently to create the highest pressure and temperature possible in the combustion chamber as the piston passes top dead centre and commences its power stroke. The distributor and ignition coil are the main components which ensure that the spark plugs ignite the charge as required.

Very high voltages need to be generated in the ignition HT (High Tension) system in order to produce the spark across the plug gap which

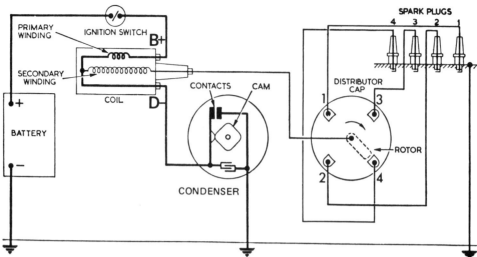

Fig. 4.1. Schematic layout of the ignition system fitted to ohv engine models (Sec. 1)

will ignite the fuel/air charge. The component in which these high voltages (several thousand volts) are generated in the coil. The coil contains two sets of windings - the primary and the secondary. A current of 12 volts is fed through the windings via the contact breaker mechanism in the distributor. When the flow is interrupted by the contact breaker a high voltage is induced in the secondary windings and that voltage is conveyed via HT leads and the rotor arm in the distributor cap to the appropriate spark plug.

It follows, therefore, that the contact breaker must part the instant a spark is required and the rotor arm must be aligned to the segment in the distributor cap which is connected to the spark plug.

The distributor shaft revolves at half the crankshaft speed, and there are four lobes on the distributor shaft and four segments in the distributor cap, to cater for the sparks which the engine requires for every two revolutions of the crankshaft.

There are two methods of controlling the ignition timing with the Marelli distributors fitted to the F I A T 131 models. The first is referred to as static timing and this is that nominal amount which corresponds to the moment of combustion at the idling speed of the engine. The second, which is fully automatic, is the centrifugal advance mechanism. This mechanism consists of two weights, which move out from the distributor shaft as the engine speed increases, owing to centrifugal force. As they move outwards they rotate the cam relative to the distributor shaft, and so advance the spark. The weights are held in position by two springs and it is the tension of the springs which is responsible for the correct spark advancement.

It is necessary, therefore, when carrying out ignition and carburation adjustments, to ensure the engine is turning at the speed appropriate to that test or adjustment.

2 Contact breaker points - adjustment

Access to the contact breaker points is limited, therefore adjustment may be easier with the distributor removed from the vehicle.

1300 and 1600 ohv engine

1 Remove the two screws and washers and lift the distributor cap off. Clean the inside and outside of the cap with a dry cloth. It is unlikely that the four segments within the cap will be badly burnt or scored, but if they are, the cap will have to be renewed. If only a small deposit has built up on the segments it may be scraped away using a small screwdriver.

2 Check that the carbon brush located in the top of the distributor cap is not broken or missing. Push the brush inwards several times to ensure that it moves freely. The brush should protrude by at least a quarter of an inch.

3 Gently prise the contact breaker points open to examine the condition of their faces. If they are rough, pitted or dirty, it will be necessary to remove them for resurfacing, or for new points to be fitted.

4 Assuming that the points are satisfactory, or that they have been cleaned and refitted, measure the gap between the points by turning

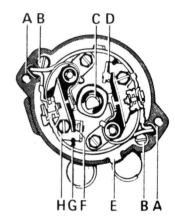

Fig. 4.2. The internal layout of the twin contact distributor fitted to the dohc engine (Sec. 2)

A   Tapped hole for cap retaining screws
B   Baseplate retaining screws
C   Rotor shaft
D   Main contact breaker points
E   Cap locating slot
F   Starting contact breaker points
G   Slotted hole for inserting screwdriver when adjusting points
H   Fixed contact plate adjuster securing screw

the engine over until the contact breaker arm is on the peak of one of the four cam lobes.

5 A feeler gauge of 0.014 - 0.017 in (0.37 to 0.43 mm) should fit between the points whilst lightly touching each face.

6 If the gap varies on this amount, slacken the contact plate securing screw and adjust the gap by inserting a screwdriver in the notched hole of the stationary point and table and turn in the required direction to increase or decrease the gap.

7 When the gap is correct tighten the contact plate screw and refit the distributor cap.

1800 dohc engine

8 Remove the distributor cap and check the condition of the cap and contact breaker points as described in paragraphs 1 - 3.

9 Remove the rotor arm and, assuming that both sets of contact breaker points are in good condition, turn the engine over until the contact breaker arm of the starting (additional) points is on the peak of one of the four cam lobes.

10 A feeler gauge of 0.012 - 0.019 in (0.31 - 0.49 mm) should fit between the points, whilst lightly touching each face.

11 If the gap varies from this amount slacken the contact plate securing screw and adjust the contact gap by inserting a screwdriver in the slot cut out and shifting the plate until the required point gap is reached.

12 Tighten the contact plate screw and recheck the gap.
13 Now turn the engine over until the contact breaker arm of the main points is on the peak of one of the lobes. Now check and adjust the gap, which should be 0.012 - 0.014 in (0.31 - 0.37 mm).
14 Finally, refit the rotor arm and secure the distributor cap with the two screws and washers.

3 Contact breaker points - removal and refitting

Access to the contact breaker points is limited, therefore removal and refitting this assembly may be facilitated by removing the distributor from the vehicle.

1300 and 1600 ohv engine
1 Remove the distributor cap.
2 Remove the two screws securing the contact points assembly to the distributor and slacken the insulated terminal in the side of the body sufficiently to release the LT lead.
3 Lift the complete contact set assembly off the pivot pin of the mounting plate.
4 If the condition of the points is not too bad, they can be reconditioned by rubbing the contacts clean with fine emery cloth or a fine carborundum stone. It is important that the faces are rubbed flat and parallel to each other so that there will be complete face to face contact when the points are closed. Generally one side of the points will be pitted while the other will have a deposit on it.
5 It is necessary to completely remove the built up deposits, but not necessary to rub the pitted point right down to the stage where all the pitting has disappeared, though obviously if this is done it will prolong the time before the operation of resurfacing the points has to be repeated.
6 Wipe the points clean and refit the assembly with the two screws. Reconnect the LT lead to the terminal.
7 Adjust the points gap as described in Section 2.

1800 dohc engine
8 Remove the distributor cap.
9 Pull off the rotor arm.
10 Slacken the LT connection screw and disconnect the LT wires.
11 Undo and remove the two hexagon-headed slotted screws which secure the contact points assembly to the base plate.
12 Check the condition of the points and renovate them as described in paragraphs 4 and 5. To ease the renovation of the contact faces the contact assembly can be divided into two parts after the circlip has been removed.
13 Repeat the procedure laid out in paragraphs 8 to 12 for the single type of contact breaker and refit the two assemblies.
14 With the two sets of contacts now refitted check and adjust the contact gaps as described in Section 2.

4 Condenser - removal, testing and refitting

1 The purpose of the condenser (sometimes termed as a capacitor) is to ensure that when the contact breaker points open there is no sparking across them which would waste voltage and cause rapid wear of the contact breaker points.
2 The condenser is fitted in parallel with the contact breaker points. If it develops a short circuit, it will cause ignition failure as the points

will be prevented from interrupting the low tension circuit.
3 If the engine becomes very difficult to start or begins to misfire after several miles of running and the contact breaker points show signs of excessive burning, then the condition of the condenser must be suspect.
4 Without the use of special electronic test equipment the only sure way of testing the condenser is to renew the suspect unit and note if there is any improvement.
5 To remove the condenser from both types of Marelli distributor it is necessary to first remove the distributor cap.
6 Slacken the LT screw connection at the contact and remove the condenser wire.
7 Remove the screw which retains the condenser to the distributor. Note that the Marelli distributor fitted to the dohc engine has the condenser units screwed to the exterior of the distributor body whereas on other models the condenser is mounted internally.
8 When fitting the condenser it is vital to ensure that the fixing screw is secure and the condenser is held tightly. The wiring connection must be secure to the LT post terminal with no chance of short circuiting.

5 Distributor - removal and refitting

1 To remove the distributor from the engine, start by removing all the HT leads from the spark plugs and remove the battery earth lead as a safety precaution.
2 Remove the two screws retaining the distributor cap and remove it.
3 Remove the HT lead from the coil, and disconnect the LT lead/s which are joined by a male and female spade connector. Note that the dohc engine will have two LT spade connectors, one for each set of contacts, housed within a plastic sleeve insulator (photo).
4 Turn the crankshaft until the rotor arm is pointing to the segment in the distributor cap which is connected to the number 1 spark plug HT lead. On the dohc engine the crankshaft pulley timing reference mark should be aligned with the tdc mark on the timing belt cover. (photo). On the ohv engines the crankshaft pulley reference timing mark should be aligned with the 10° btdc mark on the camshaft cover. The starting contact breaker points on the dohc engine and the contact breaker points on the ohv engine will be about to separate with the timing marks so aligned.
5 Mark the bottom flange of the distributor body and the adjacent cylinder block or cylinder head, which ever is applicable, with punch marks so that they may be realigned when refitting.
6 Undo the clamp securing nut and take away the clamp (photo).
7 Lift the distributor straight out (photo).
8 Refitting the unit is simply the reversal of the removal procedure. Remember to hold the rotor arm and distributor shaft aligned to No. 1 cylinder segment in the distributor cap and align the two punch marks. Provided the engine has not been turned and everything is aligned correctly no further adjustment is necessary. If the engine crankshaft has been rotated, before the distributor was refitted it will be necessary to re-time the ignition as described in Section 7.

6 Distributor - inspection and overhaul

1 Apart from the contact breaker points, the other parts of a distributor which deteriorate with age and use are the cap, the rotor arm, the

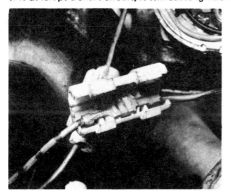

5.3 Disconnect the LT spade connectors housed within plastic sleeve insulators

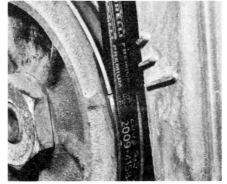

5.4 Align the crankshaft pulley reference mark with the tdc mark on the timing belt cover

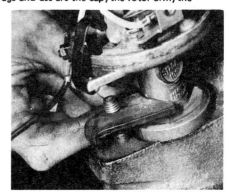

5.6 Remove the distributor clamp plate

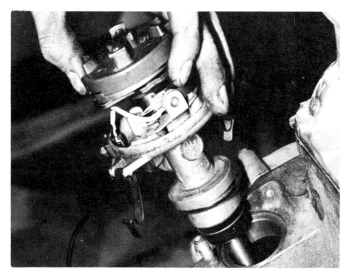

5.7 Lift the distributor straight out

shaft bushes, and the bob weight springs.

2   The cap must have no flaws or cracks and the four HT terminal segments should not be severely corroded. The centre spring loaded brush is renewable. If there is any doubt about the distributor cap fit a new one.

3   The rotor arm deteriorates minimally but with age the metal conductor tip may corrode. It should not be cracked or chipped and the metal conductor must not be loose.

4   Remove the rotor arm. On the distributor fitted to the dohc engine the rotor arm is a push-fit but on the distributor fitted to the ohv engine the rotor arm is retained by two screws.

5   Remove the contact breaker points as described in Section 3.

6   The two types of Marelli distributor are slightly different in construction and layout. The ohv engine distributor has the automatic advance and retard unit fitted above the contact breaker assembly whereas the dohc engine distributor has the reverse layout.

7   On the distributor fitted to the dohc engines, remove the two base plate retaining screws and lift the plate off to inspect the advance and retard mechanism.

8   There is no way to test the bob weight springs other than by checking the performance of the distributor on special test equipment, so if in any doubt fit new springs. If the springs are loose where they loop over the posts it is more than possible that the post grooves are worn in which case the various parts which include the shaft will need renewal. Wear to this extent would mean that a new distributor is probably the best solution in the long run. Be sure to make an exact note of both the engine number and any serial number on the distributor when ordering. When refitting the rotor arm do not force it on and ensure that it is located the correct way round. The rotor shaft fitted to the dohc engine has a flat formed on one edge so that the rotor arm is located in the correct position. The rotor fitted to the ohv engines has one round and one square locating lug to ensure that it is fitted the proper way round.

9   Some models of distributor are fitted with ball race bearings while others are fitted with plain bushes which are renewable.

10 If the main shaft is slack in its bushes allowing even the slightest sideways play it means that the contact points gap setting can only be a compromise because the cam position relative to the moving point arm is not constant. If the top of the shaft can move it means that the points gap can vary by about the same amount.

11 To further dismantle the distributor drift out the parallel pin which secures the shaft lower collar in position. Recover the washer from under the collar and slide out the shaft.

12 Examine all the components for wear and renew as necessary. Very often in fine mechanisms such as distributors several components will need renewing and individual spare parts are not always readily available. Therefore an exchange distributor should be obtained.

13 Assuming new parts are obtainable reassemble the distributor lubricating the bob weights and other parts of the advance mechanism, and the distributor centre shaft, using clean engine oil. Do not lubricate

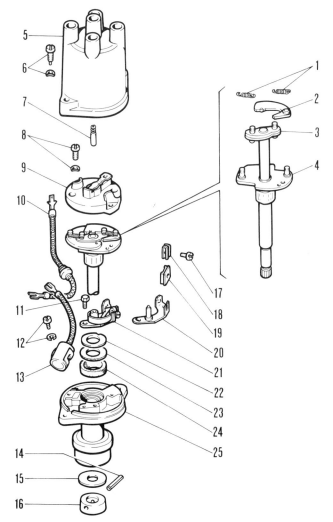

Fig. 4.3. Exploded view of the ohv engine distributor components (Sec. 6)

1 Bob weight spring	14 Roll pin
2 Bob weight	15 Thrust washer
3 Shaft	16 Retainer (oil slinger)
4 Cam and carrier plate	17 Terminal screw
5 Distributor cap	18 Bridging piece
6 Cap securing screw and washer	19 Insulation block
7 Carbon brush and spring	20 Fixed contact and plate
8 Rotor retaining screw and	21 Complete contact assembly
washer	22 Spacer washer
9 Rotor	23 Fibre washer
10 Coil LT lead	24 Felt washer
11 Contact points securing screw	25 Distributor body
12 Screw and washer securing	
condenser	
13 Condenser	

the parts excessively as the oil could get onto the contact breaker assembly and cause ignition failure.

14 Check the action of the weights in the fully advanced and fully retarded positions and ensure that they are not binding.

15 Finally, set the contact breaker gap/s as described in Section 2 and fit the distributor as described in Section 5.

7   Ignition timing - checking and adjustment

1   If the clamp plate pinch nut retaining the distributor has been loosened and the static timing lost or if, for any other reason, it is wished to set the ignition timing, proceed as follows:

2   Refer to Section 2 and check the contact breaker points gap. Set

Measuring plug gap. A feeler gauge of the correct size (see ignition system specifications) should have a slight 'drag' when slid between the electrodes. Adjust gap if necessary

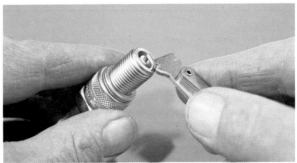

Adjusting plug gap. The plug gap is adjusted by bending the earth electrode inwards, or outwards, as necessary until the correct clearance is obtained. Note the use of the correct tool

Normal. Grey-brown deposits, lightly coated core nose. Gap increasing by around 0.001 in (0.025 mm) per 1000 miles (1600 km). Plugs ideally suited to engine, and engine in good condition

Carbon fouling. Dry, black, sooty deposits. Will cause weak spark and eventually misfire. Fault: over-rich fuel mixture. Check: carburettor mixture settings, float level and jet sizes; choke operation and cleanliness of air filter. Plugs can be re-used after cleaning

Oil fouling. Wet, oily deposits. Will cause weak spark and eventually misfire. Fault: worn bores/piston rings or valve guides; sometimes occurs (temporarily) during running-in period. Plugs can be re-used after thorough cleaning

Overheating. Electrodes have glazed appearance, core nose very white – few deposits. Fault: plug overheating. Check: plug value, ignition timing, fuel octane rating (too low) and fuel mixture (too weak). Discard plugs and cure fault immediately

Electrode damage. Electrodes burned away; core nose has burned, glazed appearance. Fault: pre-ignition. Check: as for 'Overheating' but may be more severe. Discard plugs and remedy fault before piston or valve damage occurs

Split core nose (may appear initially as a crack). Damage is self-evident, but cracks will only show after cleaning. Fault: pre-ignition or wrong gap-setting technique. Check: ignition timing, cooling system, fuel octane rating (too low) and fuel mixture (too weak). Discard plugs, rectify fault immediately

the gap as necessary.

3   Assemble the clamp plate to the distributor body but do not tighten the pinch nut fully.

4   It will be as well to remove the camshaft housing covers or valve rocker cover as applicable so that the exact position of the engine can be determined by noting the position of the valves.

5   Slowly turn the crankshaft until the groove in the pulley lines up with the tdc mark on the dohc engine, or the btdc mark on the ohv engine. Both the dohc and ohv engines have static timing reference marks representing 10° btdc, 5° btdc and tdc formed on the timing belt covers. Ensure that the valves on No. 1 cylinder are closed by observing the position of the camshaft lobes on the dohc engine and the position of the valve rocker arms on the ohv engines.

6   Alternatively it is possible to check that the No. 1 piston is coming up to its firing stroke by removing the No. 1 spark and feeling the compression from the spark plug hole as the engine is turned over. Then align the crankshaft pulley timing mark with the tdc mark on the timing belt cover.

7   Provided the distributor shaft has not been disturbed or has been refitted correctly, the rotor arm should now point to the position of the segment in the distributor cap which is connected to No. 1 spark plug.

8   If it was not found possible to align the rotor correctly with the distributor cap segments, one of two things is wrong. Either the distributor shaft has been incorrectly fitted in which case the distributor must be removed and refitted as described in Section 5; or the distributor cam assembly has been incorrectly fitted on the drive shaft. To rectify this, it will be necessary to partially dismantle the distributor and check the position of the cam assembly on the centrifugal advance mechanism; it may be 180° out of position.

9   With the distributor body lightly clamped with the retaining plate, slowly rotate the distributor body until the contact breaker points are just beginning to open. On the dohc engine the ignition static timing is set using the starting contact breaker set.

10 When you are satisfied that the timing is set correctly tighten the distributor clamping plate nut.

11 Difficulty is sometimes experienced in determining exactly when the contact breaker points open. This can be ascertained accurately by connecting a 12v bulb in parallel with the contact breaker points (one lead to earth and the other from the low tension terminal). Switch on the ignition and turn the distributor body until the bulb lights up, indicating that the points have just opened.

12 It should be noted that this adjustment is nominal and the final adjustment should be made under normal running conditions.

13 First start the engine and allow it to warm up to its normal running temperature, then in a road test accelerate the car in top gear from 30 to 50 mph whilst listening for heavy 'pinking'. If 'pinking' is heard, the ignition needs to be slightly retarded until only the faintest trace can be heard under these conditions.

14 Since the ignition advance adjustment enables the firing point to be related to the grade of fuel used, the fullest advantage of any change of fuel will only be obtained by readjustment of the ignition settings as described in paragraph 13.

8   Coil - removal and refitting

1   The high tension current should be negative at the spark plug terminals. To ensure this, check that the LT connections to the coil are correctly made.

2   The LT wires from the distributor must connect with the 'D' terminal on the coil.

3   The coil 'B+' terminal is connected ultimately to the ignition/start switch.

4   An incorrect connection can cause as much as a 60% loss of spark efficiency and can cause rough idling and misfiring at speed.

5   The coil is mounted to the left front inner wing panel and is secured by a clamp band bolted to the panel (photo).

6   The coil is easily detached after disconnecting the 'B+' and 'D' low tension cables, the main output HT lead and finally slackening off the clamp band.

7   The coil can now be slid out of the band.

8   Refitting the coil is the reverse of the removal operation. Check that the low tension cables have been correctly repositioned at the coil terminals.

9   Spark plugs and high tension (HT) leads

1   The correct functioning of the spark plugs is vital for the correct running and efficiency of the engine. The plugs fitted as standard are listed in the Specifications at the beginning of the Chapter.

2   At intervals of 6,000 miles (9600 km) the plugs should be removed and examined. The condition of the spark plug will tell much about the overall condition of the engine (see the illustrations on page 83).

3   If the insulator nose of the spark plug is clean and white, with no deposits, this is indicative of a weak mixture, or too hot a plug. (A hot plug transfers heat away from the electrode slowly - a cold plug transfers it away quickly).

4   If the insulator nose is covered with hard black deposits, then this is

Fig. 4.4. The crankshaft pulley, timing belt cover and ignition timing reference marks (ohv engines) (Sec. 7)

1   10° btdc   2   5° btdc   3   tdc

Fig. 4.5. The crankshaft pulley, timing belt and ignition timing reference marks (dohc engines) (Sec. 7)

1   10° btdc   2   5° btdc   3   tdc

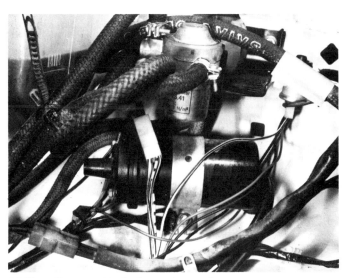

8.5 The coil mounted to the inner wing panel

indicative that the mixture is too rich. Should the plug be black and oily, then it is likely that the engine is fairly worn as well as the mixture being too rich.

5   If the insulator nose is covered with light tan to greyish brown deposits, then the mixture is correct and shows that the engine is in a good condition.

6   If there are any traces of long brown tapering stains on the outside of the white portion of the plug, then the plug will have to be renewed, as this shows that there is a faulty joint between the plug body and the insulator, and compression is being allowed to leak away.

7   Plugs should be cleaned by a sand blasting machine, which will free them from carbon more thoroughly than cleaning by hand with a wire brush. The machine will also test the condition of the plugs under compression. Any plug that fails to spark at the recommended pressure should be renewed.

8   The spark plug gap is of considerable importance, as, if it is too large or too small the size of the spark and its efficiency will be seriously impaired. The spark plug gap should be set between 0.024 and 0.027 in (0.6 and 0.7 mm) for the best results.

9   To set it, measure the gap with a feeler gauge, and then bend open, or close, the outer plug electrode until the correct gap is achieved. The centre electrode should never be bent as this may crack the insulation and cause plug failure, if nothing worse.

10 FIAT recommend that at 12,000 miles (19,000 km) intervals the plugs should be renewed. Always use the specified type in accordance with the plug manufacturer's latest recommendations.

11 Before fitting a spark plug, wipe the seat in the cylinder head clean, and apply a smear of grease to the plug threads.

12 Tighten the plug to the specified torque and reconnect the high tension leads in the correct order.

13 The spark plug leads require no attention other than being given an occasional wipe to remove any grease or dirt which might otherwise cause tracking.

---

10 Fault diagnosis - ignition system

Failure of the ignition system will either be due to faults in the HT or LT circuits. Initial checks should be made by checking the security of spark plug terminals, spade terminals, coil and battery connections. More detailed investigation, and the explanation and remedial action in respect of symptoms of ignition malfunction, are described in the following sub-sections.

Engine fails to start

1   If the engine fails to start and the car was running normally when it was last used, first check there is fuel in the fuel tank. If the engine turns normally on the starter motor and the battery is evidently well charged, then the fault may be in either the high or low tension

circuits. First check the HT circuit. **Note:** If the battery is known to be fully charged, the ignition light comes on and the starter motor fails to turn the engine, check the tightness of the leads on the battery terminals and also the security of the earth lead to its connection on the body. It is quite common for the leads to have worked loose, even if they look and feel secure. If one of the battery terminal posts gets very hot when trying to work the starter motor this is a sure indication of a faulty connection to that terminal.

3   One of the most common reasons for bad starting is wet or damp spark plug leads and distributor. Remove the distributor cap. If condensation is visible internally, dry the cap with a rag and also wipe over the leads. Refit the cap.

3   If the engine still fails to start, check that current is reaching the plugs, by disconnecting each plug lead in turn at the spark plug end, and holding the end of the cable about 3/16th inch (5 mm) away from the cylinder block. Spin the engine on the starter motor.

4   Sparking between the end of the cable and the block should be fairly strong with a regular blue spark. (Insulate the lead with rubber to avoid electric shocks). If current is reaching the plugs, then remove them and clean and regap them. The engine should now start.

5   If there is no spark at the plug leads take off the HT lead from the centre of the distributor cap and hold it to the block as before. Spin the engine on the starter motor once more. A rapid succession of blue sparks between the end of the lead and the block indicate that the coil is in order and that the distributor cap is cracked, the rotor arm faulty, or the carbon brush in the top of the distributor cap is not making good contact with the spring on the rotor arm. Possibly the contact breaker points are in a bad condition. Clean and reset them as described in Sections 2 and 3.

6   If there are no sparks from the end of the lead from the coil, check the connections at the coil end of the lead. If it is in order start checking the low tension circuit.

7   Use a 12v voltmeter or a 12v bulb and two lengths of wire. With the ignition switched on and the points open test between the low tension wire to the coil (it is marked 'B+') and earth. No reading indicates a break in the supply from the ignition switch. Check the connections at the switch to see if they are loose. Refit them and the engine should run. A reading shows a faulty coil or condenser, or broken lead between the coil and distributor.

8   Take the condenser wire off the points assembly and with the points open, test between the moving point and earth. If there is a reading then the fault is in the condenser. Fit a new condenser and the fault will be rectified.

9   With no reading from the moving point to earth, take a reading between earth and the 'D' terminal of the coil. A reading shows a broken wire which will need to be renewed between the coil and distributor. No reading confirms that the coil has failed and must be renewed, after which the engine will run once more. Remember to refit the condenser wire to the points assembly. For these tests it is sufficient to separate the points with a piece of dry paper while testing with the points open.

Engine misfires

10 If the engine misfires regularly, run it at a fast idling speed. Pull off each of the plug caps in turn and listen to the note of the engine. Hold the plug cap in a dry cloth or with a rubber glove as additional protection against a shock from the HT supply.

11 No difference in engine running will be noticed when the lead from the defective circuit is removed. Removing the lead from one of the good cylinders will accentuate the misfire.

12 Remove the plug lead from the end of the defective plug and hold it about 3/16th in (5.0 mm) away from the block. Restart the engine. If the sparking is fairly strong and regular the fault must lie in the spark plug.

13 The plug may be loose, the insulation may be cracked, or the electrodes may have burnt away giving too wide a gap for the spark to jump. Worse still, one of the electrodes may have broken off. Either renew the plug, or clean it, reset the gap, and then test it.

14 If there is no spark at the end of the plug lead, or if it is weak and intermittent, check the ignition lead from the distributor to the plug. If the insulation is cracked or perished, renew the lead. Check the connections at the distributor cap.

15 If there is still no spark, examine the distributor cap carefully for tracking. This can be recognised by a very thin black line running between two or more segments, or between a segment and some other part of the distributor. These lines are paths which now conduct

electricity across the cap thus letting it run to earth. The only answer is a new distributor cap.

16 Apart from the ignition timing being incorrect, other causes of misfiring have already been dealt with under the section dealing with the failure of the engine to start. To recap - these are that:

a) *The coil may be faulty giving an intermittent misfire.*
b) *There may be a damaged wire or loose connection in the low tension circuit.*

c) *The condenser may be short circuiting.*
d) *There may be a mechanical fault in the distributor (broken driving spindle or contact breaker spring).*

17 If the ignition timing is too far retarded, it should be noted that the engine will tend to overheat, and there will be a noticeable drop in power. If the engine is overheating and the power is down, and the ignition timing is correct, then the carburettor should be checked, as it is likely that this is where the fault lies.

Chapter 5 Clutch

For modifications, and information applicable to later models, see Supplement at end of manual

Contents

Specifications

Type	Dry single plate, diaphragm spring		
Dimensions	**1300 ohv**	**1600 ohv (four-speed)**	**1800 dohc**
Lining outside diameter	7.145 in (181.5 mm)	7.87 in (200 mm)	8.307 in (215 mm)
Lining inside diameter	5.00 in (127 mm)	5.12 in (130 mm)	5.708 in (145 mm)

Pedal free travel ... ... 1 in (25.4 mm) giving clearance of 0.077 in (2 mm) between the diaphragm spring and the release bearing

Torque wrench setting	**lb f ft**	**kg f m**
Pressure plate to flywheel bolts	22	3

1 General description

The clutch unit is fitted between the engine and gearbox and comprises an integral pressure plate and diaphragm spring assembly, a single dry plate friction disc, known as the centre or driven plate, and a release bearing assembly. The driven plate is sandwiched between the flywheel and the pressure plate assembly.

At the centre of the driven plate is an internally splined hub through which the splined gearbox primary input shaft runs. Engine torque is transmitted from the flywheel to the clutch driven plate and then to the transmission via the gearbox primary shaft.

When the clutch pedal is depressed, the clutch release bearing assembly is forced against the diaphragm spring by a cable connecting the pedal to the release bearing throw-out arm. The pressure imposed on the driven plate assembly by the diaphragm spring is released and the drive between the engine and gearbox is broken.

When the clutch pedal is released the diaphragm spring forces the

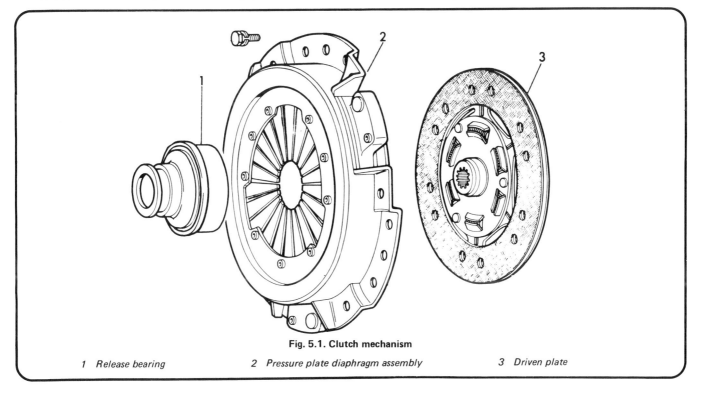

Fig. 5.1. Clutch mechanism

1 Release bearing	*2 Pressure plate diaphragm assembly*	*3 Driven plate*

pressure plate into contact with the friction lining face of the driven
plate, at the same time forcing the driven plate against the flywheel,
and so taking up the drive.

2 Clutch - adjustment

1 As wear occurs at the friction lining faces of the driven plate the
release bearing clearance and, hence, free pedal travel, will diminish.
When the clutch free pedal travel becomes less than 1 in (23 to 25
mm), the clutch cable will have to be adjusted to restore the necessary
release bearing to pressure plate clearance.
2 The clutch is adjusted at the point where the cable assembly
passes through the bulkhead within the engine compartment.
3 Slacken the locknut and turn the adjusting nut anti-clockwise until
the pedal travel is restored to approximately 1 in (23 to 25 mm). The
adjusting nut shortens the effective overall length of the outer cable
and thereby increases the available length of inner cable at the release
bearing.
4 When the required adjustment has been made retighten the
locknut.

3 Clutch cable - removal and refitting

1 Remove the clutch pedal return spring from within the car.
2 From under the car disconnect the clutch release lever return
spring.

Fig. 5.2. Clutch cable adjuster

1 Outer cable   2 Locknut   3 Adjusting nut

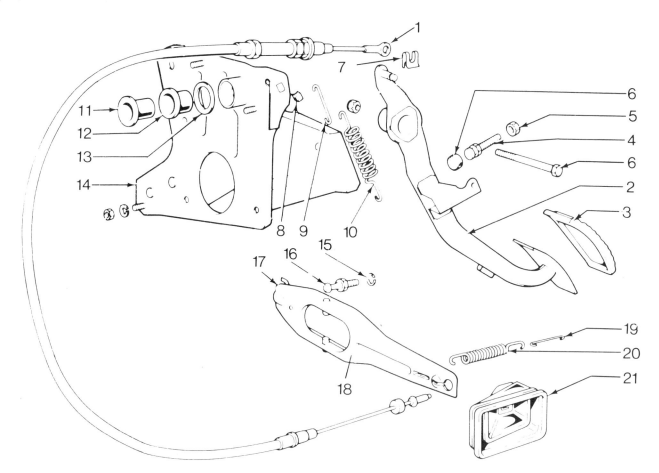

Fig. 5.3. Clutch actuating mechanism

1 Eye fastening inner cable end	8 Hook mounting point	15 Spring washer
2 Clutch pedal	9 Hook	16 Ball pivot stud
3 Pedal rubber pad	10 Pedal return spring	17 Spring clip
4 Pedal stop bolt	11 Spacer	18 Release bearing lever arm
5 Locknut pedal stop bolt	12 Bush	19 Hook
6 Stop pad	13 Washer	20 Return spring
7 Retainer clip	14 Mounting bracket	21 Rubber dust boot

3 Release the lower end of the cable from the release lever arm (photo).

4 From within the car remove the special clip which retains the cable eye fixing to the stub fixing on the pedal lever.

5 Pull the cable away from the pedal fixing stub and draw the cable through the engine bulkhead.

6 Release the cable from the bracket bolted to the bellhousing (photo).

7 Now draw the lower part of the clutch cable through the bellhousing from under the bonnet.

8 With the cable now free from the car a thorough inspection of its condition may now be carried out.

9 Refitting the cable is the reverse of the removal procedure.

10 The cable will require adjustment once installed; details are given in Section 2.

4 Clutch assembly - removal and inspection

1 Remove the gearbox as detailed in Chapter 6 (photo).

2 Mark the relative positions of the clutch assembly and flywheel.

3 Slacken off the bolts holding the pressure plate to the flywheel in a diagonal sequence, undoing each bolt a little at a time. This keeps the pressure even all around the diaphragm spring and prevents distortion.

4 With all the bolts and washers removed lift the pressure plate off the ends of the locating dowels. The driven plate will fall out at this stage (photo).

5 Examine the pressure plate for signs of scoring or abnormal wear and the springs of the diaphragm for distortion or fracture.

6 If any parts of the pressure plate assembly are found to be defective the whole unit must be renewed.

7 Examine the driven plate for indications of uneven wear and scoring of the friction surfaces. Contamination by oil will show as hard black areas which can cause slipping. If the clearance between the heads of the securing rivets and the face of the friction material is less than 0.020 in (0.5 mm) it is advisable to fit a new driven plate. Around the central hub of the driven plate are six springs acting as shock absorbers between the hub and friction faces. These springs should be intact and held tightly in position.

8 The face of the flywheel should be examined for cracks, signs of scoring or uneven wear. If these defects are evident the flywheel will have to be renewed or reconditioned. See Chapter 1 for details of flywheel removal.

5 Clutch assembly - refitting

1 Refitting of the clutch pressure plate and driven plate is the reverse of the removal procedure but not quite so straightforward, as the

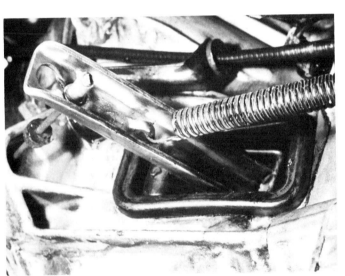

3.3 The clutch cable, release lever and return spring

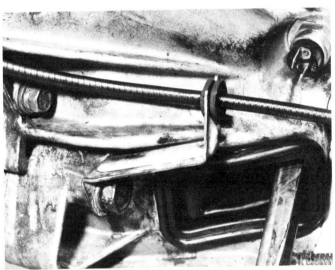

3.6 Release the cable from the bellhousing support bracket

4.1 The gearbox removed revealing the clutch

4.4 Remove the pressure plate and driven plate

following paragraphs will indicate.

2   If the clutch assembly has been removed from the engine with the engine out of the car, it is a relatively easy matter to line up the hub of the driven plate with the centre of the pressure plate and flywheel. The pressure plate and driven plate are refitted to the flywheel with the holes in the pressure plate fitting over the dowels on the flywheel. The driven plate is supported with a finger while this is done.

3   Note that the driven plate is mounted with the longer hub protrusion facing the pressure plate. Usually the new driven plate is marked to prevent a mistake being made.

4   Refit the cover mounting bolts finger tight, sufficient to just grip the driven plate. Then set the driven plate in position so that the hub is exactly concentric with the centre of the flywheel and the cover assembly. An easy way of doing this is to make a temporary mandrel, using a bar from a socket set, which should fit fairly tightly in the flywheel spigot bush. Wrap a few turns of adhesive tape round the bar near the end, which will make a snug fit inside the splined hub of the driven plate. Use this as a centering device. It is most important to get this right when refitting the clutch to an engine which is still in the car. Otherwise difficulty and possible damage could occur when refitting the gearbox.

5   Tighten up the pressure plate retaining bolts one turn at a time in a diagonal sequence to maintain an even pressure.

6   Finally tighten the bolts to the torque wrench setting specified at the beginning of the Chapter.

6   Clutch release arm and release bearing - removal and refitting

1   The clutch release arm and thrust bearing can only be removed after the engine and gearbox are separated.

2   The arm pivots on a ball ended stud screwed into the bellhousing and is held in position by a spring plate clip. To get the arm off the stud, simply pull it away, having first removed the return spring and the rubber dust boot from the bellhousing (photos).

3   The release bearing is of the 'sealed for life' type and it is moved in and out by two pegs on the release lever which engage in a peripheral groove on the sleeve. When the release lever is taken over the primary shaft of the gearbox the release bearing is freed (photo).

4   Do not attempt to wash the bearing as it cannot be repacked with grease. If the bearing is worn it should be renewed.

5   Refitting of the release arm and bearing is a direct reversal of the dismantling procedure. It is recommended that the ball pivot stud be very lightly coated with Castrol LM Grease before clipping the release lever back into place. Do not forget to refit the rubber dust boot.

7   Clutch pedal and shaft - removal and refitting

The procedure for removing the clutch pedal and shaft is described in Chapter 9, Section 18. This Section also describes the renovation of the pedal assembly.

6.2A The clutch release lever and bearing

6.2B Remove the release lever return spring

6.2C Detach the release lever from the ball pivot post

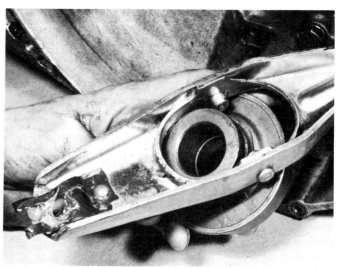
6.3 Remove the release bearing from the locating pegs of the release lever

8 Fault diagnosis - clutch

Symptom	Reason/s
Judder when taking up drive	Loose engine/gearbox mountings. Badly worn or oil contaminated friction faces of clutch centre plate. Worn splines on centre plate hub or gearbox primary shaft. Badly worn spigot bearing in end of crankshaft. Propeller shaft or rear axle mountings loose.
Clutch spin (or failure to disengage) so that gears cannot be meshed	Excessive pedal free play. Clutch centre plate sticking to pressure plate or flywheel through oil contamination. Centre plate splined hub rusted to the splined gearbox primary shaft.
Clutch slip (increase in engine speed does not result in increase in car speed - especially on hills)	Insufficient clutch pedal free play. Oil contamination of centre plate friction faces. Clutch centre plate friction faces worn out.
Noise on depressing the clutch pedal	Dry, worn or damaged clutch release bearing. Clutch centre plate worn out.

Chapter 6 Part A: Manual transmission

For modifications, and information applicable to later models, see Supplement at end of manual

Contents

Specifications

Type

1300 and early 1600 models	4 speed synchromesh and 1 reverse gear
1800 and later 1600 models	5 speed synchromesh and 1 reverse gear

Ratios

4 speed gearbox:

1st	3.667 : 1
2nd	2.100 : 1
3rd	1.361 : 1
4th	1.000 : 1
Reverse	3.526 : 1

5 speed gearbox:

1st	3.612 : 1
2nd	2.045 : 1
3rd	1.357 : 1
4th	1.000 : 1
5th	0.870 : 1
Reverse	3.244 : 1

Clearances

Backlash between gears	0.0039 in (0.10 mm)
Maximum radial movement of ball bearings	0.0020 in (0.05 mm)
Maximum axial movement of ball bearings	0.020 in (0.50 mm)
Clearance between reverse shaft and reverse bush	0.002 - 0.004 in (0.05 - 0.010 mm)

Transmission lubrication

Lubricant type	Refer to lubrication chart at beginning of manual
Lubricant capacity (approx.)	
4 speed gearbox	2.33 Imp pts (1.35 litres/2.7 US pts)
5 speed gearbox	3.2 Imp pts (1.80 litres/3.6 US pts)

Torque wrench settings

	lb f ft	kg f m
Detent ball and spring cover plate bolts	18	2.5
Bellhousing to engine bolts	61	8.5
Selector fork locking bolts	14.5	2
Layshaft bearing retainer bolt (4 speed gearbox)	69	9.5
Bellhousing to gearbox bolts	36	5
Extension housing to gearbox bolts	18	2.5

1 General description

The 1300 model and early examples of the 1600 model are fitted with the four speed manual gearbox. All later models are fitted with either a five-speed manual or three-speed automatic transmission. All the gearboxes have a reverse gear.

The arrangement and function of components in the two manual gearboxes are broadly similar, and therefore dismantling of both the four speed and the five speed gearboxes is described in Section 3 of this Chapter. The four speed gearbox differences are mentioned in all cases.

The arrangement of the gear trains is such that all forward gears are mounted within the main gearbox case while the reverse gear is located in the rear extension housing.

Drive from the engine to the gearbox is through the clutch assembly. The gearbox input primary shaft is splined on its forward end and mates with a matching set of splines in the centre hub of the clutch friction plate. The primary shaft runs in a ball race fitted into the gearbox front casing and transmits the drive through the gear trains fitted to the mainshaft and layshaft.

The gearbox mainshaft runs in a needle roller cage fitted into the end of the primary shaft, a ball race in the end of the main gearbox casing, and finally a bush fitted into the extension housing. On the four speed gearbox a ball race is used in the extension housing in place of the bush.

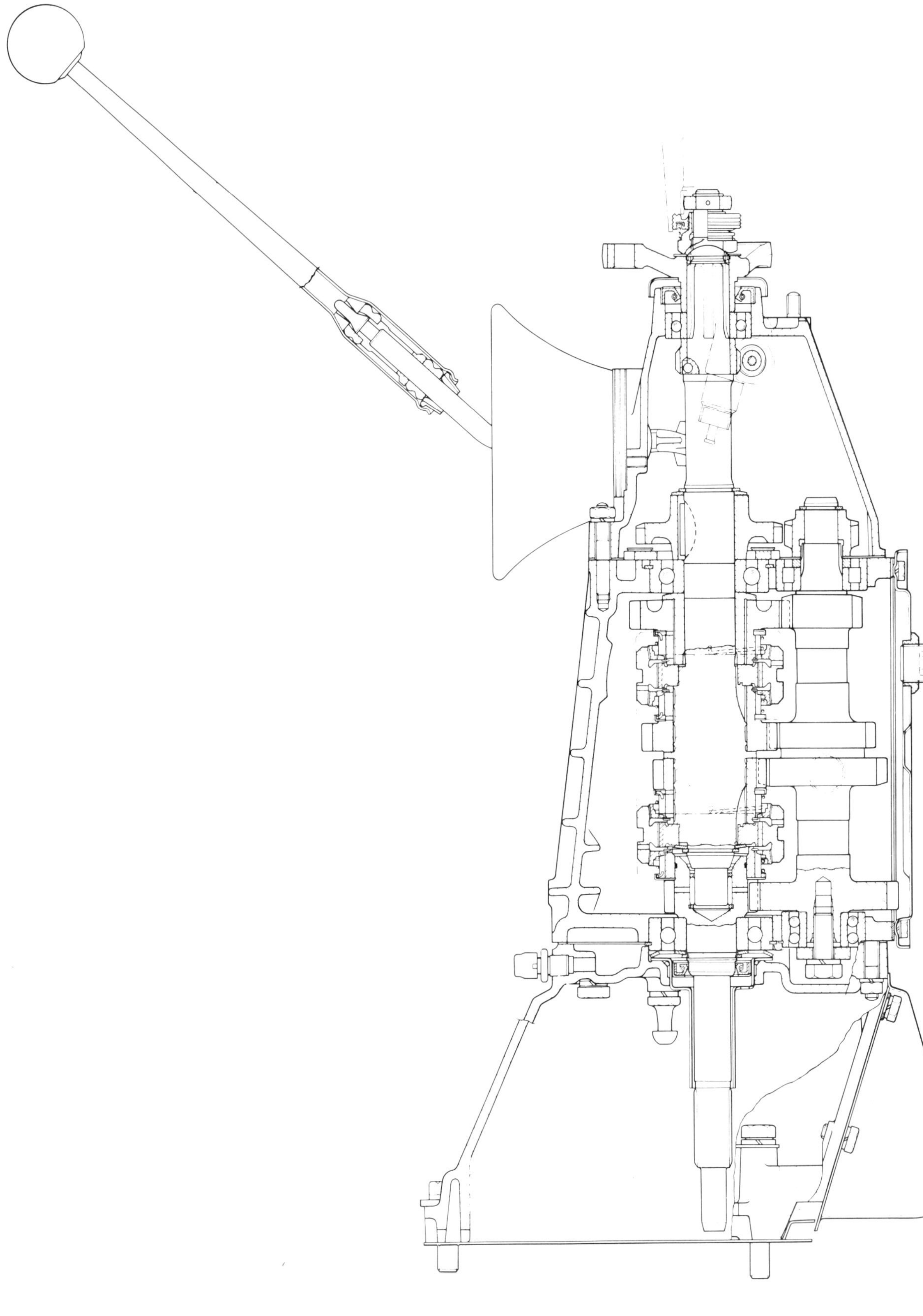

Fig. 6.1. A longitudinal cross section of the four speed gearbox assembly

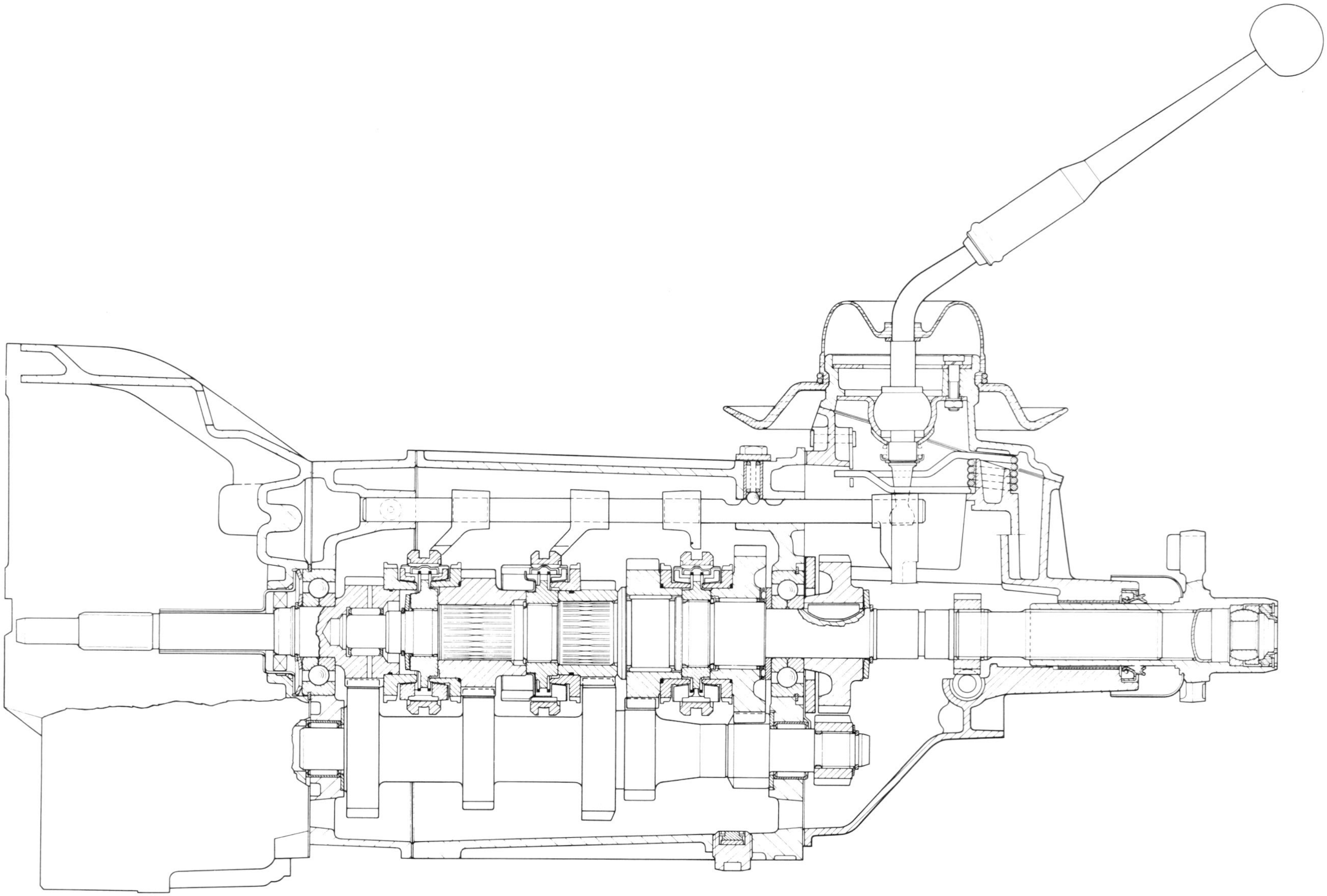

Fig. 6.2. A longitudinal cross section of the five speed gearbox assembly

All the forward gears are fitted with sliding ring and spring loaded synchromesh cone mechanisms for quick gear changing. In this mechanism the sliding ring is moved towards the gear being engaged by the selector fork. As the ring approaches the gear it passes onto the synchronising cone. The friction between the sliding ring and cone matches the rotational speeds of the two units. Once the rotational speeds are equal the sliding ring with its attached dog teeth wheel can be slid into the mating teeth machined onto the gearwheel. The gear has now been locked onto the mainshaft and the gear has been selected.

The reverse gear, mounted in the extension housing, is of the regular type using a sliding idler gearwheel to reverse the direction of drive.

The selector mechanism consists of forks held to rails by lock bolts. The ends of the rails protrude from the rear of the main casing and the gear lever, which is mounted in the rear extension housing, engages directly with the rails. The selector rails are controlled and located by conventional detent balls and springs with transverse interlocking plungers.

2 Gearbox - removal and refitting

The gearbox may be removed without disturbing the engine significantly. A special FIAT tool No. A.55035 is available to undo the bolts securing the bellhousing to the gearbox, but a socket spanner with a long extension will do the job as efficiently.

1 Raise the car so that there is approximately a two foot high space underneath the engine and gearbox region. Put chassis stands under the front of the car and chock the rear wheels. It is essential that the car is absolutely safe in the raised position, because you will be working underneath and efforts to slacken tight bolts could easily topple an inadequately supported vehicle.
2 Disconnect the battery earth lead.
3 From within the car remove the cowl around the gear lever. There is one screw underneath the soft mat just to the rear of the lever (photo).

4 Slide the rubber boot back up the gear lever (photo).
5 Remove the four screws and take away the tin cover to reveal the gear lever housing bolts. On four speed gearbox models the upper section of the gear stick can be removed (photo).
6 Slacken and remove the four housing bolts. The gear lever and housing can be lifted free on five speed gearbox models (photos).
7 Now remove the three nuts and bolts which secure the rubber coupling to the forward spider (photo).
8 On cars fitted with emission control there are two switches mounted on the gearbox. One is positioned just above the clutch lever on the bellhousing and the other is fitted to the front gearbox casing on the other side. Remove the wires from these sender switches and place them back out of the way.
9 From under the car remove the clutch cable and lever return spring. Pull the cable and sleeve clear of the bellhousing and tuck it away beside the engine.
10 Undo the nuts and bolts which secure the bottom flywheel shield to the clutch bellhousing and remove the shield.
11 Disconnect the leads from the starter motor having first identified them so that they may be connected correctly when the starter motor is refitted.
12 Undo the large bolts that secure the starter motor to the bellhousing and lift the starter motor away.
13 Undo the bolts which secure the exhaust bracket to the gearbox and remove the bracket.
14 At the tail housing remove the two wires from the reverse light switch and slacken off the knurled nut and remove the speedometer cable.
15 Some support should now be provided at the rear of the engine. A hydraulic jack and wooden packing blocks placed under the sump are ideal.
16 Remove the bolts from the safety strap crossmember.
17 The bolts can now be removed from the crossmember supporting the centre bearing and pillow block, allowing the propeller shaft to be swung across out of the way.
18 Remove the drain plug from the bottom plate of the gearbox and drain the oil into a suitable sized receptacle. When the oil has finished

2.3 The gear lever cowl with the soft mat removed revealing the retaining screw

2.4 Slide the rubber boot back up the gear lever

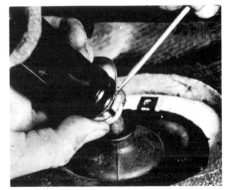

2.5 Remove the gear lever extension on the 4-speed gearbox model

2.6A Remove the tin cover plate from the transmission tunnel

2.6B Remove the upper gear lever housing on the five-speed gearbox model

2.7 Remove the three bolts joining the rubber coupling to the gearbox spider

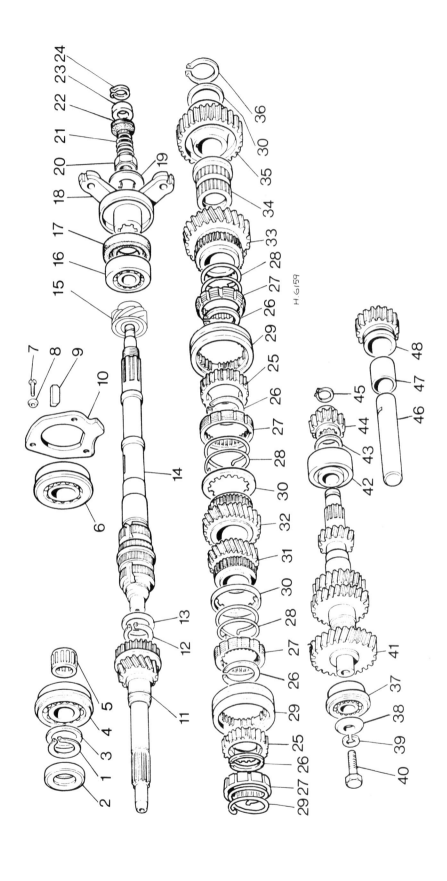

Fig. 6.3. The gear train of the four speed gearbox (Sec. 3)

1 Circlip
2 Oil seal
3 Conical washer
4 Ball bearing
5 Needle roller cage
6 Mainshaft intermediate ball
   bearing
7 Screw
8 Lockwasher
9 Woodruff key
10 Retainer plate

11 Primary (input) shaft
12 Circlip
13 Conical washer
14 Mainshaft
15 Speedometer drive gear
16 Mainshaft rear ball bearing
17 Oil seal
18 Spider sleeve
19 Lockplate
20 Nut

21 Spring
22 Seal
23 Centering ring
24 Circlip
25 Hub
26 Circlip
27 Synchronizer
28 Spring
29 Sleeve
30 Disc

31 3rd gear
32 2nd gear
33 1st gear
34 Bush
35 Reverse driven gear
36 Conical washer
37 Layshaft front ball bearing
38 Washer
39 Lockwasher
40 Bolt

41 Layshaft
42 Layshaft rear ball bearing
43 Conical washer
44 Reverse drive gear
45 Circlip
46 Reverse idler gear shaft
47 Bush
48 Reverse idler gear

H 6159

draining refit the plug.

19 A trolley jack should now be placed under the gearbox and raised to accept the weight of the box. Once the jack is in position remove the bolts securing the gearbox crossmember.

20 Having removed the crossmember, the remaining bolts retaining the gearbox to the engine can be undone and the gearbox drawn out. Take care when drawing the gearbox primary input shaft from the clutch mechanism and ensure the gearbox is kept aligned to the engine. Unnecessary tipping of the gearbox will cause damage to the primary shaft and the clutch centre friction plate.

21 Refitting the gearbox is a direct reversal of the removal sequence except that the clutch may need adjusting as detailed in Chapter 5. Remember also that the gearbox must be refilled with the correct volume and type of oil, specifications of which are given at the beginning of this Chapter. Also ensure all mounting and securing bolts are tightened to the recommended torque wrench settings, also listed at the beginning of this Chapter.

3 Gearbox - dismantling

Both the four and five speed gearboxes are similar in function and construction. The main difference, other than those already mentioned, is that the four speed gearbox has a detachable baseplate but does not have an intermediate gearbox case (between the bellhousing and main gearbox casing) as does the five speed. The dismantling sequences described in this Section are primarily for the five speed gearbox. However, as both gearboxes are similar this dismantling procedure can also be applied to the four speed gearbox, any variations between the two being noted where possible.

1 Before commencing the dismantling procedure the exterior of the gearbox must be cleaned. Temporarily refit the gear lever housing and bolts. A solvent, such as paraffin or Gunk, is ideal for cleaning the exterior of the gearbox and, when applied, it must be left to soak into the oil and dirt deposits for a while and then hosed off.

2 Wipe the gearbox off with a non-fluffy rag before removing the gear lever housing.

3 With the gearbox on a bench remove the spider coupling. On the five speed gearbox the spider can be simply pulled off. On the four speed gearbox the centring ring and its retaining circlip must first be removed. The spider is retained by a nut and locking tab washer.

4 With the spider now released remove the bolts retaining the tail housing in place. Draw the tailhousing off. On four speed gearboxes it may be necessary to remove the speedometer drive connection from the tailhousing before withdrawing the casing.

5 Now remove the clutch release lever arm and bearing from the bellhousing as detailed in Chapter 5, Section 6.

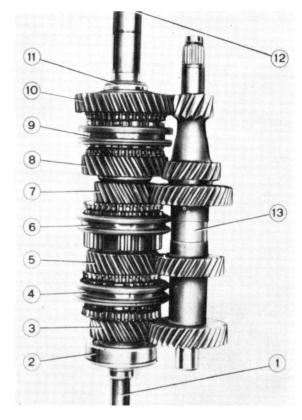

Fig. 6.4. The five-speed gearbox mainshaft and layshaft gear clusters (Sec. 3)

1 Primary shaft	8 2nd gear
2 Primary shaft bearing	9 1st and 2nd gear
3 4th gear	synchronizer hub
4 3rd and 4th gear synchronizer	10 1st gear
hub assembly	11 Inner race of split
5 3rd gear	mainshaft bearing
6 5th gear synchronizer hub	12 Mainshaft
assembly	13 Layshaft
7 5th gear	

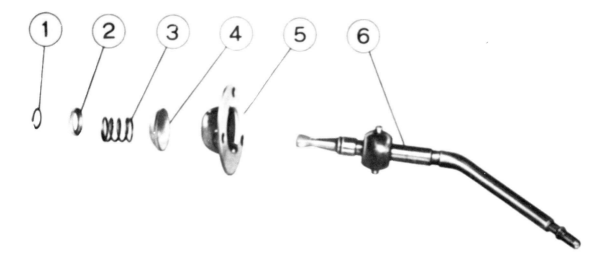

Fig. 6.5. Gearchange lever assembly (5 speed gearbox) (Sec. 3)

1 Circlip	3 Spring	5 Ball socket
2 Spring retaining cup	4 Domed cap	6 Gearchange lever

6   The bolts securing the bellhousing can now be removed and the bellhousing released.

7   On four speed gearboxes the detachable baseplate should now be removed.

8   The speedometer drive gear can now be removed from the mainshaft after having first removed its retaining snap-ring (photo). On the four speed gearbox the drive gear is locked in place by a ball bearing.

9   Remove the locking bolt from the reverse gear selector fork and slide the selector fork, spacer and sliding idle gear out.

10 On four speed boxes remove the third and fourth gear selector fork locking bolt. This will enable two gears to be selected at the same time thus locking the gear trains. With the two gears now selected remove the layshaft bearing securing bolt.

11 The reverse gear is secured to the mainshaft by a snap-ring under which is positioned a conical washer. The conical washer imposes a great deal of pressure on the snap-ring. To remove the snap-ring use a pair of snap-ring pliers assisted by a screwdriver (photo).

12 With the snap-ring and washer now released, slide the gear off its mainshaft locating key (photo).

13 Now remove the Woodruff key from the mainshaft keyway.

14 The snap-ring and conical washer can now be removed from the smaller reverse gear fitted to the end of the layshaft and the gear withdrawn (photo).

15 On four speed gearboxes the selector fork and rods can now be removed having first removed the locking bolts from the selector forks. Take care and note the positions of the interlocking pins when withdrawing the selector rods.

16 On the four speed box carefully tap out the layshaft rear bearing and then the forward bearing. The layshaft can now be removed from the gearbox.

17 On both four and five speed boxes the three countersunk screws can be removed from the mainshaft bearing retainer plate and the plate removed (photo).

18 The five speed gearbox has a retainer plate covering the detent balls and springs. Remove the two bolts and extract first the springs and then the balls by tipping the box on its side.

19 Now remove the large snap-ring from the mainshaft bearing. On four speed gearboxes the primary shaft end can be pulled out of the gearbox casing complete with the bearing.

20 On five speed gearboxes remove the lock bolt securing the third and fourth gear selector rod extension and remove the extension piece (photo).

21 The main gearbox casing can now be lifted up off the intermediate gearbox case leaving the mainshaft and layshaft gear clusters attached to the intermediate case (photo).

22 On cars fitted with emission control equipment there is a sender switch fitted into the intermediate gearbox case. The switch can now be removed followed by the interlock ball positioned below it (photos).

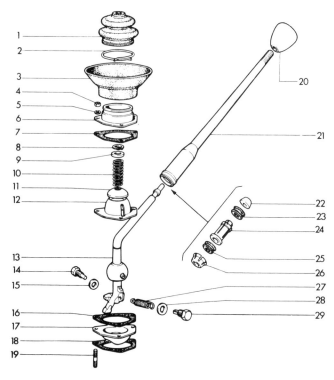

Fig. 6.6. Gearchange lever assembly (4 speed gearbox) (Sec. 3)

1	Rubber boot	16	Gasket
2	Clip	17	Plate
3	Draught excluder	18	Gasket
4	Nut	19	Stud
5	Spring washer	20	Grip
6	Mounting flange	21	Change lever extension
7	Gasket	22	Pad
8	Circlip	23	Rubber bush
9	Washer	24	Spacer
10	Spring	25	Rubber bush
11	Cap	26	Nylon securing collar
12	Ball socket	27	Spring
13	Gearchange lever	28	Washer
14	Stop screw	29	Spring retaining screw
15	Copper washer		

Fig. 6.7. Selector forks and rods - 4 speed gearbox (Sec. 3)

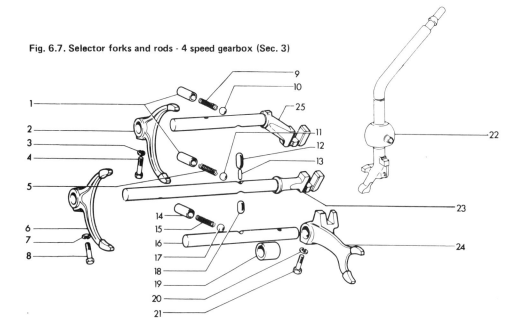

1   Bushes (in casing)
2   1st/2nd selector fork
3   Spring washer
4   Fork locking bolt
5   Detent spring
6   3rd/4th selector fork
7   Spring washer
8   Fork locking bolt
9   Detent spring
10 Detent ball
11 Detent ball
12 Interlock plunger
13 Interlock plunger
14 Bush
15 Detent spring
16 Reverse selector rod
17 Detent ball
18 Interlock plunger
19 Spacer
20 Spring washer
21 Fork locking bolt
22 Gear lever assembly
23 3rd/4th selector rod
24 Reverse selector fork
25 1st/2nd selector rod

3.8 The speedometer drive gear is retained by a snap ring

3.11 Remove the circlip from the reverse mainshaft gear using circlip pliers and a screwdriver

3.12 Slide the reverse gear off the mainshaft locating key

3.14 Remove the circlip and conical washer from the layshaft reverse drive gear

3.17 Remove the three countersunk screws and lockwashers from the mainshaft bearing retainer plate

3.20 Remove the lockbolt from the 3rd/4th selector rod extension piece

3.21 Lift the main gearbox case from the gear clusters

3.22A Removing the 3rd/4th gear sender switch from the intermediate gearbox case

3.22B Remove the interlock ball from the intermediate gearbox case

23 Remove the selector fork lock bolts and withdraw the selector rods and then the forks. Note that on the third and fourth gear selector rod there is an interlock pin fitted. There are also interlocking balls fitted between the selector rods in the intermediate gearbox cover (photo).

24 The mainshaft and layshaft can now be lifted from the intermediate case.

25 On the four speed gearbox the mainshaft has to be removed by drawing the assembly forward and up through the gearbox casing.

26 Both four and five speed mainshaft gear assemblies are retained to the shaft by locating snap-rings and conical washers. The following dismantling procedure is primarily for the five speed gearbox; however, the instructions for removing the snap-rings and gears are similar on the four speed gearbox.

27 The layshaft assembly is a one piece unit and cannot be dismantled further.

28 The intermediate gearcase comprises two sub-assemblies; the primary shaft at the forward end and the mainshaft at the rear section. Lying between the two shafts is a needle bearing cage.

29 Pull the primary shaft away from the mainshaft and extract the needle bearing cage and fourth gear synchromesh ring.

30 The mainshaft assembly can be dismantled from its forward end after having first removed the snap-ring and conical washer (photo).

31 Draw the third and fourth gear synchroniser hub assembly off the shaft, followed by the third gear (photo).

32 Remove the snap-ring which locates the fifth gear synchroniser hub and withdraw the synchroniser hub assembly followed by the synchromesh ring and finally the fifth gear (photo).

33 Working from the other end of the mainshaft remove the mainshaft bearing. The bearing can be removed in one of two ways, either it may be levered off using two screwdrivers or, the end of the mainshaft can be struck with a soft hammer while the bearing is held (photos).

34 The bearing is in three parts comprising the outer bearing and two inner split races.

35 After the bearing has been removed the thick plain washer can be removed followed by a thrust needle bearing and finally a thinner plain washer.

3.23 The interlocking pin fitted to 3rd/4th gear selector rod

3.30 Remove the circlip and conical washer retaining 3rd/4th gear synchronizer assembly and 3rd gear

3.31 The 3rd and 4th gear synchronizer assembly removed

3.32 The snap ring retaining 5th gear and synchronizer hub assembly

3.33A Remove the mainshaft rear bearing using a soft mallet

3.33B As an alternative method the rear mainshaft bearing can be levered off using two large screwdrivers

3.38 The snap ring retaining 1st/2nd gear synchronizer hub assembly and 1st gear

5.1 Install the 2nd gear onto the mainshaft and needle bearing cage

5.3 Install the 1st/2nd gear synchronizer hub assembly

5.4 Install the thick plain washer, thrust needle bearing and thick washer after the 1st gear

5.5 Fitting the outer part of the split bearing inner race

5.8 Installing the 5th gear synchronizer hub assembly

36 The first gear can now be slid from the needle roller bearing on which it runs.

37 Remove the needle bearing.

38 Now remove the snap-ring retaining the first and second gear synchroniser hub assembly (photo).

39 Withdraw the synchroniser hub assembly and synchromesh ring.

40 The second gear and synchromesh ring can now be withdrawn followed by a further needle roller bearing.

41 The mainshaft is now completely stripped and the components ready for inspection and cleaning.

4 Gearbox - inspection and renewal of components

Thoroughly clean all the gearbox components in paraffin to remove oil residue and lay them out on sheets of clean paper. Examine the gearbox casings and covers for any signs of cracks and see that the mating faces are free from burrs. The old gaskets should be removed and the mating faces cleaned with emery paper. The oil seals should be removed during the cleaning operation.

The condition of the shafts, gears and synchromesh assemblies is a question of degree. Renewal of the cones should be made if there is significant wear on the cone faces. Serious backlash of more than 0.010 in (0.25 mm) in the hubs between the inner and outer sleeves means that the whole synchromesh unit should be renewed and this can be expensive.

The gear teeth should not be chipped or excessively worn. Backlash between the gear teeth should not exceed 0.008 in (0.20 mm)

The selector rods should slide easily in the gearbox casing without any undue slackness which might cause jamming. The detent springs should not be weak and the balls not worn or pitted. The selector forks must be at right angles to the selector rods when fitted and the tongues which engage in the grooved outer sliding sleeve of the synchromesh unit must not be worn on either face. Any wear on the tongues will result in excessive clearance and consequent lost motion in gear engagement.

Finally all the gearbox bearings, races, needle roller cages and thrust washers should be inspected for wear.

It is essential when overhauling a gearbox to evaluate the cost and availability to purchase an exchange gearbox unit from a FIAT dealer.

5 Gearbox - reassembly

Reassembly of both four- and five-speed gearboxes is similar in many aspects, but to avoid confusion between the two, this Section is sub-divided accordingly.

On both gearbox types, lubricate all bearings and friction surfaces prior to assembly and, where applicable, renew the gaskets and oil seals.

Five-speed gearbox

1 Slide the needle roller cage onto the mainshaft along with the second gear (photo).

2 Fit the second gear synchromesh ring.

3 Refit the first and second gear synchroniser hub assembly (photo) and fit the snap-ring into the locating groove, followed by a spacing washer.

4 Slide the first gear needle roller cage onto the mainshaft followed by the first gear, thin plain washer, thrust needle bearing and finally a thicker plain washer (photo).

5 The inner race of the split bearing can now be refitted followed by the outer part of the bearing and the other half of the split inner race (photo).

6 The remaining gears must be fitted from the other end of the mainshaft.

7 Begin by fitting the fifth gear along with its synchromesh ring.

8 Refit the fifth gear synchronising hub assembly. There are two slots in the synchroniser hub, the large one being for the segment of the synchromesh ring (photo).

9 Refit the snap-ring which retains the synchroniser hub assembly.

10 Now slide the third gear onto the mainshaft (photo). This gear appears to be fitted the wrong way round. There is quite a large boss on the back of the gear which fits into the synchroniser hub assembly for fifth gear operation.

11 The third and fourth speed synchroniser and synchromesh ring can now be refitted.

12 Now refit the conical washer, dished face outwards, along with the retaining snap-ring. The simplest method to relocate the snap-ring in its groove is to use a socket and hammer (photo).

13 The primary shaft must now be reassembled. The bearing on the primary shaft is of the three part type already mentioned.

14 Refit the bearing assembly, conical washer and snap-ring. To fit the snap-ring in its groove, use a piece of suitably sized pipe. Slide the pipe down over the primary shaft on top of the snap-ring. Strike the end of the pipe hard to compress the conical washer which will then allow the snap-ring to seat in the groove.

15 Refit the needle roller cage to the forward end of the mainshaft and refit the mainshaft to the primary shaft having first rested the fourth gear synchromesh ring in place.

16 Fit the layshaft bearing into the intermediate gearbox case.

17 Fit the layshaft thrust washer with the oil grooves uppermost. This washer can be held in place with a little grease (photo).

18 Support the intermediate case on suitable blocks. Position one of the blocks in such a way that it will prevent the layshaft bearing from being forced out when the gear assemblies are refitted.

19 Refit the assembled mainshaft and layshaft into the intermediate casing.

20 Fit the fifth gear and reverse gear selector rod into the fifth gear selector fork (photo).

21 Refit the interlocking ball between the selector rod holes (photo).

22 Now refit the third and fourth gear selector fork and selector rod. On fitting the selector rod, push the rod part way down and refit the interlocking pin in the hole provided (photo).

23 Locate the 1st/2nd gear selector rod and fork in a similar manner, and also refit the Allen screw into the housing.

24 Fit the selector fork locating bolts and tighten them to the specified torque.

25 Refitting of the layshaft is the reversal of its removal. However, take care when refitting the bearings and tighten the front bearing lock bolt to the torque wrench setting as specified at the beginning of this Chapter.

26 Refit the detent balls and springs. The correct positioning of the colour coded springs is important. Facing the gearbox, the left-hand spring is blue, the centre spring dark green and the right-hand spring light green.

5.10 Installing 3rd gear

5.12 Use a socket and hammer to relocate the circlip

5.17 Fit the layshaft thrust washer with the oil grooves uppermost

5.20 Install the 5th and reverse gear selector rod into the 5th gear selector fork

5.21 Refit the interlock ball between the selector rod holes

5.22 The interlock pin location in the 3rd/4th gear selector rod

5.37 Relocate the circlip on the mainshaft using a pipe and a hammer

5.38 Refit the reverse gear selector fork and sliding idler gear

5.41A The rear housing oil seal installed

5.41B Refitting the gearbox spider on the five-speed gearbox

5.44 The bellhousing oil seal installed

Four-speed gearbox

27 Reassemble the 3rd/4th and 1st/2nd synchro hub units.
28 Grease the mainshaft and slide onto it the 2nd gear, 1st/2nd synchro hub unit, then the 1st gear and bush (refer to Fig. 6.3).
29 Locate the Woodruff key into the groove in the mainshaft, slide the 2nd gear into position and secure it with a washer and circlip.
30 Invert the mainshaft and assemble the 3rd gear and 3rd/4th synchro hub unit. Retain this with a washer and circlip, fitted in a similar manner to that described in paragraph 12.
31 The mainshaft assembly is now refitted into the gearbox, along with its rear bearing and retainer plate.
32 The selector forks can now be rested in their positions and the 1st and 2nd gear selector rod, its interlocking pin, and fork relocated. Refit the selector fork locking bolt.
33 Now refit the 3rd and 4th gear selector rod.
34 Refit the needle roller bearing cage into the end of the mainshaft and fit the primary shaft and its attached bearing through the gearbox casing into location with the mainshaft.
35 Insert the layshaft into position in the gearcase then fit the front

ball bearing, tapping it carefully into position. Fit and tighten the bearing lockbolt to the specified torque of 69 lbf ft (9.5 kg fm).

Four- and five-speed gearboxes

36 The fitting of the reverse gear and selector assemblies is almost identical for both four- and five-speed gearboxes. On the five-speed gearbox, refit the mainshaft Woodruff key, then refit the 3rd/4th gear selector extension and retain it with a lockbolt.
37 Slide on the reverse gear, conical washer and snap-ring. Use a piece of suitable length pipe placed over the mainshaft and resting directly on top of the snap-ring. Strike the end of the pipe hard with a hammer to compress the conical washer enabling the snap-ring to reseat itself in the mainshaft groove (photo).
38 Now refit the spacer on the reverse gear selector rod and refit the selector fork together with the sliding gear (photo).
39 Tighten the selector fork locking bolt.
40 The speedometer drive mainshaft gear can now be refitted along with its retaining snap-ring.

41 Fit a new oil seal in the tailhousing and refit the tailhousing, followed by the spider coupling (photos).
42 Refit the speedometer external drive unit.
43 On four-speed gearboxes, the spider is retained by a nut and tab washer, followed by the centring ring and a snap-ring.
44 Fit a new oil seal into the bellhousing and refit the bellhousing to the gearbox (photo).
45 Finally, on the four-speed gearbox, fit a new gasket to the bottom plate and refit it to the gearbox.
46 The gearbox is now ready for refitting in the vehicle, after having refitted the clutch release lever and bearing assemblies in the bellhousing.

6 Fault diagnosis - manual transmission

Symptom	Reason/s
Weak or ineffective synchromesh	Synchromesh cones and rings worn or damaged. Baulk rings worn. Defective synchromesh.
Jumps out of gear	Worn interlock plunger. Worn detent ball. Weak or broken detent spring. Worn selector fork or synchromesh sleeve groove. Worn gear.
Excessive noise	Incorrect grade of oil being used. Oil level too low. Worn gear teeth. Worn mainshaft bearings. Worn thrust washers. Worn primary shaft splines. Worn mainshaft splines.
Difficult gear changing or selection	Incorrect clutch pedal free play.

Chapter 6 Part B: Automatic transmission

For modifications, and information applicable to later models, see Supplement at end of manual

Contents

Specifications

Type	GMS, three forward speeds and reverse, three element torque converter with planetary geartrain

Ratios

1st	2.4 : 1	
2nd	1.48 : 1	converter ratios
3rd	1.0 : 1	
Reverse	1.92 : 1	

Torque ratio in converter	2 : 4 - 1 : 1
Fluid capacity (approx)	5 Imp pints (2.8 litres) (6 US pints)
Fluid type	Automatic Transmission Fluid Dexron

Torque wrench settings

	lb f ft	kg f m
Adjustment screw on brake band	3.3	0.46
Locknut brake band adjusting screw	15	2.1
Servo cover plate bolts	19	2.6
Transmission sump pan bolts	16 - 19	2.3 - 2.6
	7 - 9	1.0 - 1.3

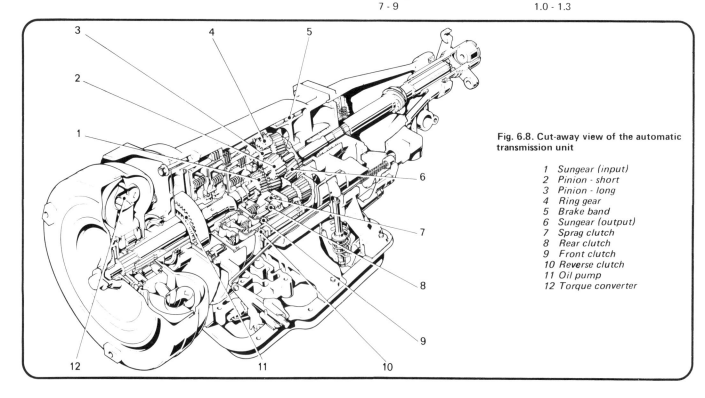

Fig. 6.8. Cut-away view of the automatic transmission unit

1 Sungear (input)
2 Pinion - short
3 Pinion - long
4 Ring gear
5 Brake band
6 Sungear (output)
7 Sprag clutch
8 Rear clutch
9 Front clutch
10 Reverse clutch
11 Oil pump
12 Torque converter

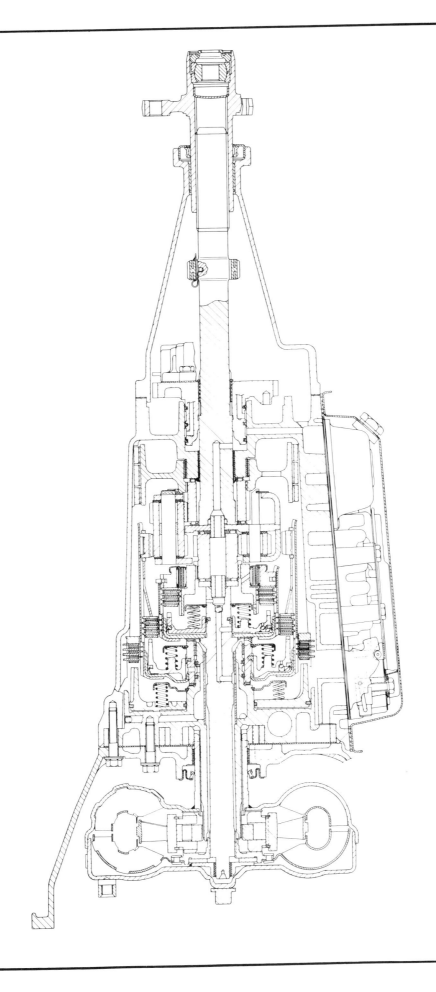

Fig. 6.9. A longitudinal sectioned view of the automatic transmission unit

7 General description

An automatic transmission is offered as an option on the Fiat 131,
when it is fitted with the 1600 or 1800 engines. The GMS type of automatic transmission comprises two main components: a three element
hydrokinetic torque converter coupling capable of torque multiplica-
tion at an infinitely variable ratio between 2.4 : 1 and 1 : 1; and a
hydraulically operated epicyclic gearbox providing three forward
ratios and one reverse.

The control lever (which is mounted on the floor) has six positions:
Position 'P' locks the transmission for parking; 'R' is for reverse; 'N' is
neutral; 'D' is the normal drive position; '2' stops the gearbox from
engaging its third gear; '1' keeps the gearbox in first gear.

8 Automatic transmission - general repair and maintenance

Because of the complexity of this unit, it is recommended that the
owner should not attempt to dismantle the automatic transmission
unit himself. If performance is not up to standard or some fault occurs,
your FIAT agent should be entrusted to carry out the necessary
repairs. The agent will have special equipment for accurate fault
diagnosis and rectification. Many tests of the unit are best carried out
when it is still in the car, so if you have (or suspect) trouble, do not
remove the unit from the car before placing it in the hands of the
repairer.

The following Sections, therefore, are confined to adjustments
and servicing information. Instruction for removal is given because
this is essential when removing the engine unit.

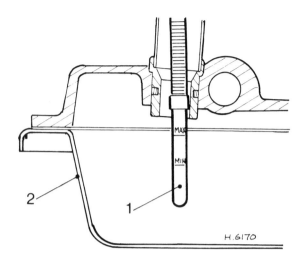

Fig. 6.10. Checking the automatic transmission fluid level (Sec. 9)

1   Dipstick   2   Transmission sump pan

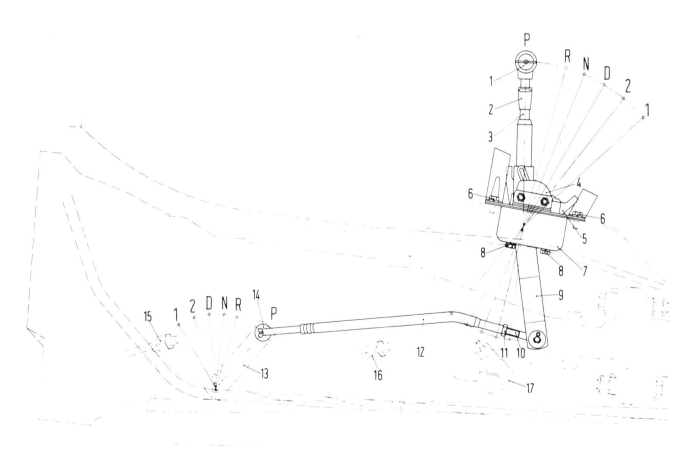

Fig. 6.11. Layout of the selector linkage of the automatic transmission (Sec. 10)

1 Lever 'T' handle	5 Gate	9 Selector arm lever	13 Cross shaft
2 Gate release lever	6 Support bracket bolts	10 Adjustable end of link rod	14 Washer
3 Lever	7 Support	11 Locknut	15 Oil cooler pipe outlet
4 Inhibitor switch	8 Saddle bolts	12 Link rod	16 Oil cooler pipe inlet

9 Fluid level - checking

1 At the intervals specified in the Routine Maintenance Section check the fluid level in the automatic transmission unit.
2 To do this, first drive the car for about 6 miles (9.6 km) to reach the normal operating temperature of the unit. Stop the car on level ground and with the engine still running at idling speed select 'P'.
3 Withdraw the dipstick, wipe it clean, re-insert it and withdraw it again and read off the oil level.
4 If necessary, top up to the 'MAX' mark through the filler tube.
Note: The utmost care should be taken to ensure that both the funnel and containers used for topping up are absolutely clean. Also ensure that the correct automatic transmission fluid is used. See the beginning of this Chapter for the correct fluid recommendation.
5 It is recommended by FIAT that the fluid is drained every 25,000 miles or two years. The fluid should be drained with the transmission warm and if it is noted that the fluid is heavily soiled then the filter in the valve assembly, along with the seal, should also be renewed.

10 Selector linkage - adjustment

1 The selector linkage may need adjustment when engine and gearbox mountings settle or free play occurs in the mechanism. These factors will effect the selector lever position in relationship to the manual valve position.
2 To adjust the linkage disconnect the adjustable link rod from the lower selector arm lever.
3 Put the hand selector lever in the 'P' position.
4 On the gearbox pull the cross shaft fully back into the 'P' position. To check that the cross shaft is in the 'P' position, check that the transmission is locked.
5 If the link rod adjustment is correct it should be just long enough to be relocated in the lower selector arm lever. Adjust the link rod as necessary until it can be relocated.
6 With the adjustable link now reconnected test the selection operation by lifting the gate release lever and selecting gear position '1'.
7 Release the gate lever and the engagement of the lock tooth in the gate should take place without any further movement of the selector lever.
8 Check the lever in the remaining selector positions and adjust the link rod as necessary.
9 Note that any part of the linkage mechanism that is worn must be renewed to ensure effective operation.

11 Automatic transmission - kickdown, accelerator cable and telescopic link adjustments

A cable connected between the carburettor and transmission operates a kickdown valve which, when activated, automatically selects a lower gear or holds a suitable gear engaged to achieve maximum acceleration.
The accelerator pedal travel can be divided into three principle stages:
The first stage position (fully released); the carburettor throttle valves are fully closed as when the engine is idling.
The second stage position (full power); the carburettor throttle valves are fully open as when achieving maximum road speed.
The third stage position (kickdown); the carburettor throttle valves remain in the fully open position but extra accelerator pedal travel is felt as a hard spot as the telescopic link is stretched and the kickdown cable is brought into operation.

Fig. 6.12. The three selector positions at the pivot quadrant (Sec. 11)

1 Accelerator cable adjustable end	7 Telescopic link locknut
2 Accelerator inner cable	8 Ball pin end on throttle lever
3 Return spring	9 Guide pin
4 Stop bracket	10 Kickdown inner cable
5 Telescopic link locknut	11 Kickdown inner cable end
6 Telescopic link	nipple
	12 Pivot quadrant

C = 0.039 to 0.118 in (1 to 3 mm)

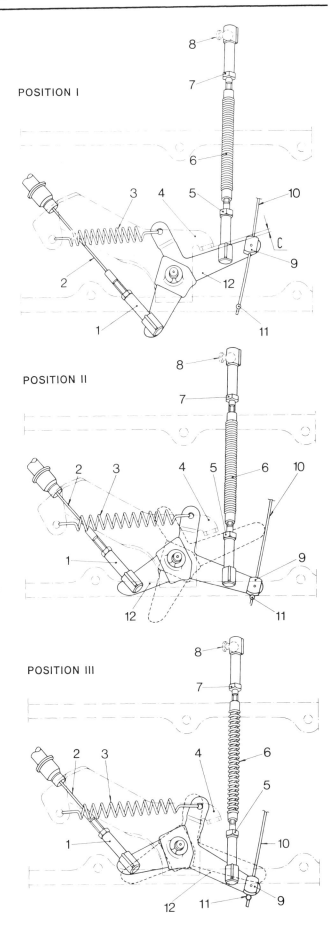

POSITION I

POSITION II

POSITION III

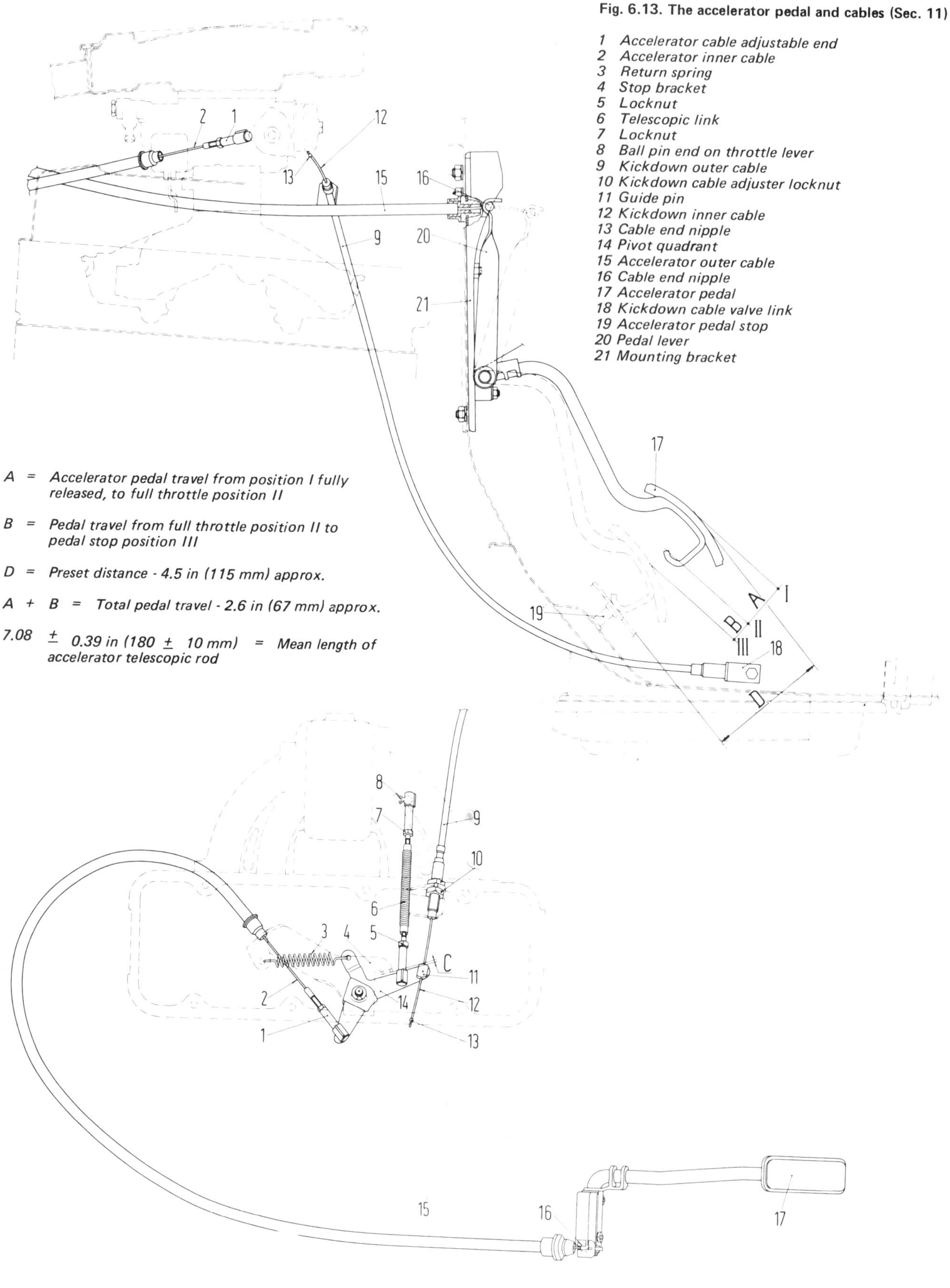

Fig. 6.13. The accelerator pedal and cables (Sec. 11)

1 Accelerator cable adjustable end
2 Accelerator inner cable
3 Return spring
4 Stop bracket
5 Locknut
6 Telescopic link
7 Locknut
8 Ball pin end on throttle lever
9 Kickdown outer cable
10 Kickdown cable adjuster locknut
11 Guide pin
12 Kickdown inner cable
13 Cable end nipple
14 Pivot quadrant
15 Accelerator outer cable
16 Cable end nipple
17 Accelerator pedal
18 Kickdown cable valve link
19 Accelerator pedal stop
20 Pedal lever
21 Mounting bracket

A = Accelerator pedal travel from position I fully released, to full throttle position II

B = Pedal travel from full throttle position II to pedal stop position III

D = Preset distance - 4.5 in (115 mm) approx.

A + B = Total pedal travel - 2.6 in (67 mm) approx.

7.08 ± 0.39 in (180 ± 10 mm) = Mean length of accelerator telescopic rod

Accelerator cable and telescopic link adjustments

1 Before commencing adjustments take the car on a short run to achieve its normal running temperature.
2 With the gear selector lever in the 'P' position adjust the engine idling speed, with the aid of a tachometer, until it is 800 ± 50 rpm.
3 With the engine still idling apply the footbrake and select the 'D' position. If the engine stalls adjust the idling speed but ensure that it remains within the quoted limits.
4 Stop the engine and disconnect the accelerator cable from the engine pivot quadrant.
5 Ensure that there is a clearance of 0.039 - 0.118 in (1 - 3 mm) between the pivot quadrant and the stop. Adjust the telescopic link to achieve the quoted clearance. **Note:** When adjusting the telescopic link make adjustments equally from both ends.
6 Refit the accelerator cable. The cable should fit without any undue slackness or excessive tightness. If necessary adjust the accelerator cable to achieve the desired fit.

Checking and adjusting kickdown travel

7 Disconnect the telescopic link from the carburettor end.
8 Now depress the accelerator pedal until the end stop of the inner kickdown cable is brought into contact with the guide pin on the pivot quadrant without causing the kickdown cable to be pulled.
9 Now depress the accelerator pedal until it has reached its stop and at the same time measure the increase in length of the inner cable. The increase in length should be 0.27 - 0.35 in (7 - 9 mm). To achieve this travel it may be necessary to adjust the outer kickdown cable. Take care not to stretch the inner cable when making the adjustment.

12 Brake band - adjustment

1 Drain the transmission fluid.
2 Remove the transmission sump pan.
3 Remove the servo brake cover.
4 Slacken the locknut and tighten the adjusting screw to the torque given in the beginning of this Chapter.
5 Now back the adjusting screw off five complete turns.
6 Tighten the locknut to the recommended torque setting ensuring that the adjusting screw is not rotated during this operation.
7 Refit the servo brake cover.
8 Refit the transmission sump pan along with a new gasket. Ensure that the retaining bolts are tightened to the recommended torque setting.
9 Refill the transmission with the recommended fluid as detailed in

the beginning of this Chapter.
   It should be noted that the correct adjustment of the brake band is not dependant on the clearance between the brake band and drum alone. The adjustment detailed above is in fact preloading the servo brake release spring.

13 Automatic transmission - starter inhibitor/reverse light switch

   On all models utilising the automatic transmission option there will be fitted into the gear selector mechanism, at the lever end of the mechanism, a dual purpose switch. The switch is fitted with four terminal ends and when the selector lever is placed in the 'R' position the contacts of the switch are closed and the current is fed through the switch to the reverse lamps.
   The inhibitor half of the switch is incorporated in the starter circuit and prevents the engine from being started in any gear. The switch will only pass current when the selector lever is in the 'P' or 'N' positions.

14 Automatic transmission - removal and refitting

1 Removal of the engine and transmission as a combined unit is described in Chapter 1 of this manual. Where it is decided to remove the transmission leaving the engine in place proceed as follows:
2 Disconnect the battery negative earth lead.
3 Remove the transmission level dipstick and the bolt holding the dipstick tube to the engine bracket.
4 From within the car remove the centre console and disconnect the wiring block connector for the transmission switch. Push the connector through the aperture in the floor panel.
5 Jack the vehicle to an adequate height and support it on stands or blocks. Alternatively position the vehicle over a pit.
6 Remove the drain plug from the rear of the transmission sump and catch the transmission fluid in a suitably sized container.
7 Disconnect the wiring from the starter motor and remove the three bolts retaining the starter motor to the transmission casing.
8 Disconnect the speedometer cable by slackening off the knurled nut at the extension housing.
9 Now release the speedometer cable retaining bracket where it is bolted to the lug on the transmission casing and stow the cable out of the way.
10 Remove the nut and bolt holding the fluid cooling pipes clamp in place.

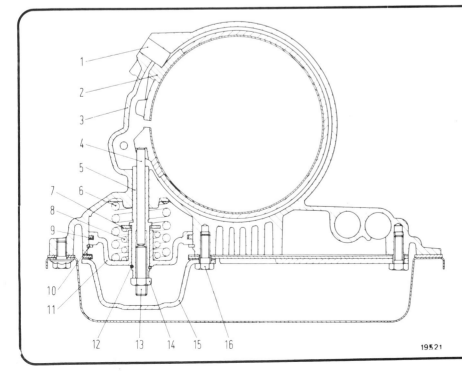

Fig. 6.14. Brake band and servo unit (Sec. 12)

1 Stop pin
2 Brake band
3 Gearbox casing
4 Pushrod
5 Guide sleeve
6 Release spring
7 Spring locating plate
8 Damping spring
9 Piston ring
10 Circlip
11 Servo piston
12 Circlip
13 Adjusting screw
14 Locknut
15 Servo cover
16 Servo cover retaining bolts

19521

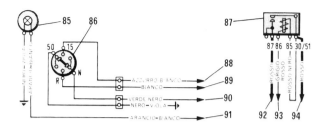

Fig. 6.15. Electrical circuits relating to the automatic transmission
(Sec. 13)

85   Gear selector lever indicator
86   Starter/Reverse inhibitor switch
87   Starter relay
88   To connector terminal 5 at rear
89   Cable to reverse lamps
90   To connector terminal 11 at rear
91   To connector terminal 12 at rear
92   To starter terminal
93   To connector terminal 21 in engine compartment
94   To the ignition switch terminal point 50
(see page 151 for colour code)

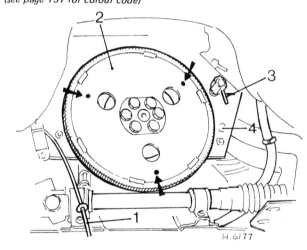

Fig. 6.16. The rear of the engine with the automatic transmission
removed (Sec. 14)

1   Speedometer cable   3   Starter motor
2   Flywheel   4   Flywheel cover
The arrows indicate the torque converter fixing points on the
flywheel plate

11 Disconnect the exhaust support bracket from the transmission
casing.
12 Remove the vacuum hose from the modulator valve and disconnect
the vacuum tube spring clip retainer from the transmission case.
13 Now remove the bolt retaining the kickdown cable bracket to the
transmission case. The bolt is positioned above the modulator valve.
14 The kickdown cable can now be disconnected from the kickdown
valve.
15 Remove the flywheel cover plate which is retained by four bolts.
16 Turn the flywheel to gain access to the three bolts which secure
the torque converter to the flywheel.
17 Now disconnect the control lever from the control rod on the
transmission.
18 Disconnect the fluid cooling pipes from the transmission casing.
19 Disconnect the propeller shaft as described in Chapter 7.
20 Support the transmission case with a jack and remove the four
bolts joining the transmission case to the engine block.
21 Finally remove the two bolts retaining the transmission support
crossmember to the body.
22 With the aid of a trolley jack or an assistant tilt the automatic
transmission down at the rear and draw it back out having first
removed the temporary support jack.
23 Refitting the automatic transmission is the reverse of the

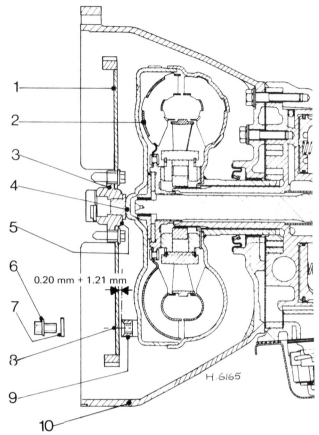

0.20 mm + 1.21 mm

Fig. 6.17. Diagram showing the reconnection of the transmission to
the flywheel (Sec. 14)

1   Flywheel   6   Bolts torque converter to
2   Torque converter   flywheel
3   Flywheel flange   7   Rubber washer
4   Contact points between   8   Fixing points torque converter
5   the torque converter and   to flywheel
     flywheel   9   Boss
                             10   Front transmission housing

dismantling procedure. Remember to feed the wiring connector for
the transmission switch up through the floor before the automatic
transmission is finally installed.
24 After bolting the transmission case to the engine block push the
torque converter against the flywheel flange and measure the gap
between the flywheel and the torque converter attachment points.
The gap at each of the three mounting points should be 0.008 - 0.048
in (0.2 - 1.21 mm). If the clearance is not within these limits the flywheel must be renewed.
25 Remember during reassembly to tighten all nuts and bolts to the
recommended torque wrench settings as given at the beginning of
this Chapter.
26 With the transmission refitted, the fluid level must be topped up.
Use only new oil of the specified type. Check that the drain plug is
securely relocated then insert about 5.28 Imp pints (2.8 litres) of
transmission fluid into the transmission, pouring through the filler
tube.
27 Check that the handbrake (park brake) is fully applied and position
a block each side of the wheels. Start the engine and allow it to run
at its normal idle speed, then select D (Drive) with the gearshift. Keep
the engine at idle speed and move the selector slowly through each
range to enable the transmission to warm up.
28 Having warmed up the transmission oil to its normal operating
temperature, select 'N' or 'P' and recheck the fluid level. Only use a
lint-free cloth to wipe the dipstick clean and, if necessary, top up
with further fluid to bring the level up to the 'MAX' mark. Do not
overfill.
29 Finally, adjust if necessary the linkages and cables as detailed in
Sections 10 and 11 respectively.

15 Automatic transmission - fault diagnosis

Symptom	Reason/s
Engine will not start in 'N' or 'P' selector positions	Faulty starter or ignition circuit. Incorrect linkage adjustment. Faulty inhibitor switch.
Engine starts in selector positions other than 'N' or 'P'	Incorrect linkage adjustment.
Severe bump when selecting 'D' or 'R' and excessive creep when idling	Idling speed too fast.
Poor acceleration and low maximum speed	Incorrect oil level. Incorrect linkage adjustment. Brake band/s worn or slipping. Torque converter faulty.

The most likely causes of faulty operation are incorrect oil level and linkage adjustments. Any other faults or malfunction of the automatic transmission unit must be due to internal faults and should be rectified by your FIAT dealer. An indication of a major internal fault may be gained from the colour of the transmission fluid which under normal conditions should be transparent red. If the fluid becomes discoloured or black then burnt clutch or brake bands can be suspected.

Chapter 7 Propeller shaft

Contents

Specifications

Type ... ...   Two piece tubular, with central support bearing and comprising a forward rubber coupling, central and rear universal joints; the rear section is bolted to the rear axle drive pinion flange

Length
Front shaft ... ...   23.169 in (588.5 mm)
Rear shaft ... ...   33.071 in (840 mm)

Clearance between universal joint spiders and needle bearings ... ...   0.004 - 0.16 in (0.01 - 0.04 mm)

Torque wrench settings

	lb f ft	kg f m
Nuts retaining front rubber coupling spider	51	7
Nuts retaining crossmember to bodyshelll	18	2.5
Bolts retaining crossmember to bodyshell	18	2.5
Bolts retaining pillow block to crossmember	18	2.5
Nut: yoke to propeller shaft	22	3
Nut: rear end of propeller shaft to axle pinion flange	25	3.5

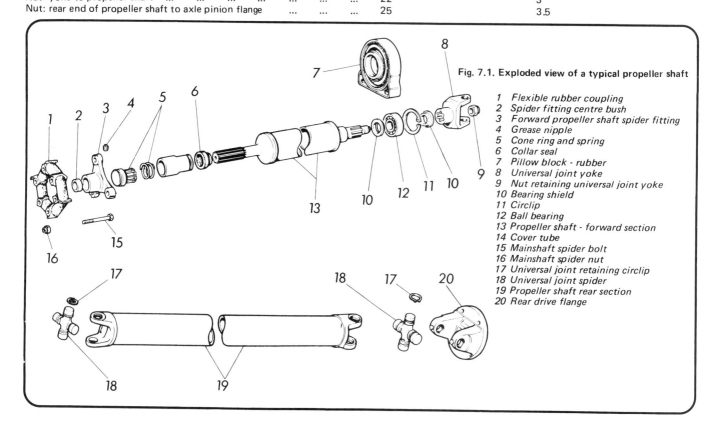

Fig. 7.1. Exploded view of a typical propeller shaft

1 Flexible rubber coupling
2 Spider fitting centre bush
3 Forward propeller shaft spider fitting
4 Grease nipple
5 Cone ring and spring
6 Collar seal
7 Pillow block - rubber
8 Universal joint yoke
9 Nut retaining universal joint yoke
10 Bearing shield
11 Circlip
12 Ball bearing
13 Propeller shaft - forward section
14 Cover tube
15 Mainshaft spider bolt
16 Mainshaft spider nut
17 Universal joint retaining circlip
18 Universal joint spider
19 Propeller shaft rear section
20 Rear drive flange

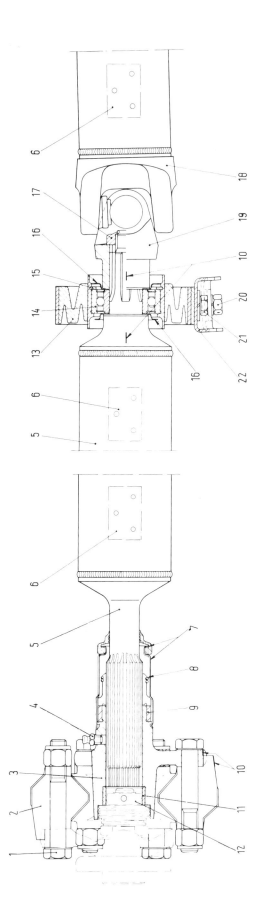

Fig. 7.2. Longitudinal section of propeller shaft
through flexible coupling and centre pillow block

1 Spider bolts
2 Flexible rubber coupling
3 Forward propeller shaft spider fitting
4 Grease nipple
5 Propeller shaft forward section
6 Balance weight
7 Seal and cover
8 Spring
9 Rubber ring
10 Balance reference marks
11 Spider fitting centre bush
12 Centre ring on mainshaft
13 Centre pillow block - rubber
14 Ball bearing
15 Bearing circlip
16 Bearing shields
17 Nut retaining universal joint yoke
18 Propeller shaft - rear section
19 Universal joint yoke
20 Crossmember to bodyshell bolts
21 Pillow block to crossmember bolts
22 Crossmember

1 General description

The FIAT 131 has a split or divided type of propeller shaft. This means that instead of having a long tubular shaft with a universal joint at each end, the 131 has a propeller shaft consisting of two short shafts with a universal joint at the centre as well as one at both ends. The advantages of this type of propeller shaft are the shallower angles at the joints, the reduced intrusion of a tunnel from the rear end of the shaft into the body floor and the greater rigidity obtained from two shafts.

The front section of the propeller shaft is joined at the gearbox end by a flexible rubber coupling. The shaft runs through a centre bearing supported in a rubber pillow block which is secured to the bodyshell by a small crossmember spanning the transmission tunnel. A universal joint yoke, splined and secured by a nut to the rear end of the front shaft, forms the front half of a universal joint which mates with the front yoke of the rear section.

The rear propeller shaft section consists of a conventional tubular type shaft with universal joint yokes welded at each end. The rear section is coupled to the axle by the rear drive flange mounted on the pinion shaft of the differential assembly.

The propeller shaft requires periodic lubrication of the splined joint of the forward shaft into the flexible coupling on the gearbox output shaft. Some makes of replacement universal joint spiders have provision for grease lubrication of the needle roller bearings on the spider.

It is essential to realise that the propeller shaft assembly is a finely balanced collection of components and that they are balanced only as they remain assembled in the alignment in which they were originally assembled.

Therefore, whenever dismantling the propeller shaft pay particular attention to the reference alignment marks on the main shaft components so that they are correctly reassembled.

It is equally important to realise that if any single or small group of major components is renewed (except universal joint spider assemblies) the whole shaft assembly must be dynamically balanced professionally.

2 Propeller shaft - removal and refitting

1 Undo the nuts and remove the three long bolts which secure the front end of the propeller shaft to the rubber coupling. If possible compress the rubber coupling with a large hose clip before removing the bolts, this will make reassembly easier. Access to the bolts can either be made from within the car after having removed the gear lever grommets and shroud, or alternatively from underneath the car (photo).
2 Remove the nuts and washers which hold the pillow block and safety strap crossmembers to the bodyshell (photos).
3 Some form of support at this stage should be provided to prevent the propeller shaft from damage if it should accidently fall to the ground.
4 Finally remove the four nuts and bolts which locate the rear section of the propeller shaft to the rear axle drive flange.
5 The shaft can now be lifted free from the vehicle.
6 The refitting procedure is the reverse of the removal sequence. If, however, the propeller shaft has been dismantled check that the balance reference marks are correctly aligned before refitting. Ensure that all

nuts and bolts are tightened to the specified torque wrench settings.

3 Universal joints - inspection and repair

1 Wear in the needle roller bearings on the central spider is characterised by vibration in the transmission, 'clonks' on taking up the drive and in extreme cases of lack of lubrication, metallic squeaking and ultimately grating sounds as the bearings disintegrate.
2 It is easy to check if the needle bearings are worn with the propeller shaft in position. Try to turn the shaft with one hand while maintaining a grip on the other side of the joint with the other hand. There should be no movement between the two.
3 If wear is apparent, the worn bearings and spiders will have to be removed and new ones fitted. A repair kit is available and consists of new universal joint spiders, bearings, seals and retainers.

Universal joints dismantling

4 Clean away all traces of dirt and grease from the snap-rings located on the bearing cups in the yokes. Remove the snap-rings by pressing their open ends together with a pair of snap-ring pliers and lift them out with a screwdriver. If they are difficult to remove, tap the bearing cup top with a mallet to ease the pressure on the snap-ring.
5 Hold one side of the joint - normally the tubular shaft side to begin with and remove the bearing cups and needle rollers by tapping the yoke at each bearing with a copper or hide faced hammer. As soon as the bearing cups begin to emerge from their bores, they can be drawn out with either your fingers or a pair of pliers. If the bearing cups refuse to move then place a small drift against the inside of the bearing and tap it gently until the cup begins to move.
6 With all four cups removed together with their needle rollers, the spider can easily be extracted from the yokes. Once the spider is free the bearing faces may be wiped clean with a petrol damped cloth and the surfaces inspected. If any grazing scores or ridges are found the spider will need renewing. On some occasions when the universal joint has failed through lack of lubricant, the bores in the yokes in which the bearing cups fit can be worn. Again once the joint has been dismantled it is easy to check the condition of the yokes.

Universal joints - reassembly

7 Thoroughly clean the yokes and bores. Remember to check that the snap-ring grooves are clear.
8 Fit new grease seals and retainers on the new spider journals and place the spider into the shaft yoke. Assemble the needle rollers in the bearing cups and hold in place by smearing them with a medium lithium based grease. In new assemblies the needles should pack so well that they each retain the other in place.
9 Carefully ease the cup, packed with the needle rollers into the yoke bore and onto the appropriate spider journal. It is all too easy to hurry and a single roller fall from place and prevent the cup from seating properly on the journal.
10 It may be necessary to tap the bearing cups home in the final stages and once the cup face has passed the snap-ring groove in the yoke refit the snap-ring.
11 Once the whole universal joint has been assembled there is provision on most makes of new universal joints for injecting extra grease into the spider bearings before the propeller shaft is refitted to the car. A

2.1 Separating the forward propeller shaft from the flexible rubber coupling

2.2A Undoing the pillow block crossmember nuts

2.2B Undoing the safety strap crossmember bolts

small grub screw in the centre of the spider can be unscrewed and a grease nipple temporarily fitted to enable the joint to be greased.

4 Rubber pillow block - removal and refitting

1 The pillow block supports a bearing in which the rear end of the front shaft turns. It is necessary to remove the propeller shaft assembly from the car and remove the centre universal joint before the block can be removed.
2 Section 2 details the removal and refitting of the shaft assembly and Section 3 describes how to remove the central universal joint.
3 With the forward shaft separated from the rear, remove the single nut from the rear end of the forward shaft and slip the universal joint yoke off the splined end of the shaft.
4 Support the inner ring of the rubber block on the shaft side. The propeller shaft may then be tapped gently out of the ball race bearing held in the inner ring of the rubber block. Use only a hide or copper hammer on the shaft, as a steel hammer will damage the shaft.
5 The bearing may be removed from the block inner ring after the snap-ring which retains it in the ring has been extracted.
6 Finally, the block outer cover is separated from the support cross-member after the two securing bolts are undone.
7 The refitting of the pillow block onto the shaft follows the reverse procedure to removal, except that the following checks and tasks must be included:

a) Ensure that the centre bearing shields are in place on each side of the bearing.
b) Check that the nut on the rear end of the forward shaft is tightened to the specified torque given at the beginning of this Chapter.
c) Make sure that the pillow block has been mounted the correct way round, with the bearing shoulder on the forward side of the assembly.

5 Forward shaft front spider - removal and refitting

The front flexible joint spider is splined onto the forward end of the front shaft.
1 The spider can be removed once its rear cover is unscrewed and slipped away down the shaft.
2 The internal splines in the spider and the splines on the shaft may be cleaned and inspected.
3 If, on inspection, wear is found on either of the items, then both

should be renewed. It is false economy to renew only one of the components as they are a matched pair.
4 It should be noted that the propeller shafts are finely balanced assemblies and it is essential to realise that the spider must be refitted on the front shaft so that the reference marks on the spider and shaft are aligned.
5 It is equally essential, if parts are renewed singularly, that the whole assembly must be balanced professionally before refitting it to the car.
6 The propeller shaft spline cover and sealing components may be slid off the shaft when the spider has been removed.
7 The bush in the forward end of the spider fitting should be inspected for wear together with the centring ring on the end of the gearbox mainshaft on which it runs. If wear is found then both centring ring and bush should be renewed.
8 The bush can be drifted out of the spider fitting and the centring ring removed from the mainshaft once the end nut has been removed. Check that the new components fit closely before assembling them onto the transmission.
9 Reassembly of the spider fitting onto the forward propeller shaft is the reverse of removal except the following checks should be included:

a) Grease the mating splines liberally with a lithium based grease.
b) Ensure that the spider is fitted to the propeller shaft with the balance reference marks aligned correctly.

6 Centre bearing - removal and refitting

1 Wear of this bearing is typified by transmission vibration and in the event of total loss of lubricant, metallic shrieking accompanied by excessive vibration. The condition of the bearing may be checked with the propeller shaft assembly in the car by shaking the shaft to discern radial play in the bearing.
2 Remove the propeller shaft assembly as described in Section 2 of this Chapter.
3 Dismantle the front universal joint as described in Section 3 of this Chapter.
4 Remove the centre pillow block assembly as described in Section 4 of this Chapter.
5 Tap the bearing out of the pillow block inner ring once the retaining snap-ring has been removed.
6 Reassembly is a direct reverse of this dismantling procedure. As with all tasks on the propeller shaft it is important to ensure that the reference marks are correctly aligned and all locating nuts and bolts are tightened to the torque wrench settings listed at the beginning of the Chapter.

7 Fault diagnosis - propeller shaft

Symptom	Reason/s
Vibration	Out of balance Wear in sliding joint splines. Loose flange securing bolts. Worn universal joints. Worn centre bearing.
Noise	Worn centre bearing.

Chapter 8 Rear axle

For modifications, and information applicable to later models, see Supplement at end of manual

Contents

Specifications

Type	Semi-floating hypoid
Oil capacity (approx)	2.3 Imp. pts (1.4 US qts) (1.3 litres)
Oil type	SAE 90EP gear oil

Final drive ratio

1300	4.1 : 1
1600	3.9 : 1
1800	4.4 : 1
1600 with automatic transmission	3.5 : 1
2000	3.9 : 1

Torque wrench settings

	lbs f ft	kg fm
Axle shaft retainer plate bolts	36	5
Panhard rod end nuts	58	8
Trailing arm end bolts	72	10
Axle case cover bolts	18	2.5
Upper arm bracket to body	36	5
Lower arm bracket to body	36	5
Shockabsorber top mounting to body nuts	18	2.5
Shockabsorber top spindle nuts	11	1.5

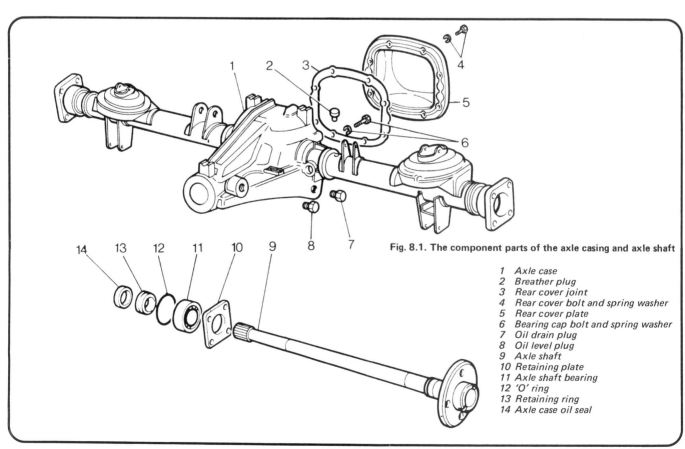

Fig. 8.1. The component parts of the axle casing and axle shaft

1 Axle case
2 Breather plug
3 Rear cover joint
4 Rear cover bolt and spring washer
5 Rear cover plate
6 Bearing cap bolt and spring washer
7 Oil drain plug
8 Oil level plug
9 Axle shaft
10 Retaining plate
11 Axle shaft bearing
12 'O' ring
13 Retaining ring
14 Axle case oil seal

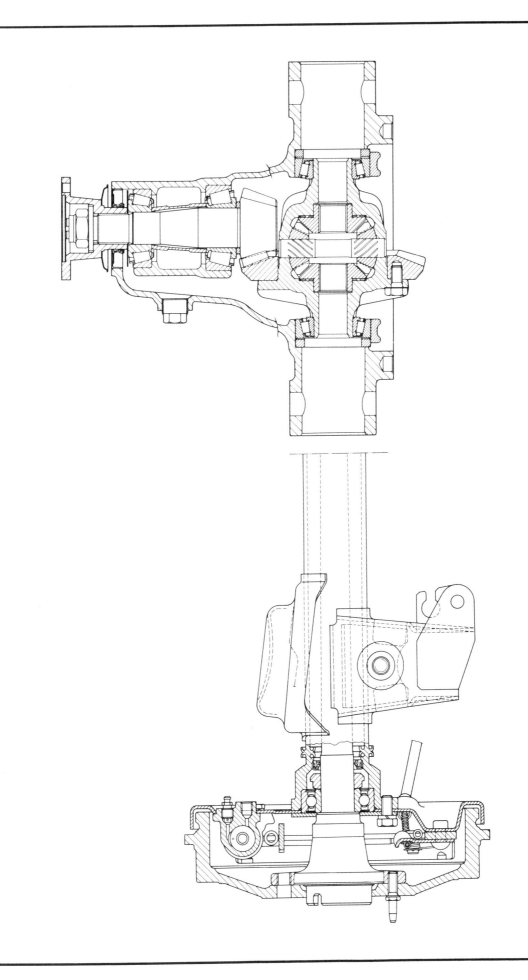

Fig. 8.2. A section through the final drive, differential assembly and the left-hand hub

1 General description

The conventional live rear axle is mounted on two coil springs with telescopic shockabsorbers and is located by four trailing arms and a Panhard (transverse) rod.

Drive to the axle is by a two-piece propeller shaft bolted to the bevel pinion drive flange. The bevel pinion input shaft runs in a pair of taper roller bearings, between which there is a 'collapsible spacer' which maintains an end thrust on the bearing rollers. The pinion meshes with the crownwheel which is bolted onto the differential cage and the whole differential cage runs in a pair of taper roller bearings.

Drive from the differential unit to the hubs is taken through a conventional axle shaft which has splines on its inner end which slide into matching splines on the differential side gear.

Axle shafts can be removed without difficulty but the removal of the differential assembly necessitates the use of a special tool to stretch the axle casing. It is therefore advisable to entrust any work connected with the removal or adjustment of the assembly to a FIAT dealer.

Some models are available with an optional limited slip differential.

2 Axle shaft, bearing and oil seal - removal and refitting

1 Loosen the wheel nuts of the wheel on the shaft to be removed and then jack up the car and support the axle casing on a stand. If both shafts are to be removed it is important that the rear axle is supported firmly on two stands.
2 Remove the wheel and brake drum.
3 Turn the axle shaft so that the large holes give access to the four bolts securing the axle shaft retainer plate and remove the bolts.
4 The axle shaft and bearings have to be drawn out together and this normally involves some form of percussion to force the bearing from the housing. If a slide hammer is available there is no problem. Otherwise an alternative is to refit the wheel (or if possible an old rim without a tyre) and strike it from the inside to draw the axle shaft out. Do not under any circumstances strike the axle shaft flange directly. It can be damaged and distorted easily.
5 With the shaft removed access can be gained to the oil seal fitted within the axle tube. There is also a rubber 'O' ring fitted between the axle shaft retainer plate and bearing.
6 Refitting of the axle shaft is a reversal of the dismantling procedure. Do not forget the oil seal and the rubber 'O' ring which should both be renewed.
7 After reassembly has taken place check, and if necessary top up, the rear axle with the correct oil as specified at the beginning of this Chapter.

3 Axle shaft bearings - renewal

1 If the ball bearing on the shaft is obviously worn and in need of renewal it is best undertaken by your FIAT dealer who will have the proper equipment. The bearing is held on the shaft by a retaining ring which requires heating to 300°C and 5 tons weight under a press to get it on. Somewhat more than 5 tons is needed to get it off and the use of hammers, cold chisels, hacksaws and the like will probably result in a ruined axle shaft. Take it along to a FIAT franchise garage who will have the part and the appropriate tools and press to fit it without damage to either the axle or bearing.

4 Rear axle - removal and refitting

1 Raise the rear of the car and fit strong chassis stands situated adjacent to the trailing arm anchorages on the bodyshell. FIAT supply special purpose-built stands for supporting the bodyshell when removing the axle assembly. The FIAT number for the stands is Ar 22908.
2 With the car safely supported remove the rear wheels.
3 Next remove the brake fluid reservoir cap and stretch a sheet of polythene over the reservoir and refit the cap. This method will prevent the excessive loss of fluid from the brake system when pipes are subsequently removed or disconnected.

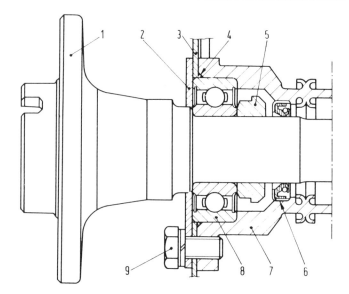

Fig. 8.3. A sectioned view of the axle shaft and its location in the axle casing (Sec. 2)

1 Axle shaft	6 Hub oil seal
2 Retainer plate	7 Rear axle end casing
3 Brake backplate	8 Axle shaft bearing
4 Rubber 'O' ring	9 Retaining plate bolt
5 Retaining plate	

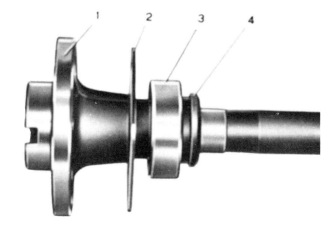

Fig. 8.4. The axle shaft and bearing assembly removed (Sec. 3)

1 Axle shaft	3 Axle shaft bearing
2 Retaining plate	4 Retaining ring

4 Disconnect the flexible hose where it joins the brake pipe on top of the rear axle casing. Tape over the ends of the pipe to prevent the ingress of dirt.
5 Remove the four bolts which secure the propeller shaft to the axle drive flange.
6 Make sure the handbrake is in the 'off' position and remove the return spring from the rear cable support bracket.
7 Slacken off the cable by turning the adjusting nut, situated just below the handbrake lever, in an anti-clockwise direction. Continue slackening the cable until it can be released from the pulley bracket.
8 The rear cable can now be dropped down from its fixing bracket complete with pulley assembly.
9 Bring a jack underneath the centre of the axle assembly and raise the jack up to take the weight of the axle.
10 Disconnect the brake regulator control rod from its mounting

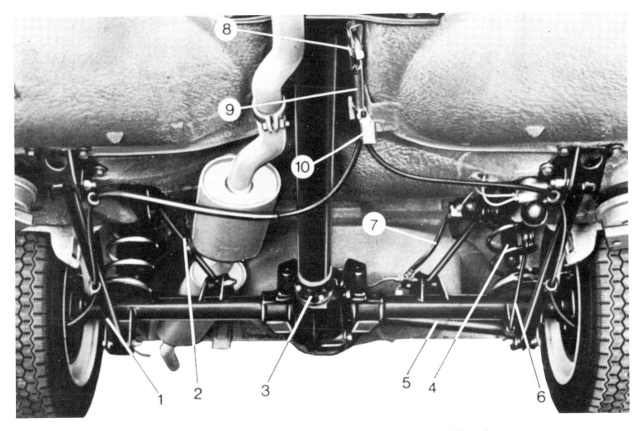

Fig. 8.5. Location of the rear axle as seen from the front (Saloon) (Sec. 4)

1 Lower trailing arm
2 Upper trailing arm
3 Propeller shaft attached to pinion drive flange
4 Shockabsorber and coil spring unit
5 Panhard rod

6 Brake regulator control rod
7 Brake flexible hydraulic hose
8 Handbrake pulley and bracket
9 Handbrake cable return spring
10 Rear cable support bracket

bracket.

11 The trailing rods and transverse Panhard rod can now be released. Long bolts secure the rubber bushed ends of these rods to the anchorage points on the bodyshell.

12 The lower trailing rods must be disconnected at their forward mounting points to avoid the necessity to remove the handbrake cables from the backplates.

13 Finally, from within the boot undo the upper securing nuts for the shockabsorber. There are three nuts keeping the mounting block in place and a further nut on top of the shockabsorber spindle which sandwiches two spacer blocks, one rubber and the other metal.

Note: On estate car models the shockabsorber is mounted independently away from the coil spring unit.

14 The jack can now be lowered down and the axle assembly drawn back from under the vehicle.

15 Refitting the axle is a reversal of the dismantling procedure.

16 Make sure the springs and their seats are properly located and move the assembly into position under the car.

17 Raise the axle up, taking care to guide the tops of the shockabsorbers through the holes in the bodyshell into the boot space.

18 Secure the shockabsorber mounting block and metal and rubber spacers, and screw the nuts down finger tight.

19 Refit the trailing arm bolts and relocate the Panhard rod. Do not tighten the nuts and bolts more than finger tight.

20 Reconnect the flexible brake pipe and refit the brake regulator control rod into its mounting bracket.

21 Rejoin the front and rear handbrake cables together and refit the return spring.

22 Bolt the propeller shaft to the rear axle pinion flange.

23 The radius rods, Panhard rod, shockabsorbers and other mountings can now be tightened to the specified torque wrench figures as listed at the beginning of this Chapter.

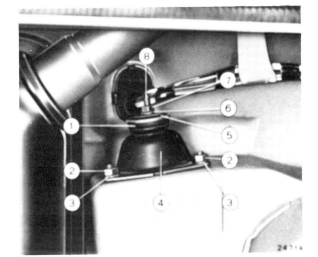

Fig. 8.6. Shockabsorber top mounting (Sec. 4)

1 Rubber spacer
2 Mounting nut
3 Spring washer
4 Upper mounting block

5 Metal spacer
6 Spring washer
7 Shockabsorber spindle nut
8 Shockabsorber spindle

5   Fault diagnosis - rear axle

Symptom	Reason/s
Vibration	Propeller shaft out of balance. Loose drive flange bolts. Wheels require balancing.
Noise	Insufficient lubrication. Worn differential gears. Centre bearing worn.
Knock when accelerating or decelerating	Excessive crownwheel to pinion backlash. Worn gears. Worn axle shaft splines. Loose drive flange couplings. Loose wheels.
Oil leakage	Faulty pinion or axle oil seals. Blocked axle breather. Defective gaskets. Oil level too high.

Chapter 9 Braking system

For modifications, and information applicable to later models, see Supplement at end of manual

Contents

Specifications

Type ... ...   Hydraulically operated dual circuit with discs at the front and drums at the rear

Front disc brake
Type ....   Single cylinder floating caliper
Disc diameter ... ...   8.94 in (227 mm)
Maximum permissible run-out ... ...   0.006 in (0.15 mm)
Minimum pad thickness (worn) ... ...   0.06 in (1.5 mm)
Minimum thickness of disc after regrind ... ... · ...   0.368 in (9.35 mm)

Rear drum brake
Drum diameter ... ...   8.9882 - 9.000 in (228.3 - 228.6 mm)
Maximum increase in drum diameter after regrind ... ...   0.003 in (0.8 mm)
Minimum lining thickness (worn) measured from lining face to rivet head or shoe in the case of bonded linings ... ...   0.08 in (2 mm)

Servo unit
Manufacturer ... ...   Master-Vac Girling Benaldi
Vacuum cylinder bore ... ...   6.2401 in (158.5 mm)
Piston rod protrusion from cover face ... ...   0.0324 - 0.04075 in (0.825 - 1.025 mm)

Master cylinder
Bore ... ...   0.75 in (19.05 mm)
Fluid ... ...   Castrol Girling Universal Brake and Clutch Fluid

Rear brake regulator
Distance from the bodyshell to the end of the control rod:
   Saloon ... ...   13.346 in (339 mm)
   Estate ... ...   12.874 ± 0.197 in (327 ± 5 mm)

Torque wrench settings

	lb f ft	kg f m
Master cylinder retaining bolts	18	2.5
Brake servo unit retaining bolts	18	2.5
Brake caliper yoke retaining bolts	36	5
Brake caliper hose union bolt	22	3
Rear drum retaining bolts	14.5	2
Front disc retaining bolts	14.5	2

1 General description

The FIAT 131 is fitted with a Girling Benaldi master/vac unit which comprises a vacuum servo unit joined to a dual circuit brake master cylinder. The servo unit is connected by a rubber hose to the inlet manifold and boosts the hydraulic pressure delivered from the master cylinder thus reducing the effort required at the brake pedal.

Application of the footbrake creates hydraulic pressure at the master cylinder and fluid travels down the two outlet pipes to the front and rear brakes. The two systems are connected together by steel pipes and flexible hoses.

The front brakes consist of two calipers (one each side), the pistons of which force friction pads into contact with a round metal disc.

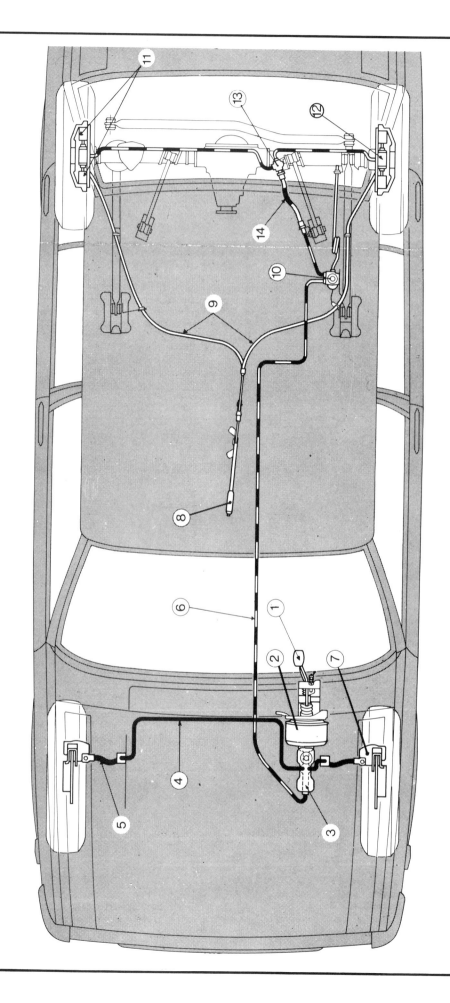

Fig. 9.1. Brake system layout (typical for all models)

1 Footbrake pedal
2 Servo unit
3 Master cylinder

4 Front brake pipe line
5 Front flexible hose
6 Rear brake pipe line

7 Front brake caliper
8 Handbrake lever
9 Rear handbrake cable

10 Brake compensator valve
11 Rear brake shoes
12 Rear brake wheel cylinder

13 Rear brake three-way connector
14 Rear flexible hydraulic hose

The rear brakes are of the self-adjusting, leading and trailing shoe type, with one brake cylinder per wheel. Connected into the rear brake line, just in front of the axle, is a brake pressure regulator valve. This device adjusts the fluid pressure applied to the rear brakes in proportion to the laden state of the vehicle.

The handbrake is of the conventional lever and cable type and is adjustable should the cables stretch.

2 Bleeding the hydraulic system

1   This without doubt will be one of the most frequent tasks to be performed on the brake system. You will require some small 1/8 or 3/16 inch bore rubber or clear plastic tubing and a clean dry glass jar. The tubing should be at least 15 inches long. You will also require a quantity of brake fluid (Castrol Girling Universal Brake and Clutch Fluid) probably between ¼ and ½ a pint.

2   It will be necessary to bleed the brakes whenever any part or all of the brake system has been overhauled or when a brake pipe connection has been undone in the course of performing tasks on other assemblies on the car. Bleeding of the brakes will also be necessary if the level of fluid in the brake system reservoirs has fallen too low and air has been taken into the system. During the task of bleeding the brakes, the level of fluid should not be allowed to fall below half way, or air will be drawn into the system again.

3   Although not necessary from the point of view of a successfully completed task, it improves access to remove the roadwheel adjacent to the brake to be bled. Beginning at the front of the car, place a jack underneath the lower arm of the suspension. Raise the roadwheel off the ground and remove the wheel. Chock the other wheels and release the handbrake.

4   Remove the rubber dust cover from the bleed screw and wipe the screw head clean. Push the rubber/plastic tubing onto the screw head and drop the other end into the glass jar placed nearby on the floor. Remove the reservoir cap and ensure that the fluid level is near the top of the reservoir. Pour a little brake fluid into the glass jar, sufficient to cover the end of the tube lying in the jar. Take great care not to allow any brake fluid to come into contact with the paint on the bodywork, it is highly corrosive.

5   Use a suitable open ended spanner and unscrew the bleed screw about one half to a full turn.

6   An assistant should now pump the brake pedal by first depressing it in one full stroke followed by three shorter more rapid strokes, allowing the pedal to return of its own accord each time. Check the level of fluid in the reservoir and replenish if necessary with new fluid. **Never re-use fluid.**

7   Carefully watch the flow of fluid into the glass jar and when the air bubbles cease to emerge from the bleed screw and braking system through the plastic pipe, tighten the bleed screw during a down stroke on the pedal. It may be necessary to repeat the pumping detailed in paragraph 6 if there was a particularly large accumulation of air in the brake system.

8   Repeat the operations detailed in paragraph 3 to 7 on the other three brakes. When bleeding the rear brakes, place the jacks under the axle casing and remove the wheels. **Do not use chassis stands acting on the bodyshell otherwise the rear brake regulator system will be brought into operation** and prevent the flow of fluid to the rear brakes. A last additional point with regard to the rear brakes, is to pump the pedal slowly and allow one or two seconds between each stroke.

9   Sometimes it may be found that the bleeding operation for one or more cylinders is taking a considerable time. The cause is probably due to air being drawn past the bleed screw threads, back into the system during the return stroke of the brake pedal and master cylinder, when the bleed screw is still loose. To counteract this occurrence, it is recommended that at the end of the downward stroke the bleed screw be temporarily tightened and loosened only when another downstroke is about to commence.

10 Once all the brakes have been bled, recheck the level of fluid in the reservoir(s) and replenish as necessary. Always use new brake fluid - **never re-use fluid.**

11 If after the bleed operation, the brake pedal operation still feels spongy, this is an indication that there is still some air in the system, or that the master cylinder is faulty.

3 Disc pads - removal, inspection and refitting

1   Before dismantling any parts of the brakes they should be thoroughly cleaned. The best cleaning agent is hot water and mild detergent. Do not use petrol, paraffin or any other solvent which could cause deterioration to the friction pads or piston seals.

2   The caliper block seats in a yoke fitting which is bolted to the stub axle casing and 'wraps around' part of the disc. The pads and their retaining springs, and the caliper block which acts on the pads, are held between the upper and lower parts of the enveloping yoke. The caliper is held so that it is free to move axially to centre itself on the pads and disc. It is retained radially by two wedges which are held axially to the caliper yoke by two cotter pins (photo).

3   The procedure for removal of the disc brake pads is as follows: Jack up the appropriate side of the car and remove the roadwheel.

4   Pull out the cotter pins which retain the caliper block wedges. Wedges are fitted above and below the caliper block. Mark the wedges before removing them to ensure that you will be able to refit them in exactly the same location (photo).

5   Once the wedges are out, the caliper block can be lifted away from the brake assembly. Be careful not to strain the flexible hydraulic hose joining the caliper to the brake system. Rest the caliper on a suitable object (photos).

6   Remove the brake pads. The pad anti-vibration springs may be removed if desired (photos).

7   Mark the pads so that they may be refitted into their exact locations.

8   On inspection, if the pads are found to be either damaged or worn to a thickness less than or near the minimum thickness, as quoted at the beginning of the Chapter, the pad set must be removed (photo).

9   Pads are sold in sets of four and it is recommended that should any pad need renewal then the whole set should be renewed.

10 It is advisable before refitting disc brake pads to check the disc for scoring or excessive wear. Section 6 of this Chapter details the checks to be carried out when inspecting the disc assembly.

11 The refitting of the disc pads follows the reverse order to the dismantling procedure (see photo sequence).

12 If new pads are being fitted the caliper piston will have to be pushed gently back into the caliper bore. This is to provide a sufficient gap between the caliper piston and outer claw when accommodating the increased thickness of the new pads. It is as well to remember that when the piston is retracted into the caliper bore brake fluid will be displaced and returned to the master cylinder reservoir. The reservoir will overflow as the piston is being retracted unless some fluid is drawn off with a device such as a pipette.

13 The caliper can now be refitted over the pads and the refitting procedure carried out.

4 Front brake caliper block and yoke - removal and refitting

1   Working inside the engine compartment, remove the cap on the brake fluid reservoir, and stretch a thin sheet of polythene over the top of the reservoir. Refit the cap. This will prevent an excessive loss of fluid when the brake hose is subsequently disconnected from the caliper.

2   Jack the car up and remove the roadwheel.

3   Remove the two bolts which secure the hydraulic hose to the caliper. The smaller bolt retains the hose locating plate while the large bolt forms the hose union joining it to the caliper. To prevent the ingress of dirt it is advisable to tape up the end of the hydraulic hose and plug the inlet port of the caliper (photo).

4   To remove the caliper follow the dismantling procedure as described in Section 3 of this Chapter.

5   The caliper can now be lifted from the car and taken to a clean bench for overhaul.

6   Refitting the caliper block follows the exact reversal of the dismantling procedure.

7   With the caliper and pads refitted the system must be bled as described in Section 2 of this Chapter.

8   To remove the caliper yoke follow the procedure as described in Section 3 of this Chapter.

9   With the pads now removed and the caliper placed out of the way the two bolts securing the yoke to the stub axle can now be removed

3.2 Front brake caliper block and yoke assembly

3.4 The caliper block wedges and retaining cotter pins

3.5A Removing the caliper block wedges

3.5B Lifting away the caliper block

3.6A Pads ready for removal

3.6B The pad anti-vibration springs

3.8 A badly worn brake pad. Note the cracks on the two friction surfaces

4.3 The hydraulic hose union at the front caliper. Note the location of the bleed nipple

and the yoke lifted away.

10 The brake anti-rattle springs should be removed and the yoke brushed clean. Renew the yoke only if cracks or serious wear is found.

11 Refitting is the reverse of removal, but remember to use new lock washers and to tighten the securing bolts to the recommended torque wrench settings as detailed at the beginning of this Chapter.

5 Front brake caliper - overhaul

1 Once the caliper block has been removed as described in Section 4 the next problem is to extract the slave piston so that the fluid seals may be removed and all components cleaned for inspection. Some times the piston may be a smooth enough fit in the bore within the caliper block to be pulled out directly. Very often however, the piston will need persuading out by force exerted by a supply of high pressure air or hydraulic fluid into the caliper block under pressure. The latter is described here as it is a technique which does not require special equipment.

2 Temporarily reconnect the caliper block to the vehicle brake system and bleed the line to the block. Having bled the line, continue to pump the brake pedal to push the large piston in the caliper block out of its cylinder. It is as well to have an old tray beneath the area of work to catch any brake fluid spilt.

3 Once the piston protrudes a half inch or so it may be pulled out with your fingers. Once the piston has been removed, disconnect the caliper block and flexible hose and transfer all the components to a clean bench for cleaning, inspection and reassembly.

4 Remove the dust seal and 'O. ring seal from the bore in the caliper block using a plastic knitting needle or similar. Take care not to scratch the surface of the bore.

5 Wash all the components in Girling Cleaning Fluid or methylated spirit. Do not use any other cleaning fluid because traces will damage the seals and contaminate the hydraulic fluid when the block is reassembled.

6 Inspect the caliper bore and piston for scoring and wear, renew the whole caliper block assembly if such wear is found.

7 To reassemble the caliper, wet the new 'O' ring seal with new brake fluid and carefully insert it into its groove near the rim of the bore in

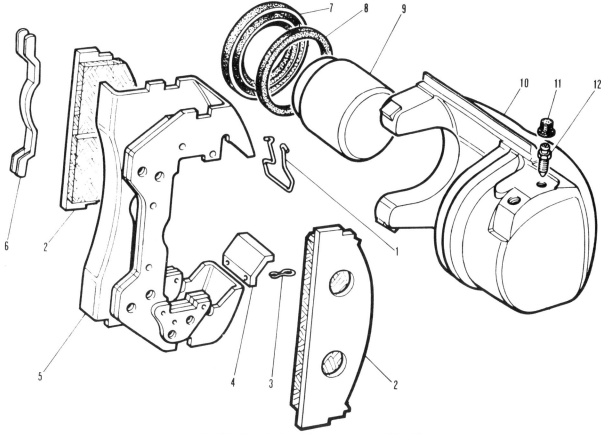

Fig. 9.2. Front brake caliper components (Sec. 5)

1	Caliper block positioning spring	4	Caliper block wedge
2	Disc pad	5	Caliper yoke
3	Cotter pin	6	Anti-vibration spring

7	Dust shield	10	Caliper block
8	Seal	11	Bleed nipple dust cap
9	Piston	12	Bleed nipple

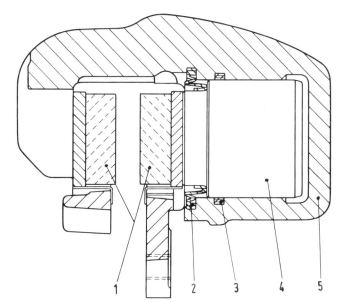

Fig. 9.3. A sectioned view of the front brake caliper block assembly (Sec. 5)

1	Disc pads	4	Piston
2	Dust shield	5	Caliper block
3	Piston seal		

the caliper.

8 Then refit the new dust seal onto its seating at the rim of the bore in the caliper. Coat the side of the piston with hydraulic fluid and carefully insert it into the bore in the caliper, until it protrudes by about one half inch. Fit the dust seal onto the top of the piston and then push the piston into the bore as far as it will go.

9 The caliper block is ready to be refitted to the brake assembly.

6 Discs - inspection and renovation

1 Discs do not last forever. However, under ideal conditions and with proper and regular maintenance of caliper pistons and brake pads they will last a long time. Under other circumstances they can warp, wear irregularly, become rusted and pitted, develop score lines and as a result provide poor braking and short pad life. Remember, disc brakes are only better than drums if they are in good condition.

2 A disc in good condition should have a smooth, shiny bright surface on the pad contact area. A deteriorated disc cannot be renovated by the burnishing effect of new pads. Another fault a disc may have, even though the surfaces are good, is warp (or run-out). This means that it does not run true. If bad it can be seen when the wheel is spun. To accurately measure the amount of run-out a clock gauge pointer should be set against one face. The actual limit of run-out is given at the beginning of this Chapter. If you do not possess a clock gauge it is worth holding a steel pointer firmly on a nearby support with the point up to the disc face. Variations can be detected quite easily in this way. Remember wheel bearings must not have any endfloat in order to check disc run-out. Worn or badly adjusted wheel bearings can be a contributory factor to disc deterioration.

3 Disc removal for renewal or machining is described in Section 7 of this Chapter. Remember also that the thickness of the disc should not

be less than the minimum thickness given at the beginning of this Chapter. If it is very deeply scored or pitted, or the run-out is excessive the only remedy is to buy a new one. If the disc is too thin it loses some of its ability to dissipate the heat generated by braking and also its rigidity.

7 Discs - removal and refitting

1 Carry out the dismantling sequences as laid out in Sections 3 and 4 of this Chapter.
2 Remove the two screws holding the retaining plate and disc to the hub and then pull off the disc (photos).
3 Refitting is a direct reversal of the dismantling procedure.

8 Rear drum and brake shoes - removal, inspection and refitting

1 Chock the front wheels.
2 Jack up the rear of the car until the roadwheels are clear of the ground.
3 Support the car on axle stands or strong wooden blocks. Never rely on the jack as being the sole method of supporting the vehicle.
4 Remove the roadwheels and release the handbrake.
5 Remove the two studs which secure the drum to the axle shaft and pull the drum off (photos).
6 If the drum is tight use a soft-faced hammer and tap the outer periphery of the drum evenly whilst rotating it.
7 When the drum has been removed it can be inspected for cracks, ovality (out of round) and scoring. Cracks and scoring can be readily seen but ovality must be measured with internal calipers. Measurements for ovality should be taken at two points at 90° to each other.
8 The brake drum can be machined to remove ovality or score marks but if deep cracks are present the drum must be renewed. As in the case of the brake disc the drum can only be machined to a certain size (see the Specifications Section of this Chapter).
9 With the drum removed inspection of the linings can take place.

10 Check first that the linings are not contaminated with oil or brake fluid. If the linings are contaminated they should be renewed and the source of contamination rectified.
11 The lining wear thickness should also be checked and if the linings have worn down to a thickness of or near to 0.059 in (1.5 mm) they should be renewed. This thickness measurement is taken from the lining face to the top of the rivets or in the case of bonded linings to the shoe.
12 To remove the brake shoes, first remove the upper shoe return spring using pliers and a screwdriver (arrowed in photo).
13 Disconnect the handbrake cable end from the rear lever arm.
14 Using a hollow rod of a suitable diameter release the two shoe retainer springs. The method of releasing the springs is to press the springs downwards and at the same time tip the rod slightly to release the spring.
15 Swing the forward lever arm back against the hub after tapping the toothed quadrant to release it.
16 Ease the brake shoes away from the wheel cylinder. Have ready a strong rubber band to wrap around the wheel cylinder to restrain the pistons from travelling outwards under the force of the spring which lies between them.
17 With the brake shoes tipped outwards pull the reaction link away from the leading shoe.
18 Reset the toothed quadrant in its initial setting position against the forward link arm.
19 Now tilt the leading brake shoe through 90° and remove the lower shoe return spring with a screwdriver (arrowed in photo).
20 The brake shoes can now be lifted from the backplate.
21 If new brake shoes are to be fitted the two lever arms and toothed quadrant must be removed and transferred to the new brake shoes after inspecting them for wear.
22 The quadrant and its spring are held in position by a special retaining fastener which can be levered carefully off.
23 Refitting the shoes is the reverse of the dismantling procedure.
24 To install the shoe retainer springs in their backplate mounting holes press them inwards and turn them through 90°.
25 Finally, before refitting the brake drum it is essential to check the

7.2A Taking off the disc retaining plate and studs

7.2B Removing the disc

8.5A Removing the studs securing the brake drum to the axle shaft

8.5B The rear drum removed

8.12 Remove the upper shoe return spring (arrowed)

8.19 Remove the lower shoe return spring (arrowed)

Section A-A

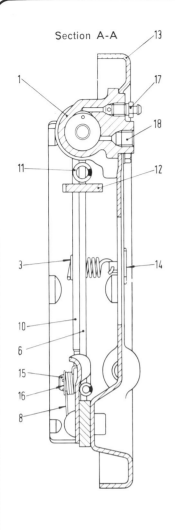

Section G-G

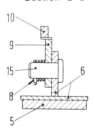

Section C-C

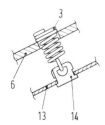

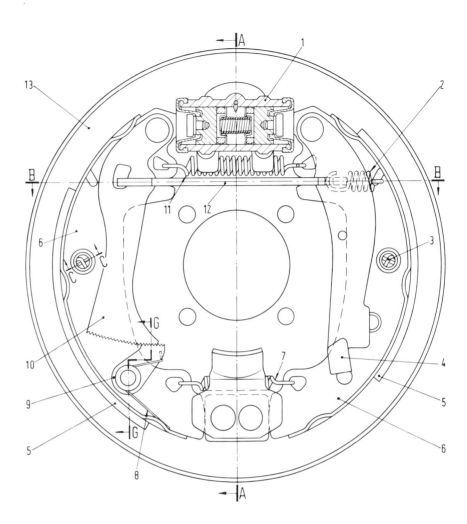

Section B-B

H = .039 to .047 in (1 to 1.2 mm)

Fig. 9.4. Sectioned views of the rear brake components (Sec. 8)

1 Wheel cylinder
2 Tension spring
3 Shoe retainer spring
4 Rear lever arm
5 Brake lining
6 Brake shoe
7 Lower shoe return spring
8 Quadrant spring
9 Toothed quadrant

10 Front lever arm
11 Upper shoe return spring
12 Reaction link
13 Backplate
14 Shoe retainer spring clip
15 Locating pin for quadrant spring
16 Retaining fastener for spring
17 Bleed nipple
18 Brake pipe connection

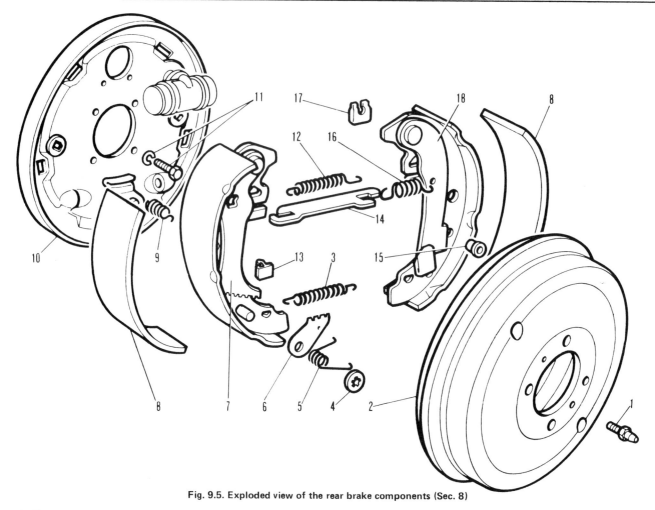

Fig. 9.5. Exploded view of the rear brake components (Sec. 8)

1	Drum retaining stud	6	Toothed quadrant
2	Drum	7	Front lever arm
3	Lower shoe return spring	8	Brake linings
4	Spring retainer	9	Shoe retainer spring
5	Toothed quadrant spring	10	Backplate

11	Bolt and washer	16	Tension spring
12	Upper shoe return spring	17	Spring clip fastener
13	Hook	18	Lever arm
14	Reaction link		
15	Plug		

initial setting of the self-adjusting mechanism.
26 Adjustment depends on the tension spring which is hooked between the link and the trailing (rear) brake shoe.
27 The tension of this spring is measured by checking the clearance between the forward edge of the link and the forward edge of the brake shoe slotted hole in which it is fitted. This clearance should be 0.039 to 0.047 in (1 to 1.2 mm)
28 If this approximate dimension is not achieved then it will be necessary to renew the tension spring and the two shoe return springs.
29 Refit the brake drum after cleaning out the brake dust and checking the drum's condition.
30 Press the brake pedal several times to centralise the brake shoes and to operate the automatic adjusters. Remember to also apply the handbrake lever to check its operation.
31 Finally, carry out a road test to ensure that the brakes operate correctly and do not pull up unevenly.

9 Rear wheel cylinder - removal, overhaul and refitting

1 Remove the drum and brake shoes as detailed in Section 8 of this Chapter.
2 Undo the metal brake pipe union at the rear of the backplate.
3 Undo the two bolts which secure the wheel cylinder to the backplate.
4 With the two bolts now removed the wheel cylinder can be lifted free.
5 Pull off the two rubber dust boots and withdraw the two hydraulic

pistons. Note the spring fitted between the pistons.
6 Inspect the bore of the wheel cylinder for score marks and pitting. If any imperfections are found then fit a new complete wheel cylinder.
7 If the cylinder is sound, thoroughly clean it with fresh brake fluid.
8 The old piston rubbers will probably be swollen or have visible score marks.
9 Remove the seal from each piston noting which way round it is installed.
10 Clean the pistons with brake fluid and install the new piston rubbers having first immersed them in clean brake fluid. When installing the new piston rubbers ensure that the lips of the rubbers face inwards.
11 Insert the pistons into the wheel cylinder bore remembering to refit the spring between the pistons. Take care when installing the pistons as any excessive force applied to the pistons when pushing them home will roll back the lip of the rubbers.
12 Refit the rubber dust boots.
13 The cylinder can now be refitted to the backplate.
14 Finally, after the brake shoes and drums have been refitted the brakes will have to be bled.

10 Brake pipes and hoses - inspection, removal and refitting

1 From time to time it is necessary to inspect the metal pipes and flexible hoses of the hydraulic braking system. Carefully check the metal pipes which run along the rear axle, under the body and in the engine compartment for damage or corrosion. Pipes showing any of the above defects should be renewed immediately. Fig. 9.1 shows

the general layout and location of the brake components.

2   Carefully inspect the three flexible hydraulic hoses. There is one flexible hose from a three-way block connector on the rear axle to the body. The remaining two hoses are mounted from the body unions to the front brake calipers.

3   If any section of the pipe line is to be removed, first of all take the fluid reservoir cap off and lay a thin piece of polythene over the top of the reservoir and refit the cap. This greatly reduces the loss of fluid when pipes or hoses are disconnected.

4   Rigid pipe removal is straightforward. The unions at each end are undone, the pipe and union pulled out, and the centre section of the pipe removed from the body clips where necessary. New complete metal pipes with unions can be purchased from a FIAT dealer or alternatively a pipe can be made up using special flaring and bending tools by a garage providing they have the old pipe as a pattern.

5   The rear flexible hose can be removed by releasing the rigid pipe from the union where it is joined at the body end. Holding a spanner on the hexagon formed on the pipe at the body end remove the two locknuts which secure the pipe to the body bracket. Slacken the hose from the three-way block connector on the rear axle and remove the hose.

6   The front flexible hoses are joined between the calipers and the metal pipes at the inner wing panel by a union (photo). The caliper end of the flexible pipe is formed into a banjo type union secured by a union bolt and an additional locking plate is provided to locate the hose. The hose can be released from the caliper by removing the two bolts mentioned. At the other end of the pipe the connection is similar to the rear flexible pipe unions.

7   Refitting of the pipes and hoses is a reversal of the dismantling procedure. Remember that the polythene must be removed from under the master cylinder reservoir cap and the brakes will have to be bled as described in Section 2 of this Chapter.

10.6 The front hydraulic hose union at the inner wing panel

11 Rear brake backplate - removal and refitting

1   Remove the brake shoes following the dismantling procedures detailed in Section 8 of this Chapter.

2   With the brake shoes removed, release the brake pipe from the union at the rear of the backplate having first placed a thin piece of polythene under the cap of the master cylinder reservoir.

3   Release the handbrake cable from the backplate as detailed in Section 16 of this Chapter.

4   Remove the four bolts which retain the axle shaft and draw the shaft out from the axle as detailed in Chapter 8, Section 2.

5   The four bolts which secure the axle shaft retaining plate also hold the backplate to the axle casing. The backplate can now be removed.

6   Refitting is a reversal of the dismantling procedure except that the brakes will have to be bled as detailed in Section 2 of this Chapter.

12 Brake pressure regulating valve - removal, overhaul, refitting and adjustment

1   As mentioned in the introduction a special valve is fitted into the rear brake hydraulic pipe line. This unit is bolted to a chassis mounting bracket which also locates the front mounting of the lower trailing arm. The unit consists of a plunger in a housing which, when released, reduces the pressure on the outlet side of the valve. The plunger is held in place by a control rod and a pivot pin. The control rod has incorporated in its length a spring coil and the rod is mounted at its lower end to the rear axle by a bracket. When the distance between the body and axle increases, as it would under sharp braking causing tail up attitude, the control rod lets the plunger out and braking pressure to the rear wheels is reduced. This prevents rear wheel lock-up and consequent skidding.

2   Before removing the unit from the car place a piece of thin polythene between the master cylinder and its cap.

3   Disconnect the two brake pipes from the regulator valve.

4   Remove the two bolts which secure the valve to its chassis mounting.

5   Lift the valve down from its mounting and draw it forward thus releasing the attached control rod from its axle locating bracket.

6   The control rod and valve, now free from the vehicle, can be dismantled.

7   Slide the rubber boot back down the control rod and remove the screw which locates the control rod in the pivot pin.

8   The control rod with rubber boot attached can now be removed. The valve block is now ready for dismantling.

9   Unscrew and remove the large end plug complete with its sealing washer.

10 Remove the bush, plunger, primary seal, large spring cup, spring, small spring cup and, finally, the secondary seal.

11 Clean all components with Castrol Cleaning Fluid or methylated spirit and wipe dry with a non-fluffy rag.

12 Inspect the seals, plunger shank and regulator bores for wear and surface deterioration. If only the seals are worn, renew the seals and reassemble the regulator. If the regulator or plunger bores are worn the regulator must be renewed as a complete assembly.

13 Reassembly of the regulator follows the reversal of the dismantling procedure, except that the primary and secondary seals should be dipped in clean brake fluid before they are refitted. It is advisable to

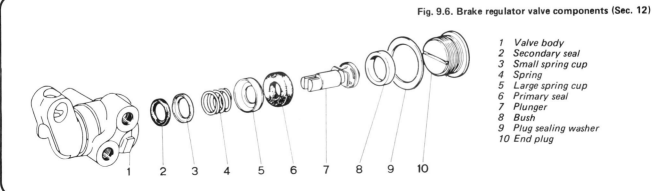

Fig. 9.6. Brake regulator valve components (Sec. 12)

1   Valve body
2   Secondary seal
3   Small spring cup
4   Spring
5   Large spring cup
6   Primary seal
7   Plunger
8   Bush
9   Plug sealing washer
10 End plug

10 Grommet

11 Point of fitting bump stop

X Distance between bar 7 (when free from bracket) and fitting
point for bump stop:

Saloon   X = 13.346 in (339 mm)

Estate Car   X = 12.874 ± 0.197 in (327 ± 5 mm)

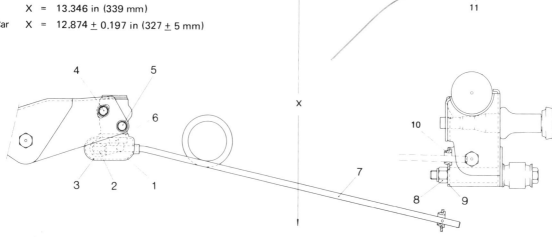

Fig. 9.7. Brake pressure regulator valve, layout and mounting (Sec. 12)

1 Control rod	4 Slotted adjustment point	7 Control rod locating bracket
2 Pivot pin	5 Fixed mounting point	8 Distance at which control rod plunger is set
3 Rubber boot	6 Plunger	9 Bump stop mounting point on bodyshell

fit a new plug seal washer on each occasion the regulator is reassembled.

14 Rejoin the control rod and pivot pin leaving the rubber boot on the
control rod.

15 The reassembled unit can now be refitted to the vehicle but only
secure the two locating bolts finger tight.

16 Do not relocate the lower end of the control rod in its bracket.

17 Slacken the nut holding the lower mounting bracket and swing it
down out of the way.

18 Remove the rubber bump stop situated directly above the axle. It
is between this mounting point and the end of the control rod that a
given measurement is made when adjusting the valve plunger and rod.
Check the measurements given at the beginning of this Chapter. The
dimensions vary between saloon and estate models.

19 Use either FIAT tool A.72265 or a piece of wood cut to the
dimension given in Specifications at the beginning of the Chapter,
placed between the bump stop mounting and the lower end of the
control rod.

20 Now with the FIAT tool or its substitute in place the regulator
valve can be adjusted.

21 One of the regulator valve mounting holes is elongated. This allows
the valve assembly to be tipped and will allow the control rod to vary
its pressure on the regulator valve plunger.

22 Turn the regulator valve assembly until the control rod rests lightly
on the plunger.

23 Tighten the two mounting bolts and refit the rubber boot.

24 Remove the FIAT tool or substitute and refit the rubber bump stop.

25 The control rod can be refitted into the lower mounting bracket
and the bracket secured.

26 Reconnect the metal brake pipes and bleed the system as detailed
in Section 2 of this Chapter. All securing nuts and bolts should be
tightened to the torque wrench settings as given at the beginning of
this Chapter.

13 Hydraulic master cylinder - removal and refitting

1   Drain the master cylinder and reservoir of fluid. This can be
achieved by pumping out the brake fluid through one of the front and
rear bleed nipples. Use a bleed tube and catch the fluid in a suitable
receptacle. Note that on USA models the master cylinder reservoir is
not mounted on top of the master cylinder (photo).

2   The master cylinder is fitted with two pistons fed from separate
halves of the fluid reservoir. One piston supplies the front brakes while
the other supplies the rear. Each system is independent of the other.

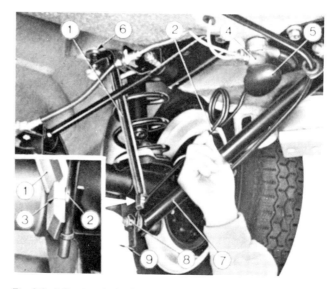

Fig. 9.8. Adjusting the brake pressure regulator valve with FIAT
tool (Sec. 12)

1 FIAT tool A72265	6 Rubber bump stop mounting
2 Control rod	7 Left-hand trailing arm
3 Measurement markings	8 Locknut
4 Brake regulator	9 Control rod locating bracket
5 Rubber boot	

3   Having covered the reservoir with polythene, remove the two feed
pipes to the master cylinder from the reservoir.

4   Undo the metal outlet feed pipe connections at the master cylinder
and pull them back a little to clear the master cylinder when it is
removed.

5   On USA models there is a four-way block connector which is
secured to the master cylinder bracket by a single nut and bolt (photo).
Pull off the wire connection at the brake low pressure warning switch
and disconnect the metal pipe connections.

6   Finally, undo and remove the two nuts securing the master cylinder
to the vacuum servo unit.

7   On British models, remove the heat shield and on USA models

remove the four-way connector bracket.

8   Now pull the master cylinder out and lift it away to a clean bench for inspection and overhaul. When lifting the master cylinder out from the engine compartment wrap it in a clean rag to prevent any brake fluid dripping out onto the paintwork. Brake fluid is highly corrosive.

9   Refitting the master cylinder is the reverse of the removal procedure except that after installation the whole braking system must be bled as detailed in Section 2 of this Chapter.

14 Hydraulic master cylinder - inspection and overhaul

1   Remove the master cylinder as detailed in Section 13 of this

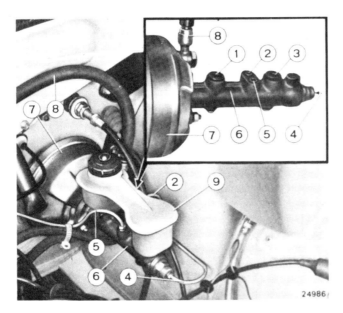

Fig. 9.9. Typical layout of the brake master cylinder mounting and pipes (Sec. 13)

1 Feed from reservoir to master cylinder for front brakes
2 Outlet port to left-hand front brake line
3 Feed from reservoir to master cylinder for rear brakes
4 Outlet port for rear brake line
5 Outlet port for right-hand front brake line
6 Master cylinder body
7 Brake servo (master/vac) unit
8 Flexible vacuum hose from inlet manifold

9 Reservoir

Chapter.

2   With the cylinder out on a clean bench lightly hold the cylinder in a vice and undo the front union nut.

3   Remove the two locating bolts which are directly under the cylinder body. These bolts project through the body into the cylinder bore and act as guides for the pistons.

4   The pistons, seals, cups and springs may now be pushed out of the cylinder from the rear end (Fig. 9.10).

5   Lay the parts out in the order in which they were removed.

6   Separate all the springs, seals, cups and springs.

7   Clean all the components with Castrol Girling Cleaning fluid or methylated spirit. Examine the master cylinder bore and the pistons for scores or wear. If either is found, then the whole master cylinder assembly must be renewed.

8   When all parts have been cleaned, gather them together for reassembly. Do not re-use seals, always obtain new ones.

9   Begin reassembly by soaking the new seals in brake fluid before fitting the secondary seals onto the rear ends of each piston. Then fit the primary seal cups and the primary seals onto their seating on the forward end of each piston. Make sure the primary seals are correctly aligned with the fine lips towards the forward end of the piston.

10 Now refit the pistons and springs in the reverse order to the dismantling procedure. Take care that the two guide bolts are located in the piston cut-out groove.

11 Reconnect the master cylinder to the vehicle as described in Section 13 of this Chapter.

15 Brake vacuum servo (master/vac) unit - removal and refitting

1   Remove the master cylinder as detailed in Section 13 of this Chapter (Figs. 9.11 and 9.12).

2   Now slacken the hose clip and remove the vacuum hose from its manifold union.

3   Remove the split pin retaining the brake pedal clevis pin and draw the clevis pin out.

4   Undo and remove the four nuts securing the servo unit to the bulkhead. Access to these nuts can be gained from within the car.

5   The servo unit can now be lifted away from the bulkhead.

6   Refitting the brake servo unit follows the reversal of the removal procedure. Remember to use new spring washers and tighten the nuts and bolts to their appropriate torque wrench setting.

16 Brake servo unit - air filter renewal

1   Under normal operating conditions the servo unit is very reliable and does not require overhaul except possibly at very high mileages. In this case it is better to obtain a service exchange unit, rather than repair the original.

13.1 The master cylinder fluid reservoir (USA models)

The four-way block connector and bracket (USA models)

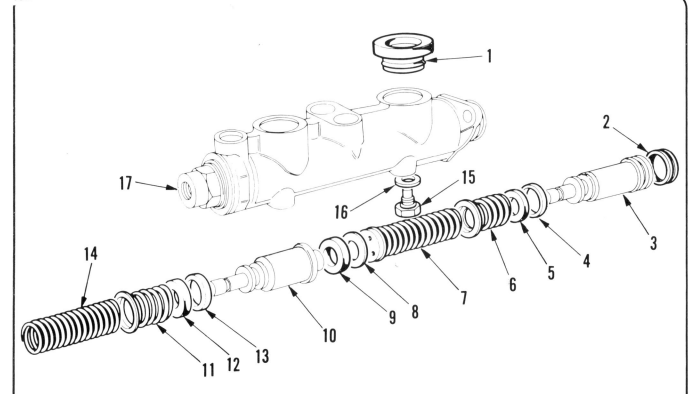

Fig. 9.10. Brake master cylinder - components (Sec. 14)

1 Reservoir connector
2 Rear seal
3 Rear piston
4 Spacer
5 Seal
6 Short spring and retaining cup
7 Long spring and cup
8 Washer
9 Seal
10 Front piston
11 Short spring
12 Seal
13 Spacer
14 Long spring
15 Locating plug
16 Gasket
17 Rear brake outlet port

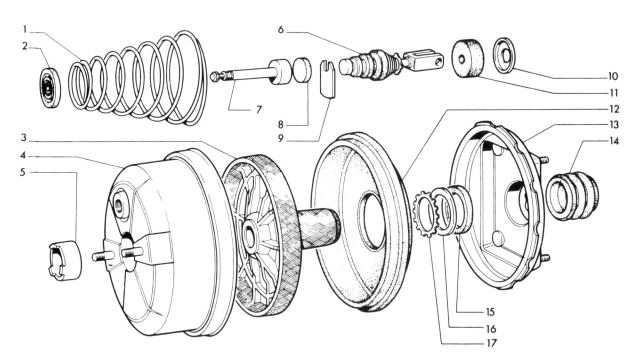

Fig. 9.11. Vacuum servo component parts (Sec. 15)

1 Diaphragm piston return spring
2 Seal
3 Diaphragm support
4 Cover
5 Seal retainer
6 Pushrod
7 Piston
8 Seal
9 Lockplate
10 Retainer
11 Air filter
12 Diaphragm
13 Backplate
14 Rubber boot
15 Seal
16 Washer
17 Retaining ring

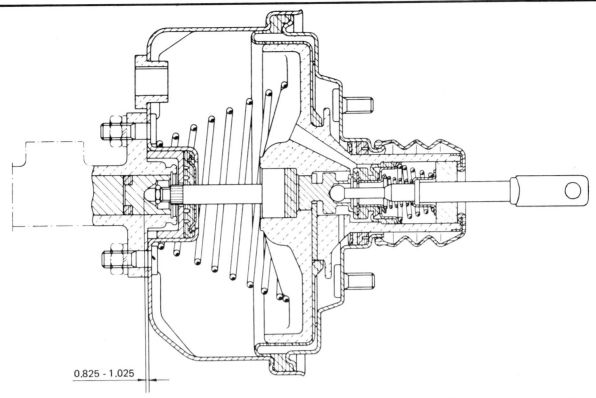

0.825 - 1.025

Fig. 9.12. Vacuum servo unit - assembled cross section indicating the piston rod protrusion from the cover face (Sec. 15)

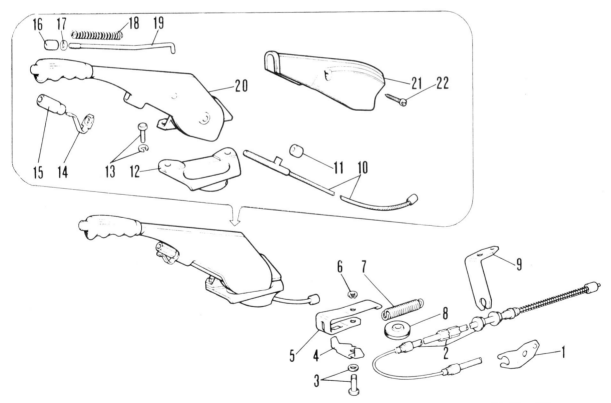

Fig. 9.13. Exploded view of the handbrake lever and forward end of the rear handbrake cable (Sec. 17)

1 Cable bracket	6 Spring clip	11 Spacer	17 Rubber ring
2 Rear adjuster	7 Return spring	12 Shield	18 Spring
3 Washer	8 Pulley	13 Bolt and spring washer	19 Release rod
4 Plate	9 Bracket	14 Front cable adjuster nut	20 Lever assembly
5 Pulley bracket	10 Front cable	lock plate	21 Shroud
		15 Front cable adjuster nut	22 Screw
		16 Release button	

2 However, the air filter may need renewal and fitting details are given below.
3 Remove the brake and clutch pedals as described in Section 18 of this Chapter.
4 Working inside the car in the driver's foot well, push back the dust cover from the pushrod and control valve housing to expose the end cap and the air filter element.
5 Using a screwdriver ease out the end cap and then with a pair of scissors cut out the air filter.
6 Make a diagonal cut through the new air filter and push the air filter over the pushrod. Hold the filter in position and refit the end cap.
7 Now pull back the dust cover over the unit body and refit the pedal assembly.

17 Handbrake cable - removal, refitting and adjustment

1 Remove the rear drums, release the cable ends from the rear lever arms and remove the brake shoes as detailed in Section 8 of this Chapter (photo).
2 The outer cable is retained in the backplate allowing a tight fitting tolerance. Take care when removing the outer cable to prevent damaging the backplate and outer cable end casing.
3 The rear cable is a one piece assembly and is restrained at its forward end by a pulley wheel which in turn is connected to the pulley support bracket and front handbrake cable.
4 Remove the cable return spring.
5 Slacken the front cable adjustment, by turning the adjusting nut at the handbrake lever in an anti-clockwise direction, until the front cable can be slipped out from the pulley support bracket.
6 The outer handbrake cable can now be released from the foward location bracket.
7 The rear cable, complete with pulley and bracket, can now be drawn forward through the retaining eyelets welded to the lower trailing arms and their attachment points.
8 Remove the bolt through the pulley and its supporting bracket.
9 The rear cable is now free, ready for inspection.
10 Refitting is a direct reversal of the dismantling procedure, but certain points must be observed.
11 Take care when fitting the outer cable into the backplate. A suitable length of tube, cut axially down the middle for a few inches, makes an ideal drift for installing the cable squarely into the backplate.
12 Before adjusting the cable check that the automatic brake adjustment is functioning correctly. Excessive pedal travel will indicate if the shoes are adjusted correctly.
13 Pull the handbrake lever on three notches. With the handbrake in this position adjust the handbrake cable until the rear wheels lock.
14 Release the handbrake lever and ensure that the rear wheels turn freely without binding.

18 Brake and clutch pedal assembly - removal, renovation and refitting

1 The brake and clutch pedals are mounted on a channel member

17.1 The cable fixing point to the rear lever arm (arrowed)

which is bolted through the bulkhead.
2 The pedals themselves pivot on bushes running on a common long bolt which passes from one side of the channel to the other.
3 It is not necessary to disturb the channel member when removing either clutch or brake pedal.
4 Begin removal of either pedal by removing the return spring acting on the clutch release lever arm, which is situated under the car by the gearbox.
5 Remove the return springs situated immediately above the clutch and brake pedals.
6 Undo and remove the nut on the end of the long bolt and then draw the bolt from the channel.
7 Remove the spring retainer clip securing the eye fixing of the clutch cable to the clutch pedal stub. Release the cable and lift the pedal clear.
8 Removal of the brake pedal necessitates the disconnection of a split pin and clevis pin which join the pedal and servo unit together via a pushrod and yoke attachment.
9 Once the pedals are free, an inspection can be made of the bolt, bushes and spacers. If the bushes are worn and oval, renew them.
10 The brake pushrod and clevis pin are available as individual spares and therefore both should be inspected for wear.
11 The reassembly procedure is the reversal of the dismantling procedure, except that it is as well to check the clutch pedal free travel as described in Chapter 5 if the pedal assembly has been repaired. Also check the operation of the brake light switch which is mounted adjacent to the brake pedal pivot.

19 Fault diagnosis - braking system

Symptom	Reason/s
Pedal travels almost to floor before brakes operate	Brake fluid level too low. Wheel cylinder leaking. Caliper leaking. Master cylinder leaking (bubbles in master cylinder fluid). Brake flexible hose leaking. Brake line fractured. Brake system unions loose. Rear automatic adjusters seized.
Brake feels 'springy'	New linings not yet bedded in. Brake discs or drums badly worn or cracked.
Brake pedal feels 'spongy' and 'soggy'	Wheel cylinder leaking. Master cylinder leaking (bubbles in master cylinder fluid). Brake pipe line or flexible hose leaking. Unions in brake system loose. Air in hydraulic system.
Excessive effort required to brake car	Pad or shoe linings badly worn. New pads or shoes recently fitted - not yet bedded in. Harder linings than standard causing increase in pedal pressure. Linings and brake drum contaminated with oil, grease or hydraulic fluid. Servo unit inoperative or faulty. One half of dual brake system inoperative.
Brakes uneven and pulling to one side	Linings and discs or drums contaminated with oil, grease or hydraulic fluid. Tyre pressures unequal. Radial ply tyres fitted at one end of the car only. Brake caliper loose. Brake pads or shoes fitted incorrectly. Different types of linings fitted at each wheel. Anchorages for front or rear suspension loose. Brake discs or drums badly worn, cracked or distorted.
Brakes tend to bind, drag or lock-on	Air in hydraulic system. Wheel cylinders seized. Handbrake cable too tight. Servo piston rod clearance insufficient. Master cylinder seized.

Chapter 10 Electrical system

For modifications, and information applicable to later models, see Supplement at end of manual

Contents

Specifications

System type	12 volt, negative earth	
Battery	45 amp hr at 20 hr rate	

Alternator

Type:

Air conditioned models only	Marelli A124-14V-60A	
Other cars	Marelli A124-14V-44A	
	60A	**44A**
Max output (watts)	1000	770
Max current output (amps)	70	53
Drive ratio, engine to alternator	1 to 2	
Field winding resistance at 20°C (ohms)	2.6 ± 0.05	4.3 ± 0.2

Voltage regulator

Type	RC2/12E	RC2/12D
Alternator speed for testing (rpm)	5000	
Control voltage (volts)	13.9 - 14.5	

Starter motor

Type:

1300 engine	FIAT E84-0, 8-12, VAR 5	
1600 and 1800 engine	FIAT E100-1, 3/12, VAR 8	
	E84	**E100**
Output (kw)	0.8	1.3
Armature endfloat	0.004 - 0.020 in (0.1 - 0.5 mm)	0.006 - 0.027 in (0.15 - 0.70 mm)
Minimum commutator thickness	0.020 - 0.027 in (0.5 - 0.7 mm)	
Brush spring pressure (new brushes)	2.53 - 2.86 lbs	1.98 - 2.42 lbs

Fuses (UK models)

	Circuits protected
No 1 (8 amps)	Reverse light, stop light, direction indicators and W/L, water temperature gauge, fuel gauge and W/L, oil pressure W/L, heater fan, panel switch light guide cable clamp*, heater dial lamp*
No 2 (8 amps)	Windscreen wiper, windscreen washer pump
No 3 (8 amps)	RH side light, LH rear light
No 4 (8 amps)	LH side light, RH rear light, number plate light, cigar lighter light, panel lights, side light W/L*
No 5 (8 amps)	LH dipped beam
No 6 (8 amps)	RH dipped beam
No 7 (16 amps)	RH outer main beam*, LH inner main beam*

No 8 (16 amps) ...	...	...	...	...	...	...	...	...	RH inner main beam*, LH outer main beam*, LH main beam, headlamp W/L
No 9 (16 amps) ...	...	...	...	...	...	...	...	...	Horn/horn relay, radiator fan
No 10 (16 amps) ...	...	...	...	...	...	...	...	...	Courtesy/interior lights, cigar lighter, clock
No 11 (16 amps) ...	...	...	...	...	...	...	...	...	Heated rear screen (option)
No 12 (16 amps) ...	...	...	...	...	...	...	...	...	Air conditioner compressor fan and heater (option)
No 13 (16 amps) ...	...	...	...	...	...	...	...	...	Air conditioner condenser cooling fan (option)

* 131 'special' model

Bulbs (UK models)

Headlamps

131 'Basic' model ...	...	...	...	...	...	...	...	Double contact 40/45W
131 'Special':								
Outer lamps ...	...	...	...	...	...	...	...	Double contact 40/45W
Inner lamps ...	...	...	...	...	...	...	...	Single contact 45W

Side/direction indicator lamps

| Direction indicator bulb | ... | ... | ... | ... | ... | ... | ... | 21W |
| Side light bulb ... | ... | ... | ... | ... | ... | ... | ... | 5W |

Repeater lamps

| Tubular type bulb ... | ... | ... | ... | ... | ... | ... | ... | 4W |

Rear light cluster

Direction indicator bulb	...	...	...	...	...	...	...	21W
Rear light bulb ...	...	...	...	...	...	...	...	5W
Stop light bulb ...	...	...	...	...	...	...	...	21W
Reversing light bulb ...	...	...	...	...	...	...	21W
Number plate lamp bulb ...	...	...	...	...	...	...	5W
Rear interior bulbs ...	...	...	...	...	...	...	4W
Heater dial bulb	...	...	...	...	...	...	1.2W
Panel switch light guide cable bulb ...	...	...	...	...	...	3W
Cigar lighter bulb ...	...	...	...	...	...	...	4W
Courtesy light bulb ...	...	...	...	...	...	...	5W
Instrument panel bulbs ...	...	...	...	...	...	...	3W
All warning light bulbs ...	...	...	...	...	...	...	3W

Fuses (USA models)

No 1 (8 amps) ...	...	...	...	...	...	...	...	Stop lights, reverse lights, brake system effectiveness and handbrake 'ON' indicator, direction indicators and W/L, fuel gauge with reserve W/L, water temperature gauge, oil pressure W/L, fasten seat belts indicator, heater fan motor, fasten belts buzzer and electronic control unit (AC cars only), temperature electronic control unit, 25,000 miles EGR and Catalyst W/L, Slow Down W/L, EGR indicator relay winding, Catalytic converter control system, odometer switch, idle stop solenoid, fast idle electrovalve, starter interlock relay (auto trans), electrovalve for diverter valve
No 2 (10 amps) ...	...	...	...	...	...	...	...	Windscreen wiper, windscreen washer pump
No 3 (10 amps) ...	...	...	...	...	...	...	...	LH rear tail light, RH front side light, RH front side marker light, LH rear side marker light
No 4 (8 amps) ...	...	...	...	...	...	...	...	LH front side light, RH rear light, number plate light, cigar lighter housing indicator, panel illumination lights, ideogram illumination light
No 5 (8 amps) ...	...	...	...	...	...	...	...	LH outer headlight - dipped beam
No 6 (8 amps) ...	...	...	...	...	...	...	...	RH outer headlight - dipped beam
No 7 (16 amps) ...	...	...	...	...	...	...	...	Inner headlights - main beams
No 8 (16 amps) ...	...	...	...	...	...	...	...	Outer headlights - main beams, main beam indicator light
No 9 (16 amps) ...	...	...	...	...	...	...	...	Horns, horn relay, engine cooling fan motor
No 10 (16 amps) ...	...	...	...	...	...	...	...	Clock, courtesy lights, cigar lighter
No 11 (16 amps) ...	...	...	...	...	...	...	...	Rear window demister
No 12 (16 amps) ...	...	...	...	...	...	...	...	Air conditioner compressor and evaporator fan (where applicable)
No 13 (16 amps) ...	...	...	...	...	...	...	...	Remove key warning buzzer, seat belt electronic control unit
No 14 (8 amps) ...	...	...	...	...	...	...	...	Fuel pump

In separate holder (3 amp) for EGR warning system

Bulbs (USA models)

Headlamps

| Outer lamps ... | ... | ... | ... | ... | ... | ... | ... | ... | Sealed beam double filament 4002 |
| Inner lamps ... | ... | ... | ... | ... | ... | ... | ... | ... | Sealed beam single filament 4001 |

Front lamps

| Direction indicator bulb | ... | ... | ... | ... | ... | ... | ... | 1034 (3/32CP) |
| Side light bulb ... | ... | ... | ... | ... | ... | ... | ... | 158 (2CP) |

Rear lamps

Direction indicator bulb	...	...	...	...	...	...	...	1073 (32CP)
Stop light bulb ...	...	...	...	...	...	...	...	1073 (32CP)
Reverse light bulb ...	...	...	...	...	...	...	1073 (32CP)
Number plate light bulb ...	...	...	...	...	...	...	67 (4CP)
Tail light bulb ...	...	...	...	...	...	...	...	67 (4CP)

Courtesy lights

Centre	12V-5W
Left and right	12V-5W
Ideogram illumination	12V-5W
Automatic transmission panel	158 (2CP)
All indicator and warning lights	158 (2CP)
Side marker lights	158 (2CP)
Glove compartment	12V-4W
Cigar lighter housing	12V-4W
Centre control panel	12V-1.2W

1 General description

The electrical system is of the 12 volt type and the major components comprise a battery of which the negative terminal is earthed, a Marelli alternator which is fitted to the front left-hand side of the engine and driven from the pulley on the front of the crankshaft, and a starter motor which is mounted on the rear left-hand side of the engine.

The battery supplies current for the ignition, lighting and other electrical circuits, and provides a reserve of electricity when the current consumed by the electrical equipment exceeds that being produced by the alternator. Normally an alternator is able to meet any demand placed upon it.

When fitting any electrical accessories to cars with a negative earth system, it is important, if they contain silicon diodes or transistors, that they are connected correctly, otherwise serious damage may result to the component concerned. Items such as radios, tape recorders, electronic tachometers, parking lights and automatic dipping should all be checked for correct polarity (earthing).

It is important that the battery leads are always disconnected if the battery is to be boost charged, or if any body or mechanical repairs are to be carried out using electric arc welding equipment, otherwise damage can be caused to the more delicate instruments, specially those containing semi-conductors.

2 Battery - removal and refitting

1 The battery is situated on the right-hand side of the engine compartment, and is held in place by a single bolt and clamping plate at its base.

2 To remove the battery begin by disconnecting the negative (−) earth lead from the battery terminal. Then disconnect the positive (+) live lead from the other battery terminal.

3 Once the leads have been removed, unscrew the single retaining bolt and remove the clamping plate.

4 Lift the battery carefully from its seating in the bodyshell, taking great care not to spill any of the highly corrosive electrolyte.

5 Any corrosion deposits on the leads or terminal posts can be removed by applying a washing soda solution.

6 Refitting the battery is the reverse of the removal procedure. Refit the positive lead first and smear the clean posts and lead clamp assembly with petroleum jelly (Vaseline) in order to prevent corrosion. **Do Not Use Ordinary Grease.**

3 Battery - maintenance and inspection

1 Check the battery electrolyte level weekly by lifting off the cover or removing the individual cell plugs. The tops of the plates should be just covered with the liquid. If not, add distilled water so that they are just covered. Do not add extra water with the idea of reducing the intervals of topping up. This will merely dilute the electrolyte and reduce charging and current retention efficiency. On batteries fitted with patent covers, troughs, glass balls and so on, follow the instructions marked on the cover of the battery to ensure correct addition of water.

2 Keep the battery clean and dry all over by wiping it with a dry cloth. A damp top surface could cause tracking between the two terminal posts with consequent draining of power.

3 Every three months remove the battery and check the support tray clamp and battery terminal connections for signs of corrosion - usually indicated by a whitish green crystalline deposit. Wash this off with clean water to which a little ammonia or washing soda has been added. Then treat the terminals with petroleum jelly and the battery mounting with suitable protective paint to prevent the metal being eaten away. Clean the battery thoroughly and repair any cracks with a proprietary sealer. If there has been any excessive leakage the appropriate cell may need an addition of electrolyte rather than just distilled water.

4 If the electrolyte level needs an excessive amount of replenishment but no leaks are apparent, it could be due to overcharging as a result of the battery having been run down and then left to recharge from the vehicle rather than an outside source. If the battery has been heavily discharged for one reason or another it is best to have it continuously charged at a low amperage for a period of many hours. If it is charged from the car's system under such conditions the charging will be intermittent and greatly varied in intensity. This does not do the battery any good at all. If the battery needs topping up frequently, even when it is known to be in good condition and not too old, then the voltage regulator should be checked to ensure that the charging output is being correctly controlled. An elderly battery, however, may need topping up more than a new one because it needs to take in more charging current. Do not worry about this provided it gives satisfactory service.

5 When checking a battery's condition a hydrometer should be used. On some batteries where the terminals of each of the six cells are exposed, a discharge tester can be used to check the condition of any one cell also. On modern batteries the use of a discharge tester is no longer regarded as useful as the renewal or repair of cells is not an economic proposition. The tables following give the hydrometer readings for various states of charge. A further check can be made when the battery is undergoing a charge. If, towards the end of the charge, when the cells are meant to be 'gassing' (bubbling), one cell appears not to be, then it indicates that the cell or cells in question are probably breaking down and the life of the battery is limited.

4 Battery - charging and electrolyte replenishment

1 It is possible that in winter when the load on the battery cannot be recuperated during normal driving time, external charging is desirable. This is best done overnight at a 'trickle' rate of 1-1.5 amps. Alternatively a 3-4 amp rate can be used over a period of four hours or so. Check the specific gravity in the latter case and stop the charge when the reading is correct. Most modern charging sets reduce the rate automatically when the fully charged state is neared. Rapid boost charges of 30-60 amps or more may get you out of trouble or can be used on a battery that has seen better days. They are not recommended for a good battery that may have run flat for some reason due to the possibility of heat buckling the plates.

2 Electrolyte replenishment should not normally be necessary unless an accident or some other cause such as contamination arises. If it is necessary then it is best first to discharge the battery completely and then tip out all the remaining liquid from all cells. Then acquire a quantity of mixed electrolyte from a battery shop or garage according to the specifications in the table. The quantity required will depend on the type of battery but three to four pints should be more than enough. When the electrolyte has been put into the battery a slow charge - not exceeding 1 amp - should be given for as long as is necessary to fully charge the battery. This could be up to 36 hours.

Specific gravities for hydrometer readings (check each cell) - with an electrolyte temperature of 60ºF (15.6ºC).

	Climate below 80ºF (26.7ºC)	Climate above 80ºF (26.7ºC)
Fully charged	*1.270 - 1.290*	*1.210 - 1.230*
Half charged	*1.190 - 1.210*	*1.120 - 1.150*
Discharged completely	*1.110 - 1.130*	*1.050 - 1.070*

Note: If the electrolyte temperature is significantly different from 60°F (15.6°C) then the specific gravity reading will be affected. For every 5°F (2.8°C) it will increase or decrease with the temperature by 0.002.

5 Alternator - general description

All the FIAT 131 models, excluding those fitted with air conditioning principally a laminated stator on which is wound a three phase nator is rated at 44 amps while the air conditioned models utilize the Marelli A124-14V-60A which is rated at 60 amps. Both alternators function in a similar way with only some constructional differences.

The alternators are of the rotating field ventilated design comprising principally of a laminated stator on which is wound a three phase output winding. In the 44 amp alternator the stator is of the 'star wound' type whereas in the 60 amp alternator the stator is of the 'delta wound' type. Each end of the rotor shaft runs in ball race bearings which are of the sealed lubricated for life type. Aluminium end brackets hold the bearings and incorporate the alternator mounting lugs. The rear bracket supports the silicon diode rectifier pack which converts AC output to DC for battery charging and output to the voltage regulator.

The rotor is belt driven from the engine through a pulley keyed to the rotor shaft. A special centrifugal action fan adjacent to the pulley draws air through the alternator. This fan forms an integral part of the alternator specification and has been designed to provide an adequate flow of air with the minimum of noise. The fan must also be able to withstand the stresses associated with the high rotational speeds of the

rotor. Rotation of the rotor is clockwise when viewed from the drive end.

The rectifier pack of silicone diodes is mounted on the inside of the rear end casing. The same mounting is utilized by the brushes which contact the slip rings on the rotor to supply the field current. The slip rings are carried on a small diameter moulded drum attached to the rotor. By keeping the circumference of the slip rings to a minimum the contact speed and therefore the brush speed is minimized.

6 Alternator - testing, removal, refitting and maintenance

1 The alternator has been designed for the minimum amount of attention during service. The only items subject to wear are the brushes and bearings.
2 If the red warning light on the instrument panel lights up indicating that the battery is no longer being charged, check the continuity of the leads to and from the alternator, voltage regulator and battery. A metal shield bolted to the rear of the alternator must be removed to inspect wiring at the alternator (photo).
3 Ensure all the connections of these leads are clean, and check for breaks in each cable by disconnecting both ends of a cable and reconnecting in series with a small battery and bulb. If the cable is complete the bulb will light up. If once the continuity checks have been completed and nothing found at fault, the alternator may be checked in situ as follows.
4 Remove the heavy brown main output cables from the alternator (photo), cover the end and stow it in a position where it will not make contact with anything metallic. Connect one end of a jumper lead from

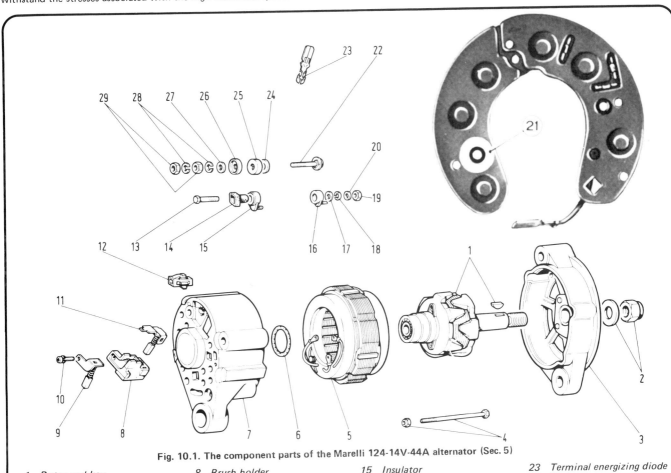

Fig. 10.1. The component parts of the Marelli 124-14V-44A alternator (Sec. 5)

1 Rotor and key
2 Nut and lockwasher
3 Front housing
4 Through bolt and nut
5 Stator
6 Seal
7 Diode end housing
8 Brush holder
9 Negative brush
10 Screw
11 Positive brush
12 Connector
13 Bolt
14 Insulator
15 Insulator
16 Insulator
17 Washer
18 Lockwasher
19 Nut
20 Washer
21 Diode support
22 Terminal 30
23 Terminal energizing diode
24 Washer
25 Insulator
26 Insulator
27 Washer
28 Lockwasher
29 Nut

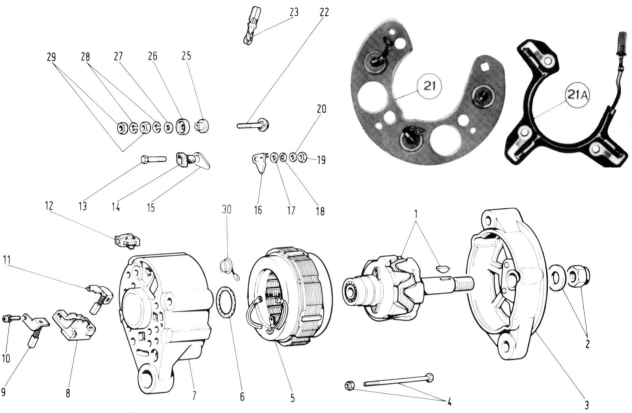

Fig. 10.2. The component parts of the Marelli 124-14V-60A alternator (fitted to air conditioned models) (Sec. 5)

1 Rotor and key	8 Brush holder	16 Insulators	23 Terminal energizing diode
2 Nut and lockwasher	9 Negative brush	17 Washer	24 Washer
3 Front housing	10 Screw	18 Lockwasher	25 Insulator
4 Through bolt and nut	11 Positive brush	19 Nut	26 Insulator
5 Stator	12 Connector	20 Washer	27 Washer
6 Seal	13 Bolt	21 Diode support	28 Lockwasher
7 Diode end housing	14 Insulator	21a Energizing diodes support	29 Nut
	15 Insulator	22 Terminal 30	30 Negative diode

Fig. 10.3. Alternator terminal connections (Sec. 6)

1 Terminal 67 (white cable connection)
2 Terminal 30 (main output heavy brown cables)
3 Energizing system plug (red, black/violet cables)
4 3-phased terminal
5 Ground (earth)

the vacant terminal and join the other end of the jumper lead to a 0 to 20V voltmeter. The remaining voltmeter terminal must now be joined to a convenient earthing point on the bodyshell. Start the engine and note the voltmeter reading as the engine speed is increased and decreased. Remove the voltmeter and reconnect the heavy brown cable to the alternator.

5 If during the voltmeter test the meter registered only a few volts, remove the alternator and inspect it more closely. If the readings obtained were between 12 and 14½ volts the alternator would seem to be functioning correctly and the voltage regulator must be suspected. It must be stated however, that the Diode Bridge network which rectifies the output of the stator make it impossible to be certain that the alternator is serviceable, even if the output appears to be between 12V and 14½ volts, therefore, if the checks detailed in paragraphs 3 and 4 do not reveal a clear fault, take the car to the nearest auto-electrician.

6 If, however, the checks in paragraph 4 did reveal a faulty alternator, begin removing the alternator by disconnecting the earth cable from the battery. Then remove the heavy brown cable from the alternator followed by the white cable and the block connector. Identify the leads and terminals so that they may be refitted correctly later.

7 Next loosen the upper and lower attachment bolts (photo) and push the alternator toward the engine. Slip the drive belt off the pulley.

8 Move the alternator away from the engine and completely expose the lower attachment bolts. Undo and remove the nuts and bolts and lift the alternator away from the engine.

9 Refitting is the reversal of the removal sequence, except that the fan belt must be tensioned as described in Chapter 2.

10 Before beginning to dismantle the alternator with a view to renewing the brushes or bearings, check that the individual spares are available. The bearings are only listed as available either with the

6.2 The alternator protective metal shield viewed from beneath

6.4 Disconnect the output cables from the alternator

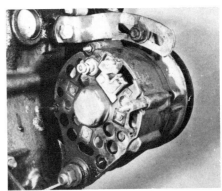

6.7 The alternator mounting bolts as viewed from the rear

rotor or with the forward casing. The alternator is usually renewed as a factory exchange unit and individual components are not readily available.

11 Assuming the brushes or bearings are available, the rear end of the alternator which houses the brushes and rear bearing is retained by four long bolts and nuts which reach to the forward end of the unit. Undo and remove the four nuts and bolts and ease the rear casing from the body. Retrieve the sealing ring which is fitted in the rear bearing housing.

12 The brushes are mounted in a plate screwed to the inside of the rear casing. Remove the plate and brushes and renew them if worn to less than 0.37 in (9.39 mm). Clean the slip rings on the rotor with a petrol damped cloth and reassemble the alternator. Take care not to damage the brushes when refitting the casing over the rotor.

13 As previously mentioned, bearings are listed as available only with the rotor or front casing, their renewal follows similar lines to that for the brushes, but the pulley and fan will need to be removed from the forward end of the rotor shaft to facilitate separation of the rotor and front casing.

7 Voltage regulator - description and testing

1   The voltage regulator is of the twin contact type and is located within the engine compartment (photo).

2   A fault in the voltage regulator may be indicated if the battery is either in a low state of charge in spite of a normal mileage being covered or if the electrolyte needs continual topping-up due to over-charging. Remember that a slack or slipping fan belt may be the cause of undercharging.

3   The only tests that the owner can successfully carry out on the voltage regulator are for open circuits using an ohmmeter.

4   Disconnect the battery negative (—) earth lead.

5   Set the ohmmeter at the most sensitive scale and connect the test probes between terminals 15 and 67 at the voltage regulator. If no reading is obtained an open circuit is present between the first stage contacts.

6   The open circuit between the first stage contacts may be the result of either oxidisation or burning of the contacts. Remove the voltage regulator cover to investigate the defect.

7   Dirty or slightly burnt contacts can be cleaned using a piece of emery or carborundum paper. Place the emery or carborundum paper between the contacts and draw it slowly through. Remove all traces of dust with a rag moistened in methylated spirits.

8   If the contact points are badly burnt then the voltage regulator unit must be renewed.

9   Now connect the ohmmeter between terminal 15 and the earth terminal. No reading on the ohmmeter indicates that an open circuit is present in the resistor or coil. Rectify this fault by renewing the voltage regulator.

10 If no faults are found after having checked the voltage regulator with the ohmmeter take the car to your nearest FIAT garage or competent auto-electrician who will be able, using special test equipment, to isolate the fault by carrying out further tests.

11 Adjustment of the voltage regulator is critical and necessitates the use of this special test equipment and is therefore beyond the scope of the D-I-Y motorist.

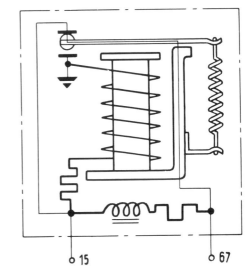

Fig. 10.4. The voltage regulator schematic wiring diagram (Sec. 7)

Fig. 10.5. The voltage regulator with the cover removed (Sec. 7)

1   1st stage fixed contact carrier
2   2nd stage fixed contact
3   1st stage fixed contact carrier adjusting screw

7.1 The voltage regulator unit located within the engine compartment

10.3 The starter motor connections removed at the solenoid

10.4 The starter motor bolted to the bellhousing

8 Starter motor - general description

1   There are two types of starter motor used in the FIAT 131 range. The 1300 model uses the E84-0, 8/12 type while the 1600 and 1800 models use the E100-1, 3/12 type. Both starters are conceptually the same, only small dimensional differences distinguishing them.
2   The starter motors are of the pre-engaged type, in which the switch solenoid is also used to physically move the drive pinion along the starter motor shaft, into contact with the ring gear on the flywheel before power is supplied to the motor for turning the engine.
3   There is a spring between the pinion and the actuating lever from the solenoid so that, as the pinion is impelled to engage with the flywheel ring gear the solenoid switch will still continue and operate the starter circuit. The pinion will become engaged as soon as the motor shaft turns.
4   The starter motor is mounted on the right-hand side of the engine, and is bolted to the clutch bellhousing. The motor/pinion projects into the bellhousing near the periphery of the flywheel.

9 Starter motor circuit - testing

1   If the starter motor fails to turn the engine when the switch is operated there are four possible reasons why:

   a) *The battery is no good.*
   b) *The electrical connections between switch solenoid, battery and starter motor are somewhere failing to pass the necessary current from the battery through the starter to earth.*
   c) *The solenoid switch is no good.*
   d) *The starter motor is either jammed or electrically defective.*

2   To check the battery, switch on the headlights. If they go dim after a few seconds the battery is discharged. If the lamps glow brightly, next operate the starter switch and see what happens to the lights. If they go dim then you know that power is reaching the starter motor but failing to turn it. Therefore, check that it is not jammed by placing the car in gear and rocking it to and fro. If it is not jammed the starter will have to come out for examination. If the starter should turn very slowly go on to the next check.
3   If, when the starter switch is operated, the lights stay bright, then the power is not reaching the starter. Check all connections from battery to solenoid switch and starter for perfect cleanliness and tightness. With a good battery installed this is the most usual cause of starter motor problems. Check that the earth link cable between the engine and frame is also intact and cleanly connected. This can sometimes be overlooked when the engine has been taken out.
4   If no results have yet been achieved turn off the headlights, otherwise the battery will go flat. You will possibly have heard a clicking noise each time the switch was operated. This is the solenoid switch operating but it does not necessarily follow that the main contact is closing properly. (**Note:** If no clicking has been heard from the solenoid it is certainly defective). The solenoid contact can be checked by putting a voltmeter or bulb across the main cable connection on the starter side of the solenoid and earth. When the switch is operated, there should be a reading or the bulb should light.
        If not, the solenoid switch is no good. (Do not put a bulb across the two solenoid terminals. If the motor is not faulty the bulb will blow). If, finally, it is established that the solenoid is not faulty and 12 volts are getting to the starter then the starter motor must be the culprit.

10 Starter motor - removal and refitting

1   Raise the front of the car onto car ramps and chock the rear wheels.
2   Continue by removing the positive connection from the battery and then stow it carefully aside. The negative earthing connection to the body may remain in place.
3   Then, working on the starter motor assembly itself, remove the heavy leads to the starter and solenoid, identifying as necessary to ensure correct refitting later (photo).
4   From underneath the car and from within the engine compartment, undo and remove the nuts and bolts securing the starter motor assembly to the bellhousing (photo).
5   The starter motor is now free to be lifted from the engine and transferred to a bench for dismantling and repair.
6   Refitting the motor assembly to the engine follows the reversal of the removal procedure. Remember to use new locking washers as appropriate and tighten the starter motor retaining nuts and bolts to their specified torques at the beginning of this Chapter.

11 Starter motor - dismantling, repair and reassembly

1   The starter motor assembly comprises three sub-assemblies: the motor itself, the solenoid switch and the pinion actuator housing. The actuator housing forms the mechanical link between the motor and the solenoid switch.
2   Such is the inherent reliability and strength of the starter motors fitted to the FIAT 131 models that it is very unlikely that a motor will need dismantling until it is totally worn out and in need of renewal as a whole.
3   The solenoid which is usually available individually as a spare is attached to the actuator housing by three nuts on three long bolts passing the length of the solenoid. Undo and remove these three nuts and lift the solenoid from the starter motor assembly.
4   There is no possibility of repairing the solenoid and therefore if after reconnecting across the battery with two stout leads the unit remains lifeless or the switch part fails to work, the whole solenoid must be renewed.
5   *Starter motor brushes.* On the forward end of the starter motor is a wide strap, with a single screw securing it in position. It covers the aperture which allows access to the motor brushes.
6   The procedure for inspection and renewal of the brushes is straightforward. With the starter removed from the car and on a bench, slacken the single screw which clamps the end strap in position and slip the strap along the motor casing to uncover the brush access apertures.
7   The brushes are retained in their mountings by spiral springs. Move

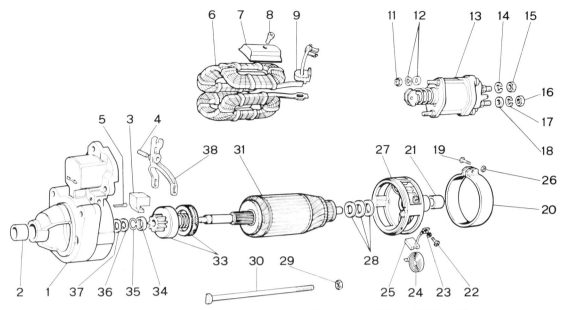
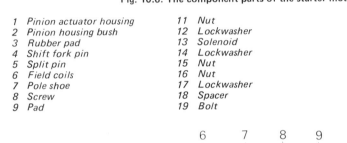
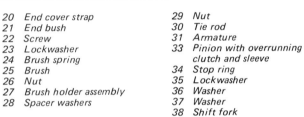

Fig. 10.6. The component parts of the starter motor fitted to the 1300 model (Sec. 11)

1	Pinion actuator housing	11	Nut	20	End cover strap	29	Nut
2	Pinion housing bush	12	Lockwasher	21	End bush	30	Tie rod
3	Rubber pad	13	Solenoid	22	Screw	31	Armature
4	Shift fork pin	14	Lockwasher	23	Lockwasher	33	Pinion with overrunning
5	Split pin	15	Nut	24	Brush spring		clutch and sleeve
6	Field coils	16	Nut	25	Brush	34	Stop ring
7	Pole shoe	17	Lockwasher	26	Nut	35	Lockwasher
8	Screw	18	Spacer	27	Brush holder assembly	36	Washer
9	Pad	19	Bolt	28	Spacer washers	37	Washer
						38	Shift fork

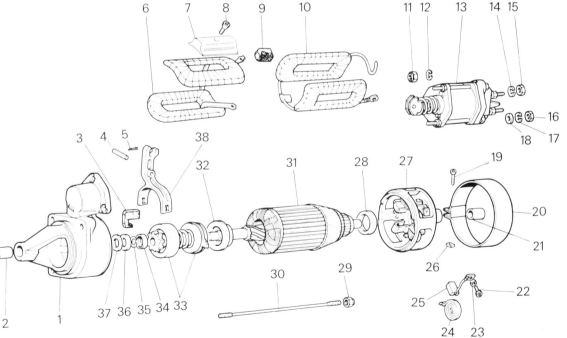

Fig. 10.7. The component parts of the starter motor fitted to the 1600 ohv and 1800 dohc
models (Sec. 11)

1	Pinion actuator housing	11	Nut	21	End bush	31	Armature
2	Pinion housing bush	12	Lockwasher	22	Screw	32	Spacer
3	Rubber pad	13	Solenoid	23	Lockwasher	33	Pinion with overrunning
4	Shift fork pin	14	Lockwasher	24	Brush spring		clutch and sleeve
5	Split pin	15	Nut	25	Brush	34	Stop ring
6	Field coils	16	Nut	26	Nut	35	Lockwasher
7	Pole shoe	17	Lockwasher	27	Brush holder assembly	36	Washer
8	Screw	18	Spacer	28	Spacer	37	Washer
9	Pad	19	Bolt	29	Nut	38	Shift fork
10	Field coil	20	End cover strap	30	Tie rod		

the ends of the spiral spring to allow the carbon brushes to be extracted from their mountings. Undo the small screw which secures the small lead from the brush to its terminal on the forward end fitting and remove the brush from the motor assembly. If the brush was worn to the extent that the spiral spring applies little force, then the brush should be renewed.

8   *Motor dismantling.* Having already removed the solenoid, the front end of the motor is the next unit to be separated from the motor assembly. The motor is held together by tie rods screwed into the actuator housing at the rear end and projecting through the front end fitting to accommodate nuts at the other.

9   Before proceeding to separate the motor it is necessary to disconnect the electrical connections. In particular the forward end cover strap should be removed along with the brushes. The electrical leads running from the field windings in the motor to the terminals in the forward end cover, should be detached from their terminals.

10   Once the nuts on the tie rods have been removed, the forward end fitting, motor casing and pinion actuator housing can be separated. The motor armature and drive pinion are mounted on a shaft which runs in bush bearings housed in the actuator housing and forward end fitting. It will be necessary to drive the pinion actuating pin from the actuator housing to permit the separation of the actuator housing and motor armature assembly.

11   Be careful to retrieve the spacer shims and thrust bearings on each end of the motor shaft when the motor shaft is freed. The spacers and thrust components should be refitted in their exact positions when the motor is reassembled.

12   The field windings are held to the inside of the motor main casing by special blocks which are in turn secured by screws passing through the casing.

13   The armature and pinion assembly will usually be separated from the motor components in order to gain access to the pinion assembly. Inspection and repair of the pinion assembly is described in Section 12.

14   Reassembly of the starter motor follows the reversal of the dismantling procedure. Fortunately there is little in the way of adjustments to make on the motor, the assemblies usually fit together to their correct relative positions.

12 Starter motor drive pinion - inspection and repair

1   Persistent jamming or reluctance to disengage indicates that the start pinion needs attention. The starter motor should be removed from the car first of all for general inspection.

2   With the starter motor removed, thoroughly clean all the grime and grease off with a petrol soaked rag. Take care to avoid any liquid running into the motor itself. If there is a lot of dirt, particularly on the pinion itself, this could be the trouble. The pinion should move freely along a spiral which is machined on the motor shaft. If the pinion motion is not smooth and easy remembering the springs which are fitted to the solenoid and pinion carriage to return it to its disengaged position - the motor should be dismantled and the armature/pinion assembly inspected and cleaned as follows.

3   Having removed the armature/pinion assembly the commutator may be cleaned with a petrol dampened rag. The pinion carriage is retained on the motor shaft by a spring ring and sleeve. The sleeve should be driven off the end of the shaft exposing the spring ring which can now be slipped out of its groove seat and off the shaft.

4   Slide the pinion carriage off the rotor shaft and then clean the spiral which is exposed. Wipe the internal spiral in the pinion carriage clean. You should not dismantle the pinion carriage. Individual parts are not listed as available and if the pinion teeth are damaged then the pinion carriage or the whole starter should be renewed.

5   The spiral splines should be lubricated with VS 10W grease before reassembly of the carriage onto the shaft. The intermediate disc that forms the thrust bearing between the actuating lever ring and the pinion carriage sleeve, should be lubricated with FIAT MR3 grease or its equivalent.

6   Reassembly of the pinion carriage onto the motor shaft follows the reversal of the removal procedure.

13 Fuses and relays

1   All circuits are fused with the exception of the charging circuit,

ignition circuit, starter motor circuits, headlamp main beam relay and side/tail lamp indicator light. The fuses are the weakest link in the circuit and any fault causing a short circuit will therefore blow a fuse rather than cause burning and a possible fire at the fault source.

2   The fuses are mounted under the glove compartment in a box along with four relay units (photo).

3   The circuits protected by each fuse are represented by symbols on the clear plastic fuse box cover. The fuse box cover is retained by a central knurled screw which can be easily undone to gain access to the fuses and relays (photo).

4   If any item of electrical equipment fails to operate first check the appropriate fuse. If the fuse has blown the first thing to do is to find out why, otherwise it will merely blow again - (fuses can blow through old age but this is the exception rather than the rule). Having found the faulty fuse, switch off the electrical equipment and then fit a new fuse. From the Specifications note which circuits are served by the blown fuse and then start to switch each one on separately in turn. (It may be necessary to have the ignition circuit switched on at the same time). The fuse should blow again when the faulty item is switched on. If the fuse does not blow immediately, start again only this time leave the circuits switched on and build up the cumulative total load on the fuse. If and when it blows you will have an indication of which circuits may be causing the problem. It may take a little longer to isolate the fault which may not be serious at this stage. If the new fuse does not blow until the car is moving then look for a loose, chaffed or pinched wire.

5   Various relays are fitted to the car, each controlling separate circuits. One bank of relays is fitted in the fuse box housing while the other bank is fitted within the engine compartment (photo). Refer to the wiring diagrams for details of which function each relay controls.

6   The relays are easily removed by simply pulling them out (photo).

7   If a fault occurs in one accessory or component and its rectification defies all efforts, always remember that it could be a relay at fault. Relays cannot be repaired or adjusted and if faulty should be renewed as a unit.

14 Headlamp unit - removal and refitting

USA versions of the FIAT 131 are fitted with sealed beam headlamp units while British versions are fitted with headlamp units which have renewable bulbs.

The Basic models are fitted with two rectangular headlamps whereas the Special models have a four round headlamp system. The headlamp removal sequence described in this Section is for the round headlamp. However, the rectangular headlamp is retained in a similar manner.

1   Lift the bonnet and remove the wiring block connections from the rear of the headlamps.

2   Remove the ten screws holding the plastic grille in place.

3   Lift the grille complete with attached headlamps clear from the car (photo).

4   Remove the screws retaining the headlamp backing plate to the grille.

5   Now lift the headlamps and backing plate away from the grille (photo).

6   To remove the headlamp retainer ring, slacken the three screws and turn the ring anticlockwise to align the screw heads with the clearance cut outs on the retainer ring (photo).

7   Lift the ring off and remove the headlamp unit (photo).

8   Refitting is the reverse of the removal sequence; ensure that the headlamps are refitted in the correct position. It will be noted that the outer headlamps have three connection points while the inner headlamps have only two. The extra connection is for dipping purposes.

15 Headlamp bulb - removal and refitting

131 Basic model (rectangular headlamps) (Fig. 10.8)

1   Access to the lamps is from inside the engine compartment.

2   Pull off the wiring block connector from the rear of the lamp.

3   Slide out the plastic shield cover.

4   Pull off the rubber cover.

5   Push in the bulb retainer spring and rotate it to release the bulb (photo).

6   Refitting the bulb is the reverse of the removal operation but remember, when inserting the bulb, to align it correctly with the location dowels.

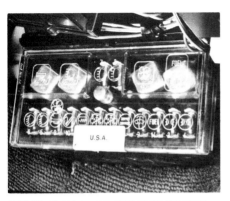
13.2 The fuse box mounted under the glove box

13.3 The fuse box cover removed (after undoing the central knurled screw)

13.5 The bank of relays fitted within the engine compartment

13.6 Removing a relay unit by pulling it out (fuse box shown)

14.3 Lift the grille complete with attached headlamps away from the car

14.5 Remove the screws and lift the headlamps and backing plate away from the grille

14.6 Turn the retainer ring anticlockwise to align the screw heads with the cut outs on the retaining ring

14.7 Lift the ring off and remove the headlamp (sealed beam unit)

15.5 Removing bulb from rear of reflector

131 Special (round headlamps) (Fig. 10.9)
7 The removal and refitting sequence is identical to the 131 basic model. However, the Special model does not have a plastic shield cover behind the lamp unit.

16 Headlamp beam alignment

1 Headlamp beam alignment is best carried out at a garage with the proper beam setting machine. However, the owner is able to do reasonably accurate setting himself provided he can arrange to line up the car on level ground facing a suitably surfaced vertical wall, at a distance of 16.5 ft (5 metres). The car should be unladen and the tyre pressures and standing heights correct.
2 On the vertical surface mark crosses in line with each headlamp centre. Taking single headlamp models first of all, mark a point 3.1 in (8 cm) below each cross. With the headlamps switched on low beam

the light zone should correspond with this point as shown in Fig. 10.10.
3 Dual headlamps are arranged so that only the outer pair dip. Having marked the four crosses on the vertical surface mark the outer lamp reference points 3.1 in (8 cm) below the crosses and the inner lamp reference points 2.4 in (5 cm) below the crosses. With the lamps on dip the outer lamp light zones should line up as indicated in Fig. 10.11. With all four lamps on the centre point of the inner lamp the pool of light must correspond with the reference.
4 There are three lamp adjusting screws on cars fitted with sealed beam headlamps. Access to these screws is through the grille (photo).
5 Cars fitted with headlamps which have bulbs installed have two lamp adjusting screws. Access to the screws is from inside the engine compartment.
6 When carrying out beam alignment checks on models which have bulbs fitted, it is essential to ensure that the manual adjuster levers are set in the normal position for use up to the medium load condition.

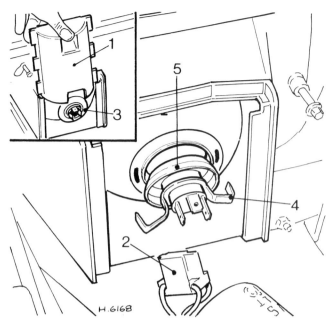

Fig. 10.8. Removing the headlamp bulb from the 131 Basic model (rectangular headlamps) (Sec. 15)

1 *Plastic cover shield*   4 *Bulb retainer spring*
2 *Wiring block connector*   5 *Headlight bulb*
3 *Weatherproof rubber cover*

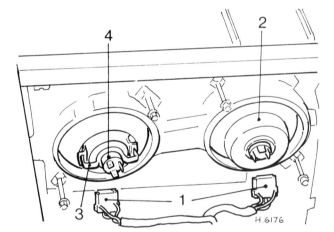

Fig. 10.9. Removing the headlamp bulb from the 131 Special (UK model) (Sec. 15)

1 *Wiring block connectors*   3 *Bulb retainer spring*
2 *Weatherproof rubber cover*   4 *Bulb*

17 Indicator side/repeater lights

1   It is a modern requirement to provide repeater indicator lights on each side of the vehicle (photo).

2   The design of these lights is conventional comprising a sealed lens and light shell. The bulb holder and bulb are a push fit into the rear of the light shell.

3   To remove the front side repeater lamps, compress the plastic retainer on the inner wing panel and pull the unit clear. Finally, disconnect the wires (photo). On some models, the bulb cannot be withdrawn from the unit and if defective must therefore be renewed complete. Push the unit into position to refit and reconnect the wires. Finally, check for satisfactory operation.

4   The rear side repeater lights have studs projecting from the light body and nuts retain the light assembly to the rear wing panels. Access

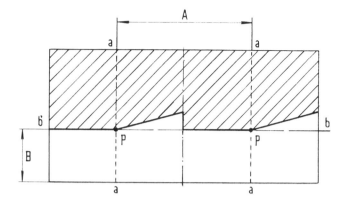

Fig. 10.10. The headlamp beam alignment diagram 131 Basic models (Sec. 16)

A = *Distance between headlamp centres*
B = *Vertical height to centre of headlamp minus 3.1 in (8 cm)*

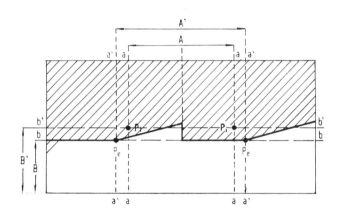

Fig. 10.11. The headlamp beam alignment diagram for 131 Special models (Sec. 16)
(RHD version shown reverse the pattern for LHD models)

A = *Distance between centres of inner headlamps*
A' = *Distance between centres of outer headlamps*
B = *Vertical height to centre of outer headlamps minus 3.1 in (8 cm)*
B' = *Vertical height to centre of inner headlamps minus 2.4 in (5 cm)*

16.4 The horizontal beam adjuster screw (USA models)

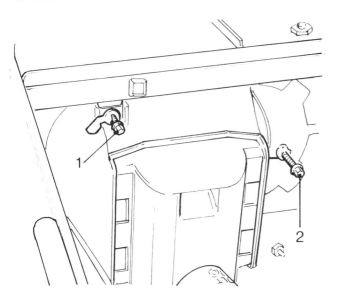

Fig. 10.12. The headlamp beam alignment adjusting screws (UK models)

1   Vertical alignment adjuster screw
2   Horizontal alignment adjuster screw

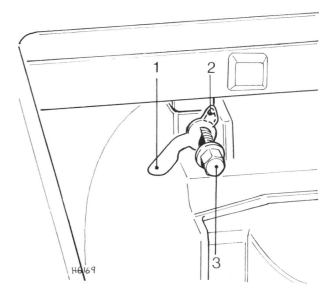

Fig. 10.13. The manual beam adjuster lever shown in the normal position for medium loads

1   Manual lever in normal position
2   Lower dipped beam position for heavy load conditions
3   Vertical adjusting screw

Fig. 10.14. The headlamp beam alignment adjusting screws (USA models)

A   Ring retaining screws and slotted holes
B   Headlamp retainer ring
C   Headlamp unit (sealed beam)
D   Vertical alignment adjuster screw
E   Horizontal alignment adjuster screw
F   Vertical alignment adjuster screw
G   Horizontal alignment adjuster screw

to the bulb holders or light securing nuts is from within the boot compartment (photo).
5   To renew the bulb simply pull the bulb holder assembly out from the rear of the light shell. The bulb is a usual push/twist fit in the holder.
6   The lens cannot be renewed singly as it is an integral part of the light assembly.

---

18 Front side and direction indicator lights

1   USA models have an amber lens and twin filament bulb fitted, whereas British models have a lens which is only half amber, the other half being clear and utilize two bulbs.
2   Both types of lamp are retained to the bumper bar fixing by two screws which also serve to locate the lens.
3   To gain access to the bulbs simply undo the two screws and lift the lens away (photo).
4   The bulbs are a bayonet fit and are easy to remove.
5   As mentioned previously, cleanliness with electrical systems is essential. Clean the bulb terminals and holder terminals. The lens gasket should always be in perfect condition; it is essential to prevent foreign matter and water entering the light assembly and corroding the electrical connections.

17.3 The later type indicator light unit (front shown)

17.4 Access to the indicator side repeater lights is from within the boot (saloon cars)

18.3 Remove the two screws and lift the lens away (USA model shown)

19 Rear lamp assembly

1 All models, excluding estate cars, have the rear stop, indicator, reverse and tail lamps incorporated in one lamp cluster.

2 Estate cars have a similar assembly fitted, but the reverse lamp is mounted independently, either to the tailgate or below the rear bumper bar.

3 Each lens making up the assembly can be detached separately (photos), with one exception, that being the combined reverse lamp.

4 To remove the clear reverse lamp lens first remove the tail lamp lens. Now remove the single screw retaining the clear lens (photo).

5 On estate car versions the reverse lamp lens is retained by two screws.

6 All the bulbs fitted to the rear lamps are of the bayonet type which are easily removed and refitted.

7 To remove the rear lamp cluster first disconnect the wiring block connector from within the boot compartment.

8 The lamp cluster is secured by nuts and washers.

9 Remove the nuts from inside the boot and draw the lamp cluster away from the body.

10 Refitting the assembly is the reverse of the dismantling procedure.

20 Number plate light

1 Some models are fitted with two number plate illumination lights. Each lamp is secured to the number plate bracket by two nuts.

2 Access to the bulb is achieved by removing the lens cover retaining screws and removing the lens (photos).

3 The bulb is the regular push/twist bayonet type.

4 Earlier British models have a single number plate lamp which is secured to a bracket bolted to the bumper bar.

5 To gain access to the bulbs the lens will have to be removed. To remove the lens simply squeeze it to release the plastic clips and lift it off. The bulb may now be removed.

21 Front and rear courtesy lights

1 The interior courtesy lights are operated by a door jam switch and a separate switch built into the light unit. This duplication of switching systems simplifies the task of identifying faulty components when there is a malfunction.

2 Quite simply, if the lights fail to shine when both switches are operated then check that the power is available on the supply leads. See circuit diagram for details.

3 The front courtesy light lens is integral with the bulb holder and is simply clipped into the light body mounting. (See Fig. 10.15).

4 To renew the bulb simply unclip the lens and release the bulb from its mounting points.

5 The rear courtesy light bulbs are removed as follows:

6 Pull out the light unit and remove the bottom wire connection.

7 Spring retainers are used to retain the bulb holder.

8 With the bulb holder now released from the light unit the bulb can be removed.

9 Refitting the unit is the reverse of the removal sequence.

22 Instrument panel, bulbs and switches - removal and refitting

1 Depending on model and year of manufacture, the rocker type switches are mounted on sub-panels either side of the speedometer/instrument panel or on a separate panel directly beneath.

2 The two sub panels are a push fit into their respective housings (photos), as are the rocker switches of the later models, where fitted into separate panels. The switches are best removed by reaching under the dashboard assembly and pushing out from inside. Finally, detach the wires.

3 When removing any of the switches note the positions of the attached wires. Some cannot be confused as they are fitted into a block connector at the rear of the switch.

4 To remove the speedometer (time clock and rev counter) panel,

19.3A The indicator lamp lens removed

19.3B The stop lamp lens removed

19.3C Alternative type of rear light cluster used on some models, with top lens removed

19.4 The side lamp and reverse lamp lens removed (saloon car model)

20.2A Remove the two lens retaining screw

20.2B The number plate lamp lens removed

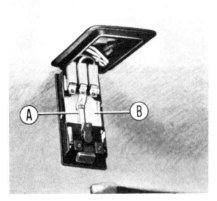

Fig. 10.15. The front courtesy light (Sec. 21)

A Plug-in type bulb
B Plug-in type lens

Fig. 10.16. The rear courtesy light (Sec. 21)

A Plug-in type lamp   C Lower wiring connection
B Spring retainer

22.2A The switch sub-panels are a push-fit into the dashboard ...

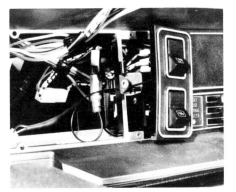

22.2B ... and cover the speedometer panel retaining screws

22.5 Removing the speedometer (time clock and rev counter) panel screws

Fig. 10.17. Remove panel surround plate (CL and Super models) (Sec 22)
A Remove both plates shown

Fig. 10.18. Remove panel surround plate (L models) (Sec 22)
B Frame to be removed

first disconnect the battery negative (−) earth lead to prevent damaging any of the electrical system by short circuits. Now pull out the two sub-panels which house the rocker type switches, (where applicable).
5   On earlier models, the speedometer/instrument panel is retained by two screws (photo). On later models, the panel surround must first be removed to gain access to the panel retaining screws (see Figs. 10.17 and 10.18).
6   With these screws now removed lift the panel outwards and disconnect the speedometer cable from the rear of the speedometer head. The speedometer outer cable is retained by a knurled collar screwed onto a threaded stub protruding from the rear of the speedometer head.
7   With the speedometer cable disconnected the panel can be pulled outwards and rested on top of the dash panel.
8   If it is desired to remove the panel completely in order to remove the printed circuit, speedometer head, rev counter or time clock then

carefully pull out the wiring block connectors and the input feed wire to the panel light rheostat switch where applicable.
9   The panel illumination and warning light bulbs are of the capless type. To remove the bulbs simply pull out the bulb holder and then withdraw the bulb from the holder.
10 The refitting of the instrument panel and its sub assemblies is the reverse of the removal operation.

23 Windscreen washer

1   The windscreen washer is electrically operated through a control lever attached to the steering column.
2   When the control lever is lifted upwards an electric current is fed to a pump unit fitted to the base of the screen washer reservoir tank.
3   The water from the reservoir is forced under pressure by the pump unit through plastic tubes to the washer jets mounted to the bulkhead.

4   The jets are adjustable and easily detached if they become clogged. To clear the jets use a needle and blow the jet through.
5   The screen washer system is generally reliable, the only attention required is to top up the reservoir with clean water and periodically clean out any algae which may collect in the reservoir.

24 Horns and horn switch

1   Two horns are fitted, one giving a high note and the other a low note.
2   The horns are operated by the horn press switch fitted to the centre of the steering wheel which activates the horn relay.
3   Both horns are fitted with volume control screws.
4   Horn failure is generally caused by a fault in the spring loaded contact ring on the horn press switch or corrosion on the switch contact faces.
5   In addition to these faults the horn may sound muffled or fail to work if water enters the horn due to driving through floods.
6   Finally, the horn relay may be suspected of malfunctioning but in most cases one of the above faults is usually the cause.

25 Speedometer cable - removal and refitting

1   The speedometer cable may break or cause erratic operation of the speedometer. To investigate, first remove the instrument panel as described in Section 21. Then undo the cable securing collar and draw out the inner cable. Note that cars fitted with a catalytic converter will have a two part cable joined at the odometer switch box.
2   If when the cable is drawn out it is found not to be broken then wash it in petrol and with some fine emery cloth smooth it down throughout its length to take off any high spots which may be causing it to 'twitch' in the outer cable. Check also the corners of the square cable drive ends and ensure that they have not become rounded and hence will slip inside of the drive housings.
3   If you are satisfied with the general condition of the cable re-grease and feed it back inside the outer cable.
4   Although it is not essential always to renew the outer cable when the inner cable breaks, it is conceivable that the outer cable could have been snagged by the broken ends of the inner cable. This may cause erratic running or even failure of a new cable fitted into it.

29 Fault diagnosis

5   When fitting a new cable disconnect the battery and feed the cable carefully through the bulkhead and secure it with the mounting clips and brackets. Avoid severe bends as they could form irrecoverable kinks in the inner cable and eventually cause failure of the inner cable.

26 Wiper blades and arms - removal and refitting

1   Whenever the wiper blades fail to clean the windscreen effectively, they must be renewed.
2   Pull the wiper arm away from the screen until it locks in position. Depress the small locking tab and pull the wiper blade from the wiper arm.
3   It may be possible to obtain new rubber inserts otherwise the wiper blade and holder will have to be renewed complete.
4   A wiper arm can be removed by lifting the small locking tab and pulling it from the splines of the driving spindle.
5   Refitting is a reversal of removal but make sure that the wiper arms are fitted to their splines in such a way that the blades are parallel with the bottom edge of the windscreen.

27 Windscreen wiper motor

Refer to Chapter 13 for information on the windscreen wiper motor and associate components.

28 Ignition switch/steering column lock - removal and refitting

1   This switch is clamped to the outer steering column and incorporates a steering column lock.
2   Disconnect the battery earth (−) lead.
3   Remove the steering column rake adjuster knob (where applicable).
4   Now remove the upper and lower halves of the plastic steering column shrouds. The shrouds are clamped together by screws.
5   Disconnect the socket plug connector which joins the ignition switch wiring to the main loom.
6   Finally remove the two bolts which clamp the assembly to the steering column.
7   Refitting the assembly is the reverse of the dismantling procedure.

Symptom	Reason/s
Starter motor fails to turn engine	
No electricity at starter motor	Battery discharged.
	Battery defective internally.
	Battery terminal leads loose or earth lead not securely attached to body.
	Loose or broken connections in starter motor circuit.
	Starter motor switch or solenoid faulty.
Electricity at starter motor: faulty motor	Starter motor pinion jammed in mesh with ring gear.
	Starter brushes badly worn, sticking, or brush wires loose.
	Commutator dirty, worn, or burnt.
	Starter motor armature faulty.
	Field coils earthed.
Starter motor turns engine very slowly	
Electrical defects	Battery in discharged condition.
	Starter brushes badly worn, sticking, or brush wires loose.
	Loose wires in starter motor circuit.
Starter motor operates without turning engine	
Dirt or oil on drive gear	Starter motor pinion sticking on the screwed sleeve.
Mechanical damage	Pinion or ring gear teeth broken or worn.
Starter motor noisy or excessively rough engagement	
Lack of attention or mechanical damage	Pinion or ring gear teeth broken or worn.
	Starter drive main spring broken.
	Starter motor retaining bolts loose.

Battery will not hold charge for more than a few days
Wear or damage

Battery defective internally.
Electrolyte level too low or electrolyte too weak due to leakage.
Plate separators no longer fully effective.
Battery plates severely sulphated.
Drive belt slipping.
Battery terminal connections loose or corroded.
Alternator not charging properly.
Short in lighting circuit causing continual battery drain.
Regulator unit not working correctly.

Ignition light fails to go out, battery runs flat in a few days
Alternator not charging

Drive belt loose and slipping, or broken.
Brushes worn, sticking, broken or dirty.
Brush springs weak or broken.
Commutator dirty, greasy, worn, or burnt.
Alternator field coils burnt, open or shorted.
Contacts in light switch faulty.

Wipers
Wiper motor fails to work

Blown fuse.
Wire connections loose, disconnected, or broken.
Brushes badly worn.
Armature worn or faulty.
Field coils faulty.

Wiper motor works very slow and takes excessive current

Commutator dirty, greasy, or burnt.
Drive to wheelboxes too bent or unlubricated.
Wheelbox spindle binding or damaged.
Armature bearings dry or unaligned.
Armature badly worn or faulty.

Wiper motor works slowly and takes little current

Brushes badly worn.
Commutator dirty, greasy, or burnt.
Armature badly worn or faulty.

Wiper motor works but wiper blades remain static

Driving cable rack disengaged or faulty.
Wheelbox gear and spindle damaged or worn.
Wiper motor gearbox parts badly worn.

Key to wiring diagram on pages 152 and 153 - USA models

1	Front park and turn lamps	32	Con. for defroster valve	64	Flasher	96	Turn signal s/w
2	Headlights (high/low beams)	33	Con. for condenser cooling fan temp. s/w	65	Fasten seat belts and remove key buzzer	97	Horns button
3	Headlights (high beams only)	34	Con. for safety temp. s/w			98	Jamb switch (driver's side) for remove key buzzer
4	Fast idle electrovalve	35	Starter r/e	66	Stop s/w		
5	'Catalyst' i/n control s/w	36	Diodes	67	Central control box	99	Button switch on driver's belt
6	Horns	37	Con. for starter inhibitor s/w (auto. trans.)	68	Lighting s/w	100	Courtesy lamps jamp s/w
7	Engine thermostatic fan s/w	38	'Catalyst' and 25.000 miles 'EGR' indicators r/e	69	Instrument cluster lights	101	Hand brake ON button s/w
8	Engine fan motor			70	Fuel reserve indicator	102	Heater/air con. controls illumination bulbs
9	Front side markers	39	Con. for fast idle electrovalve r/e	71	Instrument cluster con.		
10	'Catalyst' warning system fuse	40	Con. for condenser cooling fan r/e	72	Quartz cristal clock	103	Fast idle s/w (thru 3rd and 4th gears)
11	Fast idle	41	Con. for air conditioner master r/e	73	Instrument cluster light rheostat	104	Fast idle s/w con. (auto. trans.)
12	Ignition mode selection r/e thermostatic s/w	42	Con. for conditioner fan r/e	74	Tachometer	105	Heater fan motor
13	Ignition coil	43	Windshield wiper motor	75	Heater fan s/w	106	Cigar lighter
14	Ignition distributor	44	Diverter valve thermo s/w	76	Hazard warning signal s/w	107	Con. for starter inhibitor s/w thru reverse gear (auto. trans.)
15	Alternator	45	Horns relay	77	Park and tail lights i/n		
16	Voltage regulator	46	Headlight high beams r/e	78	Turn signal arrow i/n	108	Con. for glove compartment light
17	Battery	47	Headlight fuses	79	Headlight high beams i/n	109	Gear-engaged s/w
18	Sending unit, coolant temp.	48	Engine fan motor r/e	80	Hazard warning signal i/n	110	Con. for selected gear i/n light (auto. trans.)
19	Sending unit, oil pressure	49	Fuel pump selection r/e	81	Fuel gage		
20	Idle stop solenoid inhibitor s/w on carburetor (Catalytic Converter cars)	50	Fuses	82	Engine water temp. gage	111	Fast idle s/w thru clutch
		51	Con. for defroster valve temp. s/w	83	Back window demister i/n (where installed)	112	Con. for fast idle s/w (auto. trans.) - replaces s/w 111
		52	Con. for conditioner control board				
21	Idle stop solenoid	53	Con. for conditioner fan motor speed s/w	84	Battery charge i/n	113	Back-up light s/w
22	Spark plugs	54	Con. for conditioner cooling fan	85	Insufficient oil pressure i/n	114	Front courtesy light
23	Starter motor	55	Fuel pump relay s/w on starting	86	Brake system effectiveness/hand brake ON i/n	115	Rear courtesy lights
24	Electrovalve controlling diverter valve	56	Ignition mode selection r/e			116	Back window demister (where installed)
25	Washer pump	57	Starter inhibitor s/w con. (auto. trans.)	87	Fasten seat belts i/n		
26	Brake effectiveness and hand brake ON i/n	58	Diverter valve air feed r/e	88	Back window demister s/w (where installed)	117	Fuel gage sending unit
		59	Relay for fasten seat belts and remove key circuit	89	Light guide cables bulb	118	Fuel pump
27	Con. for condenser cooling fan (air con.)			90	'Catalyst' i/n (C.C. cars)	119	Rear side marker lights
28	Catalytic converter connector	60	Delay circuit for fasten seat belts indicator and buzzer	91	'Slow down' i/n	120	Rear turn signal lights
29	Con. for conditioner fan speed selector resistor	61	Tacho switch (C.C. cars)	92	25.000 miles 'EGR' i/n	121	Tail lights
		62	Catalytic converter electronic control circuit (C.C. cars)	93	Steering lock ignition s/w	122	Back-up lights
30	Con. for air conditioner compressor			94	Wiper/washer s/w	123	Stop lights
31	Con. for low pressure s/w	63	Back window demister r/e (where installed)	95	High/Low beam change-over and flashes s/w (0 = High beam)	124	License plate lights
						125	Catalytic converter thermocouple (where installed)

CABLE COLOUR CODE

Arancio	= Amber	Marrone	= Brown	Azzurro	= Light blue	s/w	switch
Nero	= Black	Bianco	= White	Rosa	= Pink	r/e	relay
Blu	= Dark blue	Rosso	= Red	Giallo	= Yellow	i/n	indicator
Verde	= Green	Grigio	= Grey	Viola	= Violet		

152

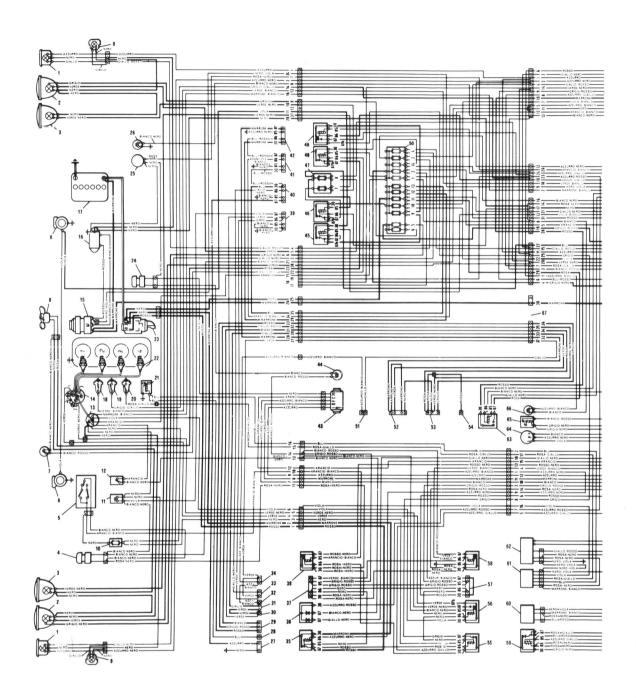

Wiring Diagram for USA - Part A

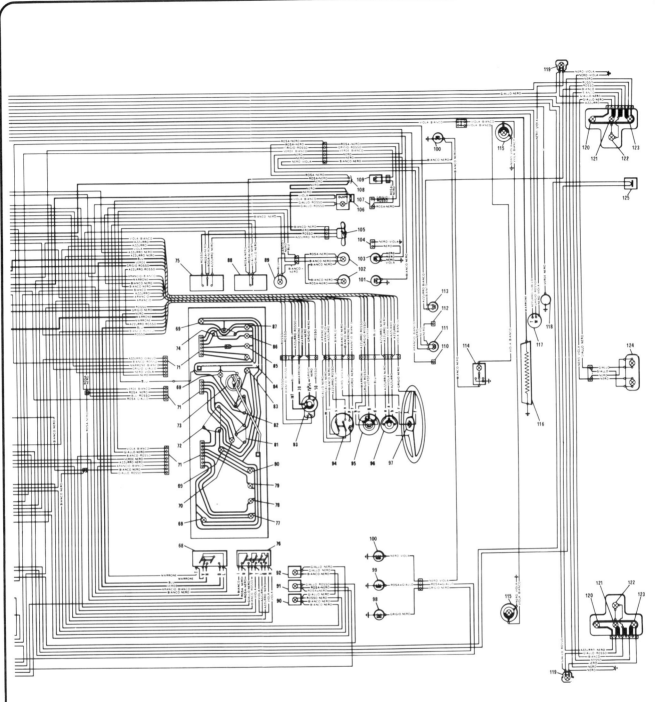

Wiring Diagram for USA - Part B

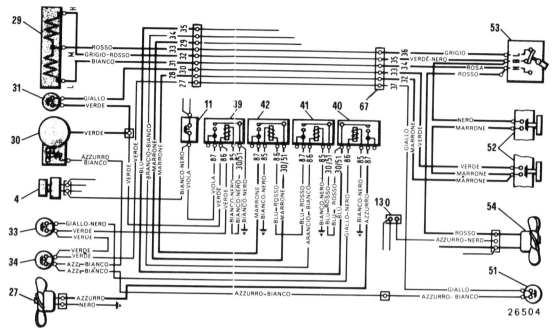

Fig. 10.17B. Air conditioner circuit (optional USA models)

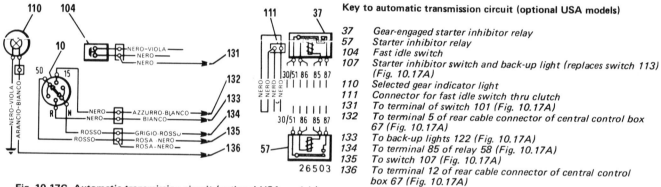

Key to automatic transmission circuit (optional USA models)

37	Gear-engaged starter inhibitor relay
57	Starter inhibitor relay
104	Fast idle switch
107	Starter inhibitor switch and back-up light (replaces switch 113) (Fig. 10.17A)
110	Selected gear indicator light
111	Connector for fast idle switch thru clutch
131	To terminal of switch 101 (Fig. 10.17A)
132	To terminal 5 of rear cable connector of central control box 67 (Fig. 10.17A)
133	To back-up lights 122 (Fig. 10.17A)
134	To terminal 85 of relay 58 (Fig. 10.17A)
135	To switch 107 (Fig. 10.17A)
136	To terminal 12 of rear cable connector of central control box 67 (Fig. 10.17A)

Fig. 10.17C. Automatic transmission circuit (optional USA models)

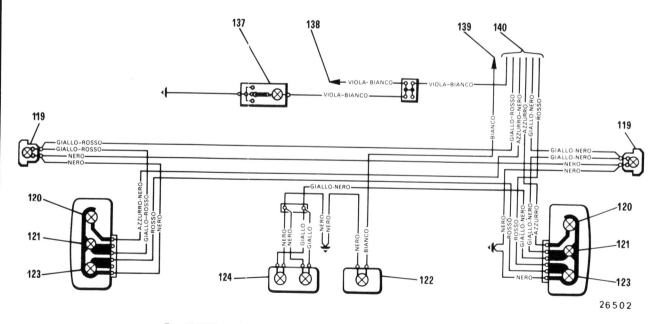

Fig. 10.17D. Supplementary wiring diagram Estate car (USA models)

Key to air conditioner circuit (optional USA models)

4	Fast idle electrovalve
11	Fast idle switch
27	Condenser cooling fan
29	Conditioner fan speed selector resistor
30	Compressor and defroster valve
31	Low pressure switch
33	Condenser cooling fan temperature switch
34	Safety temperature switch
39	Relay for fast idle electrovalve
40	Condenser cooling fan relay
41	Master relay
42	Conditioner fan relay
51	Defroster valve temperature switch
52	Conditioner control board
53	Conditioner fan motor speed switch
54	Conditioner cooling fan
67	Central control box
130	Terminal

Key to supplementary wiring diagram Estate car (USA models)

119	Rear side marker lights
120	Rear turn signal lights
121	Rear tail lights
122	Back-up light
123	Stop lights
124	License plate lights
137	Rear interior light and switch
138	To lights 115 (Fig. 10.17A)
139	To switch 112 (Fig. 10.17A)
140	To terminals of rear cable connector of central control box 67 (Fig. 10.17A)

Key to wiring diagram on pages 156 and 157 - UK models

1	Front indicators	38	Heater fan switch
2	Side lights	39	Hazard warning switch leads (if fitted)
3	Headlamp - main and dipped beams	41	Direction indicator w/l
4	Headlamp - main beams (131 Mirafiori Special)	42	Headlamp w/l
5	Horns	43	Hazard w/l
6	Rad. fan control switch (except 131 Mirafiori - 1300cc)	44	Heated rear screen w/l
7	Rad. fan motor (except 131 Mirafiori - 1300cc)	45	Ignition w/l
8	Repeater lights	46	Fuel w/l
9	Distributor	47	Oil pressure w/l
10	Ignition coil	48	Hand and foot brake w/l
11	Water temp. transmitter	49	Spare w/l
12	Oil pressure transmitter	50	Heated rear screen switch
13	Spark plugs	51	Panel switch light guide cable lamp (131 Mirafiori Special)
14	Starter motor	52	Ignition switch
15	Auto. trans. lead (optional)	53	Wiper/washer switch
16	Alternator	54	Headlamp switch
17	Voltage regulator	55	Direction indicator switch
18	Battery	56	Horn switch
19	Washer pump	57	Handbrake warning transmitter
20	Direction indicator flasher	58	Heater dial lamp (131 Mirafiori Special)
21	Brake w/l lead (if fitted)	59	Heater fan motor
22	Wiper interrupter	60	Cigar lighter/light
23	Heated rear screen relay	61	Glove box light leads (if fitted)
24	Stop light switch	62	Door switch
25	Wiper motor	63	Selector lever indicator lead
26	Central control box	64	Auto. trans. lead
27	Radiator fan motor relay	65	Courtesy light/switch
28	Headlamp relay	66	Reversing light switch
29	Fuse unit	67	Rear interior lights/switches (131 Mirafiori Special)
30	Horn relay	68	Heated rear screen (optional)
31	Wiper interrupter connector	69	Fuel transmitter
32	Lighting/panel light switch	70	Rear direction indicators
33	Panel lights	71	Rear lights
34	Connectors	72	Stop lights
35	Clock	73	Reversing lights
36	Fuel gauge	74	Number plate lights
37	Water temp. gauge	w/l	= warning light

Note: The instrument panel shown is for the 'Special model'.

CABLE COLOUR CODE

Arancio	=	Amber	Azzurro	=	Light blue	Bianco	=	White
Blu	=	Dark blue	Giallo	=	Yellow	Grigio	=	Grey
Marrone	=	Brown	Nero	=	Black	Rosa	=	Pink
Rosso	=	Red	Verde	=	Green	Viola	=	Mauve

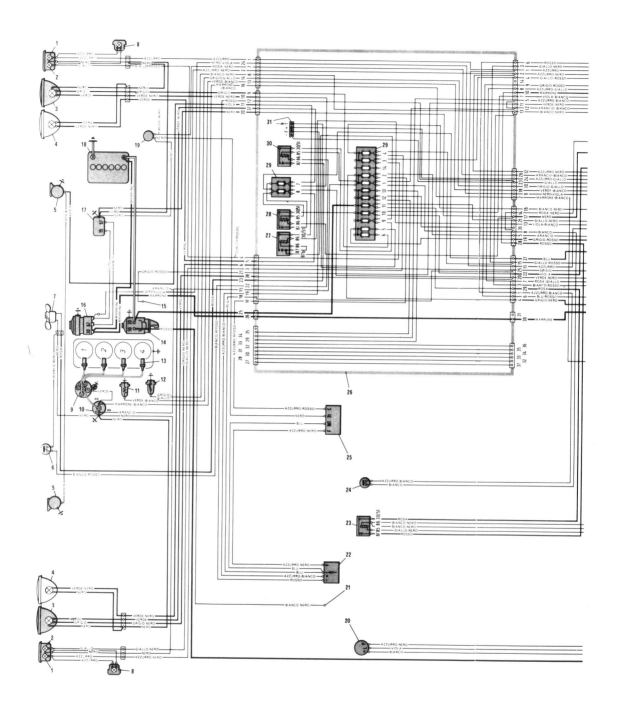

Wiring Diagram for UK models - Part A

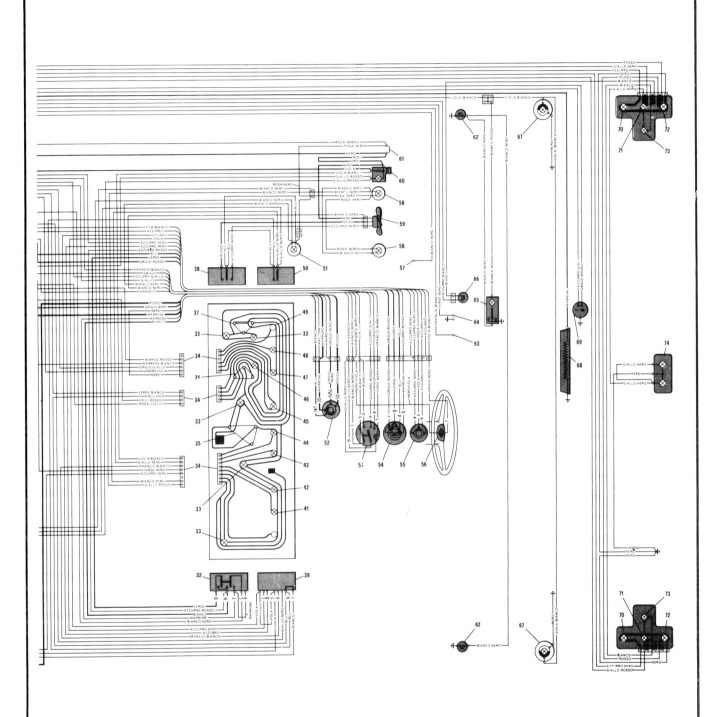

Wiring Diagram for UK models - Part B

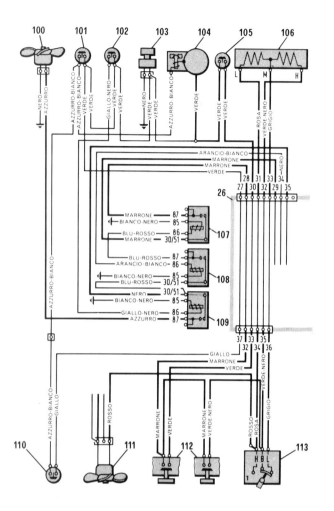

Fig. 10.18B. Air conditioner circuit (optional) (UK models)

26	Central control box
100	Condenser cooling fan
101	Radiator-mounted temperature switch
102	Condenser-mounted temperature switch
103	Fast idle solenoid valve
104	Compressor and solenoid valve
105	Low pressure switch
106	Conditioner fan speed selector resistor
107	Compressor and evaporator fan relay
108	Master relay
109	Condenser cooling fan relay
110	Compressor solenoid valve temperature switch
111	Conditioner cooling fan
112	Conditioner control board
113	Conditioner fan motor switch

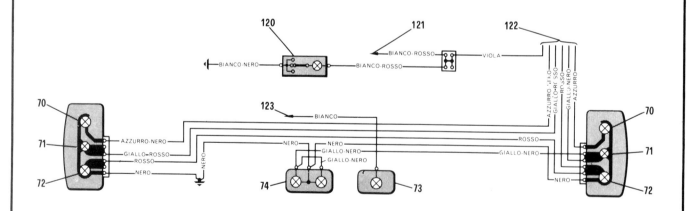

Fig. 10.18C. Supplementary wiring diagram Estate car (UK models)

70	Rear direction indicators
71	Rear lights
72	Stop lights
73	Reversing lights
74	Number plate lights
120	Interior light/switch (festoon bulb, 5W)
121	To courtesy light (see Fig. 10.18A)
122	To rear cable connector of central control box (see Fig. 10.18A)
123	To reversing switch (see Fig. 10.18A)

Chapter 11 Suspension and steering

For modifications, and information applicable to later models, see Supplement at end of manual

Contents

Specifications

Front suspension

Type	MacPherson strut incorporating a double acting shockabsorber with coil spring and utilising an anti-roll bar as a reaction member

Track (front)
Saloon	54 in (137.2 cms)
Estate	54.1 in (137.6 cms)

Rear suspension

Type	Live axle mounted on coil springs and incorporating double acting shockabsorbers. Estate car has shockabsorber mounted independently from coil spring. Axle located by four longitude trailing arms and a transverse Panhard rod

Track (rear)
Saloon	51.37 in (131.5 cms)
Estate	51.9 in (131.9 cms)

Steering

Type	Rack and pinion
Steering wheel turns, lock to lock	3.4
Steering gear lubricant type	SAE 90 gear oil
Steering gear oil capacity	0.25 Imp. pts (0.3 US pts/150 cc)

Steering geometry

Toe-in (laden)*	0.078 to 0.157 in (2 to 4 mm)
Camber angle (laden)*	0° - 1°
Caster angle (laden)*	4° - 5°
Steering pivot inclination (kpi)	6°

With 4 occupants and 110 lbs (50 kgs) of luggage.

Wheels and tyres

Type	Pressed steel, bolt fixing
Rim size	
Saloon	4½J x 13 in
Estate	5J x 13 in
Tyres	
Saloon	155 - SR13 radial ply
Estate	165 - SR13 radial ply
Tyre pressures (Saloon)	
Front	25 psi (1.8 kg/cm^2)
Rear	28 psi (2.0 kg/cm^2)
Tyre pressures (Estate)	
Front	25 psi (1.8 kg/cm^2)
Rear	31 psi (2.2 kg/cm^2)

Torque wrench settings

	lb f ft	kg fm
Track rod and nut	25	3.5
Anti-roll bar to track control arm nut	43	6
Anti-roll bar saddle bolt	65	9
Track control arm balljoint nut	58	8
Track control arm inner nut	65	9
Strut to stub axle nut	65	9
Strut upper mounting nut	43	6
Strut upper mounting support nut	18	2.5
Crossmember to chassis bolt	65	9
Rear suspension upper mounting nut	18	2.5
Rear shockabsorber upper securing nut	11	1.5
Lower shockabsorber mounting	36	5
Upper and lower trailing link nuts	58	7
Panhard rod chassis end nut	58	7
Panhard rod axle end bolt	72	10
Steering wheel nut	36	5
Steering rack to crossmember bolts	18	2.5
Steering column support bracket bolts	11	1.5
Intermediate shaft coupling nuts	18	2.5

1 General description

The front suspension is of the MacPherson strut type with telescopic shockabsorbers, coil springs and an anti-roll bar. The single lower track control arms are pivoted at their inner ends in rubber bushes and located to the front detachable crossmember assembly. The anti-roll bar is located through the track control arms at its ends and secured by two chassis mounting brackets at the front.

The rear suspension comprises a live rear axle and coil springs inside which are fitted telescopic shockabsorbers. The rear axle is located by four forward facing trailing arms and a transverse Panhard rod.

The steering is a rack and pinion system with two tie-rods connected to the steering arms through balljoints. The steering rack is mounted to the front detachable crossmember.

The steering wheel connects through a steering shaft, a universal joint, an intermediate shaft and a second universal joint to the steering gear pinion. On some models the steering column rake angle is adjustable.

The steering and suspension is maintenance-free as all ball joints are of the sealed for life type.

2 Anti-roll bar - removal and refitting

1 Apply the handbrake, then raise the front of the car, and support it on blocks or axle stands under the front crossmember. For convenience also remove the front roadwheels.
2 Now remove the four bolts which secure the anti-roll bar saddle brackets to the chassis.
3 The two nuts which secure the anti-roll bar to the track control arms can now be removed and the washers and shims removed. Note the number and positioning of the shims as on reassembly the incorrect repositioning of these shims will alter the steering caster angle.
4 Withdraw the anti-roll bar and inspect all parts for wear or deterioration. Renew parts as necessary.
5 Refitting the anti-roll bar is the reversal of the dismantling procedure. Remember to tighten all nuts and bolts to the specified torque wrench settings as listed at the beginning of this Chapter.

3 Front strut, spring and damper - removal and refitting

1 Apply the handbrake, and raise the car at the appropriate side. Support it beneath the front crossmember or bodyframe member.
2 Remove the roadwheel, followed by the anti-roll bar as described in Section 2 of this Chapter.
3 Remove the brake caliper block and secure it at a convenient point as described in Section 4, of Chapter 6.
4 Remove the two nyloc nuts from the tie-rod ball joints on the steering arms.
5 Pull back the rubber boot on the ball joint, then use a proprietary ball joint separator or split wedges to separate the ball joint from the

Fig. 11.1. The front view of the left-hand suspension assembly (Sec. 2)

1 Bolt
2 Anti-roll bar
3 Caster angle shims
4 Rubber bushes
5 Nut securing anti-roll bar to track control arm
6 Track control arm
7 Anti-roll bar saddle bracket

steering arm.
6 Remove the nut, bolt and washers holding the track control arm to the bracket on the front chassis crossmember.
7 Now support the strut and remove the three nuts and washers which secure the strut top to the inner wing panel (photo).
8 Now remove the support and withdraw the strut assembly.
9 The two nuts and bolts which retain the hub and disc assemblies to the support bracket can now be removed and the strut released.
10 Using proprietary spring compressors or FIAT tool A74277, compress the spring evenly, now remove the top retainer nut.
11 Very slowly release the compressor tool until the force exerted by the spring is fully released.
12 Now remove the top mounting and spring retainer plate.
13 Withdraw the coil spring.
14 Reassembly and refitting is the reverse of removal and dismantling sequences. Ensure that all nuts and bolts are tightened to the recommended torque wrench settings that are listed at the beginning of this Chapter (photo).

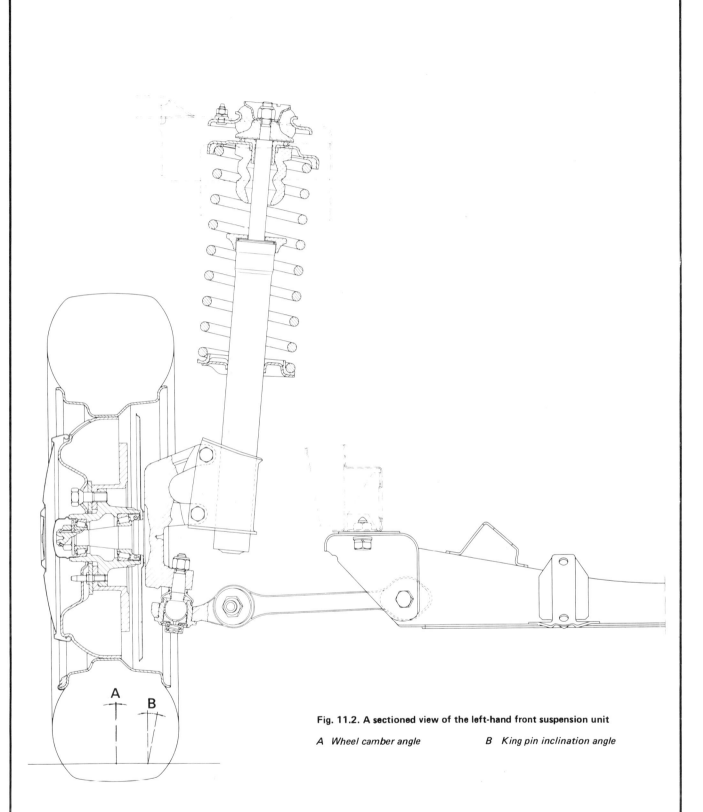

Fig. 11.2. A sectioned view of the left-hand front suspension unit

A Wheel camber angle   *B King pin inclination angle*

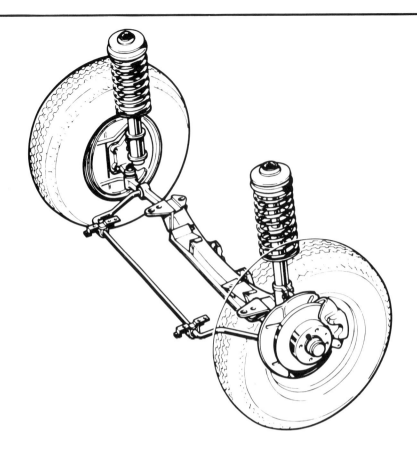

Fig. 11.3. The front suspension layout

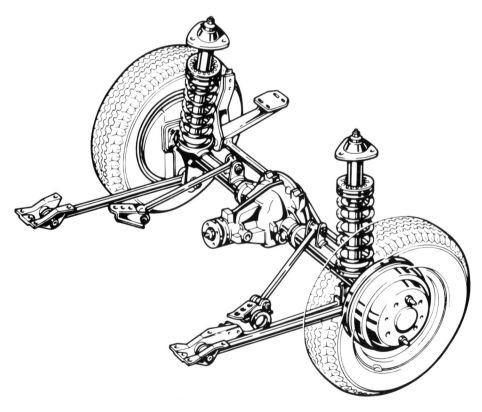

Fig. 11.4. The rear suspension layout

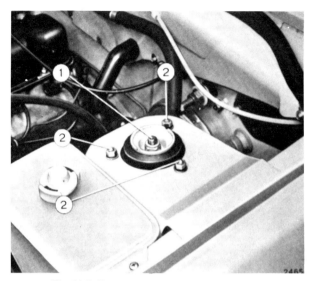

Fig. 11.5. Front strut upper mounting (Sec. 3)

1   Shockabsorber spindle and locknut
2   Retainer nuts

3.7 The upper mounting of the front strut to the inner wing panel

3.14 The front strut and coil spring in position on the car

4   Track control arm - removal and refitting

If on inspection the outer ball joint is found to have excessive play then the complete control arm must be renewed. However, if the rubber bush at the inner end is the only defective part, then a new bush can be purchased and fitted.

1   With the appropriate side jacked up and supported under the crossmember or bodyframe remove the roadwheel.

2   Remove the anti-roll bar as detailed in Section 2 of this Chapter.

3   Now remove the nut from the ball joint and using a proprietary ball joint separator or split wedges separate the ball joint from the stub axle casting.

4   Finally, remove the nut and bolt locating the track control arm to the chassis crossmember support bracket.

5   Removal of the rubber bush necessitates the use of an hydraulic press and several special FIAT tools.

6   It is as well to take the track control arm to the nearest FIAT dealer who will have the necessary equipment to fit the bush correctly.

7   Alternatively a long bolt with a nut and two large washers could be used to draw the new bush into the track control rod once the old bush has been removed.

8   Refitting the track control arm is simply the reverse of the dismantling procedure.

5   Front suspension crossmember - removal and refitting

1   Raise the front of the vehicle and support the body with axle stands or blocks.

2   Remove the front roadwheels.

3   Now support the engine, either by using a block of wood and an hydraulic jack placed under the sump or ideally by using a hoist.

4   Separate and remove the track control arms as detailed in Section 4 of this Chapter.

5   Now remove the four bolts which retain the steering rack saddle brackets to the crossmember.

6   Support the crossmember with a trolley jack and remove the nuts from the base of the two front engine mountings.

7   Remove the four bolts holding the crossmember to the chassis.

8   Lower the trolley jack and remove the crossmember.

9   Refitting the crossmember is the reverse of the removal sequence.

10 Ensure all nuts and bolts are tightened to the recommended torque settings as detailed at the beginning of this Chapter.

6   Steering rack and pinion assembly - removal and refitting

1   Raise the front of the car and support it on axle stands conveniently placed under the front crossmember or body frame.

2   Remove the front roadwheels.

3   Remove the two nyloc nuts from the tie-rod ball joints on the steering arms.

4   Pull back the rubber boot on the ball joint then, using a proprietary ball joint separator or split wedges, separate the ball joints from the steering arms.

5   Remove the nut and bolt retaining the lower universal steering joint to the steering rack pinion.

6   Undo and remove the four bolts that secure the steering rack saddle brackets to the front crossmember.

7   Lift the rack out from under the car. It may be necessary to gently lever the lower universal joint coupling off the steering rack pinion.

8   Refitting the steering rack is the reverse of the removal sequence.

9   Take care when refitting the steering column lower universal joint coupling to the steering rack pinion. The correct alignment will ensure that the roadwheels will point in the straight-ahead position when the spokes of the steering wheel are in a horizontal plane.

10 Furthermore it will be necessary to have the steering alignment checked and adjusted by a garage after refitting the steering rack assembly.

Fig. 11.6. Front suspension crossmember assembly (Sec. 5)

1   Locating brackets
2   Engine mounting nuts
3   Track control arm locating nuts and bolts

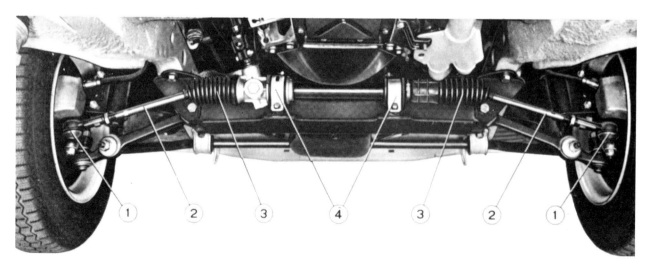

Fig. 11.7. Rear view of the suspension crossmember and steering rack and pinion (Sec. 5)

1   Tie rod ends
2   Tie rod
3   Rubber gaiters
4   Saddle brackets

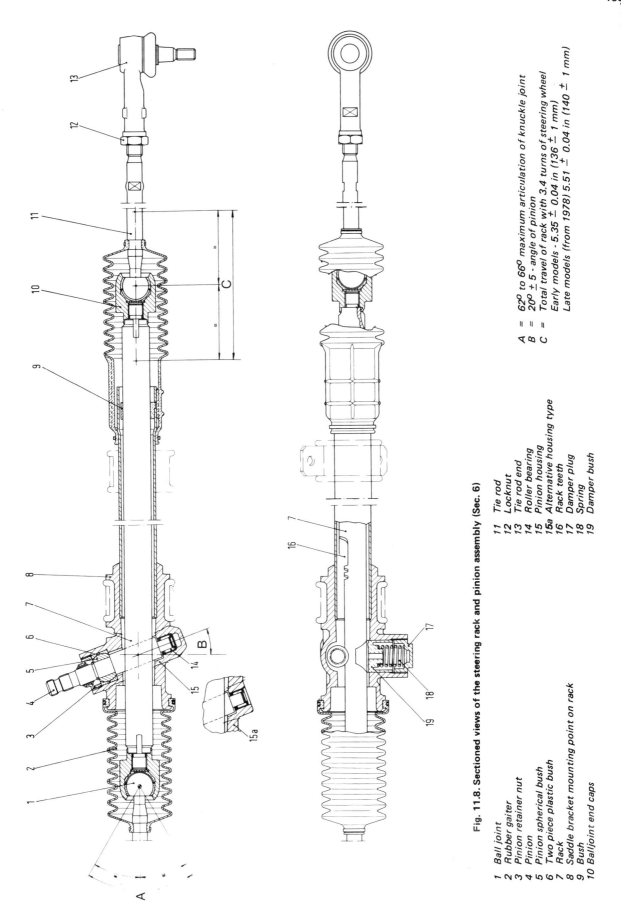

Fig. 11.8. Sectioned views of the steering rack and pinion assembly (Sec. 6)

1 Ball joint
2 Rubber gaiter
3 Pinion retainer nut
4 Pinion
5 Pinion spherical bush
6 Two piece plastic bush
7 Rack
8 Saddle bracket mounting point on rack
9 Bush
10 Balljoint end caps

11 Tie rod
12 Locknut
13 Tie rod end
14 Roller bearing
15 Pinion housing
15a Alternative housing type
16 Rack teeth
17 Damper plug
18 Spring
19 Damper bush

A = 62° to 66° maximum articulation of knuckle joint
B = 20° ± 5 - angle of pinion
C = Total travel of rack with 3.4 turns of steering wheel
       Early models - 5.35 ± 0.04 in (136 ± 1 mm)
       Late models (from 1978) 5.51 ± 0.04 in (140 ± 1 mm)

7   Steering rack and pinion - overhaul and adjustment

1   Remove the rack and pinion assembly from the car as described in Section 6 of this Chapter.

2   Tip the rack and pinion assembly so that the oil inside it is drained to one end.

3   Slacken the clips which retain the rubber gaiters and slide the gaiters back towards the tie-rods.

4   Drain the oil into a suitable receptacle.

5   Place the inner rack assembly in a vice fitted with protected jaws and using a punch and hammer knock back the crimped end caps of the ball joints. On reassembly new ball joint end caps will have to be fitted.

6   Having removed the ball joints and tie-rods now remove the damper locking plate, damper plug, damper spring and finally the plastic damper itself (photo).

7   Now remove the pinion securing nut and withdraw the pinion along with the upper half of a plastic bush.

8   Inspect the lower half of the plastic bush and remove it if necessary.

9   There is located in the bottom of the alloy casing a needle roller bearing in which the end of the pinion rotates. If it is found to be worn or damaged the needle roller bearing will have to be renewed.

10   With the pinion now removed the inner rack can be pulled out from the alloy outer housing.

11   Clean and inspect all parts for wear. Renew any damaged parts. During reassembly all moving parts should be lubricated and tightened to the torque wrench settings listed at the beginning of this Chapter.

12   Renew the inner pinion needle roller bearing if necessary.

13   Now slide the rack back into the alloy housing and ensure that the teeth of the rack face towards the pinion.

14   The lower half of the plastic two-piece bush can now be refitted followed by the pinion.

15   Refit the upper half of the plastic bush and the threaded retainer. Smear the pinion retainer with sealer Curilk 2 and tighten the nut to a torque of 22 - 23 lb f ft (3 - 3.2 kg fm).

16   Unscrew the pinion nut by approximately ¾ of a turn and check that the torque applied at the pinion to move the rack is not greater than 11 lb f ft (1.5 kg fm).

17   If the torque required to move the rack is greater than this figure the locknut can be backed off a further 1/12 of a turn.

18   Lock the pinion nut by lightly peening over the thread on the alloy casing.

19   Place the rack in the central position in relation to the pinion and refit the damper, spring and plug smearing the threads of the plug with a sealing agent. Refit the damper locking plate.

20   Refit the ball joints and end caps along with the tie-rods and

7.6 The steering rack damper plug lock plate in position

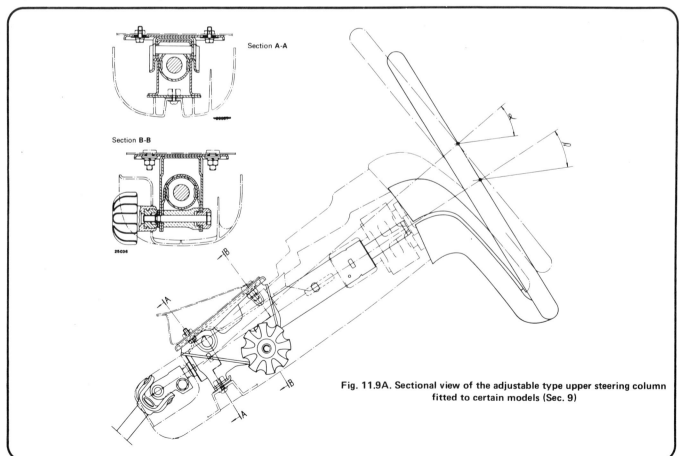

Section **A-A**

Section **B-B**

Fig. 11.9A. Sectional view of the adjustable type upper steering column
fitted to certain models (Sec. 9)

tighten the ball joint caps to a torque of 11 lb f ft (1.5 kg fm).
21 Now peen over the caps into the grooves provided on the inner rack.
22 If it is found necessary to renew the rubber gaiters, the tie-rod ends will first have to be removed to slide the old gaiters off.
23 Fit one of the gaiters and tip the rack up to fill it with the recommended volume of the correct grade of oil.
24 To speed the refilling operation, turn the pinion until the rack is extended towards the end through which it is to be filled. Slowly pour the oil into the rack housing at the same time turn the pinion which will draw the rack and oil back inside the housing.
25 When the rack has been refilled refit the other rubber gaiter and tighten the gaiter securing clips.
26 The rack and pinion assembly is now ready for refitting to the car as detailed in Section 6 of this Chapter.

8 Steering wheel - removal and refitting

1 Disconnect the battery negative earth lead.
2 Using a screwdriver prise out the horn press from the centre of the steering wheel; on models fitted with a single spoke steering wheel, the horn press pad is secured by two screws which are removed from underneath the spoke.
3 Remove the two plastic steering column shrouds which are retained by four screws. On some models there is fitted a steering column rake angle adjuster knob.
4 Remove the knob from the rake adjuster.
5 Remove the steering wheel retainer nut and washer.
6 Set the roadwheels in the straight-ahead position before drawing the steering wheel off.

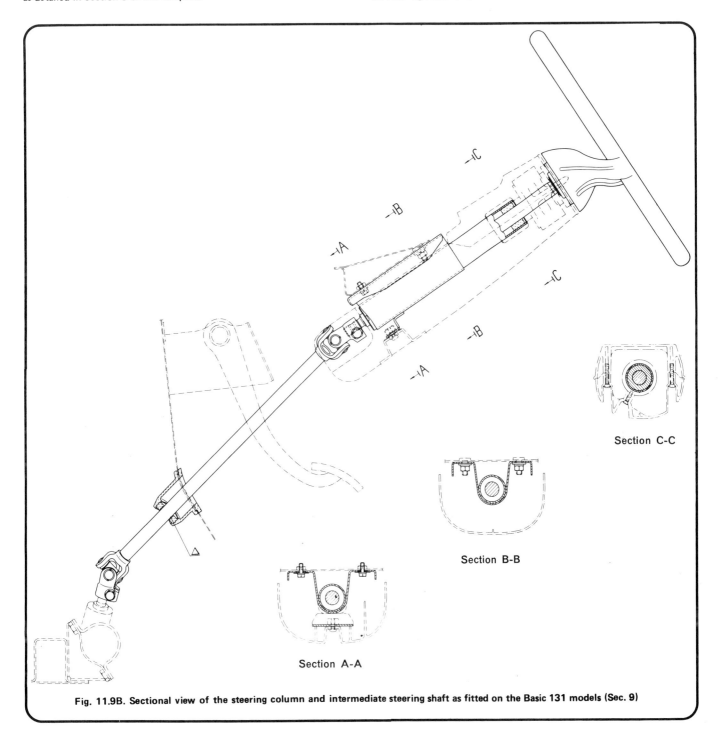

Section C-C

Section B-B

Section A-A

Fig. 11.9B. Sectional view of the steering column and intermediate steering shaft as fitted on the Basic 131 models (Sec. 9)

Fig. 11.10. The steering column and intermediate shaft assemblies (Sec. 9)

1	Universal joint coupling	4	Universal joint coupling	7	Indicator and wiper switch
2	Intermediate shaft	5	Steering column support bracket	8	Steering wheel location splines
3	Grommet	6	Ignition switch		

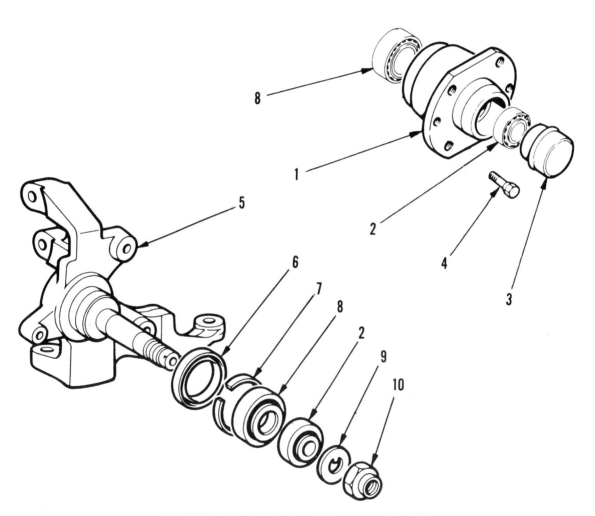

Fig. 11.11. Left-hand stub axle and hub assembly (Sec. 10)

1	Hub	4	Wheel retaining bolt	7	Retainer ring	9	Washer
2	Outer hub bearing	5	Stub axle assembly	8	Inner hub bearing	10	Hub retainer nut
3	Hub end cap	6	Hub oil seal				

7 Using a suitable extractor, pull off the steering wheel. If an extractor is not available, apply blows from the ball of the hand; do not drive or tap the wheel off in any other way.
8 Refitting the steering wheel is the reverse of the removal operation.

9 Steering column and intermediate shaft - removal, dismantling and refitting

1 Remove the steering wheel by following the instructions listed in the previous Section.
2 Disconnect the wiring harness block connectors at the steering column.
3 Remove the four nuts and washers retaining the steering column support bracket. On the 'S' models the steering column is adjustable for rake angle by slackening the large knob on the side of the column.
4 Now remove the nut and bolt retaining the upper column to the intermediate shaft universal coupling.
5 The upper column assembly can now be removed complete with the ignition switch and control levers. Further dismantling of this assembly can take place if the steering column bushes are to be renewed.
6 To remove the intermediate shaft disconnect its lower coupling at the steering rack pinion by removing the nut and bolt.
7 Now remove the large grommet in the floor through which the shaft fits.
8 The intermediate shaft complete with the grommet can now be drawn back into the car and removed.
9 Refitting of the steering column and intermediate shaft assemblies is the reverse of the dismantling procedures.

10 Front hub - removal, dismantling, reassembly, refitting and adjustment

1 Jack up the appropriate roadwheel, having first slackened the roadwheel nuts, and support the car on axle stands or packing blocks.
2 Remove the roadwheel and release the front brake caliper and pads as described in Chapter 9, Section 3.
3 Now remove the caliper yoke as detailed in Chapter 9, Section 4.
4 Remove the brake disc as described in Chapter 9, Section 7.
5 Pull off the hub end cap and using a hammer and punch, tap back the peened lip of the hub retainer nut.
6 Remove the hub nut and washer.
7 The hub assembly can now be drawn off the stub axle complete.
8 Remove the outer bearing, the inner seal and retainer, and withdraw the inner bearing.
9 Clean all the parts carefully in petrol or paraffin (gasoline or kerosene), and check for obvious wear, scoring, pits or signs of overheating (a bluish discolouration). Brown grease stains are of no importance. Renew any worn parts.
10 The bearing outer tracks can be driven out. Note that both outer bearing tracks must be driven out by passing a suitable drift through the centre of the hub in each case.
11 Check the outer races in the same way as the bearings.
12 Renew the bearings as complete assemblies where necessary. **On no account mix up parts of bearings from one side of the car to the other.**
13 Press in the bearing outer tracks, then lubricate the bearing races with a general purpose grease, working it well in with the fingers.
14 Partially pack the hub with grease, then fit the bearing races.
15 Refit the retainer ring behind the inner bearing.
16 Fit a new oil seal with the lips facing the inner bearing then push the hub onto the axle. Take care that the outer bearing is not dislodged.
17 Fit the washer to the stub axle and fit a new hub nut.
18 Initially tighten the hub nut to 14 lb f ft (2 kg fm) whilst rotating the hub.
19 Now back the nut off and retighten it to 5 lb f ft (0.7 kg f m), then loosen off the nut from the torqued position by turning it back by 30°
20 Measure the endfloat of the hub using a dial gauge. The endfloat should be between 0.001 - 0.004 in (0.025 - 0.10 mm).
21 Using a punch and hammer tap the end of the hub nut into the locking groove on the stub axle.
22 Fill the hub grease retainer with a little grease and refit it.
23 Reassembly now follows the reverse of the dismantling sequence.

11 Rear coil spring and shockabsorber - removal and refitting

1 Removal of the shockabsorbers on estate car models is a straightforward operation as they are mounted independently from the coil spring units.
2 On other models removal of the shockabsorbers necessitates the dismantling of the rear suspension.
3 Jack up the rear of the car and support its weight on axle stands or suitable packing blocks.
4 Support the axle case with either a trolley jack or two hydraulic jacks.
5 Now disconnect the three-way brake connector block at the rear axle having first placed a piece of thin polythene under the master cylinder filler cap to prevent excessive loss of brake fluid.
6 Release the rear brake pressure regulator control rod from its axle mounting point.
7 Remove the nuts and bolts securing the upper trailing arms to the body and likewise remove the nut and bolt securing the Panhard rod to its body mounting bracket.
8 Remove the lower shockabsorber mounting bolts and nuts (photo).

Fig. 11.12. Right-hand rear shockabsorber and mounting as fitted to Estate car models (Sec. 11)

1 Shockabsorber
2 Lower mounting bolt
3 Lower mounting bracket

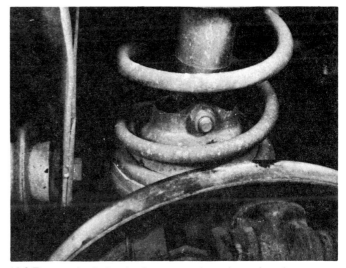

11.8 The rear shock absorber lower mounting point at the axle

12.1 The location of the Panhard rod to the chassis mounting bracket

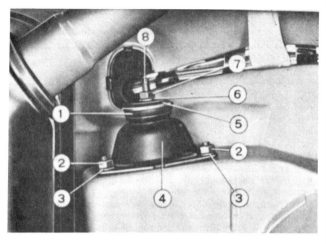

Fig. 11.13. Upper mounting of the rear shockabsorber as fitted on Saloon cars (Sec. 12)

1	Rubber block	5	Washer
2	Nut	6	Spring washer
3	Spring washer	7	Nut
4	Upper mounting turret	8	Shockabsorber spindle

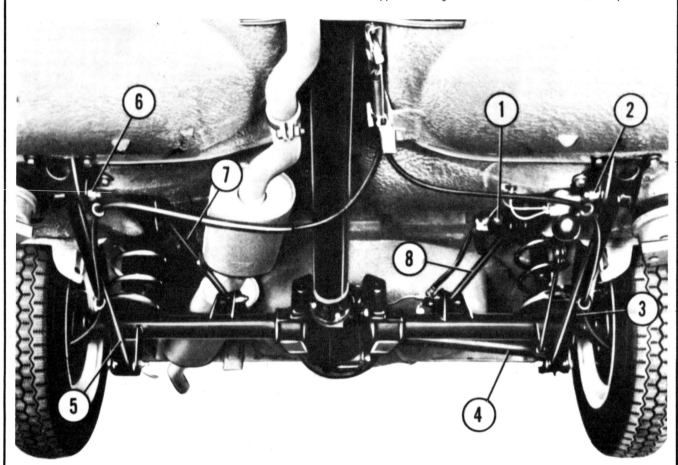

Fig. 11.14. The location of the rear axle assembly (Sec. 12)

1	Upper trailing arm locating bracket	5	Lower trailing arm right-hand
2	Lower trailing arm locating bracket left-hand	6	Lower trailing arm bracket right-hand
3	Lower trailing arm left-hand	7	Upper trailing arm right-hand
4	Panhard rod	8	Upper trailing arm left-hand

9 Remove the rear roadwheels and lower the axle gently down until the coil springs are free.
10 The upper shockabsorber mountings are within the boot and secured by a single locknut on each unit.
11 Refitting is a reversal of the dismantling procedure but do not tighten the mounting bolts and nuts until the whole assembly is in place.
12 Remember that the rear brakes will have to be bled as described in Chapter 9, Section 2.

12 Trailing arms and Panhard rod - removal and refitting

1 Removal of these units is straightforward requiring the removal of nuts and bolts (photo).
2 Likewise the chassis mounting brackets of these units are retained by bolts.
3 When removing the lower trailing arms it will be necessary to disconnect the handbrake cable at the backplate as described in Chapter 9, Section 17.
4 Refitting the units is the reverse of the dismantling procedure. Remember to tighten all nuts and bolts to the recommended torque wrench settings as specified at the beginning of this Chapter.

13 Roadwheels and tyres

1 Whenever the roadwheels are removed it is a good idea to clean the insides to remove the accumulations of mud and in the case of the front ones, disc pad dust.
2 Check the condition of the wheel for rust and repaint if necessary.
3 Examine the wheel stud holes. If these are tending to become elongated, or the dished recesses in which the retaining bolts seat have become worn or overcompressed, then the wheel will have to be renewed.
4 With the roadwheel removed, pick out any embedded flints from the tread and check for splits in the sidewalls or damage to the tyre carcasses generally.
5 Where the depth of tread pattern is 1 mm or less, the tyre must be renewed.
6 Rotation of the roadwheels to even out wear is a worthwhile idea if the wheels have been balanced off the car. Include the spare wheel in the rotational pattern.
7 If the wheels have been balanced on the car they should not be moved round the car as the balance of the wheel, tyre and hub will be upset. In fact their exact fitting positions must be marked before removing a roadwheel so that it can be returned to its original 'in-balance' state.
8 It is recommended that wheels are rebalanced halfway through the life of the tyres to compensate for the loss of tread rubber due to wear.
9 Finally, always keep the tyres (including the spare) inflated to the recommended pressures and always refit the dust caps on the tyre valves. Tyre pressures are best checked first thing in the morning when the tyres are cold.

14 Front wheel alignment - checking and adjustment

1 It is essential that the front wheel alignment is correct to ensure satisfactory steering and long tyre life. Before the steering geometry is considered, check that the tyres are correctly inflated, that the front wheels are not buckled and that the front hub bearings are not worn badly or incorrectly adjusted. The steering linkages and joints must also be in good condition, without excessive play at the joints.
2 The principle factors contributing to correct wheel alignment are:

(a) Camber angle - the angle at which the front wheels are set from the vertical when viewed from the front of the vehicle with the wheels in the straight-ahead position
(b) Castor angle - the angle between the steering axis and a vertical line viewed from each side. With positive castor, the steering axis is inclined rearward
(c) Steering axis inclination - the angle, when viewed from the front of the vehicle, between the vertical and a hypothetical line drawn through the king pin. The steering angle is the angle through which the front wheels pivot from lock to lock
(d) Toe-in - the measurable distance difference between the front inside edges of the roadwheels at hub height and the diametrically opposite distance measured between the rear inside edges of the front roadwheels (also at hub height)

3 Checking steering alignment and angles accurately requires the use of specialised equipment. It is therefore beyond the scope of the home mechanic and must be entrusted to your FIAT dealer. It is, however, possible to check the toe-in using improvised equipment in the following manner.
4 Place the vehicle on level ground with the wheels in the straight-ahead position.
5 Obtain or make a toe-in gauge. One may be easily made from tubing, cranked to clear the oil pan (sump) having an adjustable nut and setscrew at one end.
6 Using the gauge, measure the distance between the two inner wheel rims at hub height at the rear of the wheels.
7 Rotate the wheels (by pushing the car backwards or forwards) through 180° (half a turn) and again using the gauge, measure the distance of hub height between the two inner wheel rims at the front of the wheels. This measurement should be less than that previously taken at the rear of the wheel by the amount given in the Specifications, and represents the correct toe-in.
8 Where the toe-in is found to be incorrect, slacken the locknuts on the end of the trackrod, and rotate the rod until the correct toe-in is obtained. Tighten the locknuts, ensuring that the balljoints are held in the center of their arc of travel during tightening. Both rods must be adjusted equally to retain the steering wheel alignment.

15 Fault diagnosis - suspension and steering

Symptom	Reason/s
Steering feels vague, car wanders and 'floats' at speed	Tyre pressures uneven. Shockabsorbers worn. Steering balljoints worn. Steering mechanism free play excessive. Front hub bearings slack. Wheel alignment incorrect.
Stiff and heavy steering	Tyre pressures low. No oil in steering rack assembly. Front wheel toe-in incorrect. Steering gear incorrectly adjusted too tight.
Wheel wobble or vibration	Roadwheels out of balance. Wheel retainer bolts slack. Steering ball joints badly worn. Steering gear free play excessive. Broken front coil spring.

Chapter 12 Bodywork and fittings

For modifications, and information applicable to later models, see Supplement at end of manual

Contents

Specifications

Weights

4-DOOR SALOON		2-DOOR SALOON		ESTATE CAR	
131	*131 Special*	*131*	*131 Special*	*131*	*131 Special*
2172 lb	2195 lb	2128 lb	2150 lb	2249 lb	2272 lb
(985 kg)	(995 kg)	(965 kg)	(975 kg)	(1020 kg)	(1030 kg)

Kerb weight table for UK cars (add 44 lb or 20 kg for automatic transmission models).

TYPE OF TRANSMISSION UNIT FITTED	2 AND 4 DOOR SALOON	ESTATE CAR
Manual	2460 lb	2510 lb
Automatic	2490 lb	2540 lb

Kerb weight table for USA cars (add 80 lb for air conditioning equipment). The term 'kerb weight' applied in the tables above assumes that the vehicle is in an unladen state and is equipped with a spare wheel, tool kit, and the fuel, oil and water levels are correct.

1 General description

The combined body and chassis underframe is made up of steel fabrications electrically welded together to form a 'monocoque' structure. Certain areas are reinforced to provide mounting points for the suspension, steering system, engine supports etc.

Saloon versions are available as two or four door models whereas the estate car versions have four doors and a full width tailgate hinged at the top. The side doors of all models are forward opening, with anti-burst door locks and flush door handles.

UK models are available as either 'basic' or 'special' versions, whereas the USA models are all of the 'special' type. The most noticeable difference between the 'basic' and 'special' models is the headlights. The 'basic' model has a pair of rectangular shaped headlights whereas the 'special' model is fitted with a four headlight system the lights of which are round.

2 Maintenance - bodywork and underframe

1 The general condition of a car's bodywork is the thing that significantly affects its value. Maintenance is easy but needs to be regular.

Neglect, particularly after minor damage, can lead quickly to further deterioration and costly repair bills. It is important also to keep watch on those parts of the car not immediately visible, for instance the underside, inside all the wheel arches and the lower part of the engine compartment.

2 The basic maintenance routine for the bodywork is washing - preferably with a lot of water, from a hose. This will remove all the loose solids which may have stuck to the car. It is important to flush these off in such a way as to prevent grit from scratching the finish. The wheel arches and underframe need washing in the same way to remove any accumulated mud which will retain moisture and tend to encourage rust. Paradoxically enough, the best time to clean the underframe and wheel arches is in wet weather when the mud is thoroughly wet and soft. In very wet weather the underframe is usually cleaned of large accumulations automatically and this is a good time for inspection.

3 Periodically, it is a good idea to have the whole of the underframe of the car steam cleaned, engine compartment included, so that a thorough inspection can be carried out to see what minor repairs and renovations are necessary. Steam cleaning is available at many garages and is necessary for removal of the accumulation of oily grime which sometimes is allowed to become thick in certain areas. If steam cleaning facilities are not available, there are one or two excellent grease solvents available which can be brush applied. The dirt can then be simply hosed off.

4   After washing paintwork, wipe off with a chamois leather to give an unspotted clear finish. A coat of clear protective wax polish will give added protection against chemical pollutants in the air. If the paint-work sheen has dulled or oxidised, use a cleaner/polisher combination to restore the brilliance of the shine. This requires a little effort, but such dulling is usually caused because regular washing has been neglected. Always check that the door and ventilator opening drain holes and pipes are completely clear so that water can be drained out. Bright work should be treated in the same way as paintwork. Wind-screens and windows can be kept clear of the smeary film which often appears, by adding a little ammonia to the water. If they are scratched a good rub with a proprietary metal polish will often clear them. Never use any form of wax or other body or chromium polish on glass.

3   Maintenance - upholstery and carpets

1   Mats and carpets should be brushed or vacuum cleaned regularly to keep them free of grit. If they are badly stained remove them from the car for scrubbing or sponging and make quite sure they are dry before refitting. Seats and interior trim panels can be kept clean by a wipe over with a damp cloth. If they do become stained (which can be more apparent on light coloured upholstery) use a little liquid detergent and a soft nail brush to scour the grime out of the grain of the material. Do not forget to keep the head lining clean in the same way as the upholstery. When using liquid cleaners inside the car do not over-wet the surfaces being cleaned. Excessive damp could get into the seams and padded interior causing stains, offensive odours or even rot. If the inside of the car gets wet accidentally it is worthwhile taking some trouble to dry it out properly, particularly where carpets are involved. *Do not leave oil or electric heaters inside the car for this purpose.*

4   Minor body damage - repair

The photographic sequences on pages 174 and 175 illustrate the operations detailed in the following sub-sections.

Repair of minor scratches in the car's bodywork

If the scratch is very superficial, and does not penetrate to the metal of the bodywork, repair is very simple. Lightly rub the area of the scratch with a paintwork renovator, or a very fine cutting paste, to remove loose paint from the scratch and to clear the surrounding bodywork of wax polish. Rinse the area with clean water.

Apply touch-up paint to the scratch using a fine paintbrush; con-tinue to apply thin layers of paint until the surface of the paint in the scratch is level with the surrounding paintwork. Allow the new paint at least two weeks to harden: then blend it into the surrounding paintwork by rubbing the scratch area with a paintwork renovator or a very fine cutting paste. Finally, apply wax polish.

Where the scratch has penetrated right through to the metal of the bodywork, causing the metal to rust, a different repair technique is required. Remove any loose rust from the bottom of the scratch with a penknife, then apply rust inhibiting paint to prevent the formation of rust in the future. Using a rubber or nylon applicator fill the scratch with bodystopper paste. If required, this paste can be mixed with cellulose thinners to provide a very thin paste which is ideal for filling narrow scratches. Before the stopper-paste in the scratch hardens, wrap a piece of smooth cotton rag around the top of a finger. Dip the finger in cellulose thinners and then quickly sweep it across the surface of the stopper-paste in the scratch; this will ensure that the surface of the stopper-paste is slightly hollowed. The scratch can now be painted over as described earlier in this Section.

Repair of dents in the car's bodywork

When deep denting of the car's bodywork has taken place, the first task is to pull the dent out, until the affected bodywork almost attains its original shape. There is little point in trying to restore the original shape completely, as the metal in the damaged area will have stretched on impact and cannot be reshaped fully to its original contour. It is better to bring the level of the dent up to a point which is about 1/8 in (3 mm) below the level of the surrounding bodywork. In cases where the dent is very shallow anyway, it is not worth trying to pull it out at all. If the underside of the dent is accessible, it can be hammered out

gently from behind, using a mallet with a wooden or plastic head. Whilst doing this, hold a suitable block of wood firmly against the outside of the panel to absorb the impact from the hammer blows and thus prevent a large area of the bodywork from being 'belled-out'.

Should the dent be in a section of the bodywork which has double skin or some other factor making it inaccessible from behind, a different technique is called for. Drill several small holes through the metal inside the area — particularly in the deeper section. Then screw long self-tapping screws into the holes just sufficiently for them to gain a good purchase in the metal. Now the dent can be pulled out by pulling on the protruding heads of the screws with a pair of pliers.

The next stage of the repair is the removal of the paint from the damaged area, and from an inch or so of the surrounding 'sound' bodywork. This is accomplished most easily by using a wire brush or abrasive pad on a power drill, although it can be done just as effectively by hand using sheets of abrasive paper. To complete the preparation for filling, score the surface of the bare metal with a screwdriver or the tang of a file, or alternatively, drill small holes in the affected area. This will provide a really good 'key' for the filler paste.

To complete the repair see the Section on filling and respraying.

Repair of rust holes or gashes in the car's bodywork

Remove all paint from the affected area and from an inch or so of the surrounding 'sound' bodywork, using an abrasive pad or a wire brush on a power drill. If these are not available a few sheets of abrasive paper will do the job just as effectively. With the paint removed you will be able to gauge the severity of the corrosion and therefore decide whether to renew the whole panel (if this is possible) or to repair the affected area. New body panels are not as expensive as most people think and it is often quicker and more satisfactory to fit a new panel than to attempt to repair large areas of corrosion.

Remove all fittings from the affected area except those which will act as a guide to the original shape of the damaged bodywork (eg headlamp shells etc). Then, using tin snips or a hacksaw blade, remove all loose metal and any other metal badly affected by corrosion. Hammer the edges of the hole inwards in order to create a slight de-pression for the filler paste.

Wire brush the affected area to remove the powdery rust from the surface of the remaining metal. Paint the affected area with rust inhibiting paint; if the back of the rusted area is accessible treat this also.

Before filling can take place it will be necessary to block the hole in some way. This can be achieved by the use of zinc gauze or aluminium tape.

Zinc gauze is probably the best material to use for a large hole. Cut a piece to the approximate size and shape of the hole to be filled, then position it in the hole so that its edges are below the level of the sur-rounding bodywork. It can be retained in position by several blobs of filler paste around its periphery.

Aluminium tape should be used for small or very narrow holes. Pull a piece off the roll and trim it to the approximate size and shape required, then pull off the backing paper (if used) and stick the tape over the hole; it can be overlapped if the thickness of one piece is insufficient. Burnish down the edges of the tape with the handle of a screwdriver or similar, to ensure that the tape is securely attached to the metal underneath.

Bodywork repairs - filling and respraying

Before using this Section, see the Sections on dent, deep scratch, rust holes and gash repairs.

Many types of bodyfiller are available, but generally speaking those proprietary kits which contain a tin of filler paste and a tube of resin hardener are best for this type of repair. A wide, flexible plastic or nylon applicator will be found invaluable for imparting a smooth and well contoured finish to the surface of the filler.

Mix up a little filler on a clean piece of card or board — measure the hardener carefully (follow the maker's instructions on the pack) otherwise the filler will set too rapidly or too slowly.

Using the applicator apply the filler paste to the prepared area; draw the applicator across the surface of the filler to achieve the correct contour and to level the filler surface. As soon as a contour that approximates to the correct one is achieved, stop working the paste — if you carry on too long the paste will become sticky and begin to 'pick up' on the applicator. Continue to add thin layers of filler paste at twenty-minute intervals until the level of the filler is just proud of the surrounding bodywork.

This sequence of photographs deals with the repair of the dent and paintwork damage shown in this photo. The procedure will be similar for the repair of a hole. It should be noted that the procedures given here are simplified — more explicit instructions will be found in the text

In the case of a dent the first job — after removing surrounding trim — is to hammer out the dent where access is possible. This will minimise filling. Here, the large dent having been hammered out, the damaged area is being made slightly concave

Now all paint must be removed from the damaged area, by rubbing with coarse abrasive paper. Alternatively, a wire brush or abrasive pad can be used in a power drill. Where the repair area meets good paintwork, the edge of the paintwork should be 'feathered', using a finer grade of abrasive paper

In the case of a hole caused by rusting, all damaged sheet-metal should be cut away before proceeding to this stage. Here, the damaged area is being treated with rust remover and inhibitor before being filled

Mix the body filler according to its manufacturer's instructions. In the case of corrosion damage, it will be necessary to block off any large holes before filling — this can be done with aluminium or plastic mesh, or aluminium tape. Make sure the area is absolutely clean before ...

... applying the filler. Filler should be applied with a flexible applicator, as shown, for best results; the wooden spatula being used for confined areas. Apply thin layers of filler at 20-minute intervals, until the surface of the filler is slightly proud of the surrounding bodywork

Initial shaping can be done with a Surform plane or Dreadnought file. Then, using progressively finer grades of wet-and-dry paper, wrapped around a sanding block, and copious amounts of clean water, rub down the filler until really smooth and flat. Again, feather the edges of adjoining paintwork

The whole repair area can now be sprayed or brush-painted with primer. If spraying, ensure adjoining areas are protected from over-spray. Note that at least one inch of the surrounding sound paintwork should be coated with primer. Primer has a 'thick' consistency, so will find small imperfections

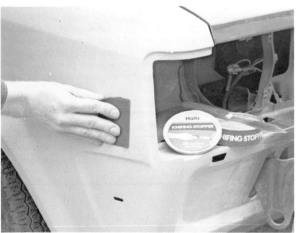

Again, using plenty of water, rub down the primer with a fine grade wet-and-dry paper (400 grade is probably best) until it is really smooth and well blended into the surrounding paintwork. Any remaining imperfections can now be filled by carefully applied knifing stopper paste

When the stopper has hardened, rub down the repair area again before applying the final coat of primer. Before rubbing down this last coat of primer, ensure the repair area is blemish-free — use more stopper if necessary. To ensure that the surface of the primer is really smooth use some finishing compound

The top coat can now be applied. When working out of doors, pick a dry, warm and wind-free day. Ensure surrounding areas are protected from over-spray. Agitate the aerosol thoroughly, then spray the centre of the repair area, working outwards with a circular motion. Apply the paint as several thin coats

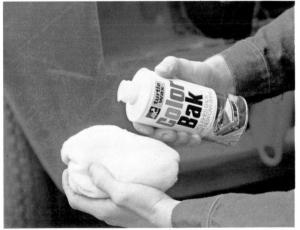

After a period of about two weeks, which the paint needs to harden fully, the surface of the repaired area can be 'cut' with a mild cutting compound prior to wax polishing. When carrying out bodywork repairs, remember that the quality of the finished job is proportional to the time and effort expended

Once the filler has hardened, excess can be removed using a metal plane or file. From then on, progressively finer grades of abrasive paper should be used, starting with a 40 grade production paper and finishing with 400 grade wet-and-dry paper. Always wrap the abrasive paper around a flat rubber, cork, or wooden block — otherwise the surface of the filler will not be completely flat. During the smoothing of the filler surface the wet-and-dry paper should be periodically rinsed in water. This will ensure that a very smooth finish is imparted to the filler at the final stage.

At this stage the 'dent' should be surrounded by a ring of bare metal, which in turn should be encircled by the finely 'feathered' edge of the good paintwork. Rinse the repair area with clean water, until all of the dust produced by the rubbing-down operation has gone.

Spray the whole repair area with a light coat of primer — this will show up any imperfections in the surface of the filler. Repair these imperfections with fresh filler paste or bodystopper, and once more smooth the surface with abrasive paper. If bodystopper is used, it can be mixed with cellulose thinners to form a really thin paste which is ideal for filling small holes. Repeat this spray and repair procedure until you are satisfied that the surface of the filler, and the feathered edge of the paintwork are perfect. Clean the repair area with clean water and allow to dry fully.

The repair area is now ready for final spraying. Paint spraying must be carried out in a warm, dry, windless and dust free atmosphere. This condition can be created artificially if you have access to a large indoor working area, but if you are forced to work in the open, you will have to pick your day very carefully. If you are working indoors, dousing the floor in the work area with water will help settle the dust which would otherwise be in the atmosphere. If the repair area is confined to one body panel, mask off the surrounding panels; this will help to minimise the effects of a slight mis-match in paint colours. Bodywork fittings (eg chrome strips, door handles etc) will also need to be masked off. Use genuine masking tape and several thicknesses of newspaper for the masking operations.

Before commencing to spray, agitate the aerosol can thoroughly, then spray a test area (an old tin, or similar) until the technique is mastered. Cover the repair area with a thick coat of primer; the thick-

ness should be built up using several thin layers of paint rather than one thick one. Using 400 grade wet-and-dry paper, rub down the surface of the primer until it is really smooth. While doing this, the work area should be thoroughly doused with water, and the wet-and-dry paper periodically rinsed in water. Allow to dry before spraying on more paint.

Spray on the top coat, again building up the thickness by using several thin layers of paint. Start spraying in the centre of the repair area and then, using a circular motion, work outwards until the whole repair area and about 2 inches of the surrounding original paintwork is covered. Remove all masking material 10 to 15 minutes after spraying on the final coat of paint.

Allow the new paint at least two weeks to harden, then, using a paintwork renovator or a very fine cutting paste, blend the edges of the paint into the existing paintwork. Finally, apply wax polish.

5 Major body damage - repair

1　Where serious damage has occurred or large areas need renewal due to neglect, it means certainly that completely new sections or panels will need welding in and this is best left to professionals. If the damage is due to impact it will also be necessary to completely check the alignment of the bodyshell structure. Due to the principle of construction, the strength and shape of the whole can be affected by damage to a part. In such instances the services of a FIAT agent with specialist checking jigs are essential. If a body is left misaligned, it is first of all dangerous as the car will not handle properly - and secondly, uneven stresses will be imposed on the steering, engine and transmission, causing abnormal wear or complete failure. Tyre wear will also be excessive.

6 Bumpers - removal and refitting

1　Some models are fitted with energy absorbing bumpers while others are fitted with the conventional chromium plated type having rubber

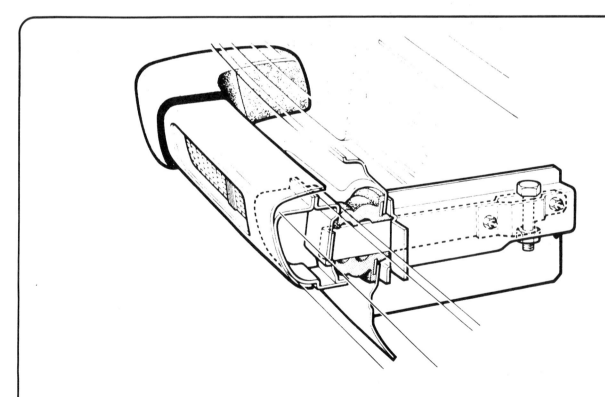

Fig. 12.1. Cross sectional view through the energy-absorbing bumper fitted as an option to some models (Sec. 6)

cappings and strips for additional protection.

2   Both front and rear bumper bars are located by brackets and bolts. There are bolts holding each bumper in place and removal is a straightforward procedure. Apply penetrating oil to rusted bolts.

3   When removing the front bumper, however, it will be found necessary to disconnect the side/indicator lamp wing connections.

4   On removing the rear bumper bar it will be found necessary to disconnect the wiring to the number plate illumination lamp.

5   Refitting the bumper bars is the reverse of the dismantling procedure.

7   Radiator grille - removal and refitting

1   Open the bonnet and disconnect the block connectors fitted to the headlamps. The basic models have two blocks while the special models have four.

2   Unscrew the radiator grille retaining screws.

3   Lift the grille out complete with the headlamp units and their attached backing plate.

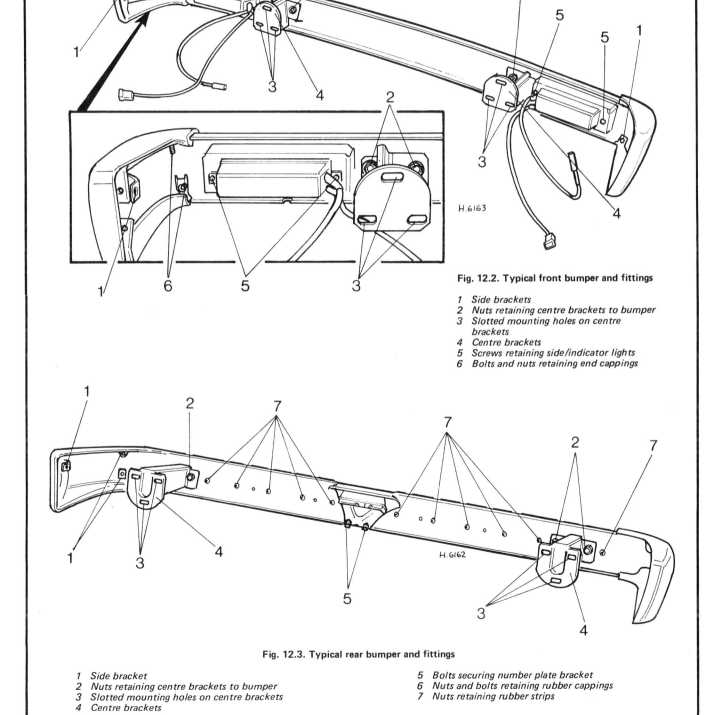

Fig. 12.2. Typical front bumper and fittings

1   Side brackets
2   Nuts retaining centre brackets to bumper
3   Slotted mounting holes on centre brackets
4   Centre brackets
5   Screws retaining side/indicator lights
6   Bolts and nuts retaining end cappings

Fig. 12.3. Typical rear bumper and fittings

1   Side bracket   5   Bolts securing number plate bracket
2   Nuts retaining centre brackets to bumper   6   Nuts and bolts retaining rubber cappings
3   Slotted mounting holes on centre brackets   7   Nuts retaining rubber strips
4   Centre brackets

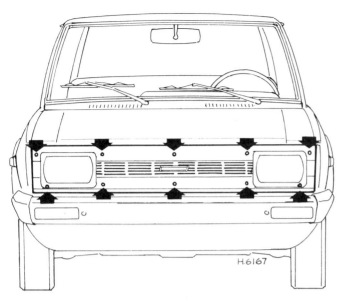

Fig. 12.4. The ten grille fixing screws (Basic 131 model shown) (Sec. 7)

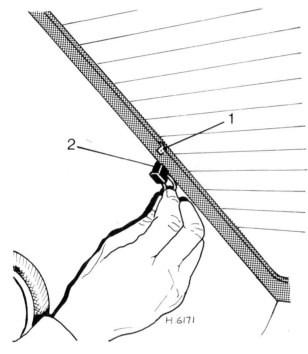

Fig. 12.5. Removing the wiring connector from the heated rear window (Sec. 8)

1 Spade terminal   2 Connector plug

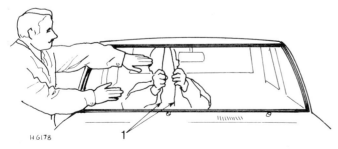

Fig. 12.6. Fitting a front screen using a length of strong cord (Sec. 8)

1 The ends of the cord

4   The headlamp units can be removed from the grille by removing their backing plate which is located by screws.
5   Refitting the grille is the reverse of the dismantling procedure.

8   Windscreen and rear window glass - removal and refitting

1   The windscreen and rear window glass are located by a rubber extrusion which slips around the mounting flange in the screen aperture and around the periphery of the glass screen. A metal chromed trim is used to lock the screen and mounting flange in the rubber extrusion on Special models.
2   The following procedure describes the removal sequence of the windscreen fitted to the Special model which is almost identical to the removal of the windscreen fitted to the Basic model. On cars fitted with a heated rear window the wiring connections must first be separated before commencing the removal sequence.
3   If the windscreen or rear window shatters, refitting a replacement is one of the tasks the average owner is advised to leave to the experienced fitter. For the owner wishing to do the job himself the following instructions are given:
4   Remove the wiper arms from their spindles, remove the interior rear view mirror and the sun visors. Cover the screen heating apertures with sticky tape.
5   Next extract the metal trim from the outside of the screen edge rubber. This trim locks the rubber extrusion around the glass screen edge.
6   Place a blanket or suitable protection on the car bonnet to prevent scoring the paintwork with the broken screen.
7   Move to the inside of the car and have an assistant outside the car to catch the screen as it is released.
8   Wearing leather gloves or similar hand protection push on the glass screen as near to the edge as possible, beginning at the top corners. The rubber extrusion should deform and allow the screen to move outwards out of the screen aperture. This of course is not applicable if the screen has shattered.
9   Remove the rubber surround from the glass or alternatively carefully pick out the remains of the glass. Use a vacuum cleaner to extract as much of the screen debris as possible.
10 Carefully inspect the rubber extrusion surround for signs of pitting or deterioration. Offer up the new glass to the screen aperture and check that the shape and curvature of the screen conforms to that of the aperture. A screen will break quite soon again if the aperture and glass do not suit, typically if the vehicle has been involved in an accident during which the screen broke. A car bodyshell can be deformed easily in such instances to such an extent that the aperture will need reshaping by a competent body repairer to ensure conformity with a new screen.
11 Position the glass into the rubber extrusion surround, remember that the groove for the metal trim needs to be on the outer side of the screen assembly.
12 With the rubber now correctly positioned around the glass, a long piece of strong cord should be inserted in the slot in the rubber extrusion which is to accept the flange of the screen aperture in the bodyshell. The two free ends of the cord should finish at either the top or bottom centre and overlap each other.
13 The screen is now offered up to the aperture, and an assistant will be required to press the rubber surround hard against the bodyshell flange. Slowly pull the cord from one end, moving around the windscreen, thereby drawing the lip of the rubber extrusion screen surround over the flange of the screen aperture.
14 Finally, ensure the rubber surround is correctly seated around the screen and then press in the metal trim strip which locks the screen in the rubber. Once the glass has been fitted satisfactorily the windscreen wipers, visors and interior mirror can be refitted. In the case of fitting the rear screen do not forget to reconnect the wires to the screen heating element.

9   Door rattles - tracing and rectification

1   The most common cause of door rattles is a misaligned, loose or worn striker plate, but other causes may be:

a) *Loose door handles, window winder handles or door hinges*
b) *Loose, worn or misaligned door lock components.*
c) *Loose or worn remote control mechanism, or a combination*
   of these.

2   If the striker catch is worn, renew and adjust, as described later in this Chapter.
3   Should the hinges be badly worn then it may become necessary for new ones to be fitted.

10 Doors and tailgate - removal and refitting

The front and rear doors can be removed in the same manner.
1   Squeeze together the legs of the check strap and release it from its bracket fixing bolted to the body.
2   With an assistant to hold the door remove the four bolts which secure the two hinges to the door frame.
3   Refitting the door is the reverse of the removal operation except that the door will require alignment and the catch will need adjusting. It will be advantageous to mark the exact position of the door hinges prior to removing the door so that it can be realigned easily.
4   The rear tailgate on estate car versions is easily removed following this procedure.
5   Disconnect the wiring connector at the heated rear screen.
6   With an assistant holding the tailgate remove the nut and washers

Fig. 12.7. The tailgate mountings (Sec. 10)

1 Nut retaining prop to tailgate	4 Connector for heated window
2 Tailgate	5 Hinge bolts
3 Prop	6 Hinge

securing the prop to it.
7   Remove the four bolts securing the two hinges to the body and lift the tailgate clear.
8   Refitting the tailgate is the reverse of the removal operation.

11 Interior handles and trim panel - removal and refitting

1   Remove the three screws holding the armrest/door pull in position. Two of the screws are located under the arm rest while the third is positioned underneath a blanking plug at the forward end of the arm rest. The plug is a push fit in the arm rest and can be gently levered out with a screwdriver (photos).
2   Depress the bezel around the window winder handle and using a piece of stiff wire, fashioned to a small hook, pull out the 'horse shoe' retainer clip. The winder handle can now be slid off (photos).
3   The bezel covering the inner door handle is retained by a plastic clip. Access to the clip is through a small slotted hole at the rear of the bezel.
4   Using a thin screwdriver press the plastic clip in and draw the bezel forward from the handle (photos).
5   The door trim panel can now be levered off carefully using a wide bladed screwdriver. This action will release the trim panel retaining clips (photo).
6   Remove the window winder spindle and inner door handle spacers (photo).
7   The inner door handle is retained by two screws and is easily removed after disconnecting the control rod at its rear (photo).
8   Refitting the components is the reverse of the removal operation.

12 Door catch and lock assemblies - removal and refitting

1   Two locking systems are incorporated in the front doors. An external key operated barrel lock is fitted into the outer door handle and operates the door catch/lock assembly through a link rod.
   The second locking system is provided by an internal sill lock button operating through another control rod acting on the catch/lock assembly.
2   To remove any of the above components the door trim panel will have to be renewed as detailed in Section 11.
3   To remove the external door handle/lock assembly, remove the two securing nuts and release the two control rods joined to it (photo).
4   The lock barrel is retained by a spring clip and a pin.
5   Drive out the pin joining the lock control lever to the lock cylinder.
6   Using a pair of long nosed pliers remove the spring clip retaining the lock barrel. Refit the lock barrel and reassemble the handle.
7   The catch/lock assembly is retained to the door by three screws and can be removed complete with interior door handle and control rods after having first removed the rear window channel.

13 Door glass and regulator - removal and refitting

Four door model
1   Remove the door trim panel and fittings as described in the previous

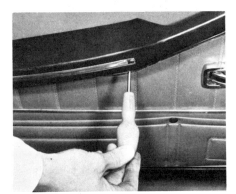
11.1A Remove the screws from the armrest/door pull

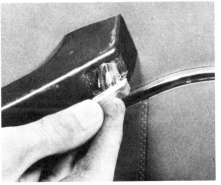
11.1B Removing the blanking plug from the front of the armrest/door pull

11.2A Sliding the winder off the spindle

11.2B The winder and the 'horse shoe' retainer clip

11.4A Use a thin screwdriver to depress the plastic clip retaining the bezel

11.4B Draw the bezel forward off the handle

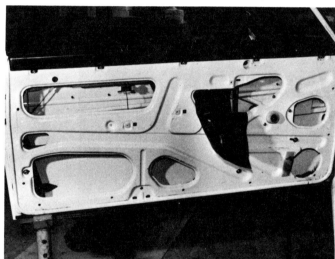

11.5 Remove the door trim panel

11.6 Remove the window winder spacer block

11.7 Remove the two screws retaining the inner door handle

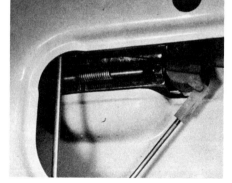

12.3 The external door handle viewed through the aperture in the inner door panel

Section.
2   Now remove the two screws holding the channel to the window regulator unit (Fig. 12.10).
3   Lift the window up at the same time tilt the glass down at the front end to release the channel from the regulator unit.
4   Remove the single lower and two upper bolts retaining the side

channel to the door frame.
5   Now remove the two bolts retaining the winder spindle mechanism to the door frame.
6   Push the clamp, situated near the bottom of the door panel, inwards.
7   The regulator assembly can now be removed through the aperture in the door frame.

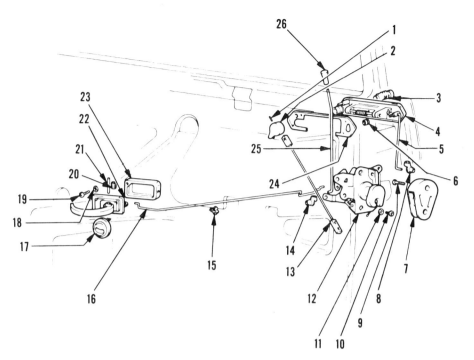

Fig. 12.8. Front door handles and catch/lock assemblies (Sec. 12)

1 Pin	7 Striker plate	13 Link rod	20 Spring
2 Control arm	8 Clip	14 Clip	21 Pin
3 Lock barrel	9 Screw	15 Clamp	22 Inner door handle
4 Outer door handle	10 Screw	16 Link rod	23 Trim fitting
5 Link rod	11 Washer	17 Trim ring	24 Gasket outer door handle
6 Nut	12 Catch	18 Washer	25 Inner lock rod
		19 Screw	26 Lock button

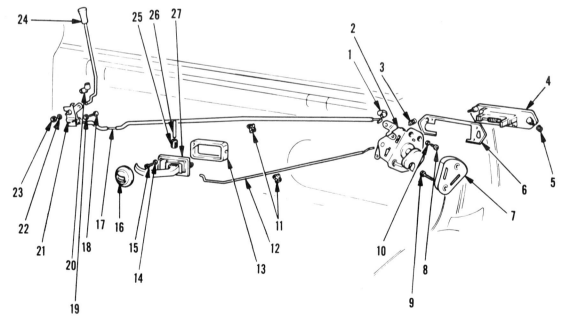

Fig. 12.9. Rear door handles and catch/lock assemblies (Sec. 12)

1 Clip	8 Screw	15 Screw	22 Washer
2 Catch/lock assembly	9 Screw	16 Trim ring	23 Nut
3 Spring	10 Washer	17 Link rod	24 Lock rod
4 Outer door handle	11 Clip	18 Screw	25 Spring
5 Nut	12 Link rod	19 Washer	26 Pin
6 Gasket outer door handle	13 Trim fitting	20 Clip	27 Inner door handle
7 Striker plate	14 Washer	21 Lock rod relay	

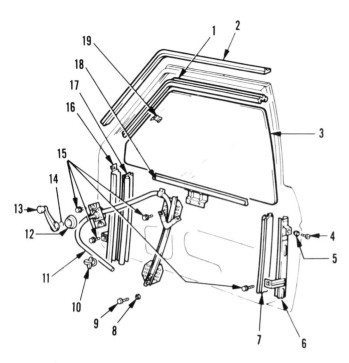

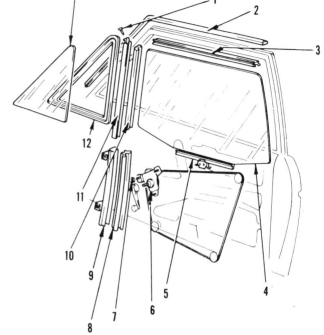

Fig. 12.10. Window and regulator as fitted to four door models (Sec. 13)

1	Weatherstrip	11	Regulator
2	Weatherstrip	12	Trim bezel
3	Glass	13	Winder handle
4	Screw	14	Horseshoe clip
5	Washer	15	Bolts
6	Rear channel member	16	Front channel member
7	Channel strip	17	Channel strip
8	Washer	18	Lifting channel
9	Bolt	19	Clip
10	Clamp		

Fig. 12.11. Window and regulator as fitted to two door models (Sec. 13)

1	Screw	8	Channel strip
2	Weatherstrip	9	Front channel member
3	Weatherstrip	10	Channel strip
4	Glass	11	Pillar
5	Lifting channel	12	Weatherstrip
6	Regulator	13	Quarterlight glass
7	Nut		

Two door model

8   The window winding mechanism on two door models is a wire rope regulator comprising a loop of wire rope which passes around four pulleys mounted in the door frame. The winder handle is geared to the top forward pulley and the window support strip is clamped onto the rear vertical length of cable. As the handle is turned the wire rope is moved around the pulleys and in so doing raises or lowers the window as appropriate.

9   To remove the window winder mechanism, lower the window to its lower position.

10 Remove the door trim panel and fittings as described in Section 12.

11 Now remove the two screws which retain the clamping plate and wire rope to the window support strip (photo). Slacken the nut and bolt on which the forward lower pulley rotates, and move the pulley and bolt rearward in the slot in the door frame, to slacken the wire rope.

12 The winder pulley and handle spindle assembly is secured to the inside of the door panel by three nuts. Undo and remove these nuts and extract the winding mechanism with the wire rope from the door structure.

13 The window glass may be extracted from the door once the quarter light and forward guide channel have been removed.

14 The quarter light is retained by a single screw through the door frame in the top corner.

15 Remove the two screws retaining the forward guide channel and remove both the quarter light and guide channel.

16 The window glass may now be lifted from the door frame.

17 Refitting the window follows the reversal of the removal sequence.

18 Refitting the winding mechanism follows the reversal of its removal sequence, except that the wire rope should be terminated before the trim panel and fittings are refitted. The tension of the wire rope with the window fitted and the winding mechanism secured, should be sufficient to limit the vertical movement midway between the two lower pulleys to approximately 0.5 inches.

13.11 Remove the two screws which retain the clamping plate

14 Bonnet and lock - removal, refitting and adjustment

1   The help of an assistant will be required to support the bonnet during the removal and refitting procedures.

2   Remove the bonnet prop retainer.

3   The four bolts and washers securing the bonnet to the hinges can now be removed.

4   Now remove the two bolts retaining the bonnet prop to the front body section.

5   The bonnet can now be lifted clear.

6   Refitting the bonnet and prop assembly is the reverse of the dismantling sequence. However, the bolts securing the bonnet must only be initially just nipped up.

7   Close the bonnet and ensure it is correctly aligned to the body and wing panels. Adjust the bonnet as necessary.

8   With the bonnet now correctly aligned the securing hinge bolts can be fully tightened.

9   The bonnet catch and release assembly can be removed by releasing the six retaining bolts and cable (photo).

10 Refitting of the assembly is straightforward except that before the six securing bolts are fully tightened the assembly must be correctly aligned.

11 Check the operation of the assembly by closing and opening the bonnet several times.

15 Boot lid and lock assembly — removal, refitting and adjustment

1   With the help of an assistant to hold the boot lid remove the four nuts and washers securing the boot lid to the two hinges.

2   Refitting is the reverse to the removal sequence. Once again before the securing nuts are fully tightened the boot lid must be correctly aligned to the body and rear wing panels.

14.9 The bonnet catch and lock assembly

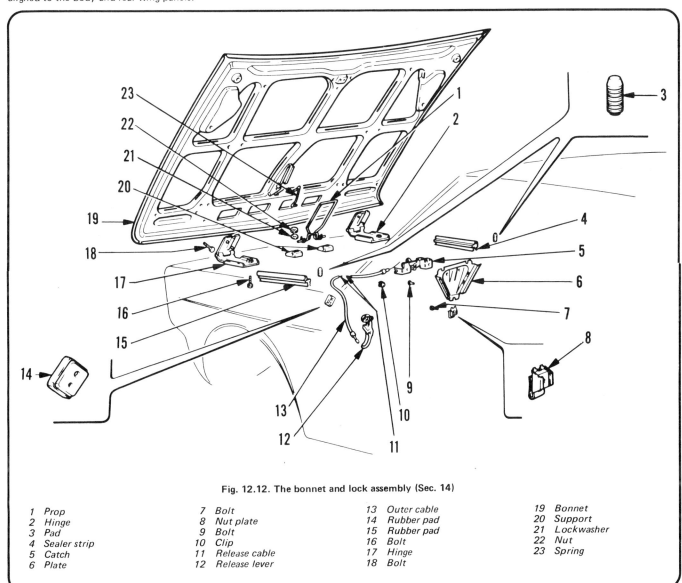

Fig. 12.12. The bonnet and lock assembly (Sec. 14)

1 Prop	7 Bolt	13 Outer cable	19 Bonnet
2 Hinge	8 Nut plate	14 Rubber pad	20 Support
3 Pad	9 Bolt	15 Rubber pad	21 Lockwasher
4 Sealer strip	10 Clip	16 Bolt	22 Nut
5 Catch	11 Release cable	17 Hinge	23 Spring
6 Plate	12 Release lever	18 Bolt	

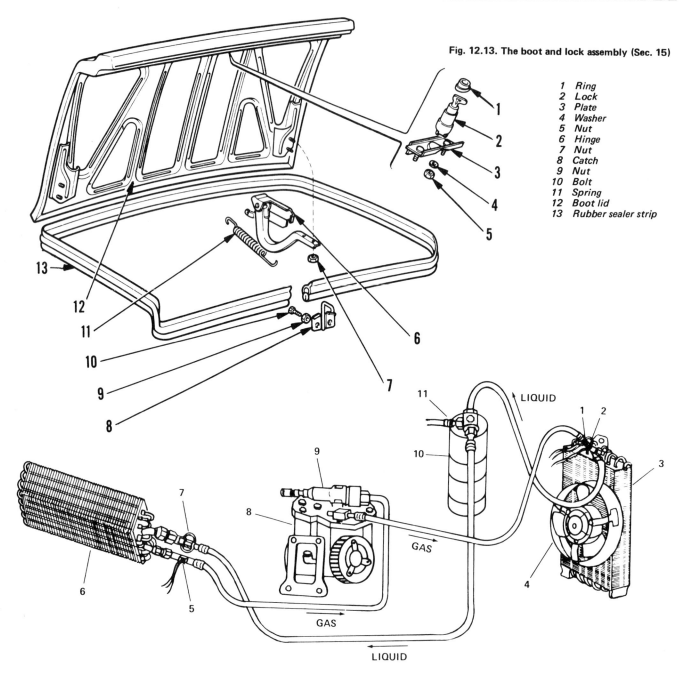

Fig. 12.13. The boot and lock assembly (Sec. 15)

1 Ring
2 Lock
3 Plate
4 Washer
5 Nut
6 Hinge
7 Nut
8 Catch
9 Nut
10 Bolt
11 Spring
12 Boot lid
13 Rubber sealer strip

Fig. 12.14. Air conditioning system (Sec. 17)

1	Condenser fan switch	4	Condenser fan	7	Expansion valve	10	Receiver/drier
2	High pressure switch	5	Frost preventing switch	8	Compressor	11	Low pressure switch
3	Condenser	6	Evaporator	9	Isobaric valve		

3   The boot lock assembly is retained to the boot lid by two nuts and washers.

4   Adjustment of the catch assembly is provided by a movable (up and down) striker post bolted to the rear bodypanel.

5   Remember to tighten the striker post retaining bolts after correct adjustment has been carried out.

16 Heater and ventilation system

Refer to Chapter 13 for information on the heater and ventilation system.

17 Air conditioning system - maintenance

1   Only two operations are possible for the home mechanic in connection with the cooling side of the air conditioning system.

2   Periodically check the security and condition of the interconnecting hoses. If they are damaged or have deteriorated, they must be renewed. **Warning:** *To do this the refrigerant gas must be discharged from the system and (later) recharged by a FIAT dealer or a competent refrigeration engineer.*

3   At regular intervals, check the tension and condition of the two compressor drivebelts. The tension of the belts should be ½ in (12.7 mm) at the longest run of the belts. Adjust the compressor position to tighten the belts.

Chapter 13 Supplement:
Revisions and information on later models

Contents

1 Introduction

Since its introduction in 1975, the FIAT 131 has undergone a number of modifications and improvements. Significant changes include the introduction of alternative power units (according to market), and the associated engine components (dependent on engine type). Wherever possible, earlier modifications have been included into the existing text in Chapters 1 to 12. This supplementary Chapter therefore gives details of those modifications made to the 131 range since 1978.

To use the Supplement to its best advantage, it is suggested that it is referred to before the main Chapters of the manual; this ensures that any relevant information applicable to your model can be collated and employed where necessary in the procedures given in the main Chapters.

2 Specifications

Engine (UK models)
B-Series

Type	In-line four-cylinder, double-overhead camshaft (dohc)		
Identification number	131 B.000*	131 B1.000	131 B2.000
Capacity	1297 cc	1585 cc	1995 cc

	131 B.000 *	131 B1.000	131 B2.000
Bore (standard)	2.992 in (76 mm)	3.307 in (84 mm)	3.307 in (84 mm)
Stroke	2.815 in (71.5 mm)	2.815 in (71.5 mm)	3.543 in (90 mm)
Compression ratio	8.9:1	9.0:1	8.9:1
Maximum power output (DIN) at 6000 rpm	57.4 kW	70.6 kW	84 kW
Maximum torque (DIN)	75.9 lbf ft (103 Nm)	94.0 lbf ft 127.5 Nm)	122.9 lbf ft (167 Nm)

In Certain territories, the 131 B7.000 engine is fitted to 1300 models. Specifications are as given above for the 131 B.000, except for the following:

Capacity	1301 cc
Bore (standard)	2.996 in (76.1 mm)

Lubrication system
Oil pump:
Type:	High capacity gear type driven by auxiliary shaft

Pump gear endfloat:
1300 and 1600	0.0012 to 0.0043 in (0.031 to 0.110 mm)
2000 engine	0.0010 to 0.0052 in (0.026 to 0.131 mm)
Gear running clearance in body	0.0043 to 0.0071 in (0.110 to 0.180 mm)
Backlash between gears	0.006 in (0.15 mm)

Oil pressure relief valve spring:
Length under load of 10 lb (45 N)	0.89 in (22.5 mm)
Minimum load to compress to above length	9.5 lb (42 N)
Lubricating pressure at 6000 rpm, with warm engine	42.6 to 71.0 lbf/in² (2.94 to 4.9 bar)

Camshafts
Journal diameters:
Front	1.1797 to 1.180 in (29.944 to 29.960 mm)
Centre	1.8027 to 1.8033 in (45.755 to 45.771 mm)
Rear	1.8185 to 1.8191 in (46.155 to 46.171 mm)

Camshaft journal clearance in head:
Front	0.0019 to 0.0035 in (0.049 to 0.090 mm)
Centre and rear	0.0011 to 0.0027 in (0.029 to 0.070 mm)

Cam lift (inlet and exhaust):
1300 and 1600	0.370 in (9.410 mm)
2000	0.390 in (9.900 mm)

Valve timing (valve clearances set at 0.031 in [0.8 mm])

	1300	1600	2000
Inlet opens	17° BTDC	12° BTDC	15° BTDC
Inlet closes	37° ABDC	53° ABDC	55° ABDC
Exhaust opens	48° BBDC	54° BBDC	57° BBDC
Exhaust closes	6° ATDC	11° ATDC	13° ATDC

Tappets
Standard bore diameter	1.458 to 1.459 in (37.000 to 37.025 mm)
Standard external diameter	1.457 to 1.458 in (36.975 to 36.995 mm)
Tappet fit clearance	0.0002 to 0.002 in (0.005 to 0.05 mm)

Shims (tappet)
Sizes available	0.128 to 0.185 in (3.25 to 4.70 mm) in increments of 0.002 in (0.050 mm)

Valves

	1300	1600 and 2000
Valve head diameter:		
Inlet	1.217 to 1.225 in (30.900 to 31.100 mm)	1.639 to 1.654 in (41.600 to 42.000 mm)
Exhaust	1.314 to 1.337 in (33.350 to 33.950 mm)	1.412 to 1.436 in (35.850 to 36.450 mm)
Valve face angle	45° 30′ ± 5′	
Valve stem diameter	0.314 to 0.315 in (7.974 to 7.992 mm)	
Valve stem clearance in guide	0.001 to 0.002 in (0.030 to 0.066 mm)	

Valve clearances (engine cold)

	1300	1600 and 2000
Inlet	0.016 in (0.42 mm)	0.018 in (0.45 mm)
Exhaust	0.019 in (0.48 mm)	0.024 in (0.60 mm)

Cylinder head
Valve guide:
    Housing bore diameter (standard) .... 0.549 to 0.550 in (13.950 to 13.977 mm)
    Interference fit .... 0.002 to 0.004 in (0.063 to 0.108 mm)
    External diameter (standard) .... 0.553 to 0.554 in (14.040 to 14.058 mm)
    Internal diameter (fitted) .... 0.316 to 0.317 in (8.022 to 8.040 mm)
Valve seat angle .... 45° ± 5'

Gudgeon pin
Standard diameter (all engines):
    Grade 1 .... 0.8664 to 0.8666 in (21.991 to 21.994 mm)
    Grade 2 .... 0.8666 to 0.8667 in (21.994 to 21.997 mm)
Oversize gudgeon pin available .... 0.0079 in (0.20 mm)

Pistons
Piston diameter (standard):
    1300 (131 B.000)* .... 2.9944 in (76 mm)
    1301 (131 B7.000)* .... 2.9983 in (76.10 mm)
    1600 (131 B1.000)* .... 3.3096 in (84 mm)
    2000 (131 B2.000):**
        Grade A .... 3.3064 to 3.3068 in (83.920 to 83.930 mm)
        Grade C .... 3.3072 to 3.3076 in (83.940 to 83.950 mm)
        Grade E .... 3.3080 to 3.3084 in (83.960 to 83.970 mm)

Measured approximately 1 in (25 mm) from piston skirt
**Measured approximately 2 in (54 mm) from piston crown*

Oversize pistons available:
    1300, 1600 and 2000 .... 0.0079, 0.0158 and 0.0236 in (0.20, 0.40 and 0.60 mm)
    1301 .... 0.0059, 0.0138 and 0.0217 in (0.15, 0.35 and 0.55 mm)
Piston-to-bore clearance:
    1300 .... 0.0024 to 0.0032 in (0.060 to 0.080 mm)
    1600 .... 0.0020 to 0.0028 in (0.050 to 0.070 mm)
    2000 .... 0.0028 to 0.0035 in (0.070 to 0.090 mm)
Piston ring groove width:
    1st (compression) .... 0.0604 to 0.0612 in (1.535 to 1.555 mm)
    2nd (oil control) .... 0.0800 to 0.0807 in (2.030 to 2.050 mm)
    3rd (oil scraper) .... 0.1563 to 0.1571 in (3.967 to 3.987 mm)

Piston rings
Thickness:
    1st (compression) .... 0.0582 to 0.0587 in (1.478 to 1.490 mm)
    2nd (oil control):
        1300 .... 0.0779 to 0.0784 in (1.978 to 1.990 mm)
        1600 and 2000 .... 0.0780 to 0.0788 in (1.980 to 2.00 mm)
    3rd (oil scraper) .... 0.1546 to 0.1551 in (3.925 to 3.937 mm)
Ring-to-groove clearance:
    1st (compression) .... 0.0018 to 0.0030 in (0.045 to 0.077 mm)
    2nd (oil control):
        1300 .... 0.0016 to 0.0028 in (0.040 to 0.072 mm)
        1600 and 2000 .... 0.0012 to 0.0027 in (0.030 to 0.070 mm)
    3rd (oil scraper) .... 0.0012 to 0.0024 in (0.030 to 0.062 mm)
Ring end gap:
    1st and 2nd:
        1300 .... 0.012 to 0.020 in (0.30 to 0.50 mm)
        1600 and 2000 .... 0.012 to 0.018 in (0.30 to 0.45 mm)
    3rd:
        1300 .... 0.008 to 0.014 in (0.20 to 0.35 mm)
        1600 and 2000 .... 0.010 to 0.016 in (0.25 to 0.40 mm)

Crankshaft and bearings
Main bearing journal diameter .... 2.0876 to 2.0883 in (52.985 to 53.005 mm)
Maximum ovality (out-of-round) .... 0.0002 in (0.005 mm)
Standard main bearing shell thickness:
    1300 and 1600 .... 0.0722 to 0.0725 in (1.834 to 1.840 mm)
    2000:
        Grade 1 .... 0.0722 to 0.0725 in (1.834 to 1.840 mm)
        Grade 2 .... 0.0724 to 0.0727 in (1.839 to 1.845 mm)
Main bearing shell undersizes .... 0.010, 0.020, 0.030 and 0.040 in (0.254, 0.508, 0.762 and 1.016 mm)
Main bearing-to-journal clearance:
    1300 and 1600 .... 0.0020 to 0.0037 in (0.050 to 0.095 mm)
    2000 .... 0.0013 to 0.0030 in (0.032 to 0.077 mm)

Big-end journal diameter:
    1300 and 1600 .... 1.9000 to 1.9008 in (48.224 to 48.244 mm)
    2000:
        Grade A .... 2.0012 to 2.0015 in (50.792 to 50.802 mm)
        Grade B .... 2.0008 to 2.0012 in (50.782 to 50.792 mm)
Big-end bearing-to-journal clearance:
    1300 and 1600 .... 0.0012 to 0.0029 in (0.030 to 0.074 mm)
    2000 .... 0.0008 to 0.0026 in (0.021 to 0.065 mm)
Big-end bearing shell thickness (standard):
    1300 and 1600 .... 0.0600 to 0.0602 in (1.524 to 1.528 mm)
    2000 .... 0.0604 to 0.0606 in (1.533 to 1.537 mm)
Big-end bearing shell undersizes .... 0.010, 0.020, 0.030 and 0.040 in (0.254, 0.508, 0.762 and 1.016 mm)
Thrust washers:
    Standard thickness .... 0.0910 to 0.0929 in (2.310 to 2.360 mm)
    Oversize range .... 0.0960 to 0.0980 in (2.437 to 2.487 mm)
Crankshaft endfloat .... 0.0022 to 0.0120 in (0.055 to 0.305 mm)
Maximum flywheel run-out .... 0.0039 in (0.10 mm)

Connecting rod

Big-end diameter:
    1300 and 1600 .... 2.0224 to 2.0230 in (51.330 to 51.346 mm)
    2000 .... 2.1235 to 2.1242 in (53.897 to 53.913 mm)
Small-end diameter (unbushed) .... 0.9432 to 0.9445 in (23.939 to 23.972 mm)
Small-end diameter (bushed):
    Grade 1 .... 0.8669 to 0.8691 in (22.004 to 22.007 mm)
    Grade 2 .... 0.8671 to 0.8672 in (22.007 to 22.010 mm)

Auxiliary shaft

Journal diameter:
    Front .... 1.8917 to 1.8927 in (48.013 to 48.038 mm)
    Rear .... 1.5732 to 1.5348 in (39.929 to 38.954 mm)
Journal clearance (fitted) .... 0.0018 to 0.0036 in (0.046 to 0.091 mm)
Journal bush internal diameter (fitted):
    Front .... 1.8945 to 1.8953 in (48.084 to 48.104 mm)
    Rear .... 1.5366 to 1.5374 in (39.000 to 39.020 mm)

Torque wrench settings

1300 and 1600 engines

	lbf ft	kgf m
Main bearing cap bolts (12 mm)	83	11.5
Main bearing cap bolt (front cap) (10 mm)	59	8.2
Engine breather-to-crankcase bolt	16	2.3
Cylinder head bolts	61	8.5
Camshaft housing bolts	16	2.2
Inlet manifold-to-cylinder head nut	18	2.5
Inlet manifold-to-cylinder head bolt	18	2.5
Exhaust manifold-to-cylinder head nut	18	2.5
Big-end bearing cap nut (9 mm)	37	5.2
Flywheel-to-crankshaft bolt (10 mm)	61	8.5
Camshaft sprocket bolt	86	12
Belt tensioner nut	32	4.5
Oil pump and pick-up-to-crankcase bolt	14	2.0
Alternator and water pump driving pulley nut	144	20
Oil filter mounting-to-crankcase bolt	36	5
Alternator-to-crankcase nut	50	7
Alternator-to-upper bracket nut	32	4.4
Alternator upper bracket-to-crankcase bolt	38	5.3*
Oil pressure switch	24	3.3

Olive green coloured bolts to be tightened to 52 lbf ft (7.2 kgf m)

2000 engine (as above except for the following)

	lbf ft	kgf m
Bolt for securing upper section of cylinder head and bracket for mounting compressor (air conditioning only)	16	2.2
Big-end bearing cap nut (10 mm)	54	7.5
Flywheel-to-crankshaft bolt (12 mm)	105	14.5
Oil pump and pick-up-to crankcase nut	14	2
Bolt securing oil filter, power-assisted steering pump and compressor to crankcase (air conditioning only)	36	5
Water pump pulley bolt	16	2.3
Nut securing alternator, water pump and power-assisted steering pump driving pulley	180	25
Bolt securing oil filter mounting and power-assisted steering pump to crankcase	36	5
Oil pressure sender unit	27	3.8
Nut securing power-assisted steering pump gear	36	5
Bolt securing power-assisted steering pump to oil filter mounting	16	2.3

C-Series

The specifications are as given for the B-Series with the exception of the following:

Type .... In-line four-cylinder, single-overhead camshaft (sohc) or double-overhead camshaft (dohc)

Identification

1300 sohc	131 C.000
1300 dohc	131 C.1000
1600 sohc	131 C.2000
1600 dohc	131 C.3000
2000 dohc	131 C.4000

Capacity

1300	1367 cc
1600	1585 cc
2000	1995 cc

Bore

1300 and 1600	3.073 in (78 mm)
1600 and 2000	3.310 in (84 mm)

Stroke

1300 and 1600	2.817 in (71.5 mm)
2000	3.546 in (90 mm)

Compression ratio

1300 sohc, 1600 and 2000 dohc	9:1
1300 dohc	8.9:1
1600 sohc	9.1:1

Camshaft (sohc)

Journal diameters (from front to rear):

No 1	1.1798 to 1.1804 in (29.945 to 29.960 mm)
No 2	0.9945 to 1.0052 in (25.50 to 25.515 mm)
No 3	0.9456 to 0.9461 in (24.00 to 24.015 mm)
No 4	0.9434 to 0.9440 in (23.945 to 23.960 mm)

Camshaft journal bore in cylinder head:

No 1 (front) for camshaft bush	1.3012 to 1.3024 in (33.026 to 33.056 mm)
No 2 (front centre) for camshaft	1.0064 to 1.0074 in (25.545 to 25.570 mm)
No 3 (rear centre) for camshaft	0.9473 to 0.9483 in (24.045 to 24.070 mm)
No 4 (rear) for camshaft bush	1.0648 to 1.0660 in (27.026 to 27.056 mm)

Camshaft bush internal diameter:

No 1 (front)	1.1816 to 1.1825 in (29.990 to 30.015 mm)
No 4 (rear)	0.9452 to 0.9461 in (23.990 to 24.015 mm)

Camshaft bush external diameter:

No 1 (front)	1.3045 to 1.3061 in (33.110 to 33.150 mm)
No 4 (rear)	1.0681 to 1.0697 in (27.110 to 27.150 mm)

Valves

Valve clearances (cold):

1300 and 1600 sohc:

inlet	0.011 in (0.30 mm)
exhaust	0.015 in (0.40 mm)

1300, 1600 and 2000 dohc:

inlet	0.017 in (0.45 mm)
outlet	0.019 in (0.50 mm)

To check valve timing:

sohc engines	0.027 in (0.70 mm)
dohc engines	0.031 in (0.80 mm)

Valve head diameter:

inlet:

1300 sohc	1.3199 in (33.50 mm)
1300 dohc	1.470 to 1.485 in (37.30 to 37.70 mm)
1600 sohc	1.548 to 1.564 in (39.30 to 39.70 mm)

exhaust:

1300 sohc	1.196 to 1.219 in (30.35 to 30.95 mm)
1300 dohc	1.314 to 1.338 in (33.35 to 33.95 mm)
1600 sohc	1.436 to 1.452 in (36.45 to 36.85 mm)

Pistons

Note: *Diameter to be measured 55.3 mm (2.178 in) below crown for 1300 and 1600 sohc, and 1 in (25 mm) from base of skirt for 1300 and 1600 dohc. To measure 2000 dohc pistons refer to B-Series specifications.*

Piston diameter:

1300 sohc:

Grade A	3.0716 to 3.0720 in (77.960 to 77.970 mm)
Grade C	3.0724 to 3.0728 in (77.980 to 77.990 mm)
Grade E	3.0732 to 3.0735 in (78.000 to 78.010 mm)

1300 dohc:

Grade A	3.0708 to 3.0712 in (77.940 to 77.950 mm)
Grade C	3.0716 to 3.0720 in (77.960 to 77.970 mm)
Grade E	3.0724 to 3.0728 in (77.980 to 77.990 mm)

1600 sohc:

Grade A	3.3080 to 3.3084 in (83.960 to 83.970 mm)
Grade C	3.3088 to 3.3092 in (83.980 to 83.990 mm)
Grade E	3.3096 to 3.3100 in (84.000 to 84.010 mm)

1600 dohc:

Grade A	3.3072 to 3.3076 in (83.940 to 83.950 mm)
Grade C	3.3080 to 3.3084 in (83.960 to 83.970 mm)
Grade E	3.3088 to 3.3092 in (83.980 to 83.990 mm)

Piston-to-bore clearance:

1300 and 1600 sohc	0.0012 to 0.0020 in (0.030 to 0.050 mm)
1300 and 1600 dohc	0.0020 to 0.0027 in (0.050 to 0.070 mm)

Piston rings

Ring thickness:

1st (all engines)	0.0582 to 0.0587 in (1.478 to 1.490 mm)
2nd (except 2000)	0.0779 to 0.0784 in (1.978 to 1.990 mm)
2nd (2000)	0.0780 to 0.0788 in (1.980 to 2.00 mm)

3rd (oil scraper):

1300	0.1545 to 0.1551 in (3.922 to 3.937 mm)
1600 and 2000	0.1546 to 0.1551 in (3.925 to 3.937 mm)

Piston ring groove clearance:

1st (all engines)	0.0017 to 0.0030 in (0.045 to 0.077 mm)
2nd (except 2000)	0.0015 to 0.0028 in (0.040 to 0.072 mm)
2nd (2000)	0.0011 to 0.0024 in (0.030 to 0.062 mm)

3rd (oil scraper):

1300	0.0011 to 0.0025 in (0.030 to 0.065 mm)
1600 and 2000	0.0011 to 0.0024 in (0.030 to 0.062 mm)

Piston ring end gap:

1300	0.011 to 0.019 in (0.30 to 0.5 mm)
1600 and 2000	0.009 to 0.015 in (0.25 to 0.40 mm)

Torque wrench settings (sohc engines only)

The specifications are the same as those given for the B-Series engines with the exception of the following:

	lbf ft	kgf m
Cylinder head bolts:		
Stage 1	14	2.0
Stage 2	30	4.1
Stage 3	Angular tightening in two stages of 90° each	
Camshaft cap nuts	14	2.0
Camshaft cover bolts	21	3.0
Camshaft front bearing housing and belt shield nut	21	3.0
Camshaft rear bearing housing bolt	21	3.0
Oil pump and distributor gear bolt	86	12

Engine (USA models)

The specifications are the same as those given for the 2 litre B-Series engine with the exception of the following:

Type

1979:

49 state version	132 C2.040
California version	132 C2.031

1980 on:

Carburettor version	132 C3.040
Fuel injected version	132 C3.031

Capacity

121.7 cu in (1995 cc)

Compression ratio

8.1:1

Horsepower rating (SAE) net

1979:

49 state version	86 hp at 5100 rpm
California version	80 hp at 5000 rpm

1980 on:

Carburettor version	80 hp at 5000 rpm
Fuel injected version	102 hp at 5500 rpm

Valve timing (valve clearances set at 0.31 in [0.8 mm])

Inlet opens	5° BTDC
Inlet closes	53° ABDC
Exhaust opens	53° BBDC
Exhaust closes	5° ATDC

Valve clearances (engine cold)

Inlet	0.018 in (0.45 mm)
Exhaust	0.020 in (0.50 mm)

Pistons

Piston diameter (standard):

Grade A	3.3076 to 3.3080 in (83.950 to 83.960 mm)
Grade C	3.3084 to 3.3088 in (83.970 to 83.980 mm)
Grade E	3.3092 to 3.3096 in (83.990 to 84.000 mm)
Piston-to-bore clearance*	0.0016 to 0.0024 in (0.040 to 0.060 mm)

Measured at right angle to gudgeon pin and 1.89 in (48 mm) from piston crown

Torque wrench settings

The settings are identical to those given for the B-Series engine with the addition of the following:

	lbf ft	kgf m
Air conditioning upper bracket nut	36	5.0
Diverter valve vacuum point union	11	1.5
Air pump bracket but	18	2.5
Air pump support stud nut	36	5.0
Air pump support nut	20	2.8
Air pump bracket bolt*	38	5.3
Air pump pulley bolt	4.0	0.6
EGR pipe fitting plug	4.0	5.5

Bolts coloured olive green have a different torque value of 52 lbf ft (7.2 kgf m)

Cooling system
Thermal fan switch

Fan cut-in temperature	90 to 94°C (194 to 201°F)
Fan cut-out temperature	85 to 89°C (185 to 192°F)

Thermostat

Opening temperature:

sohc engine	80 to 85°C (176 to 185°F)
dohc engine	83 to 87°C (181 to 188°F)
Fully open temperature (all engines)	95°C (203°F)

Radiator cap relief pressure   11 lbf in (0.8 kgf cm)

Torque wrench setting

	lbf ft	kgf m
Water temperature sender unit	36	5

Carburation (UK models)
Application and identification

Engine code and capacity	Carburettor type
131 A.000 (1297 cc ohv)	Weber 32 ADF 3/200 or Solex C32 TEIE/42
131 A7.000 (1301 cc ohv)	Solex C32 TEIE/42
131 A1.000 (1585 cc ohv)	Weber 32 ADF 3/200 or Weber 32 ADF 3/100* or Weber 32 ADFY 7/250 or Weber 32 ADF 7/150*
131 B.000 (1297 cc dohc)	Weber 32 ADF 13/250 or Solex C32 TEIE/1
131 B7.000 (1301 cc dohc)	
131 B1.000 (1585 cc dohc)	Weber 32 ADF 14/250 or Weber 32 ADF 14/150* or Solex C32 TEIE/2
131 B2.000 (1995 cc dohc)	Weber 34 ADF 15/250 or Weber 34 ADF 15/150*
131 C.000 (1367 cc sohc)	Weber 32 ADF 51/250 or Solex C32 TEIE/7
131 C1.000 (1367 cc dohc)	Weber 32 ADF 52/250 or Solex C32 TEIE/9
131 C2.000 (1585 cc sohc)	Weber 32 ADF 50/250 or Solex C32 TEIE/8
131 C3.000 (1585 cc dohc)	Weber 32 ADF 53/250 or Solex C32 TEIE/10
131 C4.000 (1995 cc dohc)	Weber 34 ADF 54/250 or Weber 34 ADF 54/150*

air conditioned models

Carburettor specifications
All dimensions given in metric

Solex C32 TEIE/1

	Primary	Secondary
Choke tube diameter	32	32
Venturi diameter	22	24
Main jet size	117.5	132.5
Idling speed jet size	52.5	52.5
Idling speed air bleed jet size	160	190

	Primary	Secondary
Accelerator pump jet size	55	
Needle valve seat size	160	
Float level	9.5*	

*Measured from float to cover gasket, in vertical position

Solex C32 TEIE/2
Specifications are as given for the Solex C32 TEIE/1 with the exception of the following:

	Primary	Secondary
Main jet size	120	132.5

Solex C32 TEIE/7

	Primary	Secondary
Choke tube diameter	32	32
Venturi diameter	23	23
Auxiliary venturi diameter	5.0	5.0
Main jet size	120	125
Air correction jet size	160	180
Emulsion tube type	86	87
Idling speed jet size	45	45
Idling speed air bleed jet size	110	70
Accelerator pump jet size	50	–
Accelerator pump discharge orifice size	45	–
Power fuel jet size	–	60
Power fuel mixture jet size	–	200
Needle valve seat size	160	–
Anti-syphon bleed size	140	–
Accelerator pump output (10 strokes)	8.5 to 10.5 cc	
Float level	9 to 10 mm*	
Float weight	7.5 g	

*See Fig. 13.7, dimension 'a'

Solex C32 TEIE/8

	Primary	Secondary
Choke tube diameter	32	32
Venturi diameter	23	23
Auxiliary venturi diameter	5.0	5.0
Main jet size	125	125
Air correction jet size	170	190
Emulsion tube type	86	87
Idling speed jet size	50	40
Idling speed air bleed jet size	100	70
Accelerator pump jet size	50	–
Accelerator pump discharge orifice size	55	–
Power fuel jet size	–	80
Power fuel mixture jet size	–	200
Needle valve seat size	160	–
Anti-syphon bleed size	140	–
Accelerator pump output (10 strokes)	8.5 to 10.5 cc	
Float level	9 to 10 mm*	
Float weight	7.5 g	

*See Fig. 13.7, dimension 'a'

Solex C32 TEIE/9

	Primary	Secondary
Choke tube diameter	32	32
Venturi diameter	22	24
Auxiliary venturi diameter	3.5	3.5
Main jet size	115	127
Air correction jet size	180	180
Emulsion tube type	86	87
Idling speed jet size	50	42
Idling speed air bleed jet size	100	70
1st progression orifice size	80	100 .
2nd progression orifice size	120	–
3rd progression orifice size	120	–
4th progression orifice size	120	–
Accelerator pump jet size	50	–
Accelerator pump discharge orifice size	45	–
Needle valve seat size	160	–
Anti-syphon bleed size	140	–
Accelerator pump output (10 strokes)	9 to 11 cc	
Float level	9 to 10 mm*	
Float weight	7.5 g	

*See Fig. 13.7, dimension 'a'

Solex C32 TEIE/10

	Primary	Secondary
Choke tube diameter	32	32
Venturi diameter	22	24
Auxiliary venturi diameter	5.0	5.0
Main jet size	115	122
Air correction jet size	180	190
Emulsion tube type	86	96
Idling speed jet size	47	55
Idling speed air bleed jet size	100	70
Idling speed calibration bush size	170	–
1st progression orifice size	120	100
2nd progression orifice size	120	–
3rd progression orifice size	100	–
4th progression orifice size	100	–
Accelerator pump jet size	50	–
Accelerator pump discharge orifice size	45	–
Power fuel jet size	–	80
Power fuel mixture jet size	–	200
Needle valve seat size	160	–
Anti-syphon bleed size	140	–
Accelerator pump output (10 strokes)	9 to 11 cc	
Float level	9 to 10 mm*	
Float weight	7.5 g	

*See Fig. 13.7, dimension 'a'

Weber 32 ADF 7/250 and Weber 32 ADF 7/150

	Primary	Secondary
Choke tube diameter	32	32
Venturi diameter	23	23
Auxiliary venturi diameter	4.5	4.5
Main jet size	117	125
Air correction jet size	165	160
Emulsion tube type	F73	F73
Idling speed jet size	50	50
Idling speed air bleed jet size	160	70
Accelerator pump jet size	50	–
Power fuel jet size	–	100
Power fuel mixture jet size	–	250
Anti-syphon bleed size	100	–
Needle valve seat size	175	–
Float level	See Fig. 13.7	
Accelerator pump output (10 strokes)	9 to 13.5 cc	

Weber 32 ADF 13/250

	Primary	Secondary
Choke tube diameter	32	32
Venturi diameter	22	24
Auxiliary venturi diameter	4.5	4.5
Main jet size	112	115
Air correction jet size	140	170
Emulsion tube type	F52	F5
Idling speed jet size	50	80
Idling speed air bleed jet size	145	80
Idling speed calibration bush size	140	–
1st progression orifice size	120	120
2nd progression orifice size	100	120
3rd progression orifice size	100	–
Anti-syphon bleed size	100	–
Accelerator pump jet size	40	–
Power fuel jet size	–	130
Power fuel mixture jet size	–	250
Needle valve seat size	175	–
Float level	See Fig. 13.7	

Weber 32 ADF 14/250 and Weber 32 ADF 14/150

	Primary	Secondary
Choke tube diameter	32	32
Venturi diameter	22	24
Auxiliary venturi diameter	4.5	4.5
Main jet size	115	115
Air correction jet size	165	170
Emulsion tube type	F20	F5
Idling speed jet size	50	80
Idling speed air bleed jet size	130	70
Idling speed calibration bush size	135	–
1st progression orifice size	120	120
2nd progression orifice size	110	120
3rd progression orifice size	110	–
4th progression orifice size	100	–

	Primary	Secondary
Anti-syphon bleed size	100	—
Accelerator pump jet size	40	—
Accelerator pump discharge orifice size	40	—
Power fuel jet size	—	130
Power fuel mixture jet size	—	250
Needle valve seat size	175	
Float level	See Fig. 13.7	
Float weight	11g	

Weber 32 ADF 50/250

	Primary	Secondary
Choke tube diameter	32	32
Venturi diameter	23	23
Auxiliary venturi diameter	4.5	4.5
Main jet size	117	120
Air correction jet size	185	170
Emulsion tube type	F73	F73
Idling speed jet size	50	60
Idling speed air bleed jet size	150	70
Accelerator pump jet size	45	—
Accelerator pump discharge orifice size	40	—
Power fuel jet size	—	130
Power fuel mixture jet size	—	250
Needle valve seat size	175	
Anti-syphon bleed size	100	—
Accelerator pump output (10 strokes)	7.5 to 12.5 cc	
Float level	See Fig. 13.7	

Weber 32 ADF 51/250

	Primary	Secondary
Choke tube diameter	32	32
Venturi diameter	23	23
Auxiliary venturi diameter	4.5	4.5
Main jet size	115	120
Air correction jet size	165	165
Emulsion tube type	F73	F73
Idling speed jet size	50	50
Idling speed air bleed jet size	160	70
Accelerator pump jet size	50	—
Accelerator pump discharge orifice size	40	—
Power fuel jet size	—	100
Power fuel mixture jet size	—	250
Needle valve seat size	175	
Anti-syphon bleed size	100	—
Float level	See Fig. 13.7	
Accelerator pump output (10 strokes)	7.5 to 12.5 cc	

Weber 32 ADF 52/250

	Primary	Secondary
Choke tube diameter	32	32
Venturi diameter	22	24
Auxiliary venturi diameter	4.5	4.5
Main jet size	107	125
Air correction jet size	180	150
Emulsion tube type	F73	F5
Idling speed jet size	52	50
Idling speed air bleed jet size	80	80
Idling speed calibration bush size	120	—
1st progression orifice size	—	—
2nd progression orifice size	110	120
3rd progression orifice size	110	—
4th progression orifice size	100	—
Accelerator pump jet size	40	—
Accelerator pump discharge orifice size	45	—
Power fuel jet size	—	80
Power fuel mixture jet size	—	250
Needle valve seat size	175	—
Anti-syphon bleed size	140	—
Accelerator pump output (10 strokes)	7.5 to 12.5 cc	
Float level	See Fig. 13.7	

Weber 32 ADF 53/250

	Primary	Secondary
Choke tube diameter	32	32
Venturi diameter	22	24
Auxiliary venturi diameter	4.5	4.5
Main jet size	107	120
Air correction jet size	160	180

	Primary	Secondary
Emulsion tube type	F20	F5
Idling speed jet size	47	50
Idling speed air bleed jet size	80	70
Idling speed calibration bush size	150	–
1st progression orifice size	100	120
2nd progression orifice size	110	120
3rd progression orifice size	110	–
4th progression orifice size	100	–
Accelerator pump jet size	40	–
Accelerator pump discharge orifice size	40	–
Power fuel jet size	–	130
Power fuel mixture jet size	–	250
Needle valve seat size	175	
Anti-syphon bleed size	140	–
Accelerator pump output (10 strokes)	7.5 to 12.5 cc	
Float level	See Fig. 13.7	

Weber 34 ADF 15/250 *and* **Weber 34 ADF 15/150**	Primary	Secondary
Venturi diameter	24	26
Main jet size	120	140
Air correction jet size	140	180
Idling speed jet size	47	90
Idling speed air bleed	100	70
Accelerator pump jet size	40	–
Needle valve seat size	175	
Float level	6 mm*	

Measured from float to cover gasket in vertical position

Weber 34 ADF 54/250 *and* **Weber 34 ADF 54/150**	Primary	Secondary
Choke tube diameter	34	34
Venturi diameter	24	26
Auxiliary venturi diameter	4.5	4.5
Main jet size	122	130
Air correction jet size	170	180
Emulsion tube type	F20	F5
Idling speed jet size	50	90
Idling speed air bleed jet size	130	70
Idling speed calibration bush size	150	–
1st progression orifice size	100	120
2nd progression orifice size	120	120
3rd progression orifice size	120	–
4th progression orifice size	100	–
Accelerator pump jet size	45	–
Accelerator pump discharge orifice size	40	–
Power fuel jet size	40	130
Power fuel mixture jet size	250	250
Needle valve seat size	175	
Anti-syphon bleed size	100	–
Accelerator pump output (10 strokes)	7.5 to 12.5 cc	
Float level	See Fig. 13.7	
Float weight	11 g	

Automatic choke settings (Weber carburettors)

All dimensions given in metric

Carb. type	Fast idle speed (dimension 'A', Fig. 13.8)	Cam setting (dimension 'B', Fig. 13.9)	Anti-flooding (dimension 'C', Fig. 13.10)	Choke min. (dimension 'D', Fig. 13.11A)	Choke max. (dimension 'E', Fig. 13.11B)
32 ADF 3/100	0.85 to 0.95	6.25 to 6.75	0.3 to 1.0	4.5	6.7
32 ADF 3/200	0.85 to 0.95	6.25 to 6.75	0.3 to 1.0	4.5	6.7
32 ADF 7/150	0.85 to 0.95			4.5 to 5.0	6.5 to 7.0
32 ADF 7/250	0.85 to 0.95			4.5 to 5.0	6.5 to 7.0
32 ADF 13/250	0.85 to 0.95			4.5 to 5.0	6.5 to 7.0
32 ADF 14/150	1.0 to 1.1			2.75 to 3.25	7.25 to 7.75
32 ADF 14/250	1.0 to 1.1			2.75 to 3.25	7.25 to 7.75
32 ADF 15/150	1.15 to 1.25			2.75 to 3.25	7.25 to 7.75
34 ADF 15/250	1.15 to 1.25			2.75 to 3.25	7.25 to 7.75
34 ADF 50/250	0.95 to 1.05	7.75 to 8.25	0.3 to 1.0	4.5 to 5	6.5 to 7
32 ADF 51/250	0.85 to 0.95	6.25 to 6.75	0.3 to 1.0	4.5 to 5	6.5 to 7
32 ADF 52/250	0.9 to 1.0	7.75 to 8.25	0.3 to 1.0	4.5 to 5	6.5 to 7.0
32 ADF 53/250	0.85 to 0.95	7.75 to 8.25	0.3 to 1.0	4.5 to 5	6.5 to 7.0
34 ADF 54/150	1.10 to 1.20	7.75 to 8.25	0.3 to 1.0	2.75 to 3.25	7.25 to 7.75
34 ADF 54/250	1.10 to 1.20	7.75 to 8.25	0.3 to 1.0	2.75 to 3.25	7.25 to 7.75

Automatic choke settings (Solex carburettors)

All dimensions given in metric

Carb type	Anti-flooding (dimension 'A', Fig. 13.13)	Fast idle speed (Dimension 'B', Fig. 13.14)
C32 TEIE/1	N/A	N/A
C32 TEIE/2	N/A	N/A
C32 TEIE/7	3 to 3.5	0.8 to 0.9
C32 TEIE/8	3 to 3.5	0.9 to 1.0
C32 TEIE/9	3 to 3.5	0.9 to 1.0
C32 TEIE/10	3 to 3.5	0.9 to 1.0
C32 TEIE/42	4 to 5	0.8 to 0.9

Torque wrench setting

	lbf ft	kgf m
Thermal valve for carburettor pneumatic pump	19	2.7

Carburation (USA models)
Application and identification

All specifications given below apply to the 2 litre engine fitted from 1979 on

1979 49 State version:
    Models with air conditioning:
Manual transmission	Weber 28/32 ADHA 1/179
Automatic transmission	Weber 28/32 ADHA 2/179

    Model without air conditioning:
Manual transmission	Weber 28/32 ADHA 1/279
Automatic transmission	Weber 28/32 ADHA 2/279

1979 California version:
    Models with air conditioning:
Manual transmission	Weber 28/32 ADHA 5/179
Automatic transmission	Weber 28/32 ADHA 6/179

    Models without air conditioning:
Manual transmission	Weber 28/32 ADHA 5/279
Automatic transmission	Weber 28/32 ADHA 6/279

1980 carburettor version:
    Models with air conditioning:
Manual transmission	Weber 28/32 ADHA 5/180
Automatic transmission	Weber 28/32 ADHA 6/180

    Models without air conditioning:
Manual transmission	Weber 28/32 ADHA 5/280
Automatic transmission	Weber 28/32 ADHA 6/280

Carburettor specifications (all dimensions in metric)

The specifications given below apply to all versions of the Weber 28/32 ADHA. All other specifications are the same as those given in Chapter 3.

	Primary	Secondary
Choke tube diameter	28	32
Venturi diameter	22	24
Main jet	120	130
Emulsion tube type	F74	F74
Float level	6 to 7 mm*	

*Measured from float to cover gasket, in vertical position

Idling speed and CO values

Normal idling speed:
Automatic transmission	800 to 900 rpm
Manual transmission	700 to 800 rpm
CO value (all models)	1.0 to 2.5%

Fuel injection system
Idling speed

Manual transmission	800 to 900 rpm
Automatic transmission	700 to 800 rpm

CO value

CO value	0.3 to 0.6%

Torque wrench setting

Lambda sensor	30 to 36 lbf ft (4.1 to 4.9 kgf m)

Ignition system (UK models)

Type

All 1300 and 1600 engines	Conventional coil and contact breaker
All 2000 engines	Electronic ignition

Spark plugs

Type:

1300 and 1600 dohc (B-series) engines	Champion N7Y, Bosch W200 T30, FIAT 1 L45J, Marelli CW 78 LP
2000 dohc (B-series) engine	Champion N7Y, Bosch W6D, FIAT 1 L45J, Marelli CW 78 LP
All C-Series engines	Champion N9Y, Bosch W7D, FIAT 1 L4J, Marelli CW 7 LP

Spark plug gap (all models)

0.024 to 0.027 in (0.60 to 0.70 mm)

Coil

Type and application:

1300 and 1600 ohv engines	Marelli BE200B, Klitz-O.E.M. G52S, Zelmot BE200B, Bosch K12Y
1300 and 1600 (B-Series) engines	Marelli BE200B or BES200A, Klitz-O.E.M. G52S or G37SU, Zelmot BE200B, Bosch K12V
1300 and 1600 (C-Series) engines	Marelli BE200B, Bosch 0.221.119.048, Klitz-O.E.M. G52S, Iskra ATA 0115
2000 engines (electronic ignition)	Marelli BAE 207A, Bosch 0.221.122.012

Coil primary winding resistance at 20°C (68°F):

Marelli BE200B	3.14 ± 0.13 ohms
Klitz-O.E.M. G37SU	Not available at time of writing
Bosch K12V	Not available at time of writing
Bosch 0.221.119.048	2.6 to 3.1 ohms
Klitz O.E.M. G52S	2.82 ± 0.14 ohms
Iskra ATA 0115	3.3 ± 0.13 ohms
Marelli BAE 207A	0.75 to 0.81 ohms
Bosch 0.221.122.012	1.2 to 1.6 ohms
Zelmot (Polmot) BE200B	Not available at time of writing

Coil secondary winding resistance at 20°C (68°F):

Marelli BE200B	9400 ± 400 ohms
Klitz O.E.M. G37SU	Not available at time of writing
Bosch K12V	Not available at time of writing
Bosch 0.221.119.048	8500 to 12000 ohms
Klitz-O.E.M. G52S	7100 ± 355 ohms
Iskra ATA 0115	7500 ± 750 ohms
Marelli BAE 207A	9500 to 11,500 ohms
Bosch 0.221.122.012	6000 to 10,000 ohms
Zelmot (Polmot) BE200B	Not available at time of writing

Distributor

Type and application:

1300 and 1600 (B-Series) engines	Marelli 404R1 or 404P1, Ducellier HUS15R or HUS15P
1300 and 1600 (C-Series) engines	Marelli S155C or S155P, Ducellier 525006A or 525322A, Femsa DI4.17 or DI4.23
2000 engines (electronic ignition)*	Marelli SM800AX, Bosch 0.237.001.002
2000 engines (electronic ignition and air conditioning)	Marelli SM 801 AX
Contact breaker points gap	0.014 to 0.017 in (0.37 to 0.43 mm)

Automatic advance:

All ohv engines	20° ± 2°
1300 and 1600 (B-Series) engines	28° ± 2°
All C-Series and 2000 engines	24° ± 2°
Reluctor-to-stator pole gap (electronic ignition) 2000 engines only	0.012 to 0.016 in (0.30 to 0.40 mm)

The distributor and electronic ignition fitted must be from the same manufacturer

Ignition system (USA models)

The specifications given below apply to the 2 litre engine from 1979 on

Type

Electronic with centrifugal and vacuum advance

Distributor

Type	Marelli 877AX
Air gap	0.012 to 0.016 in (0.30 to 0.40 mm)
Control module input voltage	6 to 18 volts
Current limiter output	4.5 to 6.0 amps
Rotor arm resistance	5000 ohms

Ignition coil
Type .... Marelli AEI200A
Winding resistance (at 20°C [68°F]):
    Primary .... 0.75 to 0.81 ohms
    Secondary .... 10,000 to 11,000 ohms

Spark plugs
Carburettor engines:

Type:	Normal	Resistor
AC	42XLS	R42XLS or R43XLS
Bosch	W175T30 (W7D)	W175TR30 (WR7D) or W160-TR30 (WR7D2)
Champion	N9Y	RN9Y or RN10Y
Marelli	CW7LP	CW7LPR or CW67LPR

Fuel injection engines:

Type:	Normal	Resistor
Champion	N/A	RN9Y

Spark plug gap:
    Normal type .... 0.023 to 0.027 in (0.6 to 0.7 mm)
    Resistor type .... 0.027 to 0.031 in (0.7 to 0.8 mm)

Static advance .... 10°

Centrifugal advance
Carburettor engine .... 28° ± 2° at 5200 rpm
Fuel injection engine .... 18° ± 2° at 3500 rpm

Vacuum advance
1979 49 State and 1980 carburettor versions .... 14° ± 2° at 12 in Hg
1979 California version .... 10° ± 2° at 12 in Hg
Fuel injection version .... 15° ± 2° at 11 in Hg

Clutch
Clutch plate dimensions
Overall diameter:
    B and C-Series engines (except 1600 ohv 5-speed and 2000) ..... 7.88 in (200 mm)
    1600 ohv 5-speed and 2000 engines .... 8.47 in (215 mm)
Internal diameter:
    B and C-Series engines (except 1600 ohv 5-speed and 2000) ..... 5.12 in (130 mm)
    1600 ohv 5-speed and 2000 engines .... 5.71 in (145 mm)

Clutch pedal
Minimum travel to release clutch (self-adjusting) .... 4.73 in (120 mm)

Torque wrench settings

Clutch pressure plate-to-flywheel bolts:	lbf ft	kgf m
1300 engines	11.5	1.6
1600 and 2000 engines	21.5	3.0

Gearbox
Ratios (4- and 5-speed)
From 1979 (five-speed only):
    5th 0.834:1
From January 1982:
    From chassis numbers*:
        Single ohc engines 820 363
        Twin ohc engines 826 478
        Twin ohc (ex 2000) engines 4 414 233
        Twin ohc 2000 engines 4 415 846
    Ratios:
        1st 3.612:1
        2nd 2.043:1
        3rd 1.363:1
        4th 1.00:1
        5th 0.8378:1
        Reverse 3.244:1

*These gearboxes are identified by a black paint spot on the gearbox support

Automatic transmission
Type and application
1600 ohv (131 A1.000) .... GMS ZL-C 12/20 (See Chapter 6B)
1600 dohc (131 B1.000) .... GMS ZR-C 11/20
1600 sohc (131 C.2000) TA-C11

Accelerator linkage adjustment
GMS ZR-C 11/20*:
    Lever to support bracket clearance .... 0.04 to 0.19 in (1 to 3 mm)
    Preset distance .... 4.7 in (119 mm)
TA-C11*:
    Total pedal travel .... 2.8 in (71 mm)
    Preset distance .... 4.7 in (119 mm)

Refer to Fig. 13.51

Torque wrench settings
The settings given below are additional to those given in Chapter 6A and 6B

Manual gearbox	lbf ft	kgf m
Reversing light switch	32	4.4
Starter motor-to-bellhousing bolt	14	2.0
Gearbox/securing plate-to-cross member bolt	36	5.0
Flexible coupling-to-gearbox nut	108	15
Automatic transmission		
Torque convertor-to-flywheel bolt	40	5.5

Rear axle
Final drive ratios (C-Series)
1300 sohc and 1600 dohc 4.1:1
1600 sohc and 2000 dohc 3.58:1
1300 dohc 4.44:1

Braking system
Front disc
Thickness .... 0.42 to 0.43 in (10.7 to 10.9 mm)

Rear brake load proportioning valve bar setting
Bumpstop-to-control rod distance (B-Series):
    Saloon .... 12.87 ± 0.19 in (327 ± 5 mm)
    Estate .... 12.20 ± 0.40 in (310 ± 10 mm)
Torque meter reading (taken at bracket end of bar) (C-Series):
    Saloon .... 1.3 to 1.75 lb (0.6 to 0.8 kg)
    Estate .... 0.4 to 0.8 lb (0.2 to 0.4 kg)

Electrical system (UK models)
Alternator
Type and application:
    A- and B-Series engines .... Marelli AA125-14V-45A, Marelli AA125-14V-55A*, Bosch K1-14V-45A24, Lucas 18ACR-14V-45A
    C-Series engines .... Marelli AA125-14V-45A, Bosch K1-14V-45A20**, Marelli AA125-14V-65A*, Bosch K1-14V-65A21*

Air conditioned models
**Not fitted to 1300 and 1600 sohc engines*

Specifications:
    Marelli AA125-14V-45A and 55A:
        Maximum output 50A
        Cut-in speed .... 900 ± 50 rpm
    Marelli AA125-14V-65A:
        Maximum output 65A
        Cut-in speed .... 1000 ± 50 rpm
    Bosch K1-14V-45A24:
        Maximum output 50A
        Cut-in speed .... 1100 ± 50 rpm
    Bosch K1-14V-45A20:
        Maximum output 47A
        Cut-in speed .... 1000 ± 50 rpm

Bosch K1-14V-65A21:
    Maximum output 70A
    Cut-in speed .... 1130 ± 50 rpm
Lucas 18ACR-14V-45A24:
    Maximum output 43A
    Cut-in speed .... 1250 rpm

Starter motor
Type and application:
  A- and B-Series engines .... E84-0.8/12 Var 5, Bosch DF 12V-0.7, E100-1.3/12 Var 9, Femsa E100-1.3/12, Bosch GF 12V-1.1

  C-Series engines:
    All models except 2000 dohc .... Marelli E95-12V-1kW, Ducellier 093.5-12V-1kW
    2000 dohc engines .... Bosch 094-12V-0.95kW, Ducellier 093.5-12-1.1kW

Bulbs
Twin-headlamp models:
  Inner (main) 55W
  Outer (main/dip) 45/40W H4
  Rear fog light 21W
  Glovebox light 3W
  Ashtray light 4W
  All warning lights 1.2W
  Ignition warning light 3W

All other bulb ratings are as per Specifications in Chapter 10

Fuses
No. 1 (8A) .... Stop lamps, direction indicators, reversing lamp, heater fan, fuel gauge and reserve warning light, handbrake 'on' and low brake fluid level warning light, brake pad wear warning light, low oil pressure warning light, temperature gauge, tachometer (131 Supermirafiori), heated rear window relay, glovebox light, heater ideogram lights, fibre optic bulbs, selector lights (automatic transmission), air conditioning compressor (where fitted)
No. 2 (8A) .... Windscreen wiper and washer pump, rear window wiper and washer pump (Estate), idle cut-out device (131 Supermirafiori 2000)
No. 3 (8A) .... Front RH side lamp, rear LH side lamp, left number plate lamp
No. 4 (8A) .... Front LH side lamp, rear RH side lamp, side indicator, instrument panel lights, right number plate lamp, cigarette lighter light, ashtray light
No. 5 (8A) .... LH headlamp dipped beam, rear fog lamps
No. 6 (8A) .... RH headlamp dipped beam
No. 7 (8A) .... RH headlamp main beam
No. 8 (8A) .... LH headlamp main beam and main beam indicator
No. 9 (16A) .... Horn, horn relay, radiator fan
No. 10 (16A) .... Cigarette lighter, courtesy lights, clock, radio/cassette player, electric aerial (where fitted)
No. 11 (16A) .... Hazard warning lamps, heated rear window and warning light
No. 12 (16A) .... Air conditioning compressor and fan (where fitted)
No. 13 (16A) .... Air conditioning condenser fan motor (where fitted)
No. 14 (16A) .... Spare fuse

Note: *There are two 16A fuses located under the dashboard for the central door locking system and electric windows.*
Circuits not protected: *Starting, ignition, charging and relay for automatic transmission (where fitted)*

Electrical system (USA models)
Alternator
Type .... Bosch K1-14V-55A20
Maximum output 70A
Cut-in speed .... 1000 ± 50 rpm

Fuses (1979 on)
No. 1 (8 amps) .... Stop lamps, reversing lamps, brake system effectiveness and handbrake 'on' warning light, direction indicator lamps and warning light, fuel gauge and reserve indicator, water temperature gauge, low oil pressure warning light, fasten seat belts indicator, heater fan motor, tachometer, relay for rear window heater, starter relay (automatic transmission), air conditioning relay, air conditioning compressor and fast idle relay, seat belt delay indicator and buzzer, fasten seat belts relay, gear selector light (automatic transmission), glove compartment light
No. 2 (8 amps) .... Windscreen wiper, windscreen washer pump, rear screen wiper and washer pump (Estate models)
No. 3 (8 amps) .... Left tail lamp, right front side lamp, right front and left rear side marker lamps, left licence plate lamp

No. 4 (8 amps)	Left front side lamp, right rear lamp, left front and right rear side marker lamps, right licence plate lamp, cigar lighter lamp, instrument cluster lamps, Ideogram illumination light source, ashtray lamp
No. 5 (8 amps)	Left outer headlamp (dipped beam)
No. 6 (8 amps)	Right outer headlamp (dipped beam)
No. 7 (8 amps)	Right inner and outer headlamps (main beam)
No. 8 (8 amps)	Left inner and outer headlamps (main beam)
No. 9 (16 amps)	Horns, horn relay, radiator fan motor
No. 10 (8 amps)	Clock, courtesy lamps, cigar lighter, 'Remove Key' buzzer, radio aerial (if fitted)
No. 11 (16 amps)	Rear screen heater, hazard warning lamps
No. 12 (16 amps)	Air conditioning compressor and evaporator fan, air conditioning fast idle electrovalve
No. 13 (16 amps)	Air conditioning condenser motor
No. 14 (16 amps)	Fuel pump
No. 15	Spare fuses

Circuits not protected: *Alternator, ignition, starting and relay, **battery** charge indicator, headlamp main beam relay, parking lamp indicator (Saloons only)*

Suspension and steering

Steering geometry:	
Toe-in (unladen car):	
1300 and 1600 sohc	0.24 to 0.31 in (6 to 8 mm)
1300, 1600 and 2000 dohc (except 2000 Sport)	0.20 to 0.28 in (5 to 7 mm)
2000 dohc Sport	0.16 to 0.24 in (4 to 6 mm)
Wheels:	
Type	Pressed steel *or* alloy (optional)
Rim size	5J x 13H2 (steel) *or* 5^{1}/2J x 14 (alloy)
Tyre sizes:	
1300 and 1600 sohc	165 SR-13 *or* 175/70 SR-13
1300 and 1600 sohc	165 SR-13, 175/70 SR-13 *or* 185/60 HR-14
2000 dohc	185/70 SR-13 *or* 185/60 HR-14
Tyre pressures:	
1300 and 1600 Saloons:	
Front and rear	25 lb/in² (1.8 kg/cm²)
1300 and 2000 Estates (fully laden):	
Front	25 lb/in² (1.8 kg/cm²)
Rear	31 lb/in² (2.2 kg/cm²)
2000 Saloons:	
Front	27 lb/in² (1.9 kg/cm²)
Rear	28 lb/in² (2.0 kg/cm²)

3 Engine

Engine removal and refitting – twin cam engines (1.3, 1.6 and 2.0 litre models)

The engine removal details for these engines is basically the same as that given for the ohv variant described in Chapter 1, Part A. However, the following points do differ from the instructions given in Chapter 1, Section 6.

1 When detaching the engine and associate fittings prior to removal, also detach the coolant pipes to/from the carburettor auto choke unit, the idle stop solenoid wire and the excess fuel return pipe.

2 It may be necessary to detach or lower the anti-roll bar to allow the engine sufficient forward movement for disconnection from the gearbox during the actual removal of the engine.

3 Later models, including the new sohc engine, have modified engine mounting brackets (photo).

Exhaust camshaft sprocket from April 1979

4 A wider exhaust camshaft sprocket was used from April 1979; modified in that whereas the earlier sprocket was previously manufactured in steel, the later types are cast iron. The later type sprocket is 1.14 in (29 mm) wide; the earlier type being 0.94 in (24 mm).

5 In view of the above, be sure to specify which type is required when ordering a new exhaust camshaft sprocket. Note that on the new type sprocket, the thrust washer originally fitted is no longer required.

Timing belt idler pulley

6 At the same time as the exhaust camshaft sprocket modification,

(see above) the timing belt idler pulley was also made wider and now measures 1.102 in (28 mm).

7 Similarly therefore, when ordering a new replacement be sure to specify which type is required; the new 28 mm type or the original 0.94 in (24 mm) type, although the two types are interchangeable.

3.3 Modified engine mountings

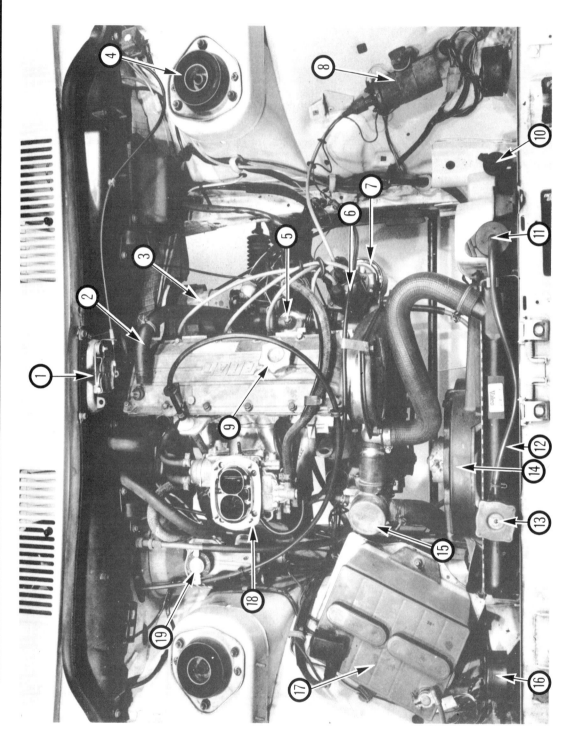

View of engine compartment from above with bonnet and air cleaner removed (1982 on)

1 Bonnet catch
2 EGR hose
3 Starter motor
4 Suspension top mounting

5 EGR control valve
6 Distributor
7 Oil filter
8 Ignition coil

9   Oil filler cap
10 Windscreen washer reservoir
11 Radiator overflow/expansion
     reservoir

12 Radiator
13 Radiator filler cap
14 Electric cooling fan
15 Thermostat housing

16 Horn
17 Battery
18 Carburettor
19 Brake fluid reservoir

View of front underbody
(1982 on)

1 Steering rack tie-rod
2 Track control arm
3 Anti-roll bar
4 Alternator
5 Oil drain plug
6 Clutch control cable
  adjustment point
7 Oil filter
8 Steering rack
9 Gearbox oil drain plug
10 Gearbox oil filler/level plug
11 Exhaust system
12 Propeller shaft flexible
   coupling

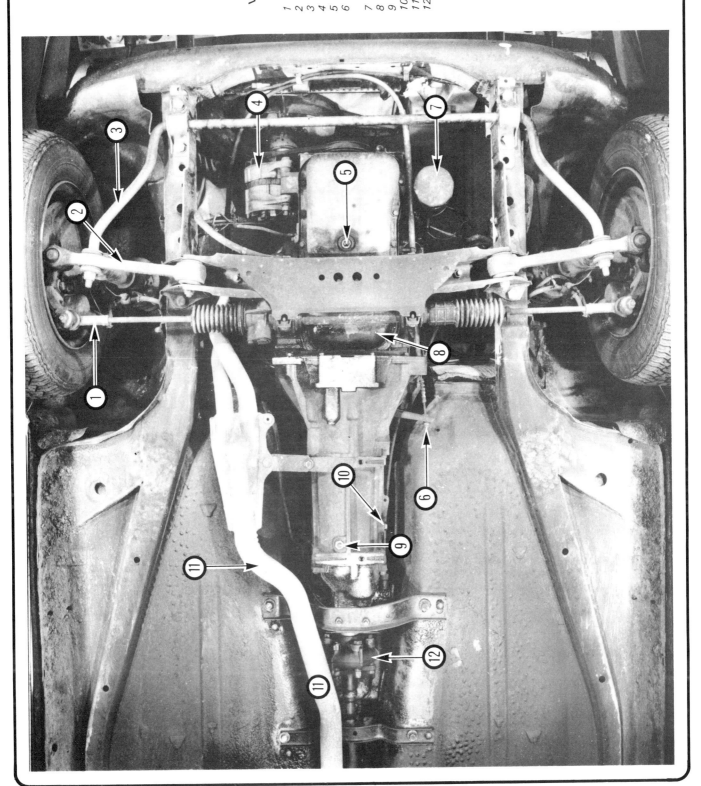

204

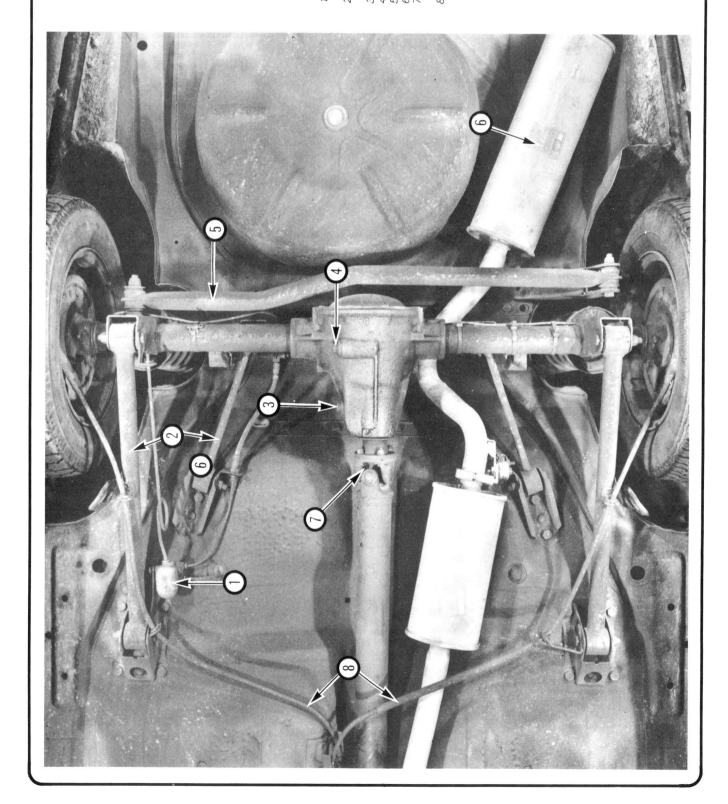

View of rear underbody (1982 on)

1 Load proportioning valve (rear brakes)
2 Upper and lower trailing arms
3 Rear axle filler/level plug
4 Rear axle oil drain plug
5 Panhard rod
6 Exhaust silencer
7 Propeller shaft universal joint
8 Handbrake control cables

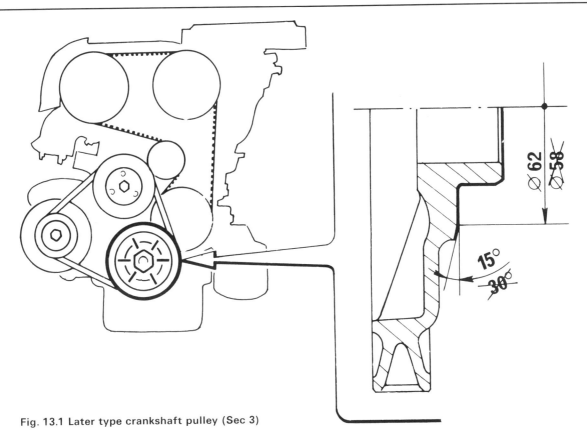

Fig. 13.1 Later type crankshaft pulley (Sec 3)

Crankshaft pulley
8   Models equipped with the later cast iron exhaust camshaft
sprocket (later models, from April 1979), are fitted with a modified
crankshaft pulley, the new pulley having a 15° chamfer as shown in
Fig. 13.1. If renewing the pulley, therefore, be sure to specify the
type required.

Crankshaft oil seal modification
9   From engine number 1 363 152 a double-lipped seal, instead of
the single lip type, is used on the 2 litre dohc engine.

Crankshaft modification – 1984 on
10 The 1600 and 2000 engines have a modified crankshaft in that
the right-hand threaded nut retaining the crankshaft pulley has been
changed for a left-hand threaded bolt and washer.

Cylinder head bolts and gasket modification
11 To improve sealing between the cylinder head and cylinder
block, new bolts and a redesigned cylinder head gasket have been
introduced. These changes required redesigned pistons to be fitted,
to prevent alteration of compression ratio.
12 Servicing operations are unaffected, except for the cylinder head
bolt tightening sequence and torque loading figures. These are
detailed under the procedure for C-Series engines, and in the
Specifications.
13 This modification is effective from the following engine
numbers:

Model	Engine serial number
131 Super 1365	1 350 245
131 Super 1600	1 362 528
131 Super 2000	1 358 246

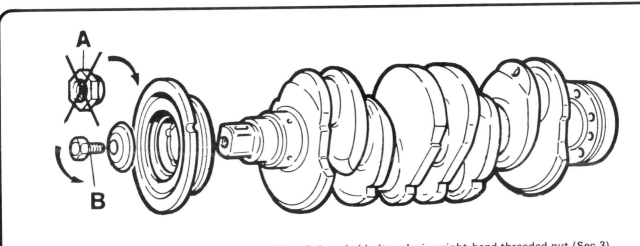

Fig. 13.2 Later type crankshaft with left-hand threaded bolt replacing right-hand threaded nut (Sec 3)

14 Where a cylinder head has been tightened down using the new torque + angle tightening procedure, it is not considered necessary to retighten the head bolts again after 700 miles (1000 km), service.

C-Series engines – 1982 on
General description
15 The C-Series engines, introduced in 1982, are available in 1367 and 1585 cc single overhead cam, and 1367, 1585 and 1995 cc double overhead cam versions, depending upon the model and market area.
16 Basically it is the same engine block as the B-series, with dimensional changes to the bore and stroke, but with a completely new alloy cylinder head in the case of the sohc version. The dohc cylinder head remains much the same as the B-Series engine and any dimensional changes will be found in the Specifications.
17 Servicing of the new engines is as described for the B-Series engine but must be used in conjunction with the Specifications given at the beginning of this Chapter, and the major changes dealt with in the following sub-Sections.
Cylinder head (sohc) – removal
Note: *The procedure given below is for the removal of the complete cylinder head. The camshaft can be removed with the cylinder head in position, in which case only those operations relevant to that operation need be carried out. There is also no need to remove the engine from the vehicle.*
18 Either prop open the bonnet or remove it completely by undoing the hinge bracket retaining bolts. Mark the position of the hinge brackets on the bonnet using a pencil.
19 Disconnect the battery leads. Disconnect the negative (earth) lead first, followed by the positive lead.
20 Drain the cooling system (refer to Chapter 2).
21 Withdraw the air cleaner assembly by undoing the three nuts which hold the cover in place, and remove the filter element. Now undo and remove the four carburettor flange plate nuts (photos).

Before the air cleaner assembly may be removed, it is necessary to disconnect all hoses, pipes and electrical leads associated with the EGR system. This will vary according to the market, and the extent of EGR equipment fitted.
22 Disconnect the spark plug leads and remove the spark plugs. Tie the leads out of the way.
23 Slacken the retaining clips and remove the hoses from the thermostat housing and radiator (photos).
24 Remove the top half of the timing cover.
25 To remove the bottom half of the timing cover, slacken the alternator tensioner bracket bolts and remove the alternator belt. (On models fitted with power steering and/or air conditioning, this may also involve removal of other drive belts.)
26 Disconnect the throttle cable by withdrawing the cable end and then depressing the spring housing to release it from its bracket.
27 Disconnect the hoses from the fuel economy device on the carburettor and inlet manifold valve, noting which way they are located.
28 Disconnect the hoses to the automatic choke and the brake servo-to-manifold vacuum pipe.
29 Disconnect the heater hose at the rear end of the cylinder head.
30 Remove the hot air collector plate from the exhaust manifold.
31 Disconnect the fuel lines to the carburettor.
32 Disconnect the electrical lead to the water temperature transmitter.
33 The carburettor may now be removed separately, or left in place on the inlet manifold and removed with it (photo).
34 Disconnect the exhaust downpipe to manifold connection (it may also be necessary to disconnect the first exhaust pipe support bracket to allow movement of the pipe).
35 To inlet manifold may now be removed.
36 To remove the exhaust manifold, first remove the coolant pipe which runs along the side of the cylinder block, then undo the remaining exhaust manifold nuts and withdraw the manifold.

3.21A Air filter cover retaining nuts

3.21B Removing the air cleaner element

3.21C Removing carburettor flange nuts

3.23A Thermostat housing hose clips

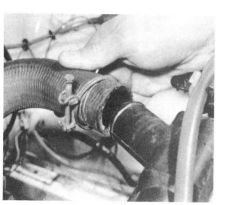
3.23B Removing top radiator hose

3.33 Removing carburettor and inlet manifold assembly

3.37 Location of support brackets and earth lead on camshaft cover (arrowed)

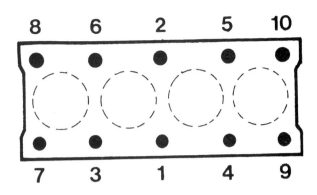

Fig. 13.3 Cylinder head bolt tightening sequence (Sec 3)

37 Remove the camshaft cover bolts, noting the location of the various support brackets and earth strap (photo).
38 Slacken the timing belt tensioner pulley bolt and its fulcrum bolt, move the tensioner to the left to release the tension, and tighten the pulley bolt again to retain the pulley. Remove the timing belt.
39 Once the timing belt has been removed do not attempt to turn either the camshaft or crankshaft, as the valve heads will strike the pistons causing damage. For this reason, removal of the camshaft sprocket should be left until the cylinder head has been removed.
40 Remove the bolt securing the top and bottom timing cover back plates together.
41 The cylinder head is now ready for removal.
42 First, mop up any oil from within the recesses in which the cylinder head bolts are located.
43 A special star-shaped drive bit is required for the cylinder head bolts.

44 Loosen the bolts evenly and progressively in the reverse order of tightening (see Fig. 13.3) and remove the bolts.
45 The cylinder head may now be carefully lifted away. If it is stuck, do not use a screwdriver to lever it off, but rather free it with a sharp blow from a hide or wooden headed mallet.
46 Place the cylinder head on a suitable working area.
Camshaft (sohc engine) – removal and refitting
47 With the cylinder head placed on a suitable surface, the camshaft sprocket can be removed.
48 A special tool is available to prevent the sprocket from turning while removing the retaining bolt, but if this is not available, wedge a suitable piece of wood under one of the camshaft lobes, or use a screwdriver inserted through the sprocket and placed under one of the camshaft front bearing housing retaining nuts. Unscrew the bolt from the camshaft and remove the sprocket (photo).
49 Remove the nuts retaining the front bearing housing (photo).
50 Lift off the camshaft dust cover top backplate.
51 Remove the bolts retaining the rear bearing housing.
52 Carefully ease out both the front and rear bearing housings.
53 The two centre bearing caps may now be removed, by undoing the four retaining nuts, slowly and evenly, until all pressure on the camshaft, exerted from the valve springs, is released (photo).
54 Remove the bearing caps from the two centre bearings and then carefully lift out the camshaft.

3.48 Removing camshaft sprocket retaining bolt using screwdriver to prevent sprocket from turning

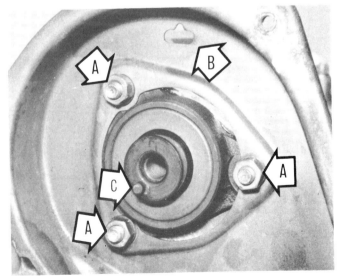

3.49 Camshaft front bearing housing retaining nuts
A Retaining nuts   C Camshaft bearing dowel
B Timing hole

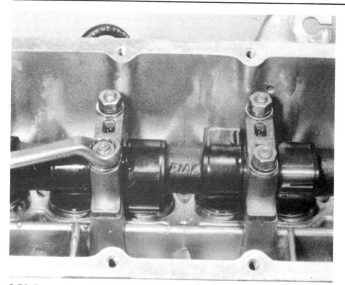

3.53 Removing centre bearing cap retaining nut

3.59 Camshaft front bearing housing and oil seal

Camshaft and camshaft bearings (sohc) – inspection

55 The camshaft should be inspected for wear as described in Chapter 1.

56 There are four camshaft bearings, one at each end and two in the centre.

57 The bearings at the front and rear of the camshaft are conventional white-metal-lined bearing shells, contained within the front and rear bearing housings.

58 If the bearing shells are worn they can be renewed by pressing out the old ones and then pressing in the new.

59 Note that only one camshaft oil seal is fitted, this being to the front bearing with its flat side facing outward (photo).

60 The two centre bearings are machined directly into the cylinder head (photo) and the bearing caps. If the bearing surfaces are in any way worn or damaged, consult your FIAT dealer.

Valves, valve guides, tappets and tappet clearances (sohc) – inspection

61 The procedures given in Chapter 1 for the inspection of the valve gear is sufficient to enable the sohc engine valve gear to be inspected.

62 Use the Specifications given at the beginning of this supplement for tolerances and clearances.

Camshaft (sohc engine) – refitting

63 When refitting the camshaft oil all parts liberally with clean engine oil.

64 Slide the camshaft into position and rest it on the two centre bearings. The internally-threaded end of the camshaft faces to the front of the cylinder head (photo).

65 Fit the front and rear bearing housings, using new gaskets. The housings will only fit one way. Do not forget to fit the camshaft dust cover upper backplate under the nuts of the front housing (photos).

66 Tighten the bearing retaining nuts and bolts, but do not torque them fully at this stage (photo).

67 Fit the centre bearing caps, ensuring the oil feed cut-outs are positioned over the oil gallery holes machined in the cylinder head (photo).

68 Tighten the bearing cap nuts slowly and progressively, to even out the load from the valve springs. FIAT produce a special tool which positions the camshaft correctly for this operation but, provided care is taken when tightening the bearing cap nuts, its use is not required.

69 The nuts and bolts retaining the two outer bearing housings should now be fully torque-tightened, followed by the centre bearing nuts. See the Specifications section for correct torque loading values.

3.60 Camshaft bearing surfaces in cylinder head (arrowed)

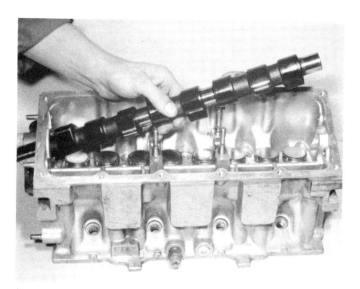

3.64 Sliding camshaft into position

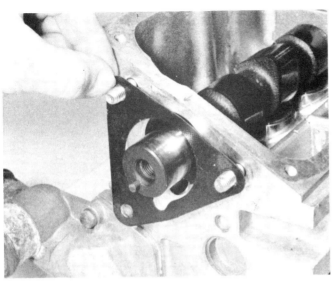

3.65A Fitting new gasket to front bearing housing location

3.65B Front bearing housing in position

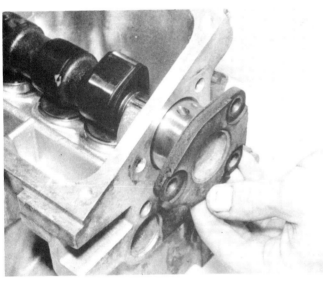

3.65C Refitting rear bearing housing

3.65D Position timing cover backplate spacing washer (arrowed), and then ...

3.65E ... fit the back plate (arrow shows fitted position of spacer)

3.66 Tightening rear bearing housing bolt

3.67 Refitting one of the centre bearing caps, showing the correct location of the oil feed cut-out (arrowed)

70 The camshaft sprocket may now be fitted, ensuring it is seated correctly on its locating dowel. Torque-tighten the retaining bolt to the correct specification while, at the same time, preventing the camshaft from rotating using one of the methods described earlier dealing with camshaft removal.

Cylinder head (sohc engine) – refitting

71 Before refitting the cylinder head, check the alignment of the timing marks on both the cylinder head and the crankshaft, and do not rotate either until the camshaft drivebelt is refitted.

72 Position a new cylinder head gasket on the cylinder block, ensuring it seats correctly over its locating dowels (photo).

73 Lower the cylinder head onto the cylinder block, ensuring it locates correctly over the dowels (photo).

74 Cylinder head bolts should only be used a maximum of four times, after which they should be renewed.

75 The bolts and washers should be well oiled, and then allowed to drain for 30 minutes before fitting.

76 Fit the cylinder head bolts and tighten them (photos) as follows in the sequence shown in Fig. 13.3, and to the torque loadings given in the Specifications at the beginning of this Chapter.

    Stage 1 –   tighten to the torque loading given for stage 1
    Stage 2 –   tighten to the torque loading given for stage 2

3.72 Fitting new cylinder head gasket (location dowels arrowed)

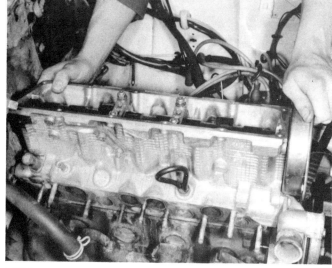

3.73 Lowering cylinder head into position

3.76A Fitting a cylinder head bolt

3.76B Tightening a cylinder head bolt using a torque wrench

The bolts must now be angular tightened, following the procedure in the next paragraph.

77 Now, using an ordinary socket wrench (ie, not a torque wrench) tighten each bolt through 90° using the sequence given in Fig. 13.3. Once this is completed, tighten the bolts again through a further 90° in sequence, so that the end result is that each bolt has been tightened a total of 180° in two stages (photo). The cylinder head retaining bolt tightening sequence is now complete, and no further re-tightening of the bolts is necessary after the engine has been run for 500 miles (800 km).

78 Ensure the reference mark on the camshaft sprocket is still lined up with the hole in the upper dust cover backplate, and that the reference mark on the crankshaft pulley is lined up with the longest mark on the cover. (The other two marks are at 5° and 10° BTDC and are used for ignition timing.)

79 Fit a new camshaft drivebelt, slipping it over the crankshaft, auxiliary drive and camshaft sprockets.

Note: *FIAT state that once a drivebelt has been removed, it should not be used again.*

80 Slacken the nut in the centre of the tensioner pulley wheel, and the fulcrum nut.

81 This will automatically tension the drivebelt.

82 Rotate the engine through several turns, in its normal direction of rotation (which is clockwise, viewed from the front).

83 Stop turning the engine with No. 1 cylinder at TDC, and tighten the tensioner pulley nut to the torque loading given in the Specifications.

84 Tighten the tensioner fulcrum nut.

85 Recheck all timing reference marks, ensuring they are still in alignment.

86 Refit the timing belt covers. It may be necessary to remove the crankshaft pulley to fit the lower cover.

87 Fit the camshaft cover using a new gasket (photo), remembering the support brackets for the throttle and fuel lines, and the earth wire located under the rear right-hand bolt.

88 Using a new gasket refit the coolant transfer pipe (photo).

89 Fit a new inlet/exhaust manifold gasket to the cylinder head (photo) and then fit the exhaust manifold.

90 Refit the coolant pipes at the rear of the engine if these were removed.

91 Refit the inlet manifold, complete with carburettor, or fit the carburettor after the manifold has been fitted.

3.77 Using a T-bar to angular-tighten a cylinder head bolt

3.87 Fitting new gasket to the camshaft cover

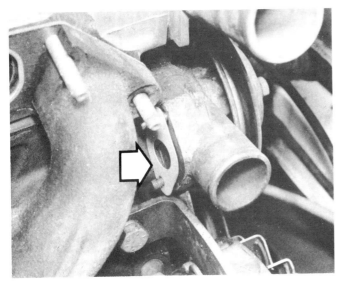
3.88 Fitting new gasket to the coolant transfer pipe (arrowed)

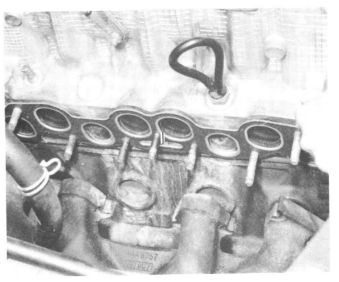
3.89 Inlet/exhaust manifold gasket correctly fitted

3.92 Tightening hose clip on automatic choke unit

3.95 Fuel supply and return hoses correctly fitted

92 Reconnect the hoses to the automatic choke (photo).
93 Reconnect the brake servo vacuum hose.
94 Fit the throttle cable into its housing bracket on the camshaft cover, and reconnect the ball-ended socket.
95 Fit the fuel supply and return lines to the carburettor (photo).
96 Reconnect the water temperature transmitter electrical lead.
97 Refit the thermostat housing and all associated hoses.
98 Connect the exhaust downpipe to the exhaust manifold, and tighten the first exhaust mounting if this was slackened during removal.
99 Refit the hot air collector to the exhaust.
100 Refit the hoses to the fuel economy device.
101 Fit the alternator drivebelt and tension the belt as described in Chapter 2.
102 Fit the hoses to the EGR system (photo).
103 Fit the air cleaner assembly to the carburettor and connect all hoses and electrical leads.
104 Fill the cooling system with coolant as described in Chapter 2.
105 Check the engine oil level.
106 Fit the spark plugs and connect the leads from the distributor.
107 Connect the battery (positive lead first).
108 Refit the bonnet if this was removed.
109 Check all connections, and refer to Chapter 1 for initial start-up procedure.

Twin overhead cam (dohc) engines – description
110 The new twin overhead cam engines are basically the same as the earlier versions, in that the twin camshafts are housed in their own cam carrier housings, which are bolted to the cylinder head.
111 Provided the instructions given in Chapter 1, Part B are followed, and used in conjunction with the Specifications and other pertinent information in this Chapter, no difficulty should be experienced in servicing.

4 Cooling system

Water pump (USA models from 1978) – removal and refitting
1 Refer to Chapter 2 and drain the cooling system.
2 Unscrew and remove the three bolts retaining the water pump pulley.
3 Withdraw the pulley and remove the drivebelt.
4 Loosen the water pump hose clip and detach the hose.
5 Unscrew and remove the four pump unit retaining bolts then withdraw the pump.
6 Refit in the reverse sequence to that given above, ensuring that

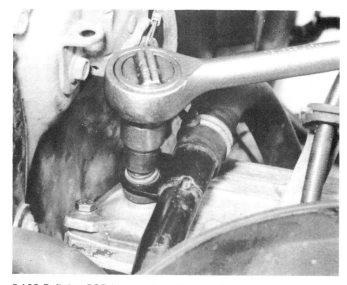

3.102 Refitting EGR hose on top of camshaft cover

the mating surfaces between the pump and engine are perfectly clean. Use a new gasket and on completion, readjust the drivebelt tension.
7 The water pump unit can be dismantled for overhaul, as given in Chapter 2, Section 9.

Coolant reservoir – later models
8 Later models are fitted with a combined radiator coolant expansion tank and windscreen wash reservoir (photo).
9 Keep the coolant level in the expansion tank filled to between the MAX/MIN marks.
10 Do not confuse the two reservoirs when topping up. Antifreeze can be very harmful to paintwork!

5 Carburation

Carburettor – 2.0 litre Sport models
Idle stop solenoid
1 The Weber carburettor fitted to the 2.0 litre Sport models now incorporates an idle stop solenoid.

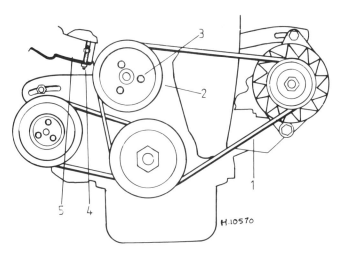

Fig. 13.4 Water pump and associated components (USA
models from 1978) (Sec 4)

1   Drivebelt   4   Hose clip
2   Pump pulley   5   Hose
3   Pulley bolts

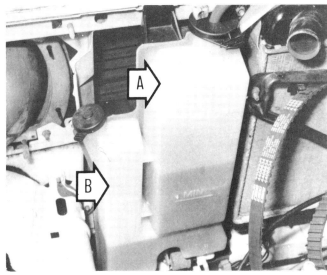

4.8 Combined coolant and windscreen wash reservoirs
A Coolant reservoir
B Windscreen wash reservoir

2   This is designed to cut the fuel supply in the carburettor as soon
as the engine is switched off, so preventing unnecessary wastage of
fuel. The solenoid consists of a coil and needle valve and is a
separate unit, being screwed into the carburettor body. The solenoid
is actuated, to open or close the fuel supply to the slow running jet,
by the ignition switch. The valve is opened when the ignition key is
switched to the 'MAR' position and closed when in the 'OFF'
position.
3   The position of the valve is shown in Fig. 13.5 and the fuel
induction route to the venturi is clearly indicated.
4   If necessary, the valve can easily be removed by simply

detaching the wire and unscrewing the unit from the carburettor
body.

Slow running jet
5   To comply with the European emission control regulations, the
slow running adjustment screw is now sealed with a tamperproof
plug (see Fig. 13.6). Should it be found that the slow running
speed is difficult to set by the throttle stop screw, the plug can be
extracted and the idle screw adjusted in the normal way in
conjunction with the throttle stop screw, as given in Chapter 3. The
plug must be refitted on completion.

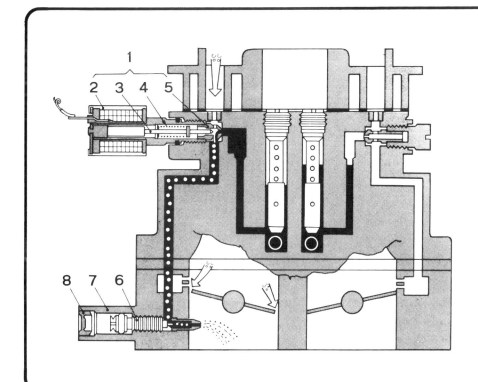

Fig. 13.5 Sectional view of
Weber carburettor fitted to
2.0 litre models (Sec 5)

1   Idle stop solenoid
2   Coil
3   Needle valve
4   Spring
5   Slow running jet
6   Slow running adjustment jet
7   Carburettor body
8   Tamperproof plug (plastic)

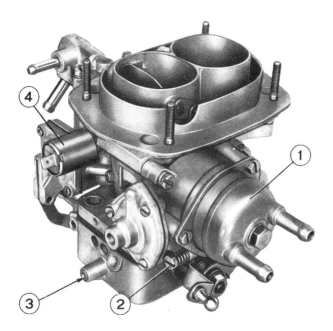

Fig. 13.6 View of the Weber carburettor fitted to 2.0 litre models (Sec 5)

1   Automatic choke unit
2   Throttle stop screw
3   Slow running adjuster screw (under plug)
4   Idle stop solenoid

Weber ADF Series carburettors adjustment
Float level adjustment
6   Remove the top cover of the carburettor.
7   With the cover gasket in position, hold the cover vertically so that the float will hang downwards under its own weight.
8   With the cover in this position, the distance between the top of the float and the underside of the cover gasket (dimension 'a', Fig. 13.7) should be as given in the specifications. It can be checked using the correct diameter drill. If it is not within limits, bend the float arm to adjust.
Float travel adjustment
9   Hold the carburettor cover horizontally, so that the float is hanging free at the full extent of its travel.
10 Measure the distance from the underside of the cover gasket to the top of the float (dimension 'b', Fig. 13.7) and check against the specifications.
11 Adjust by bending the float end.
Accelerator pump flow rate
12 Fill the float chamber with petrol and operate the main butterfly lever from its closed to fully open position several times to prime the system.
13 Operate the accelerator pump through ten successive deliveries, pausing for a few seconds between each one, and catching the expelled fuel in a calibrated jar.
14 The total should be within the specifications given.
Fast idle adjustment (Fig. 13.8, dimension 'A')
15 Close the choke flap by wrapping a strong elastic band around the control arm, simulating the action of the automatic choke bi-metallic spring.
16 Set the adjusting screw on the top step of the cam.
17 Check main butterfly valve opening clearance against that specified.
18 Obtain correct clearance by turning adjustment screw.

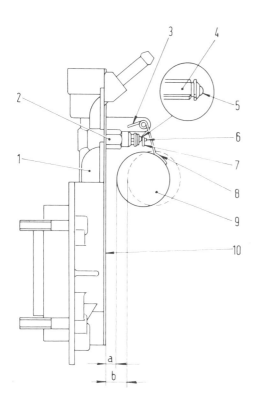

Fig. 13.7 Weber carburettor float level setting (Sec 5)

1   Cover body
2   Needle valve
3   Float end
4   Needle valve
5   Movable ball
6   Return hook
7   Tongue
8   Float arm
9   Float
10 Gasket
Dimension 'a' = 6 ± 0.25 mm
Dimension 'b' = 14 ± 0.5 mm

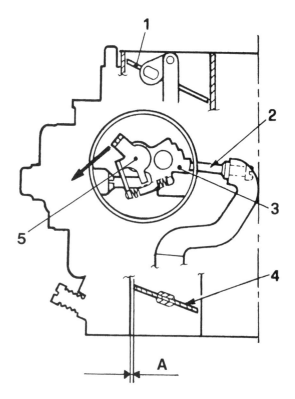

Fig. 13.8 Weber carburettor fast idle adjustment (dimension A) (Sec 5)

1   Choke flap
2   Adjusting screw
3   Cam
4   Main butterfly valve
5   Control lever

For dimension 'A' see Specifications

Setting fast idle cam (Fig. 13.9, dimension 'B')
19 With the fast idle adjusted, move the adjusting screw away from the cam to allow the choke flap to fully open. Remove elastic band used for previous adjustment.
20 Position the adjusting screw on the 3rd step of the cam.
21 In this position, the choke flap should be open by the amount specified.
22 Adjust, if necessary, by bending the control lever tongue.

Anti-flooding device adjustment (Fig. 13.10, dimension 'C')
23 Operate the throttle valve until the choke flap is fully closed.

24 Apply light pressure to the fork and check that the clearance between the bush and the tongue of the lever is as specified.
25 Adjust by bending the tongue.

Choke flap minimum opening (Fig. 13.11A, dimension 'D')
26 Exert a force on the control linkage in the direction of the arrow (this can be done by using an elastic band).
27 Operate the throttle valve several times to fully close the choke flap.
28 Bring the pneumatic weakening device stem into contact with the adjusting screw, either by applying a vacuum to the hose or mechanically.
29 Check that the choke flap opening is as specified.
30 Obtain correct opening dimension by turning adjustment screw.

Choke flap maximum opening (Fig. 13.11B, dimension 'E')
31 Prepare the carburettor as described in the previous sub-section for minimum opening, but remove the pressure applied to the bi-metallic spring fork.

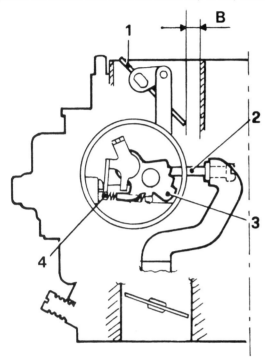

Fig. 13.9 Weber carburettor fast idle cam adjustment
(dimension B) (Sec 5)

1   Choke flap   3   Cam
2   Adjusting screw   4   Tongue

For dimension 'B' see Specifications

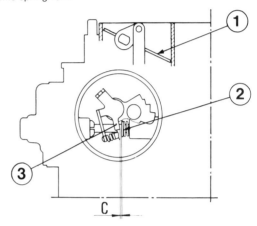

Fig. 13.10 Weber carburettor anti-flooding device clearance
(dimension C) (Sec 5)

1   Choke flap   3   Bi-metallic spring lever
2   Anti-flooding device bush

For dimension 'C' see Specifications

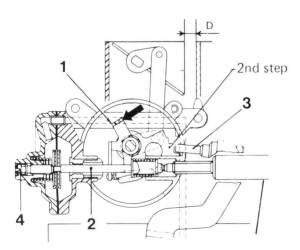

Fig. 13.11A Weber carburettor choke flap minimum opening
(dimension D) (Sec 5)

1   Control lever   3   Adjusting screw
2   Stem   4   Stem adjusting screw

For dimension 'D' see Specifications

Checking starter butterfly maximum opening

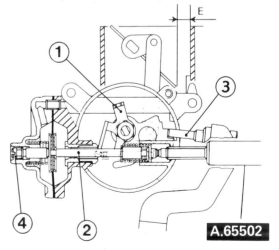

Fig. 13.11B Choke flap maximum opening (dimension E)
(Sec 5)

1   Control lever   3   Adjusting screw
2   Stem   4   Stem adjusting screw

For dimension 'E' see Specifications

32 Check the dimension is as specified.
33 If not as specified, then the diaphragm unit will require renewal, but first recheck all operations described in paras 23 to 31.

Thermostatic casing (Weber and Solex)
34 Remove the screws retaining the thermostatic casing.
35 Check inside the housing for cleanliness and freedom from deposits.
36 Check for wear and free movement of the bi-metallic spring, and that it is wound on evenly and located correctly on the centre pin.
37 Refit the casing and ensure the reference marks are aligned.
38 It is advisable to replace the thermostatic casing after 30 000 miles (50 000 km).

Solex TEIE Series carburettors adjustment
Anti-flooding device (Fig. 13.13, dimension 'A')
39 With the carburettor fitted to the engine, operate the throttle control lever until choke flap is closed.
40 Measure the choke flap opening, using a twist drill of the specified size.
41 Obtain the correct opening dimension by turning adjustment screw (2) as necessary.
Fast idle adjustment (Fig. 13.14, dimension 'B')
42 With the choke fully closed, and the adjusting screw on the highest cam step, check main butterfly valve opening is as specified.
43 Obtain the correct opening dimension by turning adjustment screw (3) as necessary.
Pneumatic accelerator pump
44 These carburettors are fitted with an extra pneumatic accelerator pump.
45 The pump is activated by a thermal-valve situated on the cylinder head.
46 Up to 55° ± 3°C (131° ± 37°F) the thermal valve remains open.
47 Above this temperature, it gradually closes, until it is fully closed at 65° ± 3°C (149° ± 37°F).
Thermostatic air filter
48 A thermal-valve fitted in the air filter housing allows warm air from the exhaust manifold to be drawn into the carburettor at temperatures below 23° to 28°C (73° to 83°F). At temperatures above these figures the valve closes and allows fresh air into the carburettor.

Fuel system – 1756 cc engine (USA model)
Fuel pump – mechanical (from 1978)
49 A mechanical fuel pump was fitted to all models in the 1756 cc engine range from 1978 on. To remove the pump, detach and plug the inlet and outlet hoses to/from the pump unit. Unscrew and remove the two pump retaining bolts (see Fig. 13.18). Withdraw the pump, together with the two gaskets and spacer.

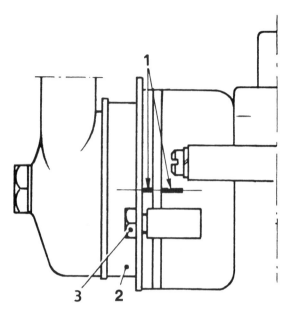

**Fig. 13.12 Automatic choke housing (Weber and Solex)
(Sec 5)**

1	Alignment marks	3	Securing bolt
2	Choke housing		

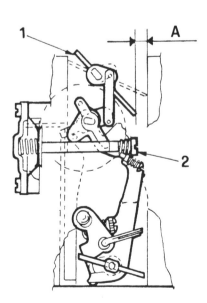

**Fig. 13.13 Solex carburettor anti-flooding device
(dimension A) (Sec 5)**

1	Choke flap	2	Adjusting screw

For dimension 'A' see Specifications

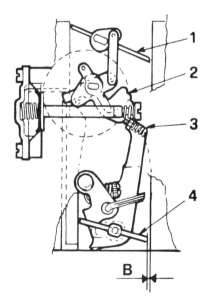

**Fig. 13.14 Solex carburettor fast idle adjustment
(dimension B) (Sec 5)**

1	Choke flap	3	Adjusting screw
2	Cam	4	Main butterfly wave

For dimension 'B' see Specifications

Fig. 13.15 Location of pneumatic accelerator pump
thermal device (arrowed) (Sec 5)

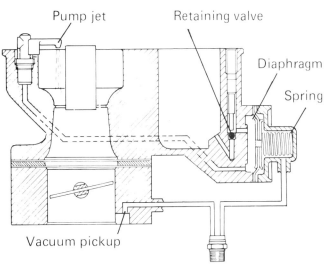

Fig. 13.16 Schematic diagram of pneumatic accelerator
pump (Sec 5)

Fig. 13.17 Air filter thermostatic valve (arrowed) (Sec 5)

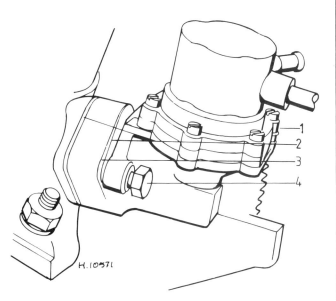

Fig. 13.18 Mechanical fuel pump fitted to later 1756 cc
engines (USA) (Sec 5)

1	Pump	3	Spacer
2	Gasket	4	Bolt

50 Refit in the reverse order, ensuring that new gaskets are used and that the flange faces are clean. Check for signs of fuel leaks at hose connections on restarting the engine.

Fuel filter

51 The later type fuel filter is shown in Fig. 13.19. To renew it, simply unscrew the inlet and outlet hose clamps then pull the hoses from the filter unit. Refit in the reverse order, ensuring filter is fitted

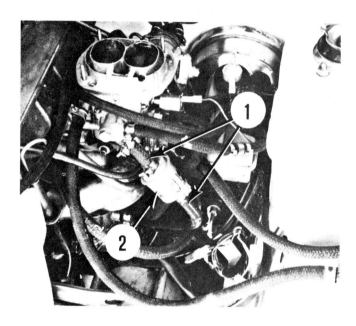

Fig. 13.19 Later type fuel filter fitted to 1756 cc engine (USA) (Sec 5)

   1   Hose connections   2   Fuel filter

(Arrow on filter must face fuel direction)

correctly by noting the fuel directional arrow on filter body, and when the engine is restarted, check the hose connections for signs of leakage. **Note:** *Do not use a plastic type filter.*

Fuel line system

52 The fuel and vapour lines between the fuel tank and the carburettor have been modified on the later models; the general layouts are shown in Figs. 13.20 and 13.21.

Fuel injection system (2.0 litre USA models – 1980 on)
Description

53 The fuel injection system is designed to ensure minimum exhaust emission levels throughout the engine speed range, as fuel is metered to the engine precisely according to load and speed.
54 To this end, the system may be divided into two main parts, the fuel injection system itself, and the electronic control system.
55 In general, servicing of the injection system requires the use of specialist equipment for testing, fault diagnosis and correct setting to comply with varying exhaust emissions control legislation.
56 It is therefore recommended that any major servicing be left to a local dealer or garage, and that only minor servicing and adjustments are carried out by the owner.
57 The operations that follow are intended only to allow the owner driver to carry out running adjustments and remove and refit various components. To prevent infringement of EEC regulations, the system should be checked by an authorised dealer after any adjustments are made or parts renewed.
Warning: *Fuel injection systems are pressurised and carry a high explosion risk due to spilt fuel. Before any part of the injection system is disturbed, the system must be depressurised, and all normal fire precautions when handling fuel observed.*

Air filter element renewal

58 The air filter element should be renewed at the mileage specified under Routine maintenance at the beginning of this manual. However, it should be noted that the mileage specified is for vehicles operating under normal conditions, and if the vehicle is driven frequently in dusty or sandy areas then the element should be renewed at half the mileage specified.
59 Using a screwdriver, release the four cover retaining clips.
60 Lift off the cover and withdraw the filter element.
61 Install new filter, replace cover and secure with retaining clips.

Idle speed adjustment

62 The engine should be at normal operating temperature and the fan switched off.
63 On cars with automatic transmission, apply the handbrake and select 'D' on gear lever.
64 Make adjustment on idle speed screw to give the correct idle speed as given in the Specifications.
65 If the correct idle speed cannot be obtained adjust the accelerator linkage stop screw as described in the next sub-section.

Accelerator linkage stop screw adjustment

Note: *Carry out this operation if the idle speed cannot be set low enough, or if the throttle linkage or inlet manifold has been disturbed.*

66 Prepare the vehicle as in paragraphs 62 and 63.
67 Turn the idle speed adjuster screw all the way in.
68 Slacken the accelerator linkage stop screw locknut and adjust stop screw to obtain idle speed given in the Specifications.
69 Prevent the stop screw from turning and tighten the locknut.
70 Carry out the idle speed adjustment as described in the previous sub-section.

Accelerator and kickdown cable adjustment

71 Ensure engine idle speed is correctly set.
72 Check the accelerator cable for slack at the cable housing support on the intake manifold.
73 Pull the accelerator cable back lightly until just before it begins to move the throttle lever.
74 Check there is a clearance of 0.04 in (1 mm), between the adjustment nuts and support.
75 Adjust the lock nuts to obtain this clearance if necessary.
76 Depress the accelerator cable until throttle lever touches the maximum opening stop.
77 Check that kickdown cable just starts to pull at this point.
78 Fully depress the accelerator. Check kickdown cable has extended by 0.35 to 0.43 in (9 to 11 mm).
79 Adjust the lock nuts to obtain correct extension of the cable if necessary.

Throttle plate switch adjustment

80 Check idle speed is correct.
81 Disconnect the multi-plug connector to the throttle plate switch.
82 Connect an ohmmeter between terminals 2 and 18 of the switch.
83 Loosen the two screws holding the throttle plate switch.
84 With the engine off, turn the switch housing clockwise until a closed circuit reading is obtained on the ohmmeter.
85 At that exact point (ie, when closed circuit is indicated) tighten the switch securing screws.
86 Re-check the adjustment.

Lambda sensor indicator reset

87 The indicator will come on at 30 000 miles (48 000 km) showing the need for renewal of the sensor.
88 To turn the indicator 'OFF', the switch unit must be reset.
89 Remove the security wire and cap screw.
90 Insert a suitable size screwdriver through the housing and press the switch contact.
91 This will reset the wheel to its high point.
92 Refit the cap screw and secure with wire.

Lambda sensor renewal

93 The Lambda sensor should be renewed every 30 000 miles (48 000 km).
94 Allow the exhaust system to cool.
95 Disconnect the electrical cable from the sensor.
96 Unscrew the sensor from the exhaust manifold.
97 Apply an anti-seize grease to the threads of the new sensor and screw it into the exhaust manifold.
98 Torque-tighten to the figure given in the Specifications.

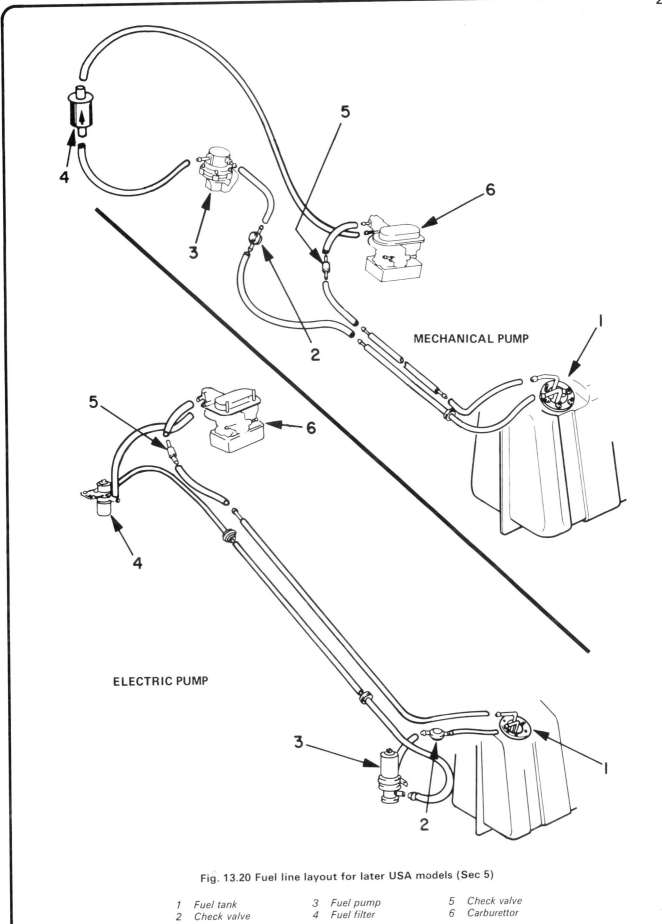

Fig. 13.20 Fuel line layout for later USA models (Sec 5)

1 Fuel tank   3 Fuel pump   5 Check valve
2 Check valve   4 Fuel filter   6 Carburettor

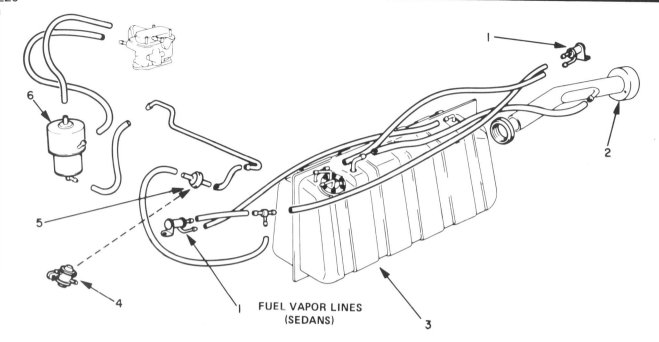

FUEL VAPOR LINES
(SEDANS)

Fig. 13.21A fuel vapour line layout for USA sedans (Sec 5)

1 Separator
2 Filler tube
3 Fuel tank
4 Three-way valve (pre-1977)
5 Two-way valve (1978)
6 Carbon trap

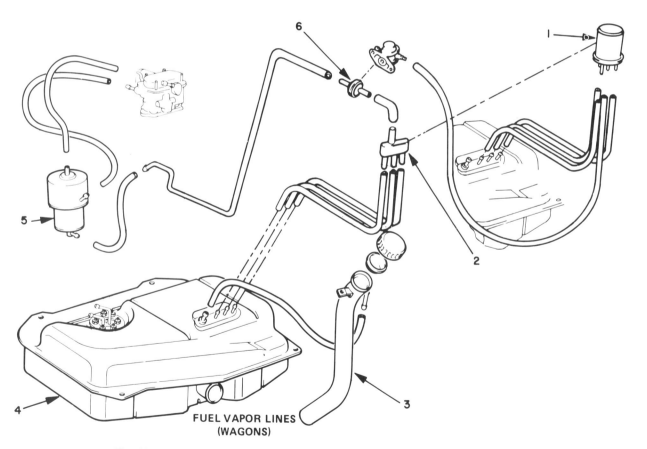

FUEL VAPOR LINES
(WAGONS)

Fig. 13.21B Fuel vapour line layout for USA Station Wagons to 1978 (Sec 5)

1 Separator (pre-1977)
2 Separator (1978 only)
3 Filler tube
4 Fuel tank
5 Carbon trap
6 Two-way valve (1978 on)
7 Three-way valve (pre-1977)

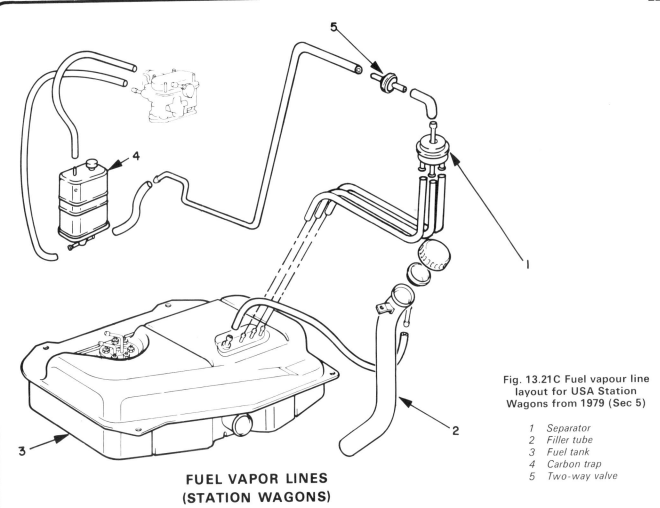

**FUEL VAPOR LINES
(STATION WAGONS)**

Fig. 13.21C Fuel vapour line
layout for USA Station
Wagons from 1979 (Sec 5)

1   Separator
2   Filler tube
3   Fuel tank
4   Carbon trap
5   Two-way valve

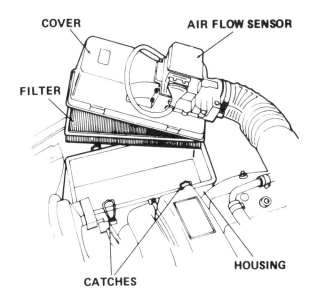

Fig. 13.22 Exploded view of air filter housing
components (fuel injection models) (Sec 5)

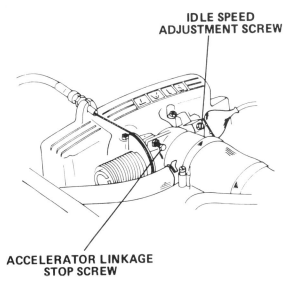

Fig. 13.23 Location of idle speed adjustment screw and
accelerator linkage stop screw (Sec 5)

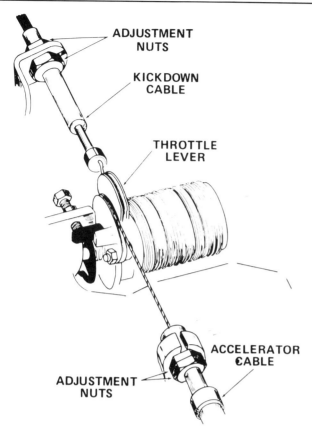

Fig. 13.24 Location of accelerator and kickdown cables adjustment points (Sec 5)

99 Reconnect the electrical cable.
100 As soon as possible, have the CO checked by an authorised dealer.
Fuel injectors – removal and installation
Caution: *Before starting work on any part of the injection system, the system must be depressurised.*
101 Remove fuel tank cap.
102 Disconnect vacuum hose from fuel pressure regulator.
103 Using a hand vacuum pump, apply a vacuum to the pressure regulator.

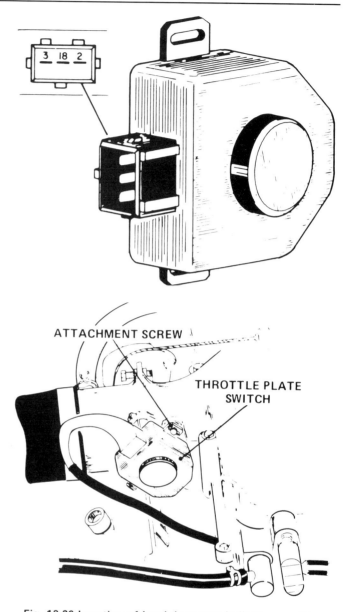

Fig. 13.26 Location of Lambda sensor indicator resetting switch housing (Sec 5)

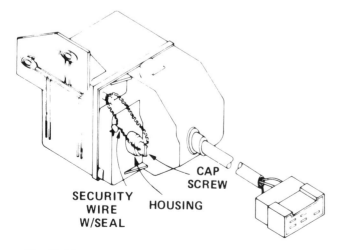

Fig. 13.25 Location of throttle plate switch adjustment screw (Sec 5)

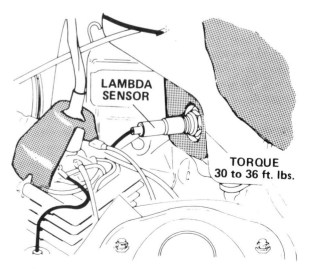

Fig. 13.27 Location of Lambda sensor (Sec 5)

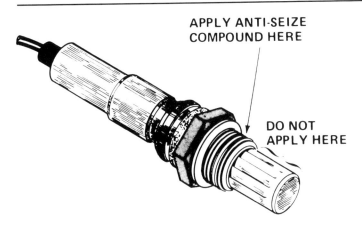

Fig. 13.28 Application area of anti-seize compound on Lambda sensor (Sec 5)

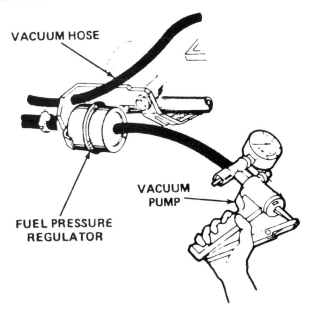

Fig. 13.29 Applying vacuum to the fuel pressure regulator (Sec 5)

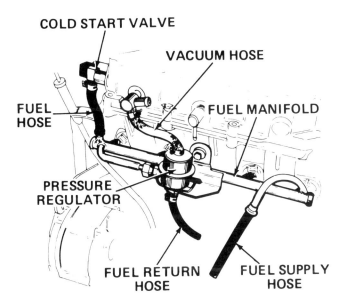

Fig. 13.30 Disconnection points for removing injectors (Sec 5)

104 Fuel pressure will then be released into the fuel tank via the fuel return hose.

105 Before removing an injector, first take precautions against fuel spillage by placing rags under each fuel hose.

106 Disconnect the wire harness from injectors.

107 Disconnect the fuel supply hose.

108 Disconnect the fuel return hose from the pressure regulator.

109 Disconnect the vacuum hose from the pressure regulator.

110 Disconnect the fuel hose to the cold start valve.

111 To remove the fuel manifold and injectors as an assembly, remove the single bolt retaining the fuel manifold to inlet manifold, and the four nuts securing the injector retainers to the inlet manifold.

112 Lift away the fuel manifold and injectors assembly, noting the positions of the rubber bushings in the inlet manifold. Retrieve any rubber bushings that may fall out.

113 Remove the four small and four large rubber bushings from the injectors together with the retainers. Inspect the rubber bushings for cracks or damage.

114 To remove an injector, pull hose from fuel manifold, noting the fitted positions of the collars.

115 The fuel injectors can be taken to a local dealer for testing if necessary.

116 When fitting new injectors, also renew the fuel hose.

117 Refitting is a reversal of the removal procedure, noting the following:

    a)   All components are clean

    b)   Rubber bushings are not damaged

    c)   Rubber bushings are correctly fitted to inlet manifold

    d)   Injectors are fitted air tight in small bushings

    e)   Injector retainer securing nuts are tight

    f)   All fuel connections are leak free.

Fuel pressure regulator – removal and refitting

118 Relieve the fuel system pressure as described at the beginning of the previous sub-section.

119 Provide a container to catch fuel spillage.

120 Disconnect the vacuum and fuel return hoses from the pressure regulator.

121 Disconnect fuel manifold pipe from pressure regulator.

122 Remove the nut holding the regulator to fuel manifold and remove the regulator.

123 Refit in the reverse order and check for leaks.

Cold start valve – removal and refitting

124 Relieve fuel system pressure described in paras 101 to 104.

125 Provide container to catch fuel spillage.

126 Disconnect the wiring lead from the cold start valve.

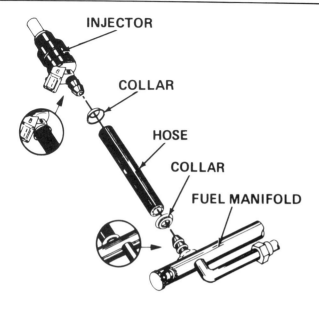

Fig. 13.31 Fuel injector assembly components (Sec 5)

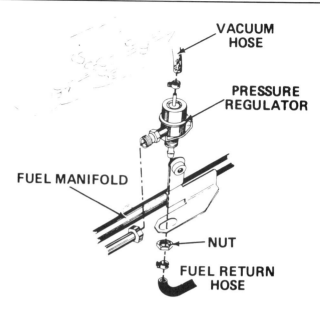

Fig. 13.32 Fuel pressure regulator components (Sec 5)

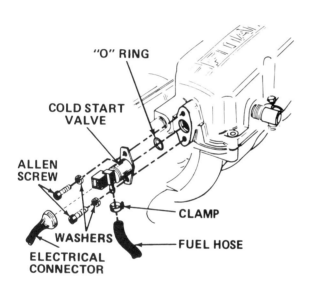

Fig. 13.33 Cold start valve components (Sec 5)

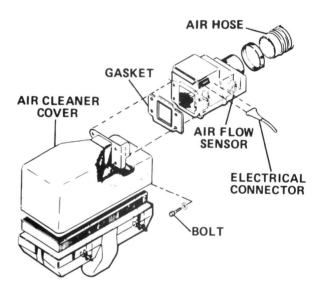

Fig. 13.34 Air flow sensor valve components (Sec 5)

127 Remove the hose clip from the fuel hose on the valve, and carefully pull the hose off the valve.

128 Remove the two Allen bolts retaining the valve to the inlet manifold.

129 Refit in the reverse order, ensuring fuel hose is pushed fully onto the valve, and that the hose clip is tight.

130 Check fuel pipe connection for leaks.

Air flow sensor – removal and refitting

131 Disconnect the electrical connections and air hose from air flow sensor.

132 Remove air cleaner cover (see paras 58 to 60).

133 Undo and remove the four retaining nuts securing the air flow sensor to the air cleaner cover.

134 Refitting is a reversal of the removal procedure, but check the air flow sensor-to-air cleaner cover gasket is correctly located and the air hose connection is tight.

Auxiliary air regulator – removal and refitting

135 Release the hose clips and remove the two air hoses.

136 Disconnect wiring lead from auxiliary air regulator.

137 Undo and withdraw the two bolts securing auxiliary air regulator to cylinder head and remove regulator.

138 Refitting is a reversal of the removal procedure, ensuring both air hose connections are tight.

Throttle plate switch – removal and refitting

139 Disconnect wiring multi-plug from throttle plate switch.

140 Undo and remove the two bolts securing the throttle plate switch to the inlet manifold and carefully withdraw the switch from the throttle shaft.

141 Refitting is a reversal of the removal procedure, ensuring the switch is located correctly on shaft and adjusted according to the procedure described in paras 80 to 86.

Fuel injection wiring diagram

142 A wiring diagram showing the various components and electrical connections has been included for reference (Fig. 13.37).

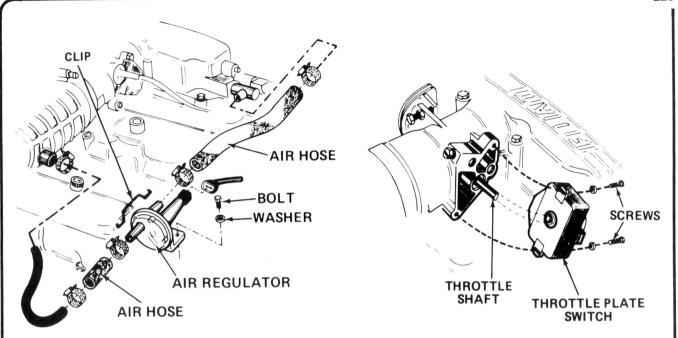

Fig. 13.35 Auxiliary air regulator components (Sec 5)

Fig. 13.36 Location of throttle plate switch (Sec 5)

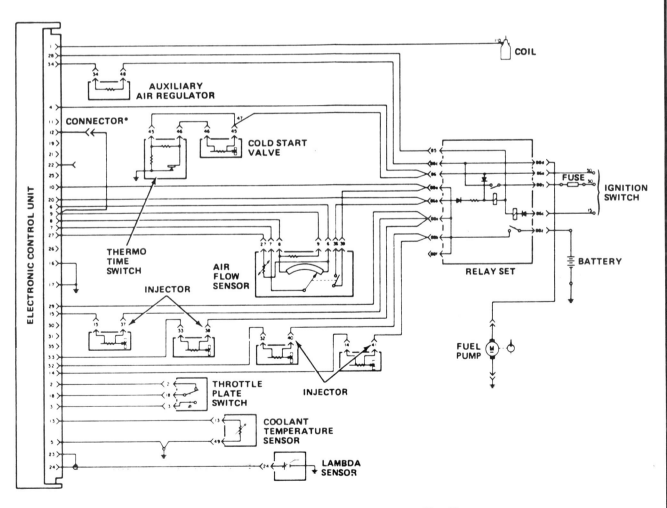

Fig. 13.37 Fuel injection wiring diagram (Sec 5)

6 Ignition system

Electronic ignition (2.0 litre models) – description and testing

1   The electronic ignition system fitted to 2.0 litre models is designed to increase engine performance whilst reducing the maintenance associated with normal distributors, by eliminating the contact breaker points, rotor arm wear and timing adjustment variation over a period of time.

2   The distributor used differs from the conventional type in that instead of having the normal fixed and moving contact points, the electronic pulses are induced by a pulse generator which comprises a magnet, fixed plate with stator pole, and a coil and reluctor which are integral with the distributor shaft.

3   The four-pole reluctor rotates, and as each point passes the stationary magnet, a magnetic pulse is created, breaks the coil primary circuit via the transistorised electronic module and generates the high voltage in the secondary winding.

4   Wiring diagrams of this type of circuit are shown in Figs. 13.38 and 13.39.

5   It is imperative, whenever this type of ignition system is being checked or worked on, that the following points are adhered to:

   (a) Never check the voltage/current of the circuit by sparking to earth!
   (b) Never remove the coil HT lead when the engine is running or in the process of being started
   (c) Do not earth the coil LT lead to the tachometer (rev-counter) black lead

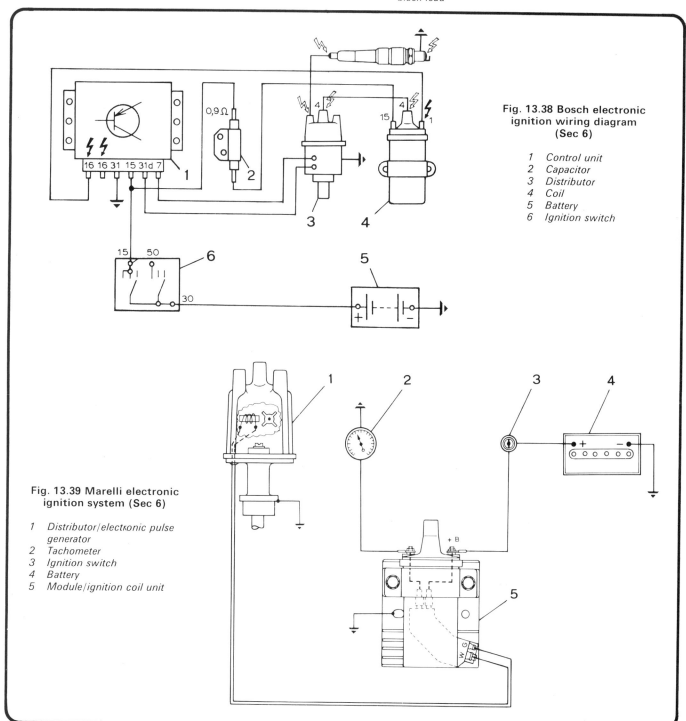

Fig. 13.38 Bosch electronic ignition wiring diagram (Sec 6)

1   Control unit
2   Capacitor
3   Distributor
4   Coil
5   Battery
6   Ignition switch

Fig. 13.39 Marelli electronic ignition system (Sec 6)

1   Distributor/electronic pulse generator
2   Tachometer
3   Ignition switch
4   Battery
5   Module/ignition coil unit

(d) Do not attempt to start the engine if the instrument panel is
     disconnected
(e) Ensure that the heat dissipator is earthed before switching on
     the ignition
(f) Never short the LT (low tension) circuit

6   To test the system, you will need a dc voltmeter and an

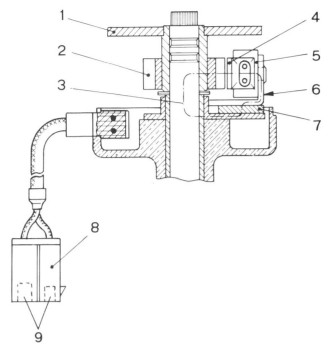

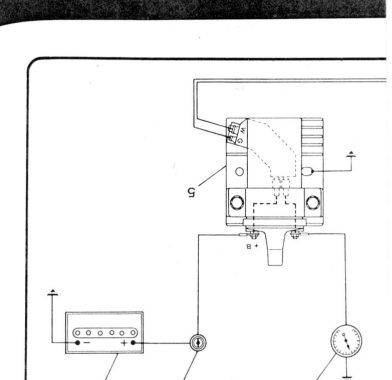

Fig. 13.40 Distributor testing – electronic ignition (Sec 6)

1	Tuning plate	6	Fixed plate
2	Reluctor	7	Magnet
3	Magnetic field	8	Connector
4	Stator pole	9	Terminals
5	Coil		

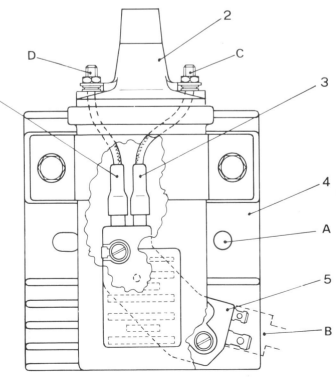

the wire terminal screw in the distributor body is secure. If these distributor checks are found to be in order, the problem must be in the electronic module attached to the coil. This cannot be repaired and must therefore be renewed if defective.

Ignition timing (2.0 litre models)

14 Where electronic ignition is fitted and a timing check is being made using a strobe light, connect the strobe lamp in accordance with the manufacturer's instructions for electronic ignition systems.

---

7 Clutch

Clutch pedal free play – 1979 on

1 Since 1979 a self-adjusting clutch has been fitted, and the requirement to adjust the clutch pedal for 'free play' does not apply.
2 The clutch cable adjustment points are situated at the release arm on the bellhousing and on the engine bulkhead where the clutch cable passes through. The bulkhead adjustment sets the outer cable length, and should be adjusted to allow proper adjustment of the inner cable.
3 The clutch cable should be adjusted to give the pedal travel dimension given in the Specifications and Fig. 13.42.

8A Manual transmission

Modifications

1 Although, mechanically, the manual gearboxes fitted to the FIAT 131 range have remained basically the same as described in Chapter 6, certain dimensional changes have taken place which affect the gear ratios.
2 It would appear from the official literature available that the 5th gear ratio was reduced during 1979 and then from January 1982, the 2nd, 3rd and 5th gear ratios were changed again. The revised ratios are given in the Specifications at the beginning of this Supplementary Chapter.
3 It is important when ordering new components for a gearbox that the chassis number and gearbox serial number are known, as those parts which affect the gear ratios are not interchangeable.

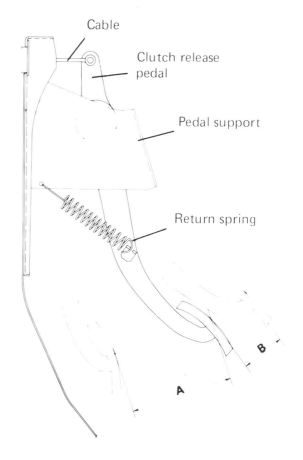

Fig. 13.42 Diagram showing self-adjusting clutch pedal travel dimensions (Sec 7)

A Minimum travel for releasing clutch = 4.7 in (120 mm)
B Pedal travel due to clutch disc wear = 2 in (50 mm)

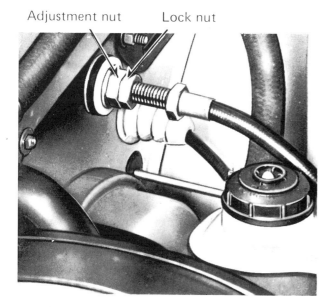

Fig. 13.43 Clutch outer cable adjustment point (Sec 7)

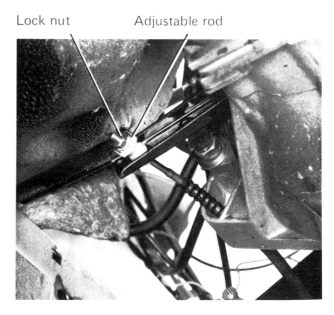

Fig. 13.44 Clutch pedal height adjustment point (Sec 7)

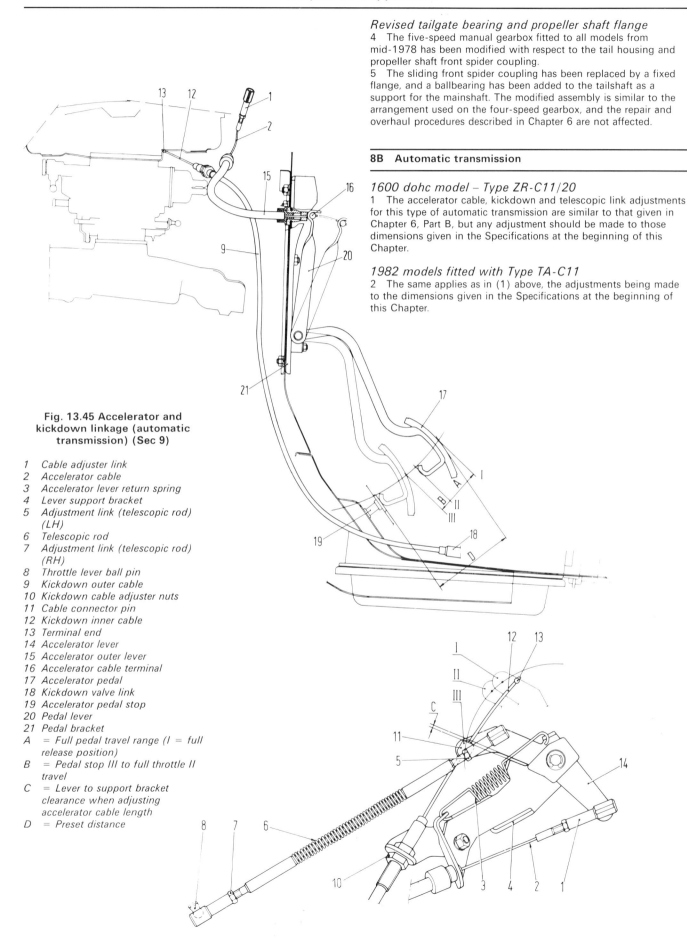

Fig. 13.45 Accelerator and kickdown linkage (automatic transmission) (Sec 9)

1   Cable adjuster link
2   Accelerator cable
3   Accelerator lever return spring
4   Lever support bracket
5   Adjustment link (telescopic rod) (LH)
6   Telescopic rod
7   Adjustment link (telescopic rod) (RH)
8   Throttle lever ball pin
9   Kickdown outer cable
10 Kickdown cable adjuster nuts
11 Cable connector pin
12 Kickdown inner cable
13 Terminal end
14 Accelerator lever
15 Accelerator outer lever
16 Accelerator cable terminal
17 Accelerator pedal
18 Kickdown valve link
19 Accelerator pedal stop
20 Pedal lever
21 Pedal bracket
A   = Full pedal travel range (I = full release position)
B   = Pedal stop III to full throttle II travel
C   = Lever to support bracket clearance when adjusting accelerator cable length
D   = Preset distance

Revised tailgate bearing and propeller shaft flange

4   The five-speed manual gearbox fitted to all models from mid-1978 has been modified with respect to the tail housing and propeller shaft front spider coupling.

5   The sliding front spider coupling has been replaced by a fixed flange, and a ballbearing has been added to the tailshaft as a support for the mainshaft. The modified assembly is similar to the arrangement used on the four-speed gearbox, and the repair and overhaul procedures described in Chapter 6 are not affected.

8B   Automatic transmission

1600 dohc model – Type ZR-C11/20

1   The accelerator cable, kickdown and telescopic link adjustments for this type of automatic transmission are similar to that given in Chapter 6, Part B, but any adjustment should be made to those dimensions given in the Specifications at the beginning of this Chapter.

1982 models fitted with Type TA-C11

2   The same applies as in (1) above, the adjustments being made to the dimensions given in the Specifications at the beginning of this Chapter.

9 Rear axle

Rear axle cover plate – sealing modification

1   On later rear axles, the method of sealing the rear cover plate has been changed.
2   This is now achieved by the use of a modified cover plate and using a silicone sealant instead of a gasket.
3   After applying sealant and fitting the cover, the rear axle differential housing should not be filled with oil for 4 to 5 hours, to allow the sealant to cure.
4   The modified cover plate may be fitted to earlier differential housings, provided silicone sealant is used, and not a gasket.

10 Electrical system

General information

1   Modifications to the electrical system consist of different types and makes of the various components.
2   Fuse ratings on different models also vary and details of these changes will be found in the Specifications at the beginning of this Chapter.
3   Information regarding the servicing of these different components was unavailable at the time of going to press although the various illustrations that were available have been included for reference.

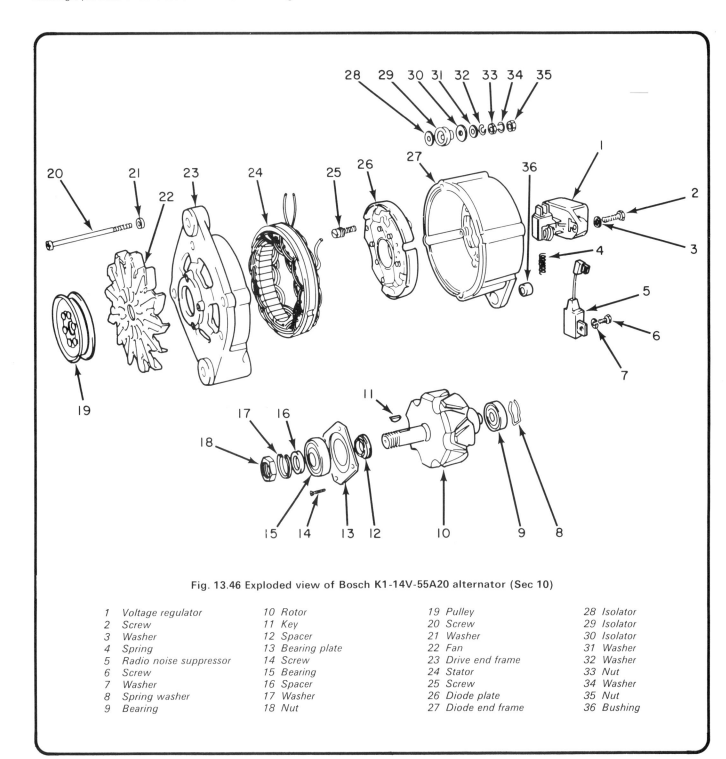

Fig. 13.46 Exploded view of Bosch K1-14V-55A20 alternator (Sec 10)

1	Voltage regulator	10	Rotor	19	Pulley	28	Isolator
2	Screw	11	Key	20	Screw	29	Isolator
3	Washer	12	Spacer	21	Washer	30	Isolator
4	Spring	13	Bearing plate	22	Fan	31	Washer
5	Radio noise suppressor	14	Screw	23	Drive end frame	32	Washer
6	Screw	15	Bearing	24	Stator	33	Nut
7	Washer	16	Spacer	25	Screw	34	Washer
8	Spring washer	17	Washer	26	Diode plate	35	Nut
9	Bearing	18	Nut	27	Diode end frame	36	Bushing

Fig. 13.47 M. Marelli AA125-14V-45A alternator (Sec 10)

Note: *the alternator to the left is shown without a diode rectifier carrier grille, and the brush voltage regulator assembly is shown separately*

Rear number plate lamp
Early models
4   On certain early model saloons and estates the number plate lamp was located in the bumper.
5   The lamp can be removed from beneath the bumper by pressing in the spring retaining clip at each end of the lamp and withdrawing the unit.
6   The bayonet type bulbs can then be removed in the normal fashion.
Various other models (pre-1982)
7   A lamp is located each side of the number plate adjacent to the rear lamp clusters.
8   The lens cover retaining screws are accessible from inside the luggage compartment through the rear panel.
9   Remove the screws and withdraw the cover from the outside to renew a bulb or lamp unit.
10 Refit in the reverse order of removal and check for correct operation on completion.
Later models
11 The number plate lamp was incorporated into the rear lamp clusters and details on gaining access are given in the following sub-section.

Rear combination lamps (1982 on)
12 To gain access to all bulbs the two sections of the lens must be removed first.
13 Remove the four retaining screws from the outside section first (photo), followed by the inside section which is held in position by two lugs (photo).

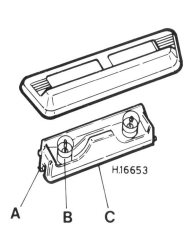

Fig. 13.48 Early bumper mounted number plate lamp (Sec 10)

10.8 Removing rear number plate light lens (pre-1982)

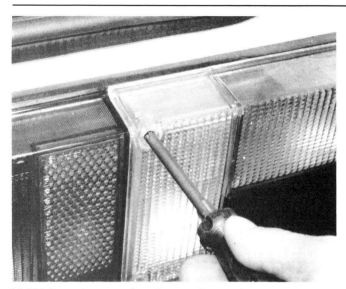

10.13A Removing screw from the outer lens section

10.13B Retaining lugs on the edge of inner lens section

14 Any defective bulbs can then be renewed (photo).
15 Refit inner lens first ensuring correct location with the two lugs, followed by the outer lens and retaining screws.
16 If the combination lamp unit is to be removed, undo and remove the retaining nuts from inside the luggage compartment and withdraw the unit from the outside of the vehicle. Disconnect the wiring to remove unit completely.

Glovebox light
17 To renew the bulb, depress the lens on either side to disengage the lugs and remove the lens (photo).
18 Refit in the reverse order and check for operation.

Headlamps – 1982 on
Bulb renewal
19 Access to the bulbs is obtained from inside the engine compartment.
20 Disconnect the multi-plug connector (photo).

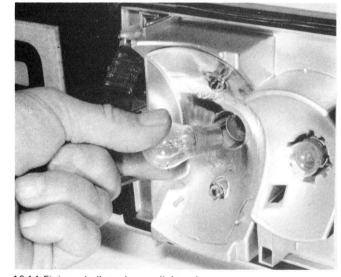

10.14 Fitting a bulb to the rear light unit

10.17 Glovebox bulb renewal
1   Retaining lugs   3   Microswitch
2   Bulb

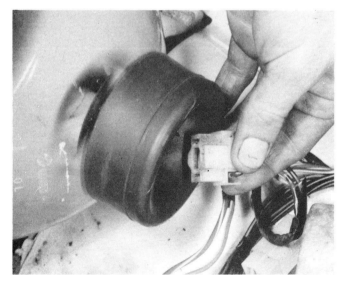

10.20 Removing the connector

21 Remove the rubber dust cover (photo).
22 Depress the retaining ring and turn anti-clockwise to remove (photo).
23 Remove the bulb (photo). If a halogen bulb is fitted, do not touch the bulb with your fingers.
24 Refit in the reverse order ensuring bulb is correctly located in lamp body.

Lens unit removal
25 Disconnect the multi-plug connector.
26 From inside the engine compartment, undo and remove the two nuts retaining the bottom edge of the lamp unit (photo).
27 From outside the vehicle, undo and remove the two retaining screws at the top front edge of the lamp unit (photo).
28 Lift out the headlamp unit.
29 Refit in the reverse order and check for correct operation.

Windscreen wiper motor and associated components
30 A general illustration of the windscreen wiper motor and its associated fitting is shown in Fig. 13.49.

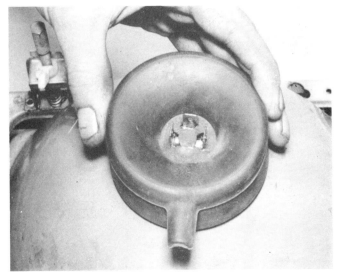

10.21 Pulling off the dust cover

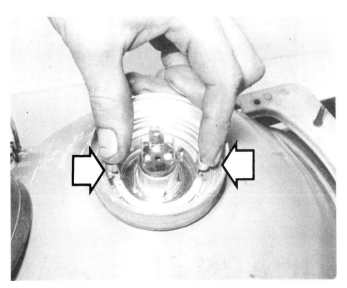

10.22 To remove retaining ring, depress in direction of arrows and turn anti-clockwise

10.23 Removing the bulb

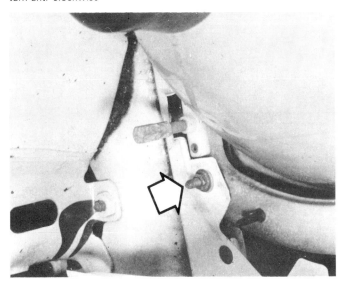

10.26 One of the headlamp unit retaining nuts in engine compartment

10.27 One of the headlamp unit retaining screws at front of car

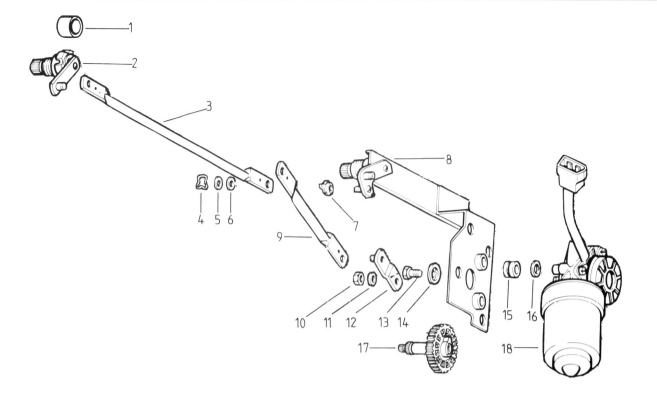

Fig. 13.49 Exploded view of windscreen wiper motor and associated components (Sec 10)

1 Bearing ring	6 Thrust ring	11 Washer	15 Bearing ring
2 Control lever	7 Socket	12 Control lever	16 Rubber ring
3 Strut	8 Supporting plate	13 Screw	17 Reduction gear
4 Clip	9 Bearing rod	14 Washer	18 Complete motor
5 Washer	10 Nut		

31 Although these components are normally reliable, the most common faults and their reasons are given below:

   (a) Blown fuse – check wiring, switch, and/or motor for fault
   (b) Control switch defective – renew
   (c) Fault in the control arm/relay rod assembly – inspect and repair as necessary
   (d) Defective wiper motor – inspect and renew as necessary; before dismantling the motor itself, ensure that parts are readily available for it
   (e) If the wipers fail to park in the normal position, it is probable that the end of travel switch is at fault. Check the contacts for corrosion and/or wear. When an intermittent wiper is fitted, its flasher unit may be at fault
   (f) If the wipers operate at low speed but do not complete each stroke fully, check the control cam and bend it to adjust as required.

With the exception of the crank transmission reduction gear, spare parts are not available; once a faulty component is traced, therefore, it must be renewed. Finally, do not rule out the possibility of broken connections when tracing a fault in the system.

Windscreen wiper motor – removal and refitting
Note: *The following procedure, together with the accompanying illustrations are for left-hand drive models. However, no difficulty should be encountered applying these instructions to right-hand drive models if it is remembered that the location of the various components may differ.*
32 Remove weatherstrip from top of cowl.
33 Detach bonnet release cable from clip.
34 Undo and remove four bolts and washers, and loosen one lower bolt, retaining protective cover to bulkhead, and remove cover.

Fig. 13.50 Removing protective cover from bulkhead (Sec 10)

1 Weatherstrip	4 Bonnet release cable
2 Retaining bolts	5 Lower protective cover bolt
3 Protective cover	

35 If possible, run wipers and stop with wiper arms in vertical position.

36 Prise off retaining clip and remove together with metal and nylon washers, and remove right wiper linkage from pin.

37 Return wipers to 'rest' position and remove left wiper arm.

38 Remove nut, spacer and rubber bush from wiper arm shaft.

39 Undo and remove two nuts and washers retaining linkage bracket to body.

40 Disconnect electrical connections and remove motor and linkage bracket assembly from vehicle.

41 Refitting is a reversal of the removal procedure ensuring motor cover is correctly positioned on motor.

Wiper motor (Estate models) – removal and refitting
See note at beginning of previous sub-section

42 Remove wiper arm from shaft.

43 Undo and remove wiper arm shaft retaining nut and spacer.

44 Prise free the six plastic retainers holding inner trim panel to tailgate and remove trim.

45 Undo and remove nut retaining wiper motor to inner panel of tailgate.

46 Lower wiper motor, disconnect electrical connectors, and remove wiper motor from tailgate.

47 Refitting is a reversal of the removal procedure.

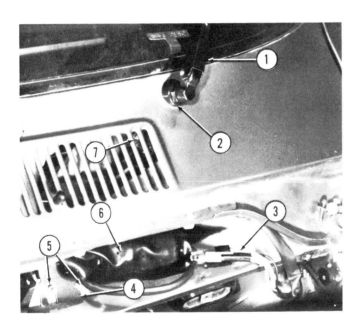

Fig. 13.51 Removing wiper motor from bulkhead (Sec 10)

1 Left wiper arm	5 Linkage bracket-to-body
2 Wiper arm shaft retaining	retaining nuts
nut	6 Wiper motor
3 Electrical connections	7 Wiper linkage retaining clip
4 Linkage bracket	

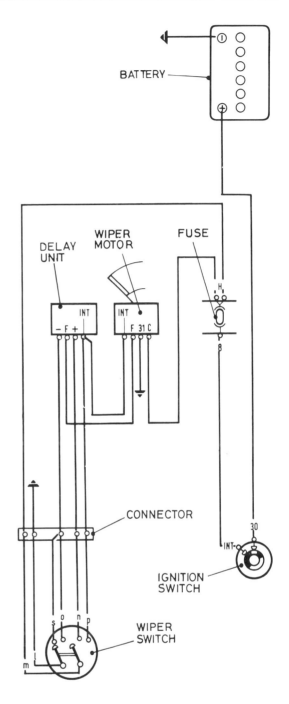

Fig. 13.52 Wiring diagram for windscreen wiper circuit (Sec 10)

Wiring diagrams overleaf

Fig. 13.53 Key to wiring diagram for Mirafiori L models up to 1982 (Sec 10)

1 Front indicators
2 Sidelights
3 Headlamp main and dipped beams
4 Horns
5 Radiator fan motor
6 Repeater lights
7 Cables preset for fitting a brake fluid level indicator switch
8 Ignition coil
9 Ignition distributor
10 Spark plugs
11 Alternator
12 Radiator fan control switch
13 Windscreen wiper interrupter
14 Battery
15 Starter
16 Oil pressure transmitter
17 Engine coolant temperature transmitter
18 Windscreen wiper motor
19 Direction indicator flasher
20 Windscreen washer pump
21 Centralised connections unit
22 Horn relay
23 Main beams relay connections
24 Fuse unit
25 Starter inhibitor switch cables (automatic transmission)
26 Heated rear screen relay
27 Fuse unit
28 Lighting/panel light switch
29 Panel lights
30 Instrument panel connectors
31 Fuel warning light
32 Fuel gauge
33 Engine coolant temperature gauge
34 Heater fan switch
35 Heated rear screen switch
36 Ignition warning light
37 Oil pressure warning light
38 Brake fluid level and handbrake 'on' warning lights

39 Heated rear screen warning light
40 Spare warning light
41 Direction indicator
42 Headlamp
43 Hazard warning light
44 Hazard warning switch
45 Rear fog lamp switch and warning light
46 Heater fan motor
47 Ignition switch
48 Windscreen wiper/washer switch
49 Headlamp control lever
50 Direction indicator lever
51 Horn control
52 LH loudspeaker cables (optional)
53 Door switch
54 Aerial motor cables
55 Handbrake 'on' switch
56 Stop light switch
57 Cigar lighter/light
58 Radio wiring
59 Radio fuse holder
60 RH loudspeaker cables (optional)
61 Door switch
62 Stop lights
63 Aerial motor cables
64 Aerial lead
65 Rear lights
66 Number plate lights
67 Rear fog lamps
68 Reversing lights
69 Direction indicator lamps
70 Fuel gauge transmitter
71 Front courtesy light/switch
72 Heated rear screen (optional)
73 Reversing light switch
74 Selector lever indicator (automatic transmission)
75 Cable preset for fitting starter reverse gear inhibitor switch (automatic transmission)

Colour codes

A = Light blue	H = Grey	R = Red
B = White	L = Blue	S = Pink
C = Amber	M = Brown	V = Green
G = Yellow	N = Black	Z = Mauve

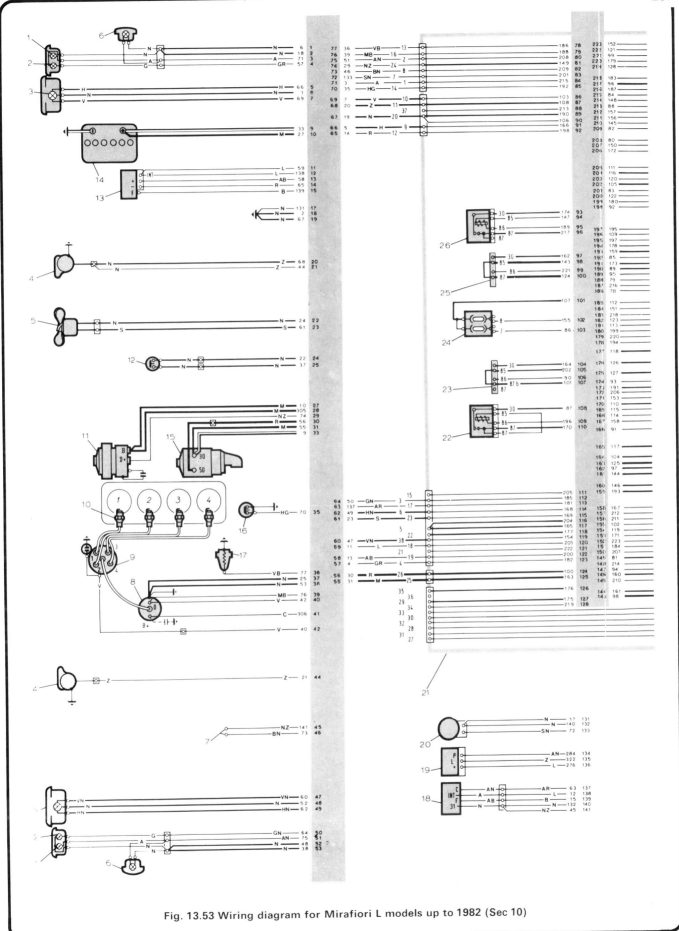

Fig. 13.53 Wiring diagram for Mirafiori L models up to 1982 (Sec 10)

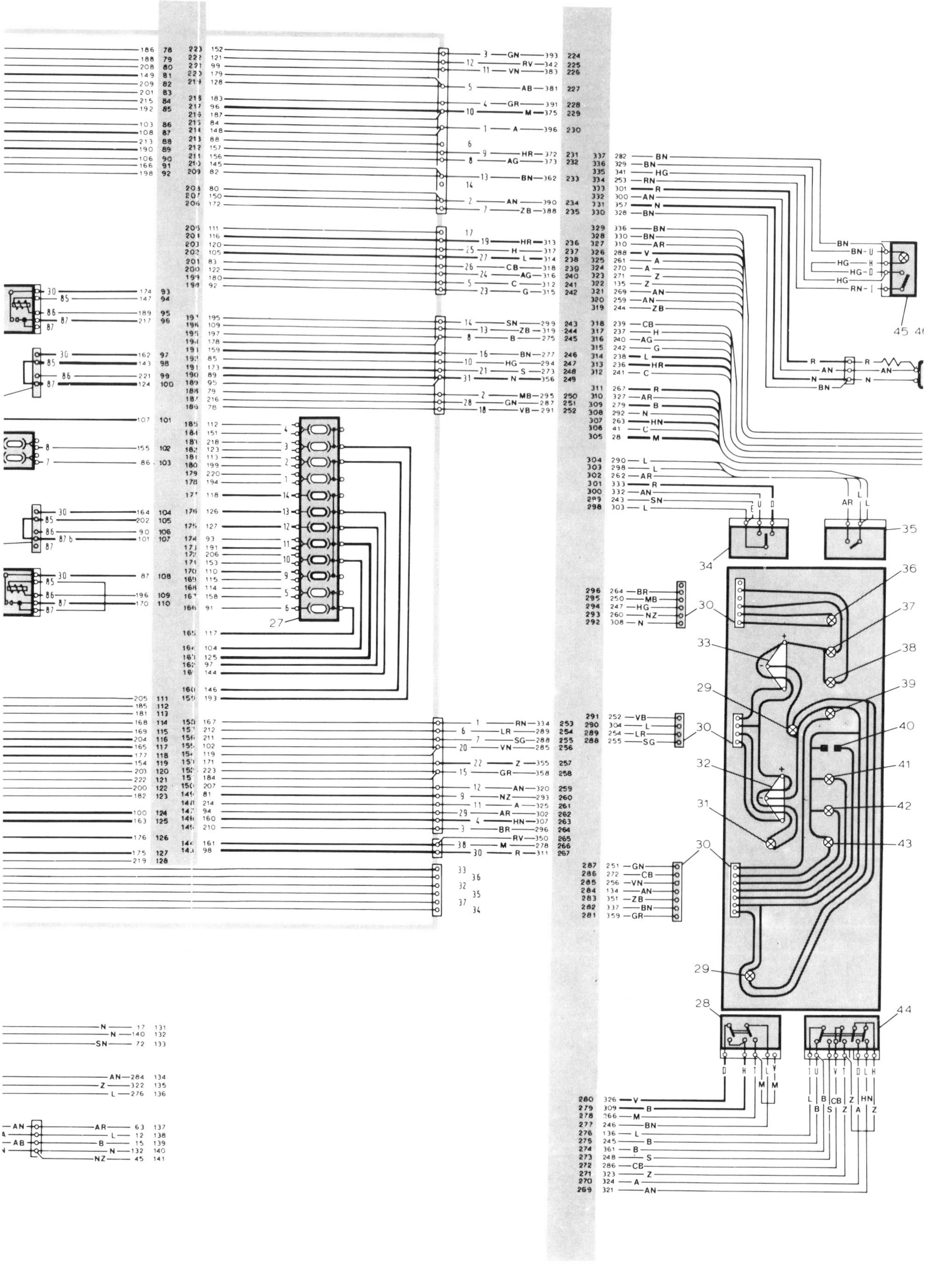

Fig. 13.53 Wiring diagram for Mirafiori L models up to 1982 (Sec 10) (continued)

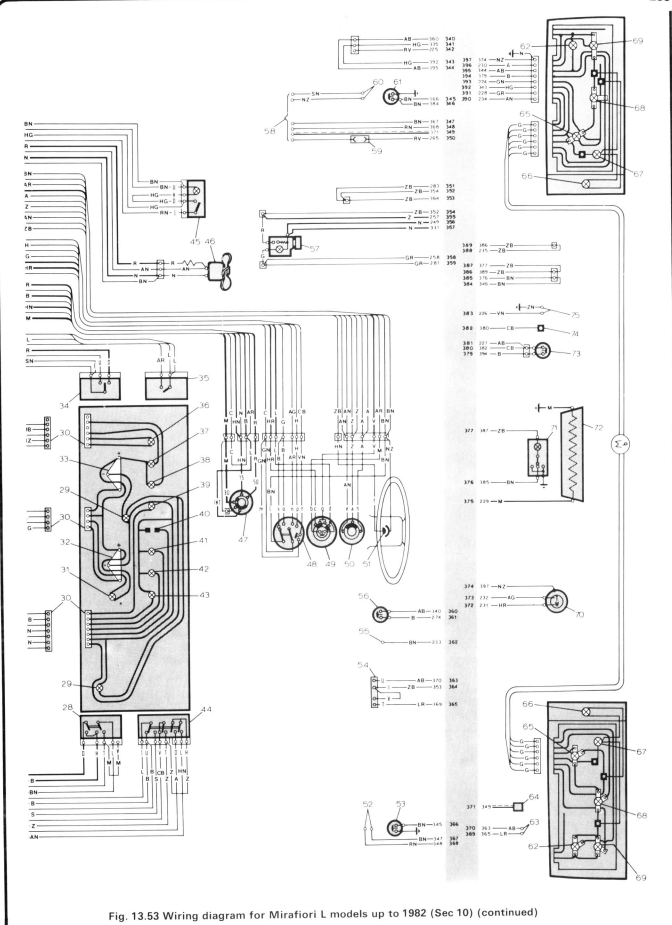

Fig. 13.53 Wiring diagram for Mirafiori L models up to 1982 (Sec 10) (continued)

Fig. 13.54 Key to wiring diagram for Supermirafiori and Mirafiori CL up to 1982 (Sec 10)

1 Front direction indicators
2 Sidelights
3 Headlamp main and dipped beams
4 Horns
5 Radiator fan motor
6 Repeater lights
7 Ignition distributor
8 Spark plugs
9 Alternator
10 Ignition coil
11 Engine coolant temperature transmitter
12 Radiator fan control switch
13 Starter
14 Windscreen wiper interrupter
15 Battery
16 Brake fluid level transmitter (where fitted)
17 Oil pressure transmitter
18 Windscreen wiper motor
19 Direction indicator flasher
20 Windscreen washer pump
21 Centralised connections unit
22 Horn relay
23 Connections preset for fitting main beam relay
24 Fuses
25 Starter relay (automatic transmission)
26 Heated rear screen relay
27 Panel lights
28 Fuel warning light
29 Instrument panel connectors
30 Quartz crystal clock
31 Electronic tachometer
32 Lighting/panel light switch
33 Heated rear screen switch
34 Rear fog lamp warning light
35 Sidelight
36 Hazard warning switch
37 Direction indicator warning light
38 Rear fog lamp switch
39 Headlamp warning light
40 Spare switch housing
41 Hazard warning light
42 Fuel gauge
43 Engine coolant temperature gauge
44 Panel light rheostat

45 Heated rear screen warning light
46 Ignition warning light
47 Oil pressure warning light
48 Brake fluid level and handbrake 'on' warning light
49 Spare warning light
50 Ideogram illumination light guide cable lamp
51 Heater fan switch
52 Heater fan motor
53 Cables preset for fitting any warning light
54 Heater ideogram lamps
55 Glovebox light
56 Ignition switch
57 Windscreen wiper/washer switch
58 Headlamp switch
59 Direction indicator switch
60 Horn control
61 LH loudspeaker cables (where fitted)
62 Door switches
63 Electric aerial connections
64 Handbrake 'on' switch (where fitted)
65 Stop light switch
66 Ashtray light
67 Cigar lighter/light
68 Glovebox light switch
69 Radio connections (where fitted)
70 Radio set fuse holder
71 RH loudspeaker cables (where fitted)
72 Stop lights
73 Aerial motor cables (preset)
74 Aerial lead
75 Rear lights
76 Number plate lights
77 Rear direction indicators
78 Reversing lights
79 Rear fog lights
80 Rear interior lights/switches
81 Fuel transmitter
82 Courtesy light/switch
83 Heated rear screen
84 Reversing light switch
85 Cable preset for fitting selector lever indicator (automatic transmission)
86 Cable preset for fitting a starter/reverse gear inhibitor switch (automatic transmission)

For colour codes, refer to Fig. 13.53

241

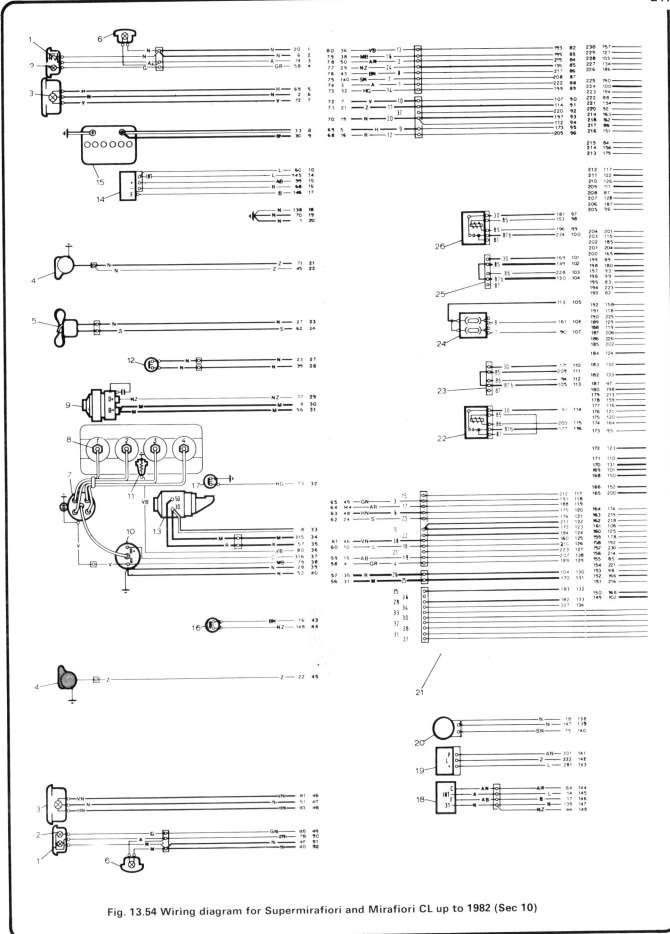

Fig. 13.54 Wiring diagram for Supermirafiori and Mirafiori CL up to 1982 (Sec 10)

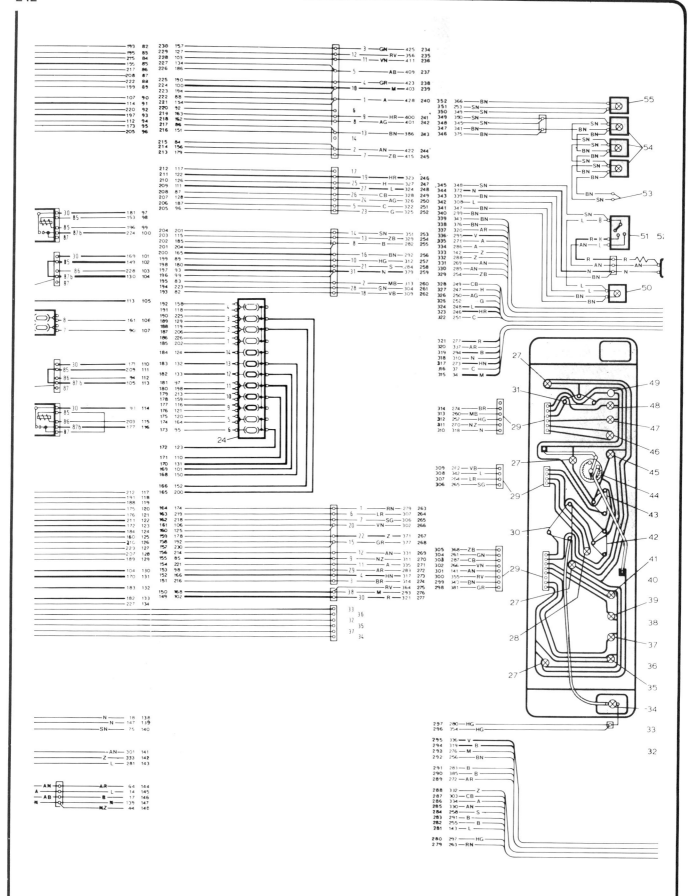

Fig. 13.54 Wiring diagram for Supermirafiori and Mirafiori CL up to 1982 (Sec 10) (continued)

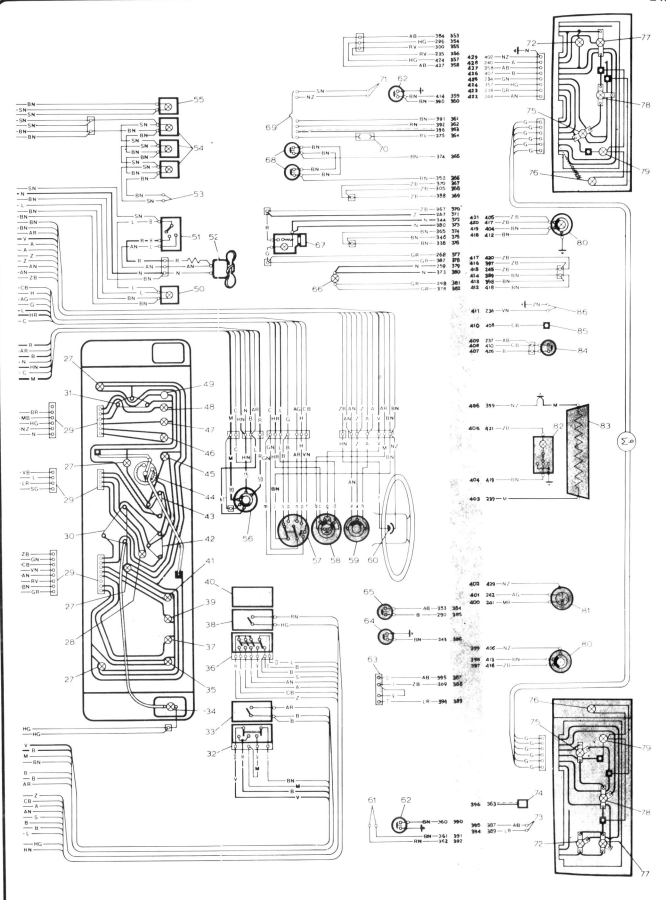

Fig. 13.54 Wiring diagram for Supermirafiori and Mirafiori CL up to 1982 (Sec 10) (continued)

Fig. 13.55 Key to wiring diagram for Panorama L (modular cable system) up to 1982 (Sec 10)

1 Front direction indicators
2 Repeater lights
3 Sidelights
4 Headlamp main and dipped beams
5 Horns
6 Radiator fan motor
7 Windscreen washer pump
8 Battery
9 Alternator and voltage regulator
10 Starter
11 Oil pressure transmitter
12 Engine coolant temperature transmitter
13 Brake fluid level transmitter
14 Spark plugs
15 Ignition distributor
16 Ignition coil
17 Radiator fan control switch
18 Modular cables identification letters
19 Standard wiring identification numbers
20 Horn relay
21 Cables, preset for fitting starter relay (automatic transmission)
22 Heated rear screen relay
23 Connections preset for fitting main beam relay
24 Fuses
25 Centralised connection unit – viewed from engine compartment
26 Centralised connection unit – viewed from passenger compartment
27 Windscreen wiper interrupter
28 Windscreen wiper motor
29 Direction indicator/hazard warning flasher
30 Rear fog lamp switch/warning light
31 Cigar lighter/light
32 Radio fuse connection
33 Connections preset for fitting a radio
34 Heater fan switch
35 Heated rear screen switch
36 Panel connector

37 Panel lights
38 Fuel gauge
39 Fuel
40 Rear screen wiper connections – preset
41 Lighting/panel light switch
42 Hazard warning switch (where fitted)
43 Stop lights
44 Hazard warning light
45 Headlamp warning light
46 Direction indicator warning light
47 Heated rear screen warning light
48 Brake fluid level and handbrake 'on' warning light
49 Oil pressure warning light
50 Ignition warning light
51 Engine coolant temperature gauge
52 Ignition switch
53 Direction indicator switch
54 Headlamp switch
55 Windscreen wiper/washer switch
56 Horn control
57 Door switches
58 Loudspeaker cables – preset
59 Cable preset for fitting a starter inhibitor switch (automatic transmission)
60 Handbrake 'on' switch
61 Reversing light switch
62 Heater fan motor
63 Cable preset for fitting selector lever indicator (automatic transmission)
64 Fuel gauge transmitter
65 Front courtesy light/switch
66 Rear courtesy light
67 Heated rear screen (optional)
68 Rear direction indicators
69 Rear lights
70 Stop lights
71 Number plate lights
72 Reversing light
73 Rear fog light

For colour codes, refer to Fig. 15.53

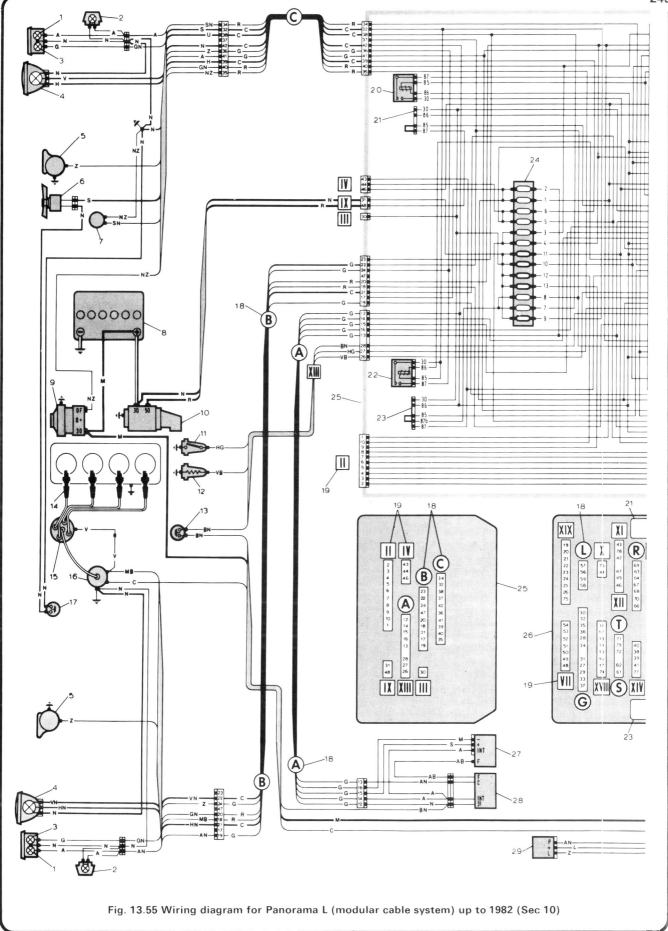

Fig. 13.55 Wiring diagram for Panorama L (modular cable system) up to 1982 (Sec 10)

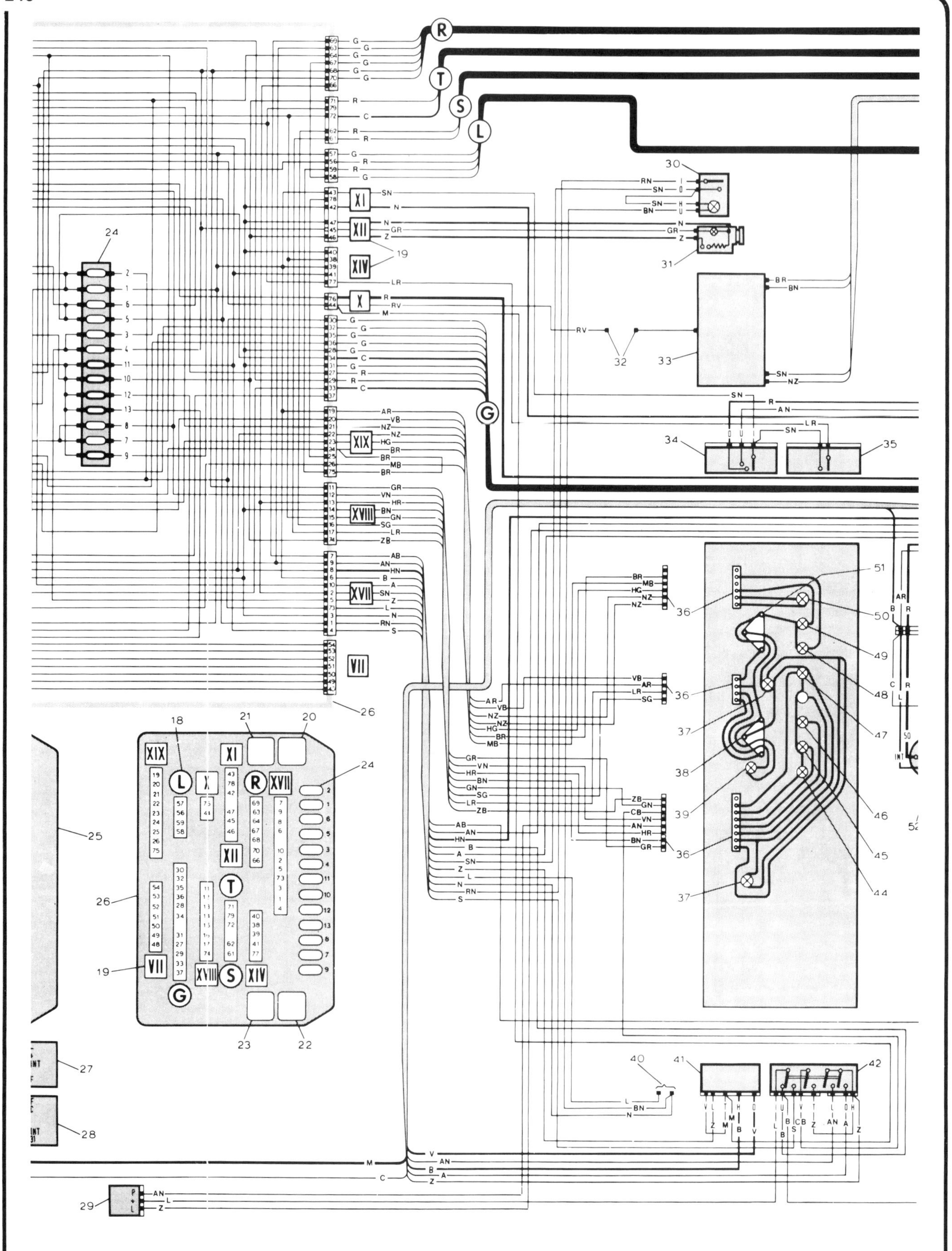

Fig. 13.55 Wiring diagram for Panorama L (modular cable system) up to 1982 (Sec 10) (continued)

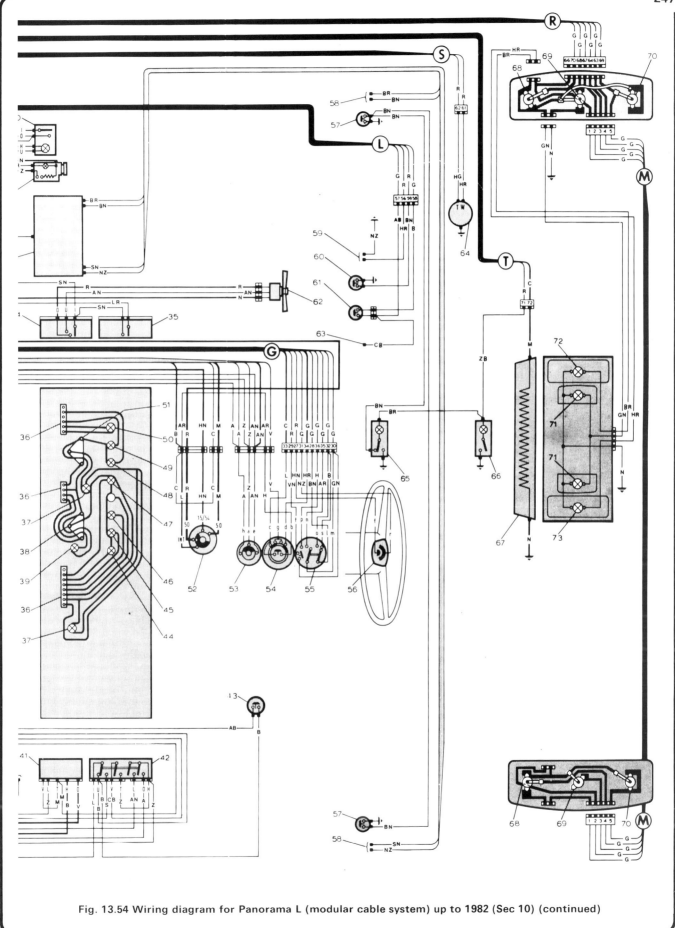

Fig. 13.54 Wiring diagram for Panorama L (modular cable system) up to 1982 (Sec 10) (continued)

Fig. 13.56 Key to wiring diagram for Panorama CL (modular cable system) up to 1982 (Sec 10)

1 Front direction indicators
2 Repeater lights
3 Sidelights
4 Headlamp main and dipped beams
5 Horns
6 Radiator fan motor
7 Windscreen washer pump
8 Battery
9 Alternator and voltage regulator
10 Starter
11 Oil pressure transmitter
12 Engine coolant temperature transmitter
13 Brake fluid level transmitter (where fitted)
14 Spark plugs
15 Radiator fan control switch
16 Ignition distributor
17 Ignition coil
18 Modular cables identification letters
19 Standard wiring identification numbers
20 Horn relay
21 Cables, preset for fitting starter relay (automatic
   transmission)
22 Heated rear screen relay
23 Connection preset for fitting main beam relay
24 Fuses
25 Centralised connection unit – viewed from engine
   compartment
26 Centralised connection unit – viewed from passenger
   compartment
27 Windscreen wiper interrupter
28 Windscreen wiper motor
29 Direction indicator/hazard warning flasher
30 Connections preset for fitting rear screen wiper
31 Stop light switch
32 Panel lights
33 Instrument panel connectors
34 Quartz crystal clock
35 Fuel gauge
36 Engine coolant temperature gauge
37 Brake fluid level and handbrake 'on' warning light (where
   fitted)
38 Oil pressure warning light
39 Fuel warning light

40 Ignition warning light
41 Heated rear screen warning light
42 Hazard warning light
43 Rear fog lamp switch
44 Headlamp warning light
45 Hazard warning switch (where fitted)
46 Direction indicator warning light
47 Heated rear screen switch (where fitted)
48 Rear fog lamp warning light
49 Lighting/panel light switch
50 Ashtray light
51 Cigar lighter/light
52 Connection preset fot fitting a fuse for radio
53 Connection preset for fitting a radio
54 Heater ideogram lamps
55 Glovebox light
56 Glovebox light push buttons
57 Heater fan switch
58 Connections preset fot fitting a starter inhibitor switch
   (automatic transmission)
59 Handbrake 'on' switch (where fitted)
60 Reversing light switch
61 Heater fan motor
62 Cable preset for fitting selector lever indicator (automatic
   transmission)
63 Light guide cable lamp for panel switch
64 Ignition switch
65 Direction indicator switch
66 Headlamp switch
67 Windscreen wiper/washer switch
68 Horn control
69 Door switches
70 Cables, preset for fitting loudspeakers
71 Courtesy light switch
72 Rear interior light
73 Heated rear screen (where fitted)
74 Fuel gauge transmitter
75 Rear direction indicators
76 Rear lights
77 Stop lights
78 Rear fog light
79 Number plate lights
80 Reversing light

For colour codes, refer to Fig. 13.53

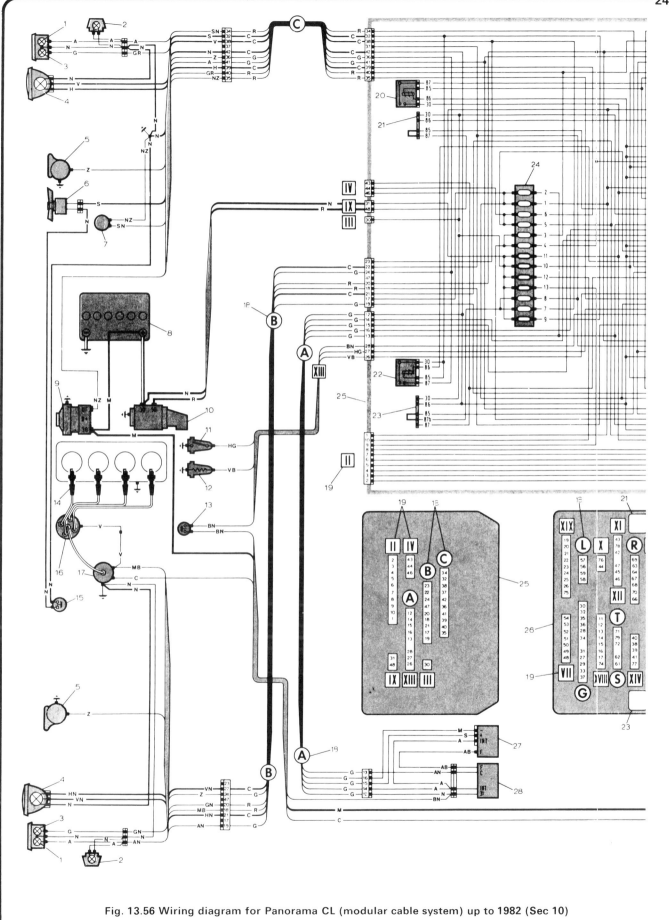

Fig. 13.56 Wiring diagram for Panorama CL (modular cable system) up to 1982 (Sec 10)

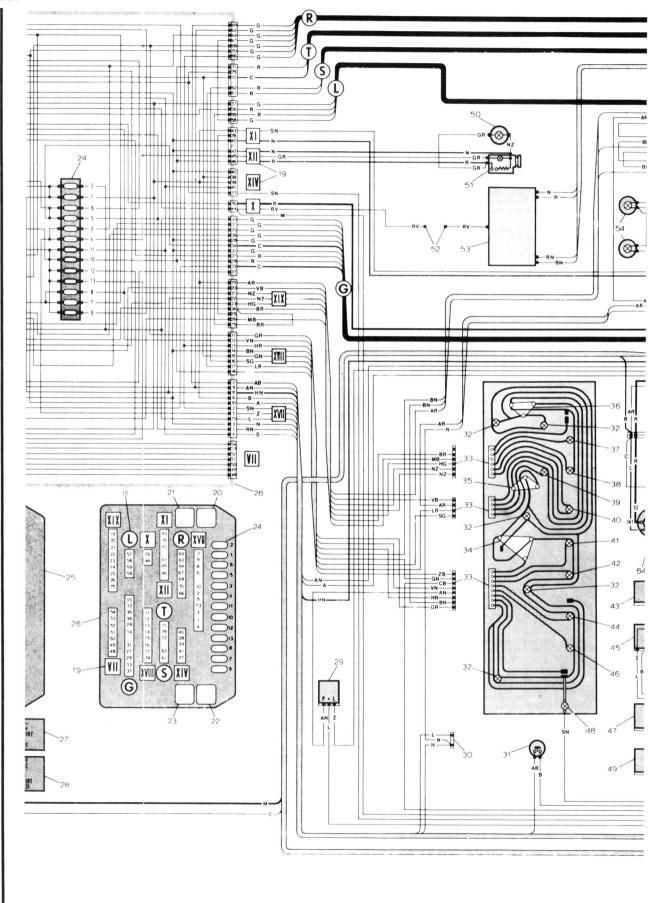

Fig. 13.56 Wiring diagram for Panorama CL (modular cable system) up to 1982 (Sec 10) (continued)

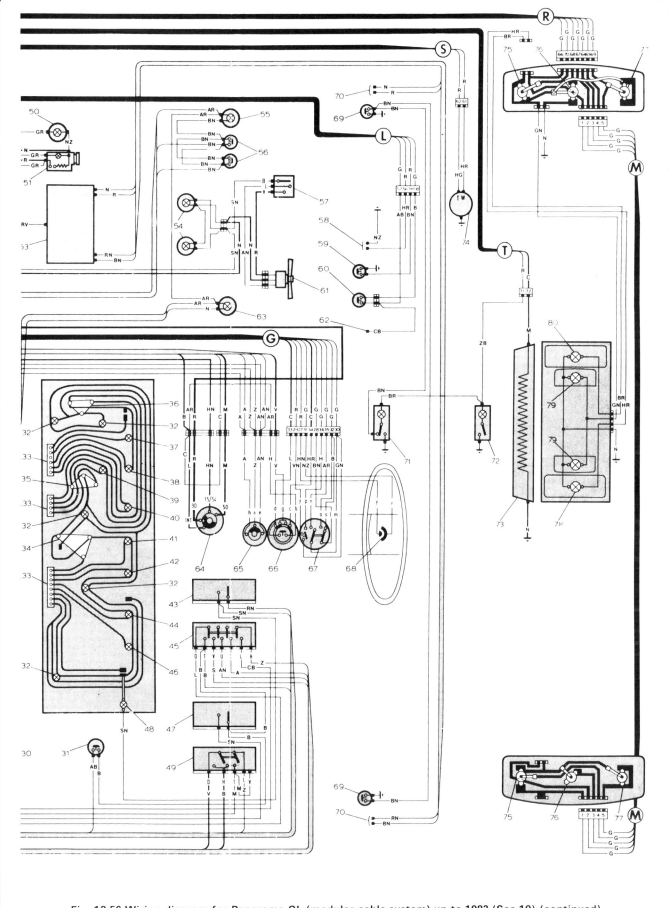

Fig. 13.56 Wiring diagram for Panorama CL (modular cable system) up to 1982 (Sec 10) (continued)

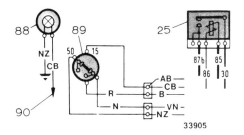

Fig. 13.57 Supplementary wiring diagram for Supermirafiori
and Mirafiori CL automatic transmission models

25 Starter relay
88 Selector lever indicator light
89 Starter/reverse gear inhibitor switch (replaces switch 84 and
makes use of cables 86)
90 To terminal 90

For colour codes refer to Fig. 13.53

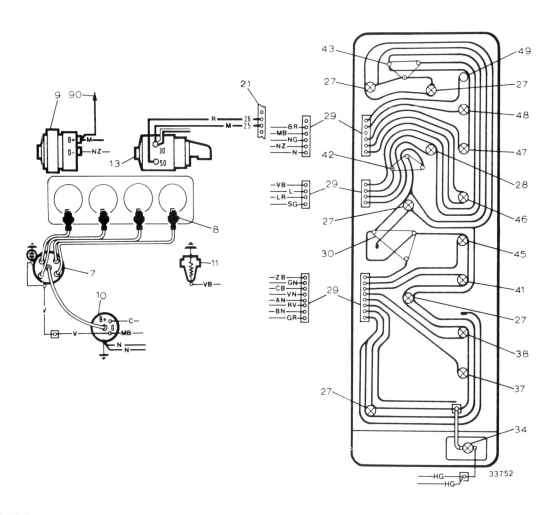

Fig. 13.58 Supplementary wiring diagram for Mirafiori CL showing differences with respect to Supermirafiori up to
1982 (Sec 10)

7	Ignition distributor	37	Indicator warning light
8	Spark plugs	39	Headlight warning light
9	Alternator	41	Hazard warning light
10	Ignition coil	42	Fuel gauge
11	Coolant temperature transmitter	43	Engine coolant temperature gauge
13	Starter	45	Heated rear screen
21	Centralised connector	46	Ignition warning light
27	Panel lights	47	Oil pressure warning light
28	Fuel warning light	48	Brake fluid level/handbrake 'on' warning light
29	Connector	49	Spare warning light
30	Quartz crystal clock	90	To ignition switch terminal 30
34	Rear fog light		

For colour codes refer to Fig. 13.53

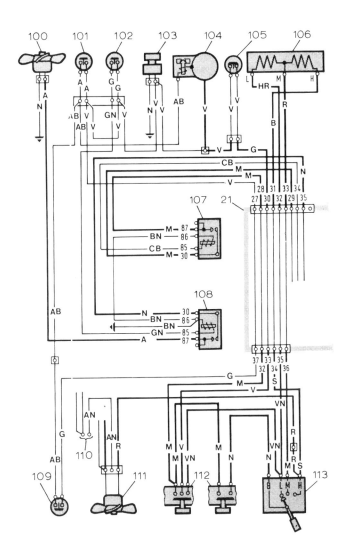

Fig. 13.59 Supplementary wiring diagram showing air conditioning circuit for Supermirafiori and Mirafiori CL up to 1982 (Sec 10)

21 Central connector	107 Compressor and evaporator fan relay
100 Condenser cooling fan	108 Condenser cooling fan relay
101 Temperature switch (radiator mounting)	109 Compressor solenoid valve temperature switch
102 Condenser mounted temperature switch	110 Heater fan switch (superseded)
103 Fast idle solenoid valve	111 Conditioner cooling fan
104 Compressor and solenoid valve	112 Conditioner control board
105 Low pressure switch	113 Conditioner fan motor switch
106 Ballast resistor	

For colour codes refer to Fig. 13.53

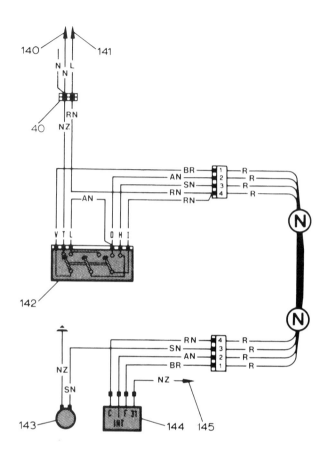

Fig. 13.60 Supplementary wiring diagram showing rear screen wiper circuit for Panorama up to 1982 (Sec 10)

30 Rear screen wiper cables
140 To terminal 3 (on connector)
141 To terminal 73 (on connector)
142 Rear screen wiper switch
143 Rear screen washer pump
144 Rear screen wiper motor
145 To heated rear screen earth

For colour codes refer to Fig. 13.53

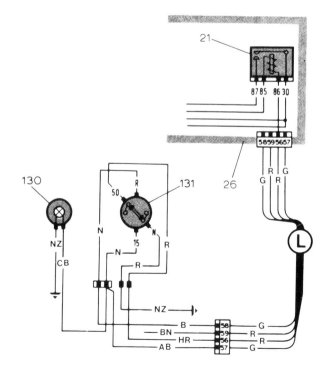

Fig. 13.61 Supplementary wiring diagram showing automatic transmission circuit for Panorama L up to 1982 (Sec 10)

21 Starter relay
26 Central connector unit – passenger side
130 Selector lever indicator
131 Starter/reverse inhibitor switch

For colour codes refer to Fig. 13.53

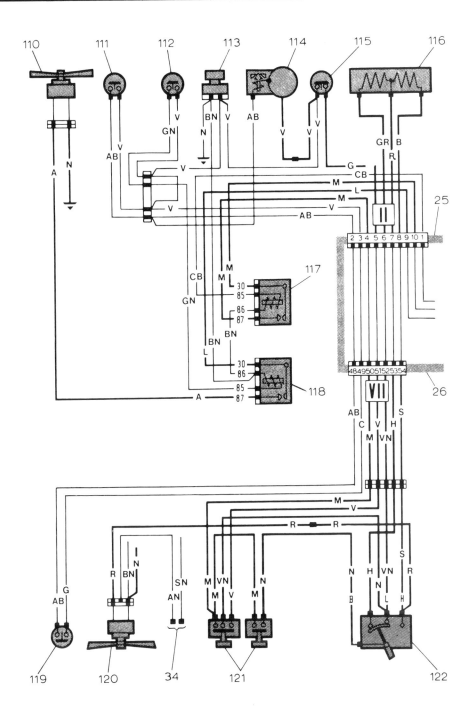

Fig. 13.62 Supplementary wiring diagram showing air conditioning circuit for Panorama L up to 1982 (Sec 10)

25 Central connector unit – engine compartment
26 Central connector unit – passenger side
34 Heater fan motor switch leads
110 Condenser cooling fan
111 Radiator mounted temperature switch
112 Condenser mounted temperature switch
113 Fast idle solenoid valve
114 Compressor and solenoid valve

115 Low pressure switch
116 Fan speed selector resistor
117 Compressor and evaporator fan relay
118 Condenser cooling fan relay
119 Compressor solenoid valve temperature switch
120 Conditioner cooling fan
121 Control board
122 Fan motor switch

For colour codes refer to Fig. 13.53

Fig. 13.63 Key to wiring diagram for Mirafiori Sport models up to 1982 (Sec 10)

1 Front indicators
2 Sidelights
3 Headlamp main and dipped beams
4 Headlamp main beams
5 Radiator fan control switch
6 Radiator fan motor
7 Alternator
8 Ignition distributor and reluctor
9 Control box and ignition coil (Magneti Marelli electronic ignition)
10 Repeater lights
11 Windscreen wiper interrupter
12 Battery
13 Engine coolant temperature transmitter
14 Spark plugs
15 Oil pressure transmitter
16 Starter
17 Horn compressor
18 Brake fluid level transmitter
19 Heated rear screen relay
20 Connections – preset for fitting starter relay (automatic transmission models)
21 Fuses
22 Main beam relay
23 Horn relay
24 Windscreen wiper motor
25 Direction indicator flasher (and hazard warning lights, where mandatory)
26 Windscreen washer pump
27 Centralised connections unit
28 Panel lights
29 Electronic tachometer
30 Instrument panel connectors
31 Quartz crystal clock
32 Fuel warning light
33 Spare warning light housing
34 Brake fluid level and handbrake 'on' warning light
35 Oil pressure warning light
36 Ignition warning light
37 Heated rear screen
38 Panel light rheostat
39 Engine coolant temperature gauge
40 Fuel gauge
41 Hazard warning light (where mandatory)
42 Headlamp warning light
43 Direction indicator warning light
44 Sidelight warning light
45 Rear fog lamp
46 Spare switch housing
47 Rear fog lamp switch
48 Hazard warning switch (where mandatory)
49 Heated rear screen switch
50 Lighting/panel light switch
51 Ideogram illumination light guide cable lamp
52 Heater ideogram lamps
53 Heater fan switch
54 Cables – preset for fitting light at guide cable lamp (air conditioned models)
55 Cables – preset for fitting radio (optional)
56 Heater fan motor
57 Glove compartment light switch
58 Radio fuse holder
59 Glovebox light
60 Cigar lighter/light
61 Ashtray light
62 Ignition switch
63 Windscreen wiper/washer switch
64 Headlamp switch
65 Direction indicator switch
66 Horn control
67 Cables – preset for fitting RH loudspeaker (optional)
68 Door switches
69 Cable – preset for fitting selector lever indicator (automatic transmission)
70 Cable – preset for fitting a starter/reverse gear inhibitor switch (automatic transmission)
71 Handbrake 'on' signal switch
72 Reversing light switch
73 Stop light switch
74 Connection preset for fitting an electric aerial
75 Cables – preset for fitting LH loudspeaker (optional)
76 Rear interior lights/switches
77 Courtesy light/switch
78 Heated rear screen
79 Fuel transmitter
80 Aerial lead
81 Cables – preset for fitting an aerial motor
82 Stop lights
83 Number plate lights
84 Rear direction indicators
85 Reversing lights
86 Rear lights
87 Rear fog lights

For colour codes refer to Fig. 13.53

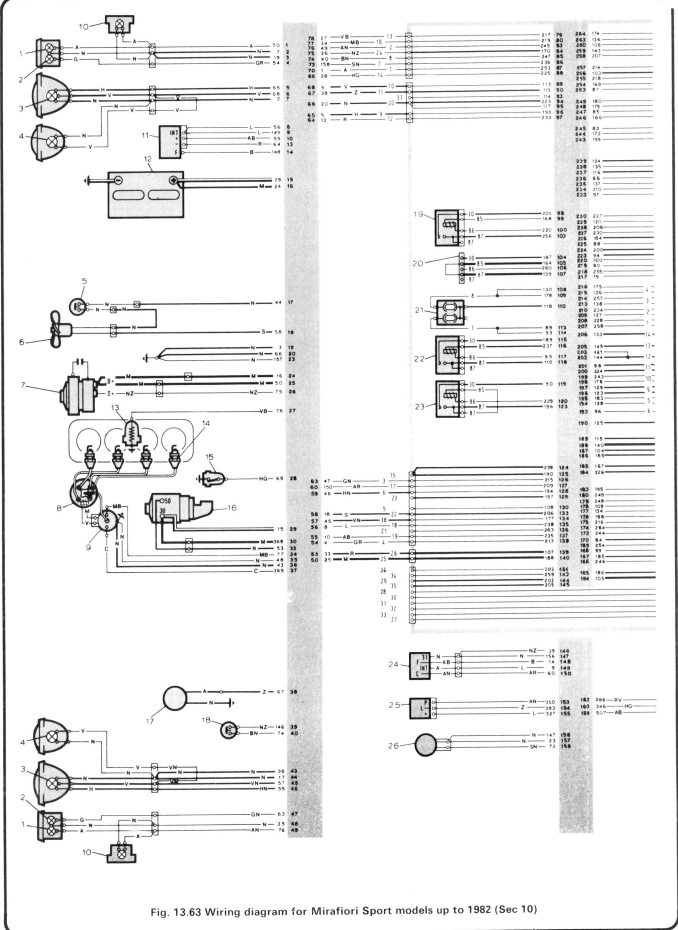

Fig. 13.63 Wiring diagram for Mirafiori Sport models up to 1982 (Sec 10)

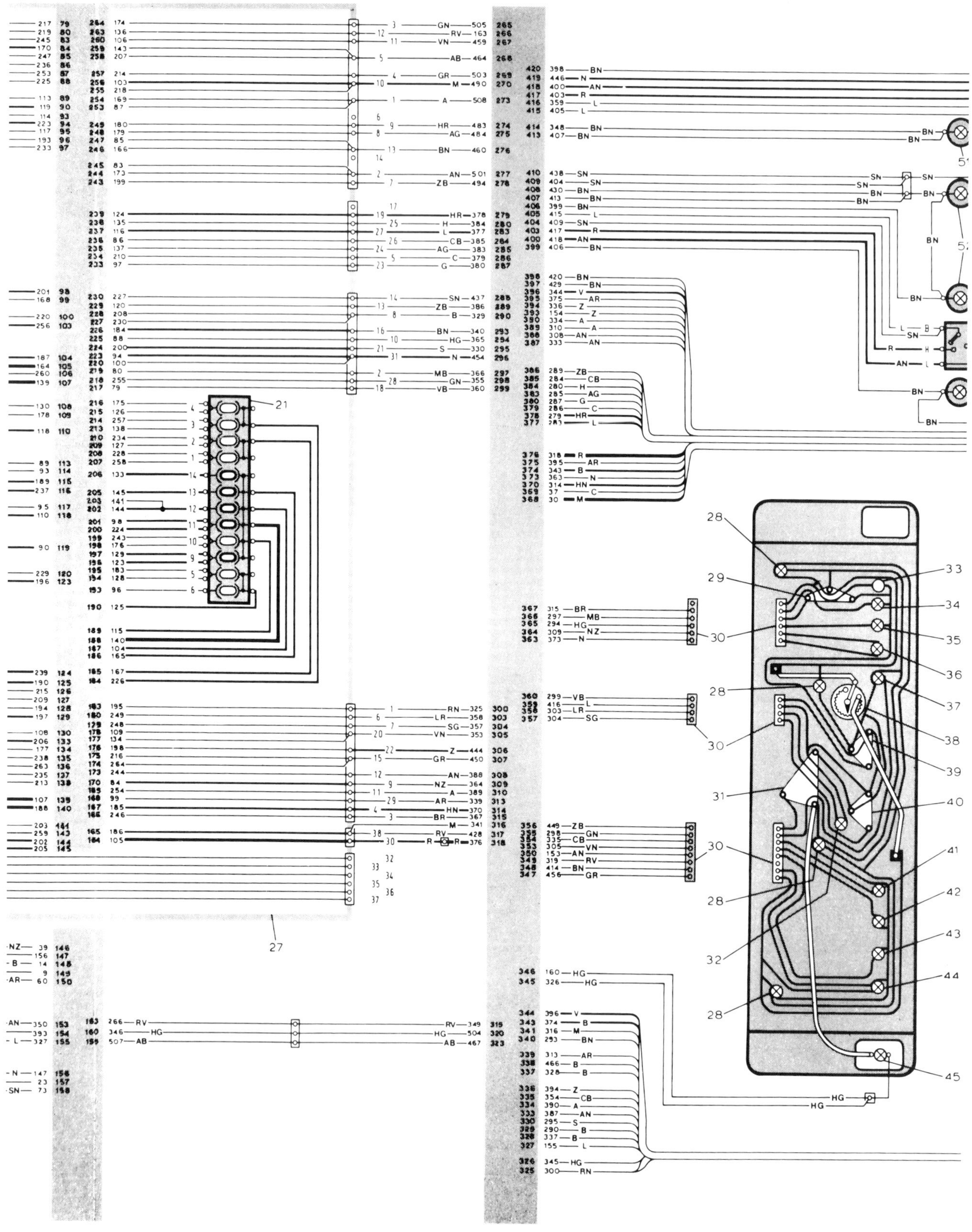

Fig. 13.63 Wiring diagram for Mirafiori Sport models up to 1982 (Sec 10) (continued)

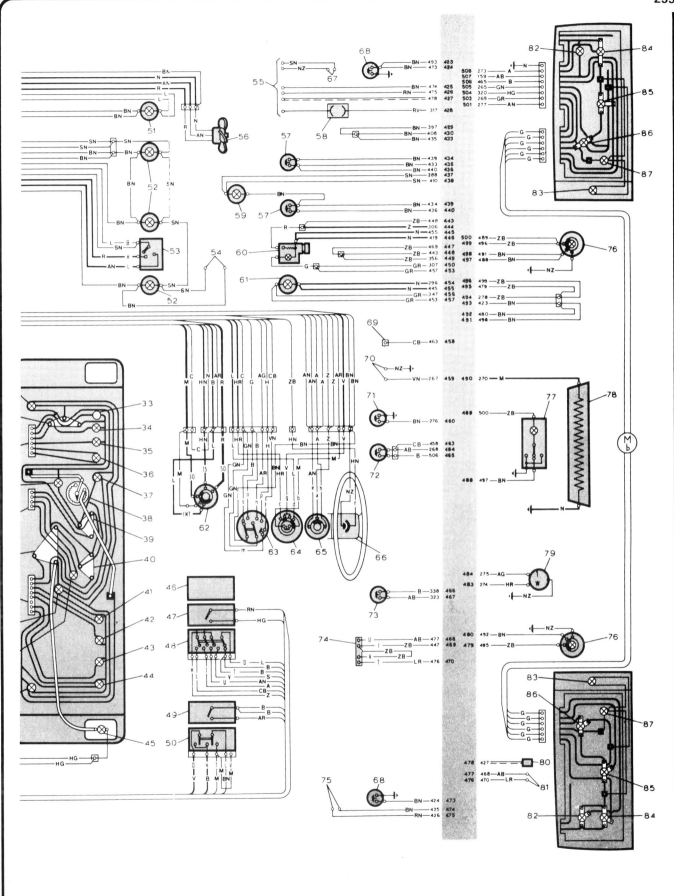

Fig. 13.63 Wiring diagram for Mirafiori Sport models up to 1982 (Sec 10) (continued)

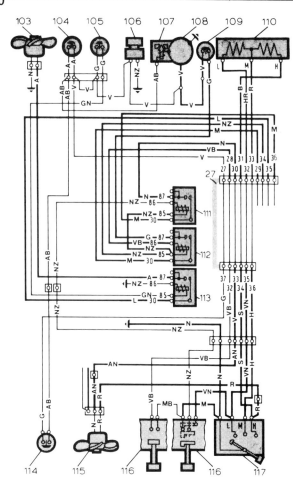

Fig. 13.64 Supplementary wiring diagram showing air conditioning circuit for Mirafiori Sport models up to 1982 (Sec 10)

27   Centralised connections unit
103   Cooling fan condenser
104   Temperature switch (radiator mounted)
105   Temperature switch (condenser mounted)
106   Fast idle solenoid valve
107   Anti-frost valve
108   Compressor
109   Low pressure switch
110   Conditioner fan speed selector resistor
111   Evaporator relay
112   Master relay
113   Condenser cooling fan relay
114   Compressor solenoid valve temperature switch
115   Conditioner cooling fan
116   Conditioner control board
117   Conditioner fan motor switch

For colour codes refer to Fig. 13.53

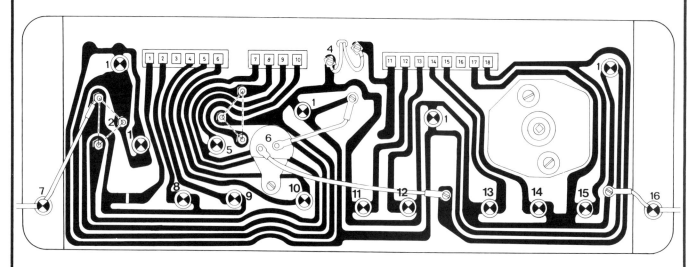

Fig. 13.65 Instrument panel circuit diagram for Mirafiori CL models from 1982 on (Sec 10)

1   Instrument panel illumination
2   Coolant liquid thermometer
3   Fuel gauge
4   Quartz clock
5   Fuel reserve warning light
6   Instrument panel light rheostat
7   Brake pad wear warning light
8   Low brake fluid and handbrake 'on' warning light
9   Low oil pressure warning light
10   Charging system warning light
11   Heated rear screen warning light
12   Hazard warning lights indicator
13   Headlamp, main beam indicator
14   Direction indicators indicator
15   Side lights indicator
16   Rear fog light indicator

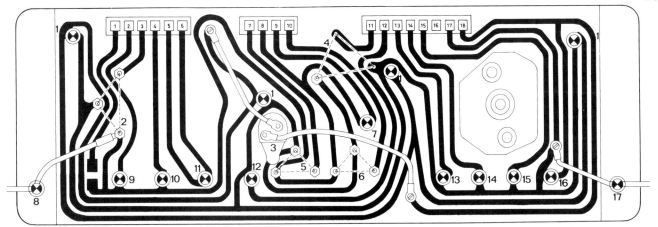

Fig. 13.66 Instrument panel circuit diagram for Supermirafiori models from 1982 on (Sec 10)

1 Instrument panel illumination
2 Tachometer
3 Instrument panel light rheostat
4 Quartz clock
5 Coolant thermometer
6 Fuel gauge

7 Fuel reserve
8 Brake pad wear warning light
9 Low brake fluid and handbrake 'on' warning light
10 Low oil pressure warning light
11 Charging system warning light

12 Heated rear screen warning light
13 Hazard warning lights indicator
14 Headlamp, main beam indicator
15 Direction indicators indicator
16 Side lights indicator
17 Rear fog light indicator

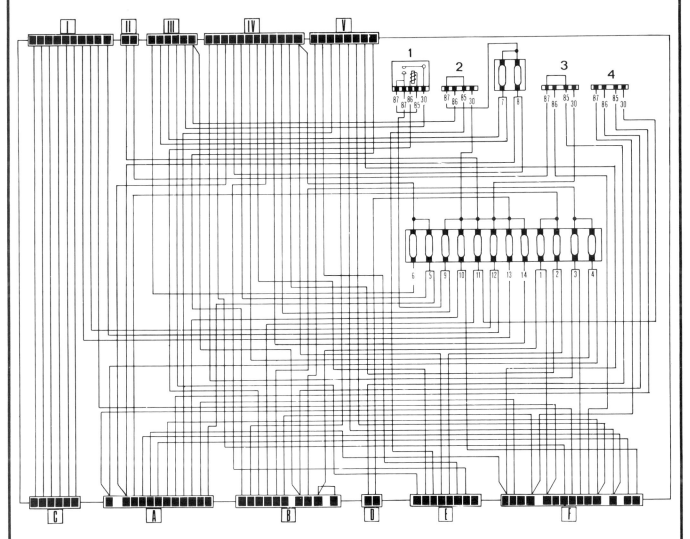

Fig. 13.67 Wiring diagram showing fuses and relay feed circuits for all models 1982 on (Sec 10)

1 Horn relay feed
2 Headlamp main beam relay feed

3 Automatic transmission relay feed
4 Heated rear screen relay feed

262

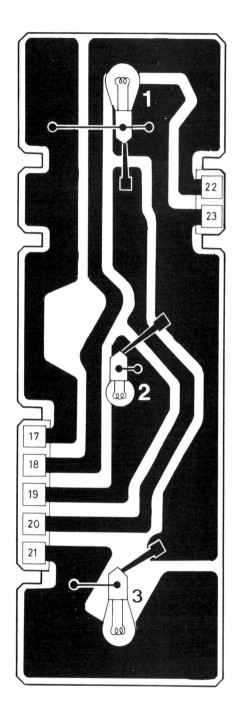
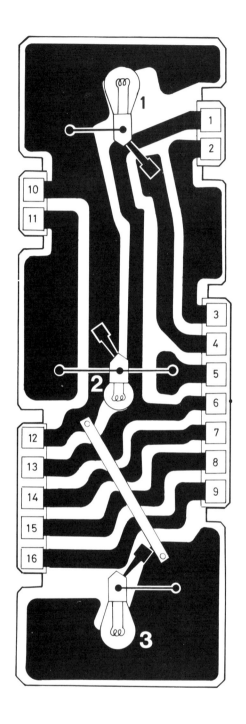

Fig. 13.68 Rear light cluster circuits for Panorama models 1982 on (Sec 10)

1 Direction indicators
2 Side lights
3 Brake lights
A Left-hand side
B Right-hand side

Key to wiring diagrams 13.69 to 13.89 inclusive

Location of connectors
1   In engine compartment near windscreen wiper intermittent device
2   Under dashboard near ignition switch
3   Under dashboard near ignition switch
4   In engine compartment near distributor
5   Under dashboard near interior fan controls
6   Under dashboard near ignition switch
7   Under dashboard near heater
8   Under dashboard near heater
9   Under dashboard right side near air duct
10 In engine compartment near left wheel arch
11 In engine compartment near battery
12 In luggage compartment near left light cluster
13 In luggage compartment near right light cluster
14 Under dashboard near ignition switch
15 In engine compartment near radiator
16 In engine compartment near lower front crossmember
17 In engine compartment near lower front crossmember
18 In engine compartment near windscreen wiper motor
19 Under dashboard near ignition switch
20 In engine compartment near alternator
21 Under dashboard near heater
22 Under dashboard near heater
23 Under dashboard near heater
24 Inside car near rear seat right side
25 Under centre tray near gear lever
26 Under dashboard near control panel
27 Under dashboard right side
28 In engine compartment near brake pump
29 In engine compartment near brake pump
30 In engine compartment near left wheel arch
31 Under dashboard near ignition switch
32 Under dashboard near control panel
33 In engine compartment near alternator
34 Inside car under front cover right side
35 Inside car under front cover left side
36 Inside car under front cover right side
37 Inside car under front cover right side
38 Inside front right door
39 Inside front right door
40 Inside front right door
41 Inside rear right door
42 Inside front left door
43 Inside front left door
44 Inside front left door
45 Inside rear left door
46 Inside car under front cover left side
47 Inside front right door
48 Inside front left door
49 Inside car under front cover right side
50 Inside car under centre tray
51 Inside car under centre tray
52 Inside car under centre tray
53 Inside car under centre tray
54 In engine compartment near compressor
55 In engine compartment near compressor
56 In engine compartment near compressor
57 In engine compartment near dehumidifier filter
58 In engine compartment near lower front crossmember
59 In engine compartment near dehumidifier filter
60 In engine compartment near radiator
61 Under dashboard near heater
62 Under dashboard near heater
63 In engine compartment near ignition coil
64 In engine compartment near ignition coil
65 Under dashboard near heater

Location of connectors
66 Under dashboard near heater
67 In engine compartment near electronic ignition control unit
68 In engine compartment near electronic ignition control unit
69 Inside car near right rear light cluster
70 Inside car near right rear light cluster
71 Near rear screen wiper motor
72 Under dashboard near control panel
73 Under dashboard near control panel

Components
100 Coolant temperature sender unit
101 Oil pressure switch
102 Glovebox light
103 Ideogram fibre optic light
104 Direction indicators and hazard warning lights flasher unit
105 Radiator fan thermostatic switch
106 Interior fan motor
107 Heater control lights
108 Windscreen wiper intermittent switch
109 Windscreen washer pump
110 Glovebox light switch
111 Ashtray light
112 Courtesy light switches
113 Rear courtesy lights
114 Centre courtesy light
115 Reversing light switch
116 Rear fog light indicator
117 Left brake pad wear sensor
118 Right brake pad wear sensor
119 Handbrake 'on' switch
120 Brake lights switch
121 Brake pad wear warning light
122 Aerial motor
123 Fuse box for electric windows and door locking system
124 Electric windows relay feed
125 Remote control door locking switch (closing)
126 Remote control door locking switch (opening)
127 Window opening motor
128 Front door locking motor
129 Front door locking switch
130 Rear door motor
131 Reversing light switch
132 Gear selector panel light
133 Air conditioning compressor
134 Anti-frost valve
135 Safety thermal switch
136 Thermal switch for condensor cooling fan
137 Pressure switch on air conditioning compressor
138 Resistor for reducing fan speed
139 Fast idle electro-valves
140 Compressor remote control switch
141 Condenser and engine cooling fan relay
142 Compressor relay
143 Air conditioning fan relay
144 Air conditioning control lights
145 Air conditioning switches
146 Thermal switch for anti-frost valve
147 Ignition coil with control module
148 Idle cut-out device
149 Ignition coil preresistor
150 Electronic ignition control unit
151 Rear courtesy light
152 Rear screen washer pump

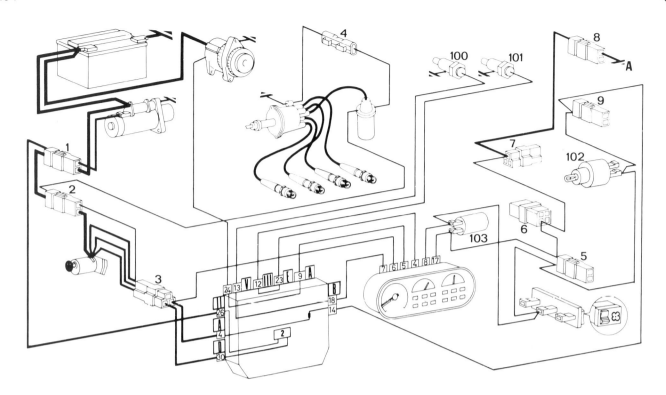

Fig. 13.69 Wiring diagram showing ignition, charging, low oil pressure, coolant temperature and Ideogram fibre optic bulb circuits for 1982 on models. For key see page 263 (Sec 10)

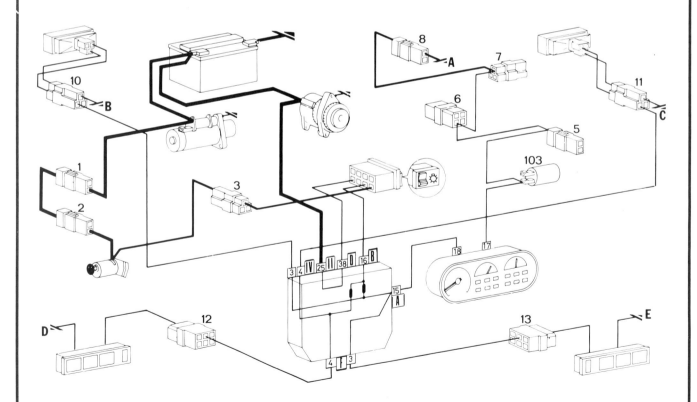

Fig. 13.70 Wiring diagram showing sidelight, number plate and instrument panel light circuits for 1982 on models (except Panorama). For key see page 263 (Sec 10)

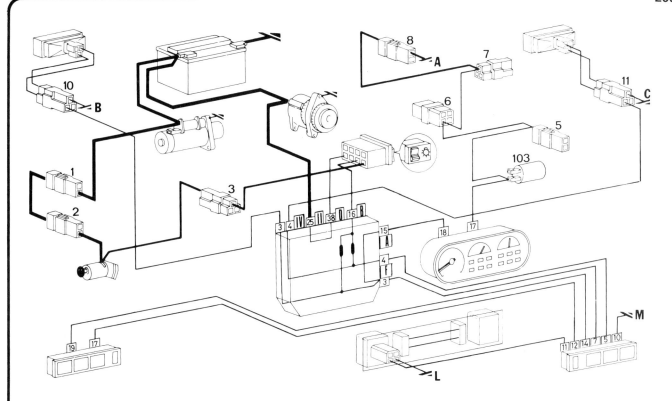

Fig. 13.71 Wiring diagram showing sidelight, number plate and instrument panel light circuits for 1982 on Panorama models. For key see page 263 (Sec 10)

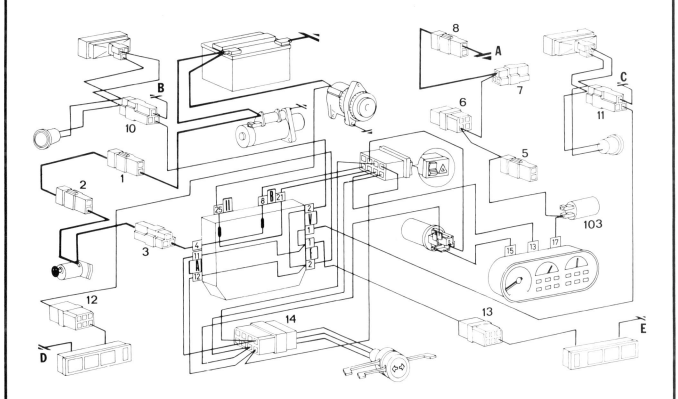

Fig. 13.72 Wiring diagram showing direction indicator and hazard warning light circuits for 1982 on models (except Panorama). For key see page 263 (Sec 10)

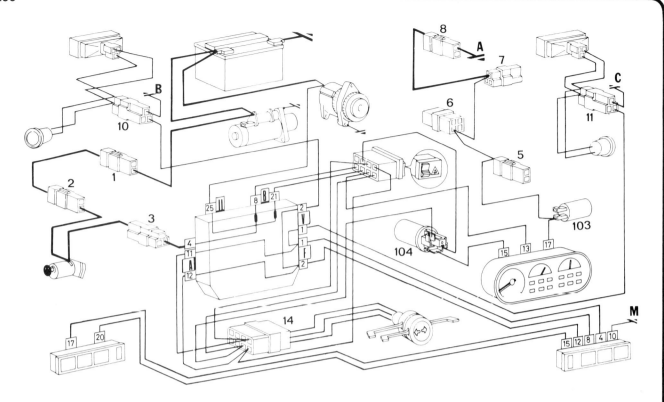

Fig. 13.73 Wiring diagram showing direction indicator and hazard warning light circuits for **1982** on Panorama models. For key see page 263 (Sec 10)

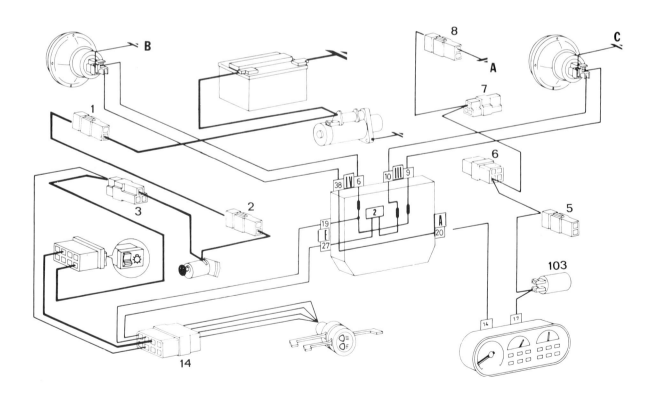

Fig. 13.74 Wiring diagram showing headlamp dip and main beam circuits for **1982** on models. For key see page 263 (Sec 10)

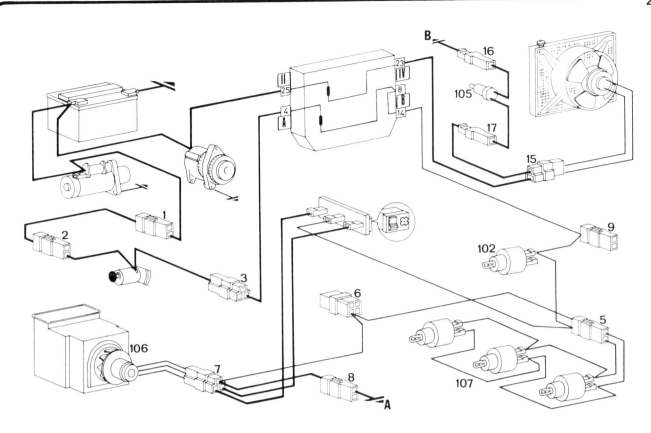

Fig. 13.75 Wiring diagram showing radiator fan motor, heater fan motor and heater Ideogram illumination circuits for 1982 on models. For key see page 263 (Sec 10)

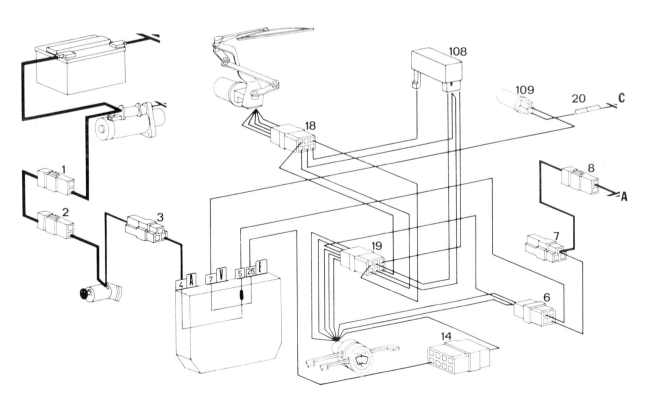

Fig. 13.76 Wiring diagram showing windscreen wiper and washer pump circuits for 1982 on models. For key see page 263 (Sec 10)

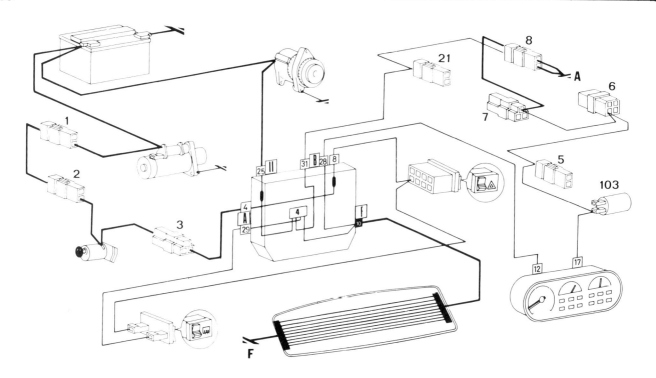

Fig. 13.77 Wiring diagram showing heated rear screen circuit for 1982 on models. For key see page 263 (Sec 10)

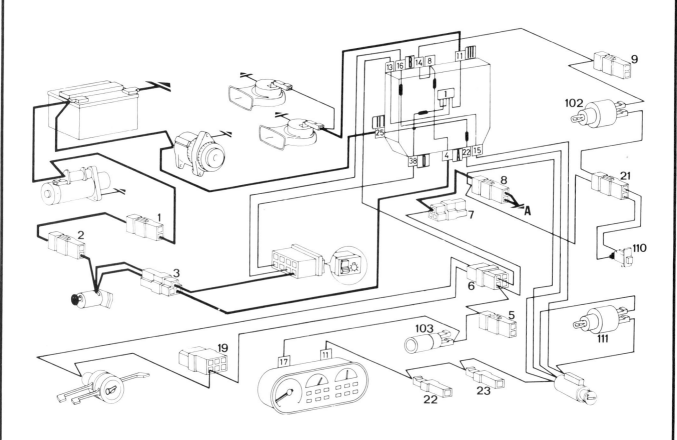

Fig. 13.78 Wiring diagram showing horn, cigarette lighter, clock, glovebox light and ashtray light circuits for 1982 on models. For key see page 263 (Sec 10)

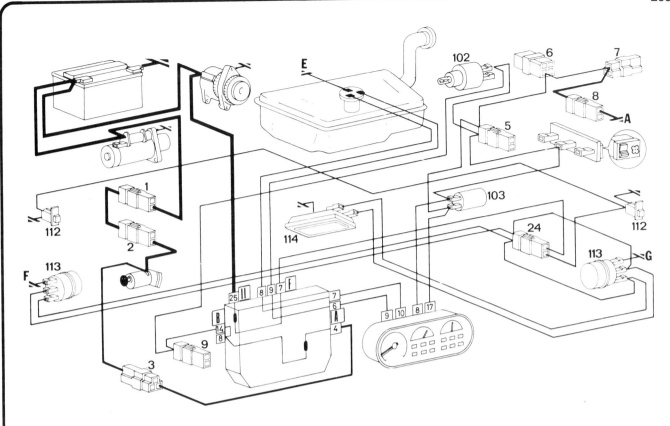

Fig. 13.79 Wiring diagram showing courtesy light, fuel gauge and reserve circuits for 1982 on models.
For key see page 263 (Sec 10)

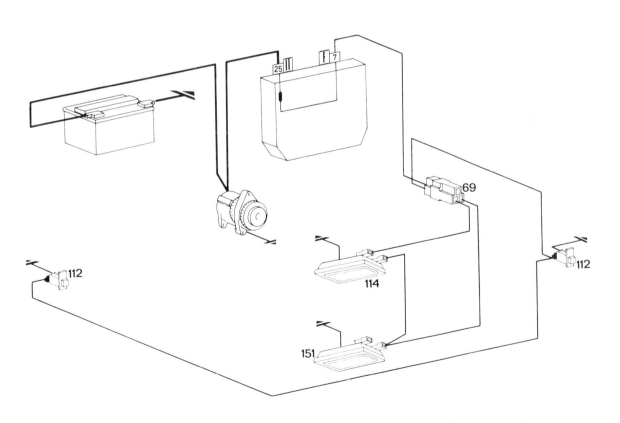

Fig. 13.80 Wiring diagram showing courtesy light circuits for 1982 on Panorama models.
For key see page 263 (Sec 10)

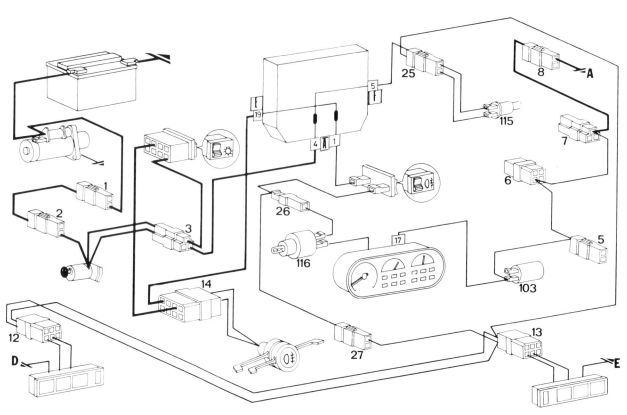

Fig. 13.81 Wiring diagram showing reversing light and rear fog light circuits for 1982 on models (except Panorama). For key see page 263 (Sec 10)

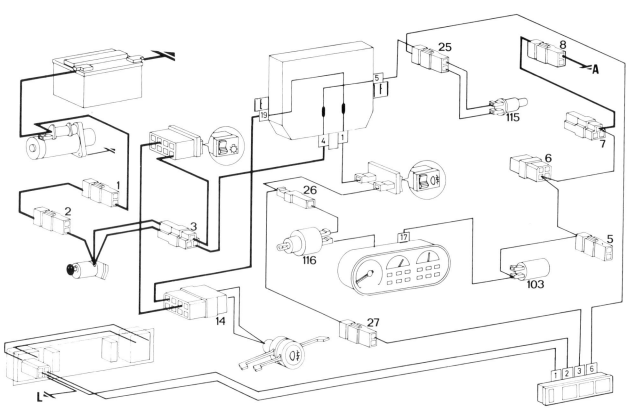

Fig. 13.82 Wiring diagram showing reversing light and rear fog light circuits for 1982 on Panorama models. For key see page 263 (Sec 10)

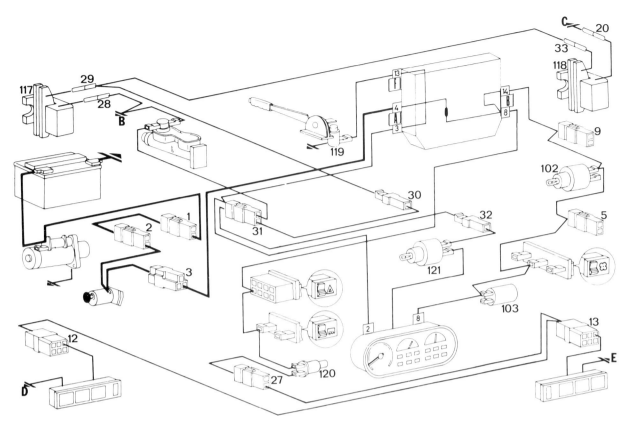

Fig. 13.83 Wiring diagram showing brake light, low brake fluid level, handbrake 'on' and brake pad wear circuits for 1982 on models (except Panorama). For key see page 263 (Sec 10)

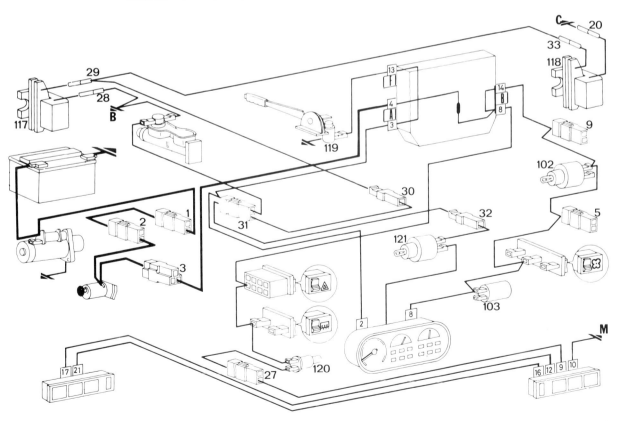

Fig. 13.84 Wiring diagram showing brake light, low brake fluid level, handbrake 'on' and brake pad wear circuits for 1982 on Panorama models. For key see page 263 (Sec 10)

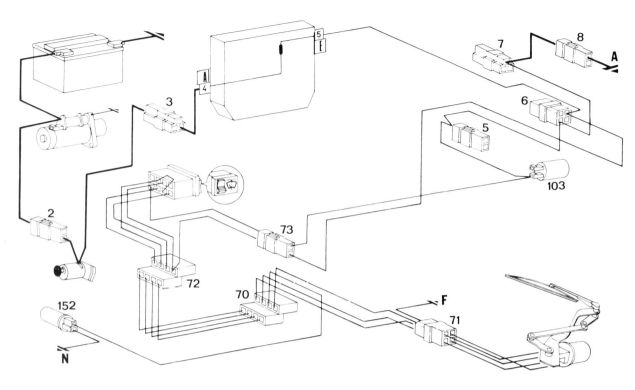

Fig. 13.85 Wiring diagram showing rear screen wiper and washer pump circuits for 1982 on Panorama models.
For key see page 263 (Sec 10)

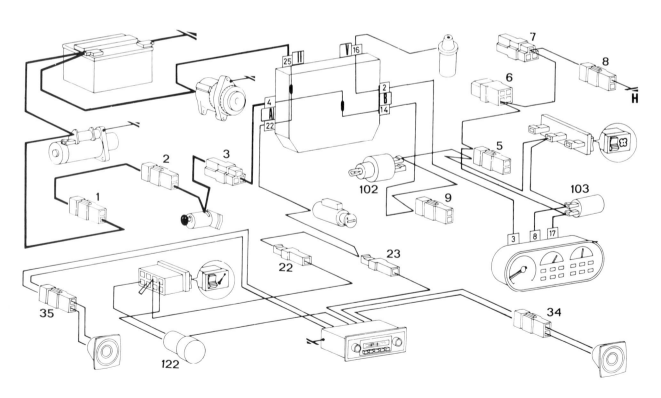

Fig. 13.86 Wiring diagram showing radio, electric aerial and tachometer circuits for 1982 on models.
For key see page 263 (Sec 10)

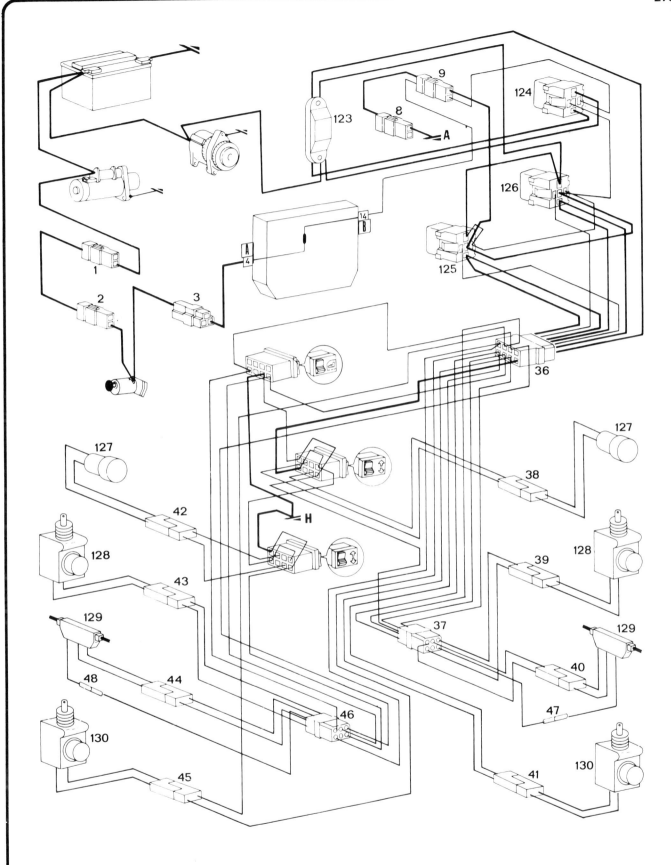

Fig. 13.87 Wiring diagram showing electric window and central door locking circuit for 1982 on models.
For key see page 263 (Sec 10)

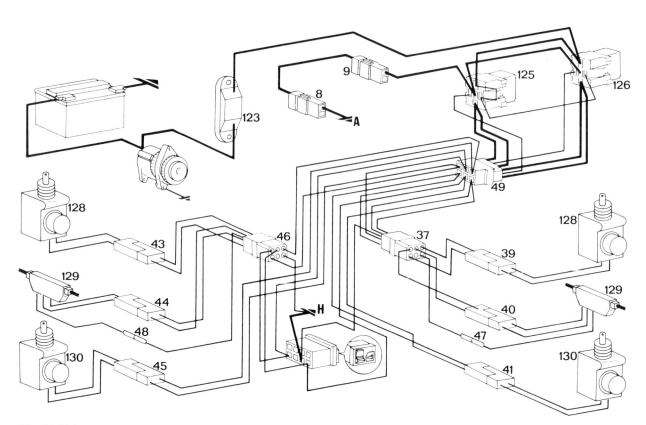

Fig. 13.88 Wiring diagram showing central door locking circuit for 1982 on models. For key see page 263 (Sec 10)

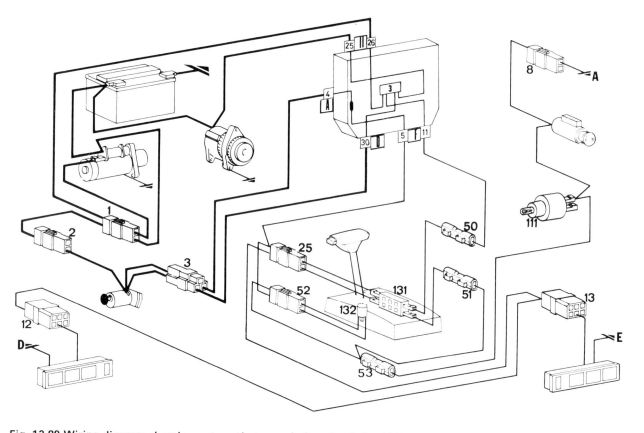

Fig. 13.89 Wiring diagram showing automatic transmission circuit for 1982 on models. For key see page 263 (Sec 10)

11 Suspension and steering

Front and rear suspension units – modification
1 From chassis numbers 943017 and 942926, FIAT have introduced a rubber spring shim to the front and rear right-hand suspension units only, as shown in Fig. 13.90.

Power assisted steering – general description and servicing
2 The power assisted steering gear is basically the same mechanically as the system described in Chapter 11 apart from the hydraulic part of the system.
3 The pump is driven by belt from the crankshaft pulley, and produces pressure for the hydraulic system, which, through the

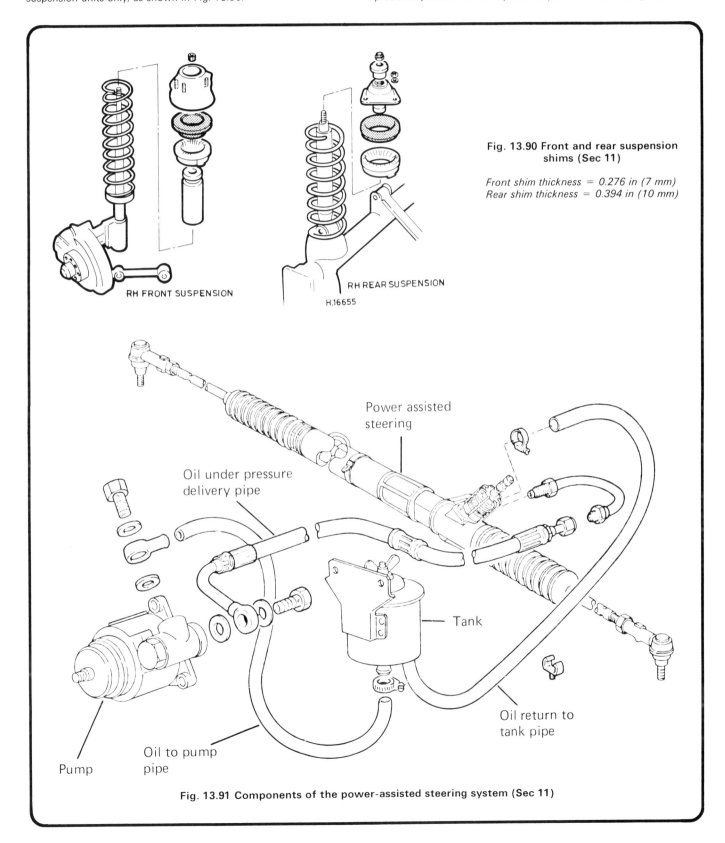

Fig. 13.90 Front and rear suspension shims (Sec 11)

Front shim thickness = 0.276 in (7 mm)
Rear shim thickness = 0.394 in (10 mm)

RH FRONT SUSPENSION

RH REAR SUSPENSION

H.16655

Power assisted steering

Oil under pressure delivery pipe

Tank

Oil return to tank pipe

Pump

Oil to pump pipe

Fig. 13.91 Components of the power-assisted steering system (Sec 11)

action of the valve gear on the rack housing and operation of the steering wheel, causes the wheels to turn.

4   Overhauling of the valve group and steering pump should be left to a local dealer, as special tools and equipment are needed.

5   Servicing of the hydraulic part of the system should be limited to checking the level in the steering pump fluid reservoir, the condition of the drivebelt, and the hydraulic pipelines for cracks, splits or fraying.

6   When checking the reservoir fluid level, the engine should be stopped and the level should reach the mark on the reservoir.

7   If the fluid is hot, the level may increase beyond this point but this is acceptable and no action should be taken to reduce the level.

8   If, with the engine running, the fluid level drops more than 0.4 in (10 mm) below the mark, then the system should be inspected by a local FIAT dealer.

9   Servicing of the mechanical components, ie, the steering rack, tie-rods and steering wheel will be found in Chapter 11.

12   Bodywork and fittings

Front spoiler (Sport models) – removal and refitting

1   Unscrew and remove the spoiler retaining screws from underneath.

2   Unscrew and remove the spoiler upper retaining screws from behind the number-plate mounting and lower the spoiler.

3   Refit in the reverse order and check for security.

Front wing moulding (Sport models) – removal and refitting

4   Unscrew and remove the moulding clamp screws around the wheel arch concerned. Remove the two retaining bolts within the forward section of the wing panel as shown (see Fig. 13.92) and the retaining screw from the underside front (where the moulding meets the spoiler). Remove the wing moulding.

5   Refit in the reverse order and check for security.

Interior handles and trim panel – removal and refitting

6   The door trim and handles on the later models have been redesigned; they are removed as follows.

7   To remove the armrest/door pull, prise the blank panel free and unscrew the two armrest retaining screws now exposed. At the rear end of the armrest, unscrew and remove the third retaining screw underneath; withdraw the armrest (photos).

8   The window regulator handle and door catch handle trim can be removed by following the procedure given in Chapter 12, Section 11. Also see photo 12.8.

9   The trim panel can now be removed by prising free the retaining clips, using a flat-bladed screwdriver, and releasing any screws that

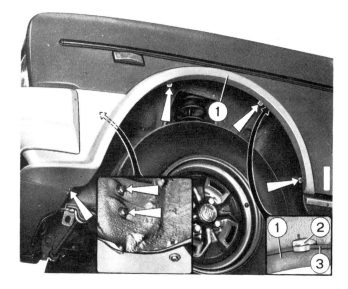

Fig. 13.92 Front wing moulding attachment points – Mirafiori Sport (Sec 12)

1 Moulding	*3 Wing panel*
2 Fasteners	

may also be used to retain the trim. Withdraw the trim panel, guiding it over the door catch handle, and releasing it from under the upper trim panel.

10   The upper trim panel is retained in position by pop rivets and should not normally need removing; but if necessary, the rivets can be drilled through using an $1/8$ in drill. The lock button is secured by a single screw.

11   Refitting is a reversal of the removal procedure. Before refitting the window regulator handle, locate the spring clip on the handle so that it snaps into position as the handle is fitted.

Centre console – removal and refitting

12   Unscrew and remove the gear lever knob. Prise free the rubber dust boot and remove it from the lever.

13   Remove the ashtray from the console and disconnect the ashtray light wiring connections, then unscrew the retaining nut from the bracket within the ashtray housing aperture. Unscrew and remove the retaining screw from the console rear face.

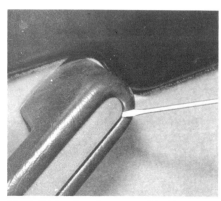

12.7A Prising free the armrest blanking panel

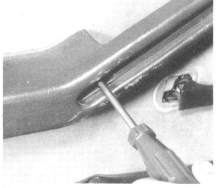

12.7B Removing armrest retaining screw

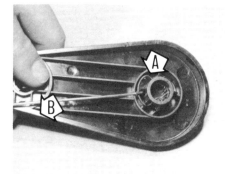

12.8 Removing window winder handle retaining spring using a piece of bent wire (handle removed for photographic purposes)
A Retaining spring
B Pull off clip in direction of arrow

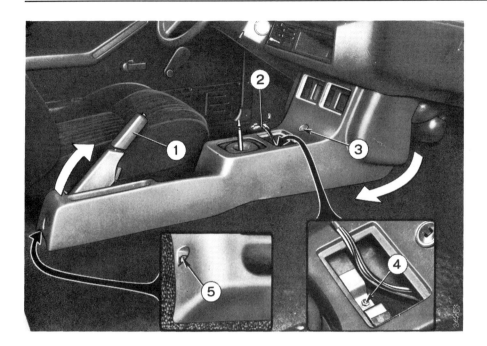

Fig. 13.93 Centre console removal (Sec 12)

1 Handbrake lever
2 Ashtray light wires
3 Cigar lighter housing
4 Forward retaining screw position
5 Rear retaining screw position
Note: certain models have two additional screws retaining front of console to lower facia panel.

14 Remove the centre vents from the console and as the console is lifted clear, disconnect the cigar lighter wiring. The handbrake must be in the 'ON' position to remove the console, which is tilted upwards at the rear to clear the handbrake lever and then rearwards for withdrawal.
15 For access to the gearbox remote control selector housing and/or forward propeller shaft coupling, remove the gearbox guard plate which is secured by five setscrews.
16 Refitting is a reversal of the removal procedure.

Later models
17 Removal of the centre console is similar to that described above except that there are two additional screws at the front retaining the console to the lower facia panel.
18 Depending upon the model, additional switchgear may be found on the console which will require disconnection of the wiring leads before the console can be lifted away.

Heater control unit – removal and refitting
19 Disconnect the battery earth (ground) lead, then remove the instrument cluster, as given in Chapter 10.
20 Pull the knobs from the console levers and when they have all been detached, unclip and withdraw the control facia panel.
21 Unscrew and remove the control unit-to-dash retaining screws.
22 Disconnect the control cables by extracting the roll pins from the spring clips and remove the clips (see Fig. 13.94).
23 Disconnect the control cables and, carefully, withdraw the control unit from the aperture in the dash.
24 Refit in reverse order and ensure full travel of the control levers on completion.

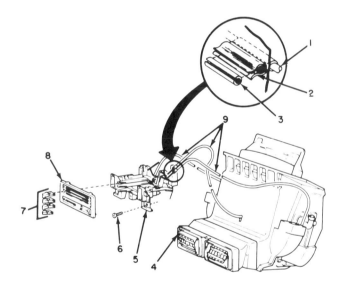

Fig. 13.94 Exploded view of heater controls and associated components (Sec 12)

1 Control cable	6 Screw
2 Spring clip	7 Knob
3 Roll pin	8 Panel
4 Heater unit	9 Wiring
5 Control unit	

Heater ducting – removal and refitting
The instructions given below apply to both the right- and left-hand ductings. Refer to Fig. 13.95.
25 Unclip the collar securing the ducting to the diffuser and detach the ducting.
26 Prise the deflector plate from the diffuser vent.
27 Unscrew and remove the diffuser retaining screws then detach the diffuser, together with its spacer gasket at the bottom. Remove the ducting and connector.
28 Prise free the heater valve endplate, remove the four securing screws at the rear and single side screw then remove the heater valve.
29 Refit in the reverse order to removal.

Heater blower motor – removal and refitting
30 Disconnect the battery earth (ground) lead.
31 Working in the engine compartment, unbolt and remove the bulkhead protective cover.
32 Remove the bonnet (hood) latch support, which is secured by three bolts.
33 Disconnect the wire connector to the blower motor unit, then release the spring clips securing the blower motor to its mounting (see Fig. 13.96).
34 The fan blade can be detached from the blower motor spindle by unscrewing the retaining nut.
35 Refit in the reverse order to removal.

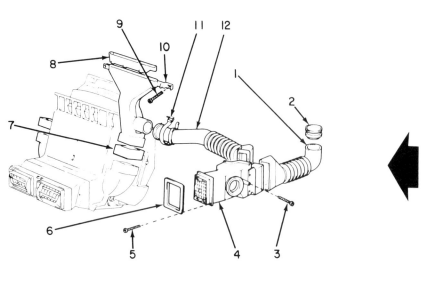

Fig. 13.95 Exploded view of heater
ducts and associated components
(Sec 12)

1 Ducting
2 Connector
3 Screw
4 Heater valve
5 Screw
6 Plate
7 Gasket
8 Deflector plate
9 Screw
10 Diffuser
11 Collar
12 Ducting

Fig. 13.96 Exploded view of heater
blower motor and associated
components (Sec 12)

1 Blower motor
2 Spring clip
3 Nut
4 Fan blades
5 Mounting plate
6 Connector

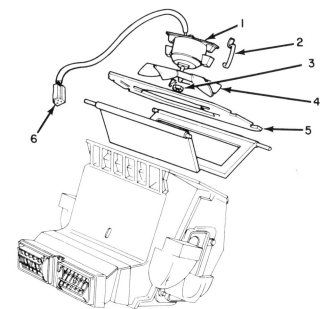

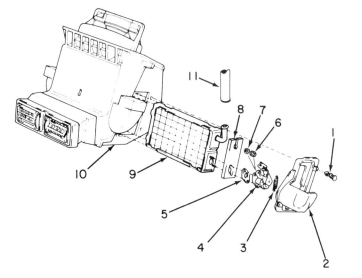

Fig. 13.97 Exploded view of heater core
unit and associated components
(Sec 12)

1 Plug
2 Cover
3 Spring
4 Control valve
5 Gasket
6 Nut
7 Washer
8 Plate
9 Heater core
10 Heater unit
11 Hose

Heater core – removal and refitting

36 Refer to Chapter 2 and drain the cooling system.
37 Detach the hose to the heater core (see Fig. 13.97), catching coolant spillage in a suitable container.
38 Prise free the three cover plugs and detach the cover. Now detach the control cable from the control valve and withdraw the heater core.
39 To dismantle the core, remove the nuts and washers, the water control valve and the plate with its gasket.
40 Refit in the reverse order to removal, taking care not to damage the core. Use a new plate gasket and renew any worn or defective items.

Air conditioning system

41 Although similar in layout, the air conditioning circuit for models from 1978 onward differs slightly from the earlier type, and this is shown in Fig. 13.98. The principal difference is the compressor which is now a Sankyo rotary type, and the isobaric valve, previously attached to the compressor unit, which is now separate

and secured to a bracket on the inner fender (wing).
42 Two later type air conditioning wiring diagrams are shown in Figs. 13.99 and 13.100. The following information may be of use, and refers to Fig. 13.99.

1   When the frost preventative valve is activated, the refrigerant flow is reduced by two thirds.
2   The pressure switch closes when the freon pressure is greater than 40 ± 5 lbf/in².
3   The condenser fan thermo switch shuts when the temperature of the outlet is 200 to 250°F.
4   The high pressure switch shuts when the pressure on the outlet exceeds 350 ± 10 lbf/in², and opens when pressure drops below 150 ± 10 lbf/in².
5   The frost prevention switch shuts when the evaporator outlet temperature falls below 32°F (0°C).
6   The fast idle electrovalve increases the engine rpm when activated.

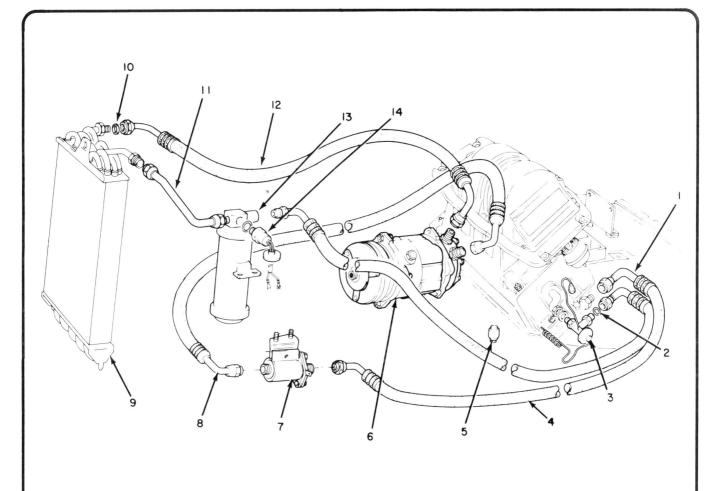

Fig. 13.98 Exploded view of air conditioning components from 1978 on (Sec 12)

1 Low pressure gas hose	6 Compressor	11 Delivery tube
2 Gasket	7 Isobaric valve	12 High pressure gas hose
3 Expansion valve	8 Return hose	13 Receiver/dryer
4 High pressure liquid hose	9 Condenser	14 Low pressure switch
5 Thermostatic sending unit	10 Gasket	

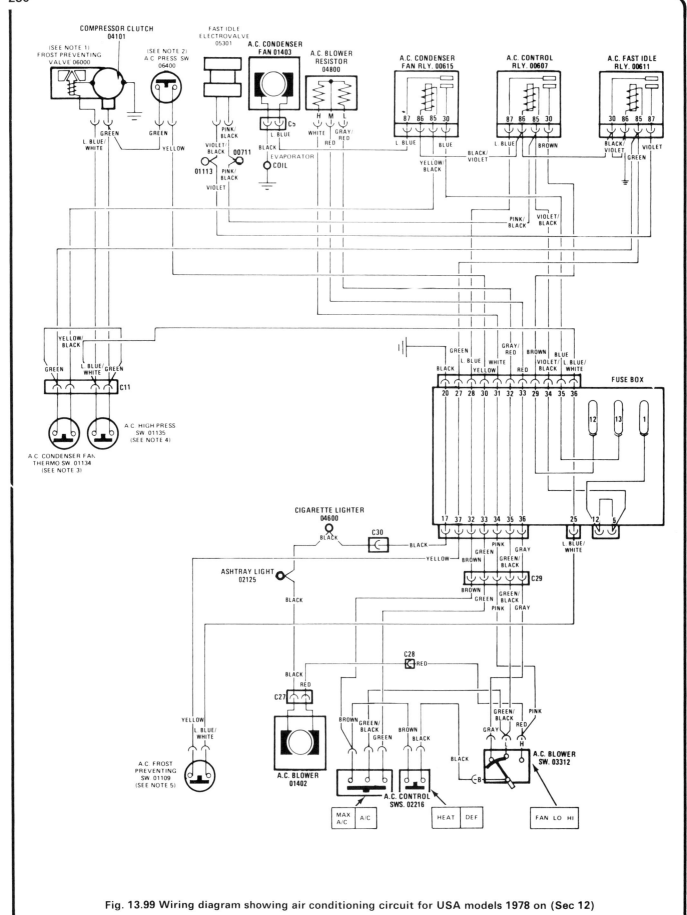

Fig. 13.99 Wiring diagram showing air conditioning circuit for USA models 1978 on (Sec 12)

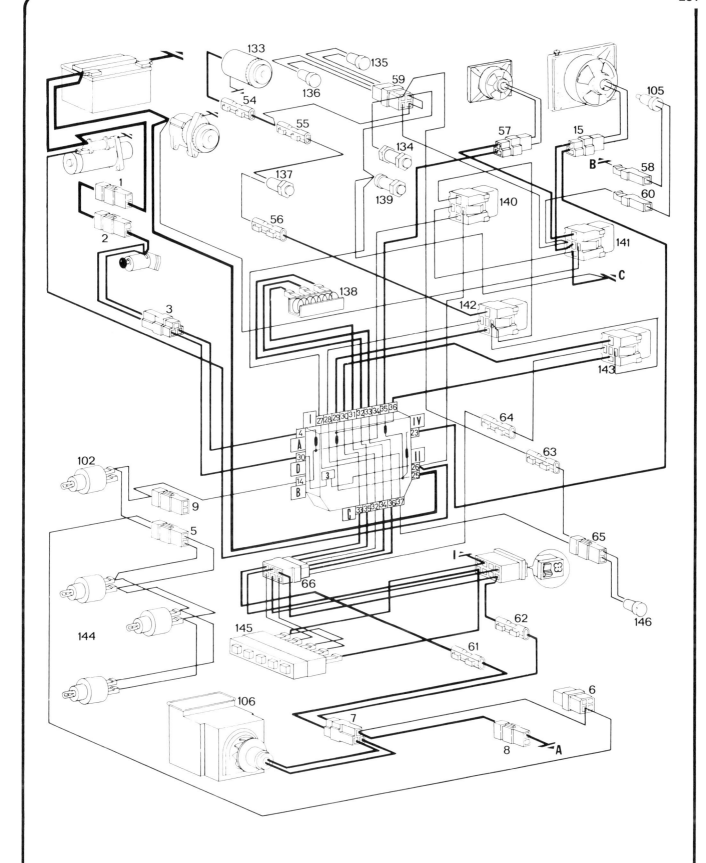

Fig. 13.100 Wiring diagram showing air conditioning circuit for UK models 1982 on. For key see page 263 (Sec 10)

Radiator grille (1982 on) – removal and refitting
43 The new style radiator grille is held in place by three screws and two clips along its lower edge and five clips on its upper edge (Fig. 13.101).

44 Remove the three screws and then carefully prise each clip from its slot (photos).
45 The chrome embellishing strips are removed with the grille.
46 Refit in the reverse order of removal.

12.44A Radiator grille centre clip

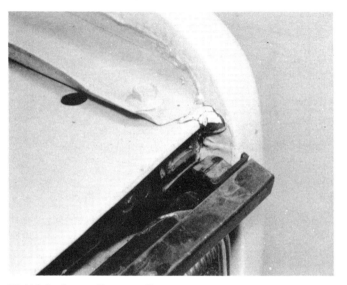

12.44B Radiator grille outer clip

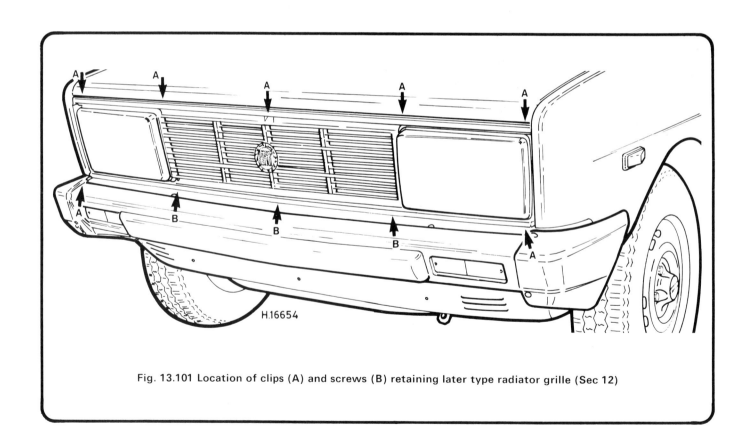

Fig. 13.101 Location of clips (A) and screws (B) retaining later type radiator grille (Sec 12)

Conversion factors

Length (distance)

Inches (in)	X	25.4	= Millimetres (mm)	X 0.0394	= Inches (in)
Feet (ft)	X	0.305	= Metres (m)	X 3.281	= Feet (ft)
Miles	X	1.609	= Kilometres (km)	X 0.621	= Miles

Volume (capacity)

Cubic inches (cu in; in^3)	X	16.387	= Cubic centimetres (cc; cm^3)	X 0.061	= Cubic inches (cu in; in^3)
Imperial pints (Imp pt)	X	0.568	= Litres (l)	X 1.76	= Imperial pints (Imp pt)
Imperial quarts (Imp qt)	X	1.137	= Litres (l)	X 0.88	= Imperial quarts (Imp qt)
Imperial quarts (Imp qt)	X	1.201	= US quarts (US qt)	X 0.833	= Imperial quarts (Imp qt)
US quarts (US qt)	X	0.946	= Litres (l)	X 1.057	= US quarts (US qt)
Imperial gallons (Imp gal)	X	4.546	= Litres (l)	X 0.22	= Imperial gallons (Imp gal)
Imperial gallons (Imp gal)	X	1.201	= US gallons (US gal)	X 0.833	= Imperial gallons (Imp gal)
US gallons (US gal)	X	3.785	= Litres (l)	X 0.264	= US gallons (US gal)

Mass (weight)

Ounces (oz)	X	28.35	= Grams (g)	X 0.035	= Ounces (oz)
Pounds (lb)	X	0.454	= Kilograms (kg)	X 2.205	= Pounds (lb)

Force

Ounces-force (ozf; oz)	X	0.278	= Newtons (N)	X 3.6	= Ounces-force (ozf; oz)
Pounds-force (lbf; lb)	X	4.448	= Newtons (N)	X 0.225	= Pounds-force (lbf; lb)
Newtons (N)	X	0.1	= Kilograms-force (kgf; kg)	X 9.81	= Newtons (N)

Pressure

Pounds-force per square inch (psi; lbf/in^2; lb/in^2)	X	0.070	= Kilograms-force per square centimetre (kgf/cm^2; kg/cm^2)	X 14.223	= Pounds-force per square inch (psi; lbf/in^2; lb/in^2)
Pounds-force per square inch (psi; lbf/in^2; lb/in^2)	X	0.068	= Atmospheres (atm)	X 14.696	= Pounds-force per square inch (psi; lbf/in^2; lb/in^2)
Pounds-force per square inch (psi; lbf/in^2; lb/in^2)	X	0.069	= Bars	X 14.5	= Pounds-force per square inch (psi; lbf/in^2; lb/in^2)
Pounds-force per square inch (psi; lbf/in^2; lb/in^2)	X	6.895	= Kilopascals (kPa)	X 0.145	= Pounds-force per square inch (psi; lbf/in^2; lb/in^2)
Kilopascals (kPa)	X	0.01	= Kilograms-force per square centimetre (kgf/cm^2; kg/cm^2)	X 98.1	= Kilopascals (kPa)

Torque (moment of force)

Pounds-force inches (lbf in; lb in)	X	1.152	= Kilograms-force centimetre (kgf cm; kg cm)	X 0.868	= Pounds-force inches (lbf in; lb in)
Pounds-force inches (lbf in; lb in)	X	0.113	= Newton metres (Nm)	X 8.85	= Pounds-force inches (lbf in; lb in)
Pounds-force inches (lbf in; lb in)	X	0.083	= Pounds-force feet (lbf ft; lb ft)	X 12	= Pounds-force inches (lbf in; lb in)
Pounds-force feet (lbf ft; lb ft)	X	0.138	= Kilograms-force metres (kgf m; kg m)	X 7.233	= Pounds-force feet (lbf ft; lb ft)
Pounds-force feet (lbf ft; lb ft)	X	1.356	= Newton metres (Nm)	X 0.738	= Pounds-force feet (lbf ft; lb ft)
Newton metres (Nm)	X	0.102	= Kilograms-force metres (kgf m; kg m)	X 9.804	= Newton metres (Nm)

Power

Horsepower (hp)	X	745.7	= Watts (W)	X 0.0013	= Horsepower (hp)

Velocity (speed)

Miles per hour (miles/hr; mph)	X	1.609	= Kilometres per hour (km/hr; kph)	X 0.621	= Miles per hour (miles/hr; mph)

Fuel consumption*

Miles per gallon, Imperial (mpg)	X	0.354	= Kilometres per litre (km/l)	X 2.825	= Miles per gallon, Imperial (mpg)
Miles per gallon, US (mpg)	X	0.425	= Kilometres per litre (km/l)	X 2.352	= Miles per gallon, US (mpg)

Temperature

Degrees Fahrenheit = ($^\circ$C x 1.8) + 32   Degrees Celsius (Degrees Centigrade; $^\circ$C) = ($^\circ$F - 32) x 0.56

*It is common practice to convert from miles per gallon (mpg) to litres/100 kilometres (l/100km),
where mpg (Imperial) x l/100 km = 282 and mpg (US) x l/100 km = 235

General repair procedures

Whenever servicing, repair or overhaul work is carried out on the car or its components, it is necessary to observe the following procedures and instructions. This will assist in carrying out the operation efficiently and to a professional standard of workmanship.

Joint mating faces and gaskets

Where a gasket is used between the mating faces of two components, ensure that it is renewed on reassembly, and fit it dry unless otherwise stated in the repair procedure. Make sure that the mating faces are clean and dry with all traces of old gasket removed. When cleaning a joint face, use a tool which is not likely to score or damage the face, and remove any burrs or nicks with an oilstone or fine file.

Make sure that tapped holes are cleaned with a pipe cleaner, and keep them free of jointing compound if this is being used unless specifically instructed otherwise.

Ensure that all orifices, channels or pipes are clear and blow through them, preferably using compressed air.

Oil seals

Whenever an oil seal is removed from its working location, either individually or as part of an assembly, it should be renewed.

The very fine sealing lip of the seal is easily damaged and will not seal if the surface it contacts is not completely clean and free from scratches, nicks or grooves. If the original sealing surface of the component cannot be restored, the component should be renewed.

Protect the lips of the seal from any surface which may damage them in the course of fitting. Use tape or a conical sleeve where possible. Lubricate the seal lips with oil before fitting and, on dual lipped seals, fill the space between the lips with grease.

Unless otherwise stated, oil seals must be fitted with their sealing lips toward the lubricant to be sealed.

Use a tubular drift or block of wood of the appropriate size to install the seal and, if the seal housing is shouldered, drive the seal down to the shoulder. If the seal housing is unshouldered, the seal should be fitted with its face flush with the housing top face.

Screw threads and fastenings

Always ensure that a blind tapped hole is completely free from oil, grease, water or other fluid before installing the bolt or stud. Failure to do this could cause the housing to crack due to the hydraulic action of the bolt or stud as it is screwed in.

When tightening a castellated nut to accept a split pin, tighten the nut to the specified torque, where applicable, and then tighten further to the next split pin hole. Never slacken the nut to align a split pin hole unless stated in the repair procedure.

When checking or retightening a nut or bolt to a specified torque setting, slacken the nut or bolt by a quarter of a turn, and then retighten to the specified setting.

Locknuts, locktabs and washers

Any fastening which will rotate against a component or housing in the course of tightening should always have a washer between it and the relevant component or housing.

Spring or split washers should always be renewed when they are used to lock a critical component such as a big-end bearing retaining nut or bolt.

Locktabs which are folded over to retain a nut or bolt should always be renewed.

Self-locking nuts can be reused in non-critical areas, providing resistance can be felt when the locking portion passes over the bolt or stud thread.

Split pins must always be replaced with new ones of the correct size for the hole.

Special tools

Some repair procedures in this manual entail the use of special tools such as a press, two or three-legged pullers, spring compressors etc. Wherever possible, suitable readily available alternatives to the manufacturer's special tools are described, and are shown in use. In some instances, where no alternative is possible, it has been necessary to resort to the use of a manufacturer's tool and this has been done for reasons of safety as well as the efficient completion of the repair operation. Unless you are highly skilled and have a thorough understanding of the procedure described, never attempt to bypass the use of any special tool when the procedure described specifies its use. Not only is there a very great risk of personal injury, but expensive damage could be caused to the components involved.

Safety first!

Professional motor mechanics are trained in safe working procedures. However enthusiastic you may be about getting on with the job in hand, do take the time to ensure that your safety is not put at risk. A moment's lack of attention can result in an accident, as can failure to observe certain elementary precautions.

There will always be new ways of having accidents, and the following points do not pretend to be a comprehensive list of all dangers; they are intended rather to make you aware of the risks and to encourage a safety-conscious approach to all work you carry out on your vehicle.

Essential DOs and DON'Ts

DON'T rely on a single jack when working underneath the vehicle. Always use reliable additional means of support, such as axle stands, securely placed under a part of the vehicle that you know will not give way.

DON'T attempt to loosen or tighten high-torque nuts (e.g. wheel hub nuts) while the vehicle is on a jack; it may be pulled off.

DON'T start the engine without first ascertaining that the transmission is in neutral (or 'Park' where applicable) and the parking brake applied.

DON'T suddenly remove the filler cap from a hot cooling system – cover it with a cloth and release the pressure gradually first, or you may get scalded by escaping coolant.

DON'T attempt to drain oil until you are sure it has cooled sufficiently to avoid scalding you.

DON'T grasp any part of the engine, exhaust or catalytic converter without first ascertaining that it is sufficiently cool to avoid burning you.

DON'T syphon toxic liquids such as fuel, brake fluid or antifreeze by mouth, or allow them to remain on your skin.

DON'T inhale brake lining dust – it is injurious to health.

DON'T allow any spilt oil or grease to remain on the floor – wipe it up straight away, before someone slips on it.

DON'T use ill-fitting spanners or other tools which may slip and cause injury.

DON'T attempt to lift a heavy component which may be beyond your capability – get assistance.

DON'T rush to finish a job, or take unverified short cuts.

DON'T allow children or animals in or around an unattended vehicle.

DO wear eye protection when using power tools such as drill, sander, bench grinder etc, and when working under the vehicle.

DO use a barrier cream on your hands prior to undertaking dirty jobs – it will protect your skin from infection as well as making the dirt easier to remove afterwards; but make sure your hands aren't left slippery.

DO keep loose clothing (cuffs, tie etc) and long hair well out of the way of moving mechanical parts.

DO remove rings, wristwatch etc, before working on the vehicle – especially the electrical system.

DO ensure that any lifting tackle used has a safe working load rating adequate for the job.

DO keep your work area tidy – it is only too easy to fall over articles left lying around.

DO get someone to check periodically that all is well, when working alone on the vehicle.

DO carry out work in a logical sequence and check that everything is correctly assembled and tightened afterwards.

DO remember that your vehicle's safety affects that of yourself and others. If in doubt on any point, get specialist advice.

IF, in spite of following these precautions, you are unfortunate enough to injure yourself, seek medical attention as soon as possible.

Fire

Remember at all times that petrol (gasoline) is highly flammable. Never smoke, or have any kind of naked flame around, when working on the vehicle. But the risk does not end there – a spark caused by an electrical short-circuit, by two metal surfaces contacting each other, or even by static electricity built up in your body under certain conditions, can ignite petrol vapour, which in a confined space is highly explosive.

Always disconnect the battery earth (ground) terminal before working on any part of the fuel system, and never risk spilling fuel on to a hot engine or exhaust.

It is recommended that a fire extinguisher of a type suitable for fuel and electrical fires is kept handy in the garage or workplace at all times. Never try to extinguish a fuel or electrical fire with water.

Fumes

Certain fumes are highly toxic and can quickly cause unconsciousness and even death if inhaled to any extent. Petrol (gasoline) vapour comes into this category, as do the vapours from certain solvents such as trichloroethylene. Any draining or pouring of such volatile fluids should be done in a well ventilated area.

When using cleaning fluids and solvents, read the instructions carefully. Never use materials from unmarked containers – they may give off poisonous vapours.

Never run the engine of a motor vehicle in an enclosed space such as a garage. Exhaust fumes contain carbon monoxide which is extremely poisonous; if you need to run the engine, always do so in the open air or at least have the rear of the vehicle outside the workplace.

If you are fortunate enough to have the use of an inspection pit, never drain or pour petrol, and never run the engine, while the vehicle is standing over it; the fumes, being heavier than air, will concentrate in the pit with possibly lethal results.

The battery

Never cause a spark, or allow a naked light, near the vehicle's battery. It will normally be giving off a certain amount of hydrogen gas, which is highly explosive.

Always disconnect the battery earth (ground) terminal before working on the fuel or electrical systems.

If possible, loosen the filler plugs or cover when charging the battery from an external source. Do not charge at an excessive rate or the battery may burst.

Take care when topping up and when carrying the battery. The acid electrolyte, even when diluted, is very corrosive and should not be allowed to contact the eyes or skin.

If you ever need to prepare electrolyte yourself, always add the acid slowly to the water, and never the other way round. Protect against splashes by wearing rubber gloves and goggles.

When jump starting a car using a booster battery, for negative earth (ground) vehicles, connect the jump leads in the following sequence: First connect one jump lead between the positive (+) terminals of the two batteries. Then connect the other jump lead first to the negative (–) terminal of the booster battery, and then to a good earthing (ground) point on the vehicle to be started, at least 18 in (45 cm) from the battery if possible. Ensure that hands and jump leads are clear of any moving parts, and that the two vehicles do not touch. Disconnect the leads in the reverse order.

Mains electricity

When using an electric power tool, inspection light etc, which works from the mains, always ensure that the appliance is correctly connected to its plug and that, where necessary, it is properly earthed (grounded). Do not use such appliances in damp conditions and, again, beware of creating a spark or applying excessive heat in the vicinity of fuel or fuel vapour.

Ignition HT voltage

A severe electric shock can result from touching certain parts of the ignition system, such as the HT leads, when the engine is running or being cranked, particularly if components are damp or the insulation is defective. Where an electronic ignition system is fitted, the HT voltage is much higher and could prove fatal.

Index

Printed by
J H Haynes & Co Ltd
Sparkford Nr Yeovil
Somerset BA22 7JJ England